THE INVENTION OF COMFORT

The Invention of Comfort

SENSIBILITIES & DESIGN IN EARLY

MODERN BRITAIN & EARLY AMERICA

JOHN E. CROWLEY

THE JOHNS HOPKINS UNIVERSITY PRESS

BALTIMORE

© 2001 The Johns Hopkins University Press

All rights reserved. Published 2000

Printed in the United States of America on acid-free paper

Johns Hopkins Paperback
edition, 2010

2 4 6 8 9 7 5 3 1

The Johns Hopkins University Press

2715 North Charles Street

Baltimore, Maryland 21218-4363

www.press.jhu.edu

Library of Congress Cataloging-in-Publication Data will be found at the end of this book.

A catalog record for this book is available from the British Library.

ISBN 13: 978-0-8018-7315-7
ISBN 10: 0-8018-7315-0

For Marian

CONTENTS

PREFACE AND ACKNOWLEDGMENTS

HOW DID the concept of "comfort" come to have its modern emphasis on self-conscious satisfaction with the relationship between one's body and its immediate physical environment? For the past twenty years economic and social historians have been emphasizing how propertied households through-out postmedieval northwestern Europe gave increasing priority in their con-sumption patterns to domestic enhancements that provided more privacy, cleanliness, warmth, and light. Historians usually label these enhancements "comfort" and, by a questionable circularity, often point to the desire for com-fort as an explanation for their development. After considering these matters from the perspectives of a variety of disciplines and subdisciplines—cultural anthropology, material culture studies, historical archaeology, the history of technology, and the comparative history of domestic relations—I have be-come convinced that interpretations of comfort in material culture have depended too uncritically on naturalistic assumptions that are liable to be unhistorical, ethnocentric, and teleological.

How natural is the desire for physical comfort? If comfort were a specific response to material living conditions, we should be able to measure it, but architects have found it difficult to specify, much less to design, a uniformly comfortable environment. According to one prominent critic, architecture schools avoid the topic. In contrast, anthropologists expect to find people in different cultures and in the past to have varying ideas of what constitutes satisfactory relations of body, material culture, and environment. They have found that technology, social structures, and belief systems dictate widely varying designs in domestic environments. Take chairs, for example. In recent centuries European culture has defined them as the appropriate furniture for private and social leisure, and the design of comfortable chairs is a strong theme in much of the history of modern furniture. But there are orthopedic reasons to think that the effort is chimerical: all chairs are bad for our backs. Yet we have learned to sit comfortably in them, episodes of back spasms aside.[1]

This study concentrates on architectural designs for the elementary comforts of light and warmth in early modern British and Anglo-American domestic environments. The first third of this book describes and interprets the material culture of heating and illumination in British and Anglo-American domestic environments during the centuries before physical comfort had much emphasis as an explicit value. With the medieval predominance of the hall and open hearth as a baseline, it considers the postmedieval changes in vernacular architecture that provided more interior illumination (through glazed windows) and more privacy with warmth (by the use of chimney fireplaces in place of the open hearth). These changes became popularized in seventeenth-century Britain and Anglo-America through vernacular appropriation of cosmopolitan features in housing, but resistance to them is apparent as well, and equally demanding of explanation. For much of the early modern period there were wide, and in large part discretionary, social variations in consumption patterns regarding heating and lighting.

The second third of the book deals with comfort as it became a crucial value in eighteenth-century material culture. Physical comfort, as a highly explicit concept, took account of changes in domestic material culture by a redefinition of the value into something close to its modern meaning. Previously, *comfort* was primarily a moral term indicating personal support. Its material connotations were liable to negative associations from Christian and classical disparagements of luxury. Much of the cultural originality of early political economy stemmed from an intellectual effort to legitimize popular consumption, especially when it involved new types of goods. The term *convenience* initially conveyed this legitimation: when Adam Smith forthrightly asserted that the whole point of economic life was consumption, he referred to people's open-ended aspirations with the phrase "necessaries and conveniencies of life."[2] As liberal political economy came to terms with the consumer revolution, it practically eliminated the traditional dichotomy between necessity and luxury in material culture. The improvement of people's immediate physical circumstances became a major cultural project of French, British, and American philosophes.

The concluding third of the book shows how landscape architecture and the picturesque aesthetic refined the crucial values and designs of a comfortable domestic environment. The content of the picturesque aesthetic, with its emphasis on the subjectivity of taste, rusticity of design, and exoticism of style, provided an alternative to the symmetry, hierarchy, and canonical style of Georgian residential architecture. As personal sensibility became critical to taste, landscape architecture shaped the identification of the cottage as the archetypal comfortable house. With the cottage as a metonym, domestic comfort began to be asserted as a right and an obligation.

THE FOLLOWING institutions supported research for this book with grants and fellowships: the Dalhousie University Faculty of Graduate Studies, the Huntington Library, the National Humanities Center, the National Endowment for the Humanities, the Social Sciences and Humanities Research Council of Canada, and the Winterthur Museum, Garden and Library. Participants in the Dalhousie University Faculty-Student History Seminar helpfully discussed early versions of most of these chapters, and my Dalhousie colleagues Alan Andrews, Marian Binkley, Cynthia Neville, Shirley Tillotson, and Daniel Woolf also reviewed final drafts. Anne Whitmore showed that heroic editing continues at the Johns Hopkins University Press.

Some of the material in this book has appeared in earlier forms in other publications, including the *Winterthur Portfolio* (vol. 32, 1997), *American Historical Review* (vol. 104, 1999), *Travail et Loisir dans l'Amérique Pré-industrielle*, edited by Barbara Karsky and Elise Marienstras (Presses Universitaires de Nancy, 1991), *American Material Culture: The Shape of the Field*, edited by J. Ritchie Garrison and Ann Smart Martin (Winterthur Museum, 1997), and *Gender and Material Culture: Historical Perspectives*, edited by Moira Donald and Linda Hurcombe (Macmillan [London], 2000).

There are two words in their language on which these people pride themselves, and which they say cannot be translated. *Home* is the one, by which an Englishman means his house. . . . The other word is *comfort;* it means all the enjoyments and privileges of *home;* and here I must confess that these proud islanders have reason for their pride. In their social intercourse and their modes of life they have enjoyments which we never dream of.

ROBERT SOUTHEY,

Letters from England: By Don Manuel Alvarez Espriella. Translated from the Spanish (1807)

All the arts, the sciences, law and government, wisdom, and even virtue itself tend all to this one thing, the providing meat, drink, rayment, and lodging for men, which are commonly reckoned the meanest of employments and fit for the pursuit of none but the lowest and meanest of the people. All the several arts and businesses of life tend to render the conveniencies and necessaries of life more attainable.

ADAM SMITH, "Report of 1762–63," *Lectures on Jurisprudence*

It must be remembered, that life consists not of a series of illustrious actions, or elegant enjoyments; the greater part of our time passes in compliance with necessities, in the performance of daily duties, in the removal of small inconveniencies, in the procurement of petty pleasures; and we are well or ill at ease, as the main stream of life glides on smoothly, or is ruffled by small obstacles and frequent interruption. The true state of every nation is the state of common life.

SAMUEL JOHNSON, *A Journey to the Western Islands of Scotland* (1773)

PART ONE

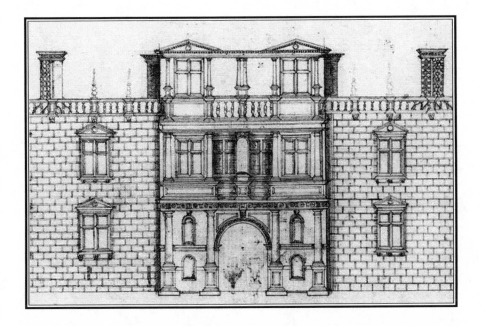

Traditional Architectural Amenity

1

COMMODIOUS COMFORT

Hall and Hearth, Chamber and Chimney

MEDIEVAL DEFINITIONS of domestic amenity gave priority to social status over personal physical comfort. For example, fourteenth-century ecclesiastical records on the condition of clerical housing used the term *competent* or its Latin form *competens* to approve a particular residence's suitability for a benefice's status and wealth. Similarly, a chronicle reported that Archbishop (of York) George Neville furnished his newly remodeled courtyard manorhouse "ryghte *comodiously* and plesauntly"—in hopes of a royal visit. These terms assigned a greater value to the harmony of domestic environment and social status than to a subjective physical standard.[1]

Physical comfort lacked priority as a value or a problem in medieval material culture. Ulrich Wyrwa has observed that medieval European languages "had no special term for the provision of the basic needs of food, clothing, and shelter"; the terminology for the consumption of goods initially developed in mercantilist discussions of fiscal issues, as "that which is taxed." *Comfort* in English derived from the medieval French *conforter/confort* (*soutenir/ encouragement*, meaning physical and emotional support). Before the middle of the eighteenth century, when used as a noun with physical reference, *comfort* usually had medicinal or nutritional connotations.[2]

Medieval articulations of *dis*comfort emphasized dirtiness, because it implied disrespect. The thirteenth-century "Dream of Rhonabwy" in the collection of Welsh tales known as *The Mabinogion* describes such discomfort on a heroic scale as Rhonabwy enters a nearly deserted longhouse and byre:

> [Rhonabwy and two companions] came to the house of Heilyn Goch son of Cadwgawn son of Iddon for lodgings. And as they came towards the house, they could see a black old hall with a straight gable end, and smoke a-plenty from it. And when they came inside, they could see a floor full of holes and uneven. Where there was a bump upon it, it was with difficulty a man might stand thereon, so exceedingly slippery was the floor with cow's urine and their dung. Where there was a hole, a man would go over the ankle, what with the mixture of water and cow-dung; and branches of holly a-plenty on the floor after the cattle had eaten off their tips. And when they came to the main floor of the house they could see bare dusty dais boards, and a crone feeding a fire on the one dais, and when cold came upon her she would throw a lapful of husks on to the fire, so that it was not easy for any man alive to endure that smoke entering his nostrils. . . .
>
> And when their resting-place was examined there was nothing on it save dusty flea-ridden straw-ends, and branch butts a-plenty throughout it, after the oxen had eaten all the straw that was on it above their heads and below their feet. A grayish-red, threadbare, flea-infested blanket was spread thereon, and over the blanket a coarse broken sheet in tatters, and a half-empty pillow and filthy pillow-case thereon, on top of the sheet. And they went to sleep.

Medieval housekeeping advice gave a high priority to preventing such interior filth as Rhonabwy and his companions endured. The most thorough such book is *Le ménagier de Paris* (c. 1393), presented as the advice of an elderly "bourgeois" to his young wife. It gives an unusually rich and specific assessment of physical amenities and discomforts:

> Wherefore love your husband's person carefully, and I pray you keep him in clean linen, for that is your business, and because the trouble

and care of outside affairs lieth with men, so must husbands take heed, and go and come, and journey hither and thither, in rain and wind, in snow and hail, now drenched, now dry, now sweating, now shivering, ill-fed, ill-lodged, ill-warmed and ill-bedded. And naught harmeth him, because he is upheld by the hope that he hath of the care which his wife will take of him on his return, and of the ease, the joys and the pleasures which she will do him, or cause to be done to him in her presence; to be unshod before a good fire, to have his feet washed and fresh shoes and hose, to be given good food and drink, to be well served and well looked after, well bedded in white sheets and nightcaps, well covered in good furs, and assuaged with other joys and desports, privities, loves and secrets whereof I am silent. And the next day fresh shirts and garments. . . .

. . . remember the rustic proverb, which saith that there be three things which drive the goodman from home, to wit a leaking roof, a smoky chimney and a scolding woman.

A man's physical requirements for comfort were clean clothes, a well-appointed bed, a fire, and someone to serve him these amenities. By far his major discomforts came from the bugs that infested his bedding and chamber—fleas, mosquitoes, and flies—and the author gave dozens of remedies to eliminate them.[3]

In books of courtesy, which became numerous in the fifteenth century, the terms assessing physical amenity dealt particularly with cleanliness and orderliness, especially of fabrics. Attention to tidiness maintained security over valuables in a open household and kept multiuse spaces available for different activities. The "dressing" of tables and chambers was critical for their satisfactoriness. The serving of meals emphasized scrupulousness in setting the table, particularly in having a smooth, white tablecloth. Thus, it was permissible to throw unwanted food on the floor for the attendant dogs but not to spit on the table nor to clean teeth with the tablecloth. The provision of facilities for washing was a crucial element of hospitality, requiring that guests be able to wash their hands before meals. As guests entered to dine, a servant called a ewer assisted with a pitcher and basin, while another provided a towel for drying. As an alternative there might be a *lavour* (basin) near or in the hall for washing oneself. As with most aspects of physical amenity, personal sanitation had a more elaborate priority in ecclesiastical institutions than in secular households. All monasteries had *lavatoria,* rooms in which the monks washed their hands before entering the refectory, and some had running water controlled by spigots. Monasteries also had latrines, and garde-robes (small rooms for a privy) were much more likely to be found in clerical housing, even at the level of parish priests, than in civilian dwellings.[4]

But among the laity, even people of means did not require much furniture for personal accommodation. *Le ménagier de Paris* mentions none, and Heilyn Goch's hall was empty because its furniture had gone with him elsewhere. Medieval vocabularies give us some idea of the items required or desired for domestic amenity, though their compilers probably exaggerated for peda-gogical purposes. John of Garland, an Englishman teaching in France in the early thirteenth century, listed furnishings necessary for a gentleman's house: "a decent table, a clean cloth, hemmed towels, high tripods, strong trestles, firebrands, fuel logs, stakes, bars, benches, forms, armchairs, wooden frames and chairs made to fold, quilts, bolsters, and cushions." Most of the English words for the amenities of household accommodation—such as *chamber, tester* (bed canopy), and *parlor*—were Norman French in origin, which implies their newness and their noble associations in English medieval culture. Medieval furnishing design gave priority to portability, so that amenities could follow the nobles' itinerant households—hence *meubles* and *mobilier* as generic terms for what would later be furnishings that stayed in one house and made it liv-able. Security, too, had a high priority in the need for and design of furni-ture. In medieval domestic environments the archetypal item of furniture was the chest, which was used to transport other items of household accom-modation, notably textiles, and provided a place to sit or sleep when travel stopped.[5] Having a seat was a sign of status, so domestic space had few chairs, and most other seating furniture—stools and benches—lacked backs.

Medieval peasant households often lacked seating furniture altogether, while their furnishings for food preparation were proportionately more im-portant than in aristocratic households. Given the vast disparities of wealth between the peasantry and the aristocracy, however, the *types* of furnishings are more striking in their similarities than in their differences. A prosperous peasant, able to maintain his household from his landholdings, could have "the usual table and pots and pans [and also] a towel, a silver spoon, a four-gallon and a twelve-gallon brass pot, a stool, a goblet, a blanket and two pairs of sheets, a mattress, a chest, a coffer, various serving utensils, a lamp, and a kiln or oven."[6] From the prosperous peasantry upward, the real disparities were in amounts and quality, not kind, of furnishings.

Spending on domestic furnishings went primarily into fabrics, for bedding and clothing, rather than on furniture. The fabrics in beds and clothing provided psychological and physical satisfactions: they asserted status, displayed wealth, and provided protection from the elements. From the twelfth through the seventeenth centuries the crucial household amenity was bedding. In Anglo-Saxon society the bed was a stuffed sack placed on a board or bench in an alcove. It was as much a place as a thing. The Normans developed the *tester* bed as a fixture that supported a tentlike enclosure of fabrics. From at least the thirteenth century it was desirable to have bedding stuffed with feathers or down rather than straw and to cover it with several layers of specialized textiles: "First, a *quilte* was spread over the bed; on this the bolster was placed; over this was laid a *quilte poynte* or *raye* (*counterpointe*, or counterpane); and on this, at the head of the bed, was placed the pillow. The sheets were then thrown over it, and the whole was covered with a coverlet." The bedding, not the bedstead, gave the bed value and prestige. Until the early nineteenth century, innovations in bedding involved the display of fabrics, not the design of mattresses or their supports. The display of bedding crucially communicated status because the bed was a place for social interaction, not just privacy. In the centuries before seating furniture became frequent, the bed provided a place to converse and to receive guests, who remained standing or sat on whatever horizontal surface was available, including the floor.[7]

Clothing provided the essential thermal protection from the elements. Just as housing and furniture were relatively homogeneous in type across the social spectrum—with enormous variation in cost of finish and scale—so most clothes worn in medieval Europe were of the same type, with great variations in their numbers and the expense of their materials. Women and men, civilians and religious, rich and poor—all wore shiftlike tunics of varying lengths over a shirt and hose. Cloaks provided further protection, especially if lined with fur, which could be anything from sable to fleece. Variations in these basic garments allowed for gender distinctions in aristocratic dress, with female clothing being more fitted to the upper body from the twelfth century on and men's tunics becoming shorter after the middle of the fourteenth century.[8] Comfort was associated primarily with fabrics and their cleanliness, rather than with the house itself.

Social Inclusion by the Hearth and Hall

The medieval hall and its open, chimneyless, hearth provide a baseline for studying the architecture of early modern comfort, particularly the elementary comforts of warmth and illumination. For a very long period, from the early Middle Ages after the decline of the Roman Empire through at least the sixteenth century, Europeans' domestic space had a common feature in most regions and social groups: the *hall*. Regardless of the size of a residence, this single room provided the crucial space for domestic, social, productive, and administrative purposes.[9] Though alternative spaces (the chamber) and facilities (the chimney fireplace) developed, and their priority in housing culture increased, they did not divert architectural focus from the hall and hearth combination until the sixteenth century. Instead, both combinations—hall with hearth and chamber with chimney fireplace—remained viable alternatives in designing the domestic environment in the late Middle Ages. Indeed, among the yeomanry and lesser gentry, designs of the hall/hearth became more elaborate in the fifteenth century. These patterns suggest that the hall/hearth was a discretionary feature of domestic architecture, and not inherently retrograde.

The elementary amenity of the hall was an open, central hearth—an unenclosed fire on the floor near the center of the room. Most rural houses in medieval Europe were chimneyless. Halls with an open central hearth were open up to the roof, where shuttered smoke holes overhead or in the gable exhausted the smoke. Windows on the wall opposite the hearth and a cross passage with opposing doors at one end of the hall provided some control over draft and a balancing of needs for air and light. The fire drew air from the door, and then the smoke exhausted through the windows as well as the smoke hole and *louver* (Fr. *louvre* = barred opening). (See Figure 1.1.) The open central hearth implied an unmediated relationship between the elements of heat and light—between the open fire and either darkness or direct sunlight admitted from out-of-doors through the smoke hole, windows, or doorways. This elemental quality of household amenity is apparent in the etymology of the English word *hearth*, which derives from *heorþ* in Anglo-Saxon, a word referring to *earth*. Aristocratic as well as peasant culture readily involved exposure to the elements. If people could be outside, they were—to work (including cooking, baking, and brewing), to play, to enter-

Figure 1.1. Hall and open hearth at Pennshurst, Kent. The magisterial view from the dais took in the passage screen, the massive roof beams, the *tables dormants*, and the hearth. John Henry Parker, *Some Account of Domestic Architecture in England from Edward I to Richard II* (Oxford: John Henry Parker, 1853), frontispiece.

tain, and to hunt. The open central hearth also suited medieval leisure activities indoors, such as chess and music, which did not require sharp viewing.[10]

Most historians of material culture treat the open hearth as an irrational and dysfunctional design. Lacking a flue to control sparks and smoke, open hearths seem inherently liable to cause house fires and respiratory ailments. With the open hearth in the middle of the hall, people were likely to set their clothes on fire as they moved about the room, while infants could burn themselves as they crawled about the floor. An open hearth supposedly resulted in a sooty, smoke-filled house. In fact, the anthropology of household ventilation in relation to heating and illumination shows that many cultures have developed sophisticated designs for heating spaces with open hearths while maintaining fresh air. It also shows that in some cultures a smoky interior is considered desirable.[11]

Historians' ethnocentric and anachronistic understandings of the open central hearth discount its symbolic importance in northern European cultures and its positive role in defining household amenity. The conjunction of the hall and the open central hearth were the literal and figurative center of medieval households. One of the earliest recorded English proverbs (c. 1300) refers to the happiness associated with one's hearth: "Este bueth one brondes" (One's own fire is pleasant). "Hearthmen" were retainers who had the privilege to sit by the fire with their lord. In customary law among English peasants, tenements descended to heirs by identification with the hearth not the dwelling: they were *astriers* (*astre* = hearth). Similarly, a term for widows' dower rights, *free bench,* referred to their privileged place near the hearth. Hearth-evoking terms such as *fire-house* identified the hall as an architectural space, while *hall* designated entire domestic complexes. Pre-Conquest Welsh and Anglo-Saxon poetry closely associated a hall's fire with the vitality of the lord who occupied it. In a frequently cited analogy, Bede's eighth-century history recounted a comparison of human life with a bird that passes momentarily through a noble's hall during a crowded meal:

> The present life of man, O king, seems to me, in comparison of that time which is unknown to us, like to the swift flight of a sparrow through the hall where you sit at your meal in winter, with your chiefs and attendants, warmed by a fire made in the middle of the hall, whilst storms of rain or snow prevail without; the sparrow, flying in at one door and immediately out at another, whilst he is visible is safe from the wintry storm, but after this short space of fair weather, he immediately vanishes out of your sight, into the dark winter from which he had emerged.

Bede assumed his listeners' ease in imagining a bird flying in one side of a house and out the other.[12]

Bede's analogy also shows how the open central hearth suited aristocratic patronage. The longitudinal axis of the hall established a superiority of the "upper" end of the hall, away from the entrance, over the lower end, where people entered. The head of the household could preside at the upper end, where there was often a dais, sometimes covered with a cloth or wooden canopy. The hearth in the center divided the rest of the company into symmetrical rankings by proximity to the lord of the house, while simultaneously providing a focus for a corporate group. The spatial relations of the open hearth were inherently sociable and hierarchical: it defined a single space with varying degrees of privilege and status. The hall marked the reciprocation of lordly patronage and personal service. From Carolingian times onward a symmetry of spatial and domestic organization of aristocratic households schematized the personal service of lesser nobles in attendance on their lord—at the dining table, and in the bedchamber, cellar (for drinks), and stables.[13]

As a social space the hall facilitated the feudal exercise of public power in private hands. Correspondingly, what had in Roman society been the private function of eating took place in the medieval hall in the company of non–family members. Eating in public (feasting) was the crucial design consideration of the aristocratic hall, the atom of medieval domestic architecture. Dining in the hall required elaborate and careful ritual with food and drink in order to observe status within and without the household. The door into the hall remained open during the day, to provide light and to indicate hospitality. The imperative to provide hospitality applied to townspeople and monastic communities as well as rural households: they too needed a hall-like space that provided flexible accommodation, and from the late thirteenth through the fifteenth centuries medieval town houses typically had open hearths.[14]

The architectural priority of the hall/hearth combination continued throughout the medieval period, even as the design of housing underwent basic changes in materials, structure, and plan. Building materials became heavier investments as stone foundations replaced post-in-hole framing, and timber framing became more extensively used in place of walling by semipermanent materials such as wattle-and-daub, mud, and cob. These materials corresponded to new structural designs, particularly upstairs chambers and halls of a single span with massive and elaborately framed roof timbers. House plans devised more specialized space, with parlors and great chambers for entertaining, and unitary plans that included service areas for cooking and food storage apart from the hall but in the same building.

Anglo-Saxon had lacked a term to designate a single building as a house. *Heorþ* (hearth) and *búr* (bower) served as metonyms for domestic space. The Anglo-Saxon hall was a modular building, with posts set in the ground as the

main structural members and walls of daubed wattling or turf-banked plank-
ing. Households replicated these barnlike buildings as needed for sleeping,
cooking, and keeping livestock and provisions. Visitors and retainers slept in
the hall, while the lordly family of the household slept in a separate building. In northern France, unlike in England until just before the Conquest,
magnates often associated two-story masonry "chamber blocks" with separate ground-level halls. This French preference apparently originated in Carolingian palaces, with their *aula* for services on the ground floor and *salle* for
hospitality on the second story.

Such stone two-story chambers, which often drew on monastic models,
became prestigious designs for aristocratic dwellings in thirteenth-century
England and Wales, but lesser knights seldom had them as accommodation.
Instead, twelfth- and thirteenth-century manor houses in England recalled
Anglo-Saxon designs with barnlike ground-floor halls and nearby ground-
level chambers. Otherwise, manor houses sometimes used a bay of their hall
to provide a chamber under the same roof as the hall's hearth. This "unitary
plan" became increasingly frequent for lesser manor houses. Persistence of
the Anglo-Saxon term *hall* corresponds with a continuation of ground-floor
halls with vestibules, despite the prestige of second-story accommodation
from French examples. *Salle*, the Norman French word for upper-level hall,
was not adopted in Middle English, while *manor* (Fr. *manoir*) became the term
for the whole residential complex.[15]

In the late twelfth century bishops' palaces began to provide more elaborate examples for the design of halls, on the principle that domestic spaces
for sleeping and food preparation should be subsidiary to and separate from
the hall and its hearth. To halls they added separate butteries (for the storage and service of drinks), often with solars (private upper chambers) above
them, either as an attachment to one of the gable walls or as a subdivision
of one of the hall's bays. A screen partitioned these additional domestic spaces
from the main space of the hall, and a door through the screen opened into
a cross passage that provided access from outside to both hall and service
end. As halls of a single span superseded aisled halls in the fourteenth century, manor houses typically separated spaces for sleeping and for services at
opposite ends of the hall. A passage entry separated the hall with its open
hearth from the space "below" the hall (i.e., beyond the lower end) which did
not need to be heated. In aristocratic households these were the buttery and
pantry. In agricultural households these could be service rooms for house-

hold production such as dairying, brewing, or weaving; or there could be a byre for cattle. This configuration corresponded with late medieval analogies between the dwelling and the body. The fourteenth-century French surgeon Henri de Mondeville distinguished two hierarchical parts of the body comparable respectively to the hall and the service spaces of an aristocratic household. In the lower, elemental, part of the body was a fire that prepared nourishment for the noble, upper part of the body and that eliminated what was not noble: "The purpose of the lower oven is to cook the nutritive humors, and, rather like a great kitchen fire, it is designed for slow combustion, for simmering soups and other peasant dishes; whereas the upper story contains a roaring fire to light the heart with joy."[16]

In the thirteenth century both barns and manor halls began to be built for permanency, with stone walls supporting massive timbers over aisled halls. Farming of demesnes (manor lands worked directly for the lord's income) became more intensive as grain prices rose, and lords concentrated their investment on fewer manors and larger barns. Having as large an open space as possible continued to be lords' priority in the design of their dwellings, especially after the previously aisled hall of Westminster was rebuilt with a single span in the middle of the fourteenth century. The hammer beam roof marked the eclipse of the aisled hall, as house carpenters increasingly used it to construct entirely open halls rather than aisled halls with their rows of posts to support the roof. Larger manor houses began to have their solar and service rooms at opposite ends of the hall in two-storied wings. Admiration for the massive woodwork associated with the aisled hall continued, however, and much of the energy invested in aristocratic domestic architecture focused on the design of roof timbers visible from within the open hall.[17]

Most of these supersessions of the aisled hall retained central open hearths as the source of heat in the hall. The prestige associated with impressive roof timbers encouraged use of the open hearth, since their display required a room open to the rafters. The introduction in the late thirteenth century of elaborate pottery louvers as ventilators for the hall (Figure 1.2) marked the persistent accommodation of the central open hearth. Such remodelings imply that the open hearth was an alternative to the chimney fireplace rather than a retrograde facility. Inconsistency in terminology for the louver (*fumatorium, fumerillum, fumericios*) marked the newness of this architectural improvement. The louver was a development beyond unglazed windows as a source of ventilation and light; in addition to exhausting smoke from the open

Figure 1.2. Louvers. Louvers announced a hall with an open central hearth; they exhausted smoke and admitted light while sheltering people below from the rain and wind. L. A. Shuffrey, *The English Fireplace* (London: B. T. Batsford, 1912), 7.

hearth, the louver admitted light from overhead while protecting the interior from rain and cross drafts. In the late Middle Ages the open hearth was not an archaism. On the contrary, halls open to the roof continued to be built, both by their traditional group, the aristocracy, and by the gentry and yeomanry.[18]

THE CHAMBER AND SPATIAL EXCLUSION

In its relative specialization of domestic space, the chamber was exceptional but necessary in medieval residential architecture. English housing culture held that there should be a domestic space separate from the hall. Thus, in the "Nun's Priest's Tale" Chaucer gives even the poor widow a private space in her "narwe cotage": "Ful sooty was hir boure and eek hire hall." In Anglo-Saxon *búr* (bower) referred to a space distinct from the hall and used particularly for the sequestration of women and their activities and for storage. In Anglo-Saxon and immediately post-Conquest England noble households typically had separate buildings for the feudal hall and for women's household space. When Chaucer used *chamber* as well as *bower* for a space apart from the hall, he was using a new English word. *Chamber* derived from the French *chambre*, whose Latin root (*camera* = vaulted ceiling) referred to any room. In medieval French domestic architecture, from the eleventh century on, second-story domestic spaces were associated with wealthy, nonagricultural households. Initially the stairs to these solars were outside, in order to inhibit casual entrance from the hall and to enhance their defensibility. Post-Conquest manor houses in England carried over this design. In the thirteenth century, when English manorial halls were usually at ground level, chambers remained on the second floor, with associations of greater status and wealth, whether noble, urban, or monastic. English usage of the word began in the early fourteenth century, when it referred to a private place, usually with bedding. *Chamber* and *solar* became synonyms during the fourteenth century, since chambers, like solars, could be upstairs while bowers were ground-level rooms. In the Midlands and the North, *chamber* was not used before the fifteenth century; then the word distinguished an upstairs room from the parlor, and *parlor* began to designate a first-floor room for sleeping and entertaining. Apparently halls in these regions had previously contained beds.[19]

The purposes of the hall and chamber were in tension as well as being complementary, and their respective designs could change independently. The status functions of the hall changed less over the medieval period than did application of the principle of female seclusion to the increase of chambers. The aristocracy collectively had reasons to enforce the relative exclusion of women from their households: negative reasons in that women were viewed as a catalyst for conflict in a household with many single men; positive reasons in terms of maximizing the opportunities for those men to serve the lord in order to enjoy his patronage. The medieval aristocratic household was over 90 percent male, from the steward to the cooks. Even senior household officials were discouraged from having wives in the household, and women, even as wives accompanying noble visitors, were seldom guests. Besides the noblewomen, the only women likely in a household were a few laundresses and the attendants on the lord's wife and daughters. Women did not often attend banquets; instead they were acknowledged to be eating simultaneously in chambers. When women took part in feasts in the hall, they left before the drinking that followed.[20]

Privacy in a separate household space had a close association with women, since it was otherwise contrary to the noblesse oblige associated with the hall. An 1117 description of an especially impressive Norman house in Flanders refers to a second-story hall with an adjacent "great chamber in which the lord and his wife slept." Next to the hall was a "dormitory of the waiting maids and children," and within the great chamber itself was "a certain private room, where at early dawn or in the evening or during sickness or at time of blood-letting or for warming the maids and weaned children," they had a fire. Whether the fire burned in an open hearth or a chimney fireplace—or most likely, a brazier, given its episodic use—was not indicated, but its warmth was apparently subsidiary to concerns about privacy based on the occupants' maturity and gender.[21]

Use of the "chamber" in the castle keep highlighted its function in separating women, especially the lord's wife and daughters, from the hall in the overwhelmingly male population of the castle. In thirteenth-century poetry the castle figures as a place for the supervision of alluring women. In the later Middle Ages a household's capacity to provide separate domestic space for women continued to connote high social status. Investment in women's household furnishings corresponded with their being less mobile than noblemen and hence more fully resident. Given the itinerancy of the barons through their domains in the thirteenth century, noblewomen were especially likely to be the long-term occupants of any particular castle (Figure 1.3).[22]

Chambers eventually became spaces associated with physical comfort, but in medieval England they primarily served principles of security and female seclusion that were applicable to all households. The chamber provided a space for withdrawal from the hall by the lord and/or lady of a household and their privileged company and attendants. Increased importance of the chamber's furnishings and activities did not imply informality or casual comfort. Household ritual and ceremony became more elaborate and precise in

Figure 1.3. Chamber and female privacy. Fabrics sumptuously accommodate Christian de Pisan, Isabeau of Bavaria, and their attendants. Manuscript collection, Harley MS 4431: f. 3, the British Library.

the fourteenth and fifteenth centuries as the great chamber became a space for selective entertainment.[23]

THE BYRE AND VERNACULAR WELL-BEING

Subsidiary spaces in the houses of peasants and lords in Anglo-Norman England differed in their implications of social status. For the lord the important subsidiary space was the chamber, for domestic sequestration; for the peasant it was the byre, where animals were kept and raw materials were processed. At the village level of society, having animals under the same roof was a sign of wealth, not poverty. The major design change in English peasant housing after the Norman conquest involved the connection of the byre to a hall-like "longhouse." The house with byre was rare in Britain before the twelfth century, but by the fourteenth century it was found nearly throughout southern England. The frequency of such "byre-houses" increased with prosperity. Before the drop in population after the Black Death the holders of longhouses with byres were likely to be enserfed, but they were better off materially than many of their free neighbors. Longhouses marked the prosperity of cattle-owning peasants in relation to poorer peasants, who lived in small one- or two-roomed *cotts.* Cottars' households, which might make up the majority of a thirteenth-century village, lacked the capability in animals and plows to cultivate the village's fields. By comparison, the longhouse represented economic competency, even though its level of domestic accommodation was little different from that of the cottars. The domestic space in both cases was about the same size and layout, with an open hearth in a hall-like room and a vestibule at a gable end (Figure 1.4).[24]

Longhouses with byres, accommodating animals and humans under the same roof, appeared at the same time that priorities in construction shifted toward greater permanency. Turf houses had no windows or special facilities to exhaust smoke. Houses with stone walls now had openings for light, and some had wattle-and-daub fire hoods over their hearths. Architectural features also increasingly differentiated human spaces from animal spaces. Early byres usually lacked partitions to separate the human area from the livestock, but in stone buildings partitions of various heights or full walls with doors could be built to divide the house and byre while allowing direct communication between them. Opposing doorways to the entry passage could be staggered so that the wider door for the animals was nearer the byre. Longhouses with byres often had a separate and raised space at their "upper" end (opposite the end draining the byre), for sleeping and/or storage. As these differentiations took place, the term *home* shifted its reference from the agricultural community to the residences of individual households.[25]

Just as with nobles' halls, the spatial functions and physical accommodations of medieval peasant houses changed much less than the standards for their construction. Many of the more permanently constructed houses were longhouses, and most continued to use central open hearths and to have earthen floors and unglazed windows. The improvements were in the quality of construction, especially in the carpentry associated with crucks, doors, and shutters. Crucks provided the equivalent of both wall and roof framing in a single massive timber and manifested the prosperity of a landholder

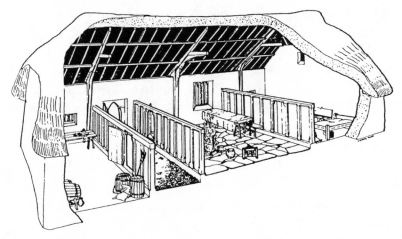

Figure 1.4. Longhouse with open hearth. This sketch of a medieval house in east Devon shows all the elements of a classic longhouse: cross-passage between service and living areas, a single open hearth in the paved hall, a chamber separated from the hall by a half-wall that allowed it to share the hall's heat, unglazed barred windows, a vent in the gable to exhaust smoke, and massive roof timbers. M. W. Barley, *Houses and History* (London: Faber & Faber, 1986), 159. Reprinted by permission.

who could afford even the minimum of two pairs of crucks required for a building. Timber roofing emphasized the heightened priority for permanency in the construction of peasant houses. Before large timbers came into use peasants had roofed their houses with roughly cut branches covered with thatch or turf.[26]

Permanency in the construction of dwellings gained strong associations with social status in the twelfth and thirteenth centuries, a period when masonry castles had architectural priority among secular buildings. Before the Norman invasion impermanent construction characterized nearly all domestic architecture in Britain, including manors and palaces. Virtually no peasant dwellings survive from before the thirteenth century in southeastern England, and in some areas of upland England and Wales there are none from before the seventeenth century—rough measures of the chronology of permanent construction in those regions. Archaeological remains from preceding periods show houses of impermanent materials—cob or turf walls, reinforced by light poles set in the ground. Such houses typically required rebuilding every ten to twenty years.[27]

The commencement of permanent construction of peasant houses in the thirteenth century corresponded with higher grain prices, prompted by increased demand in long-settled areas, and with more intensive exploitation of agricultural holdings in areas where common lands and wastes could be enclosed. This new permanency in construction also corresponded to increased social differentiation at the village level, as a few families in each village accumulated land and took on profitable leases from local manors and monasteries. In the early fourteenth century such families typically ceased to live in longhouses with attached byres and began to occupy courtyard complexes of house, barn, and byre. These "farmhouses" separated the living and agricultural spaces into separate buildings. As their numbers became greater the prevalence of longhouses with byres declined. But in upland England, houses with byres continued in use into the seventeenth century, and their numbers increased in some areas of the North.[28]

After the Black Death, tenants, being in lower supply relative to the availability of leaseholds, could negotiate more secure tenures, which further encouraged investment in permanent housing and outbuildings. Investment in permanent house construction saved the costs of maintenance associated with earthfast construction. Vernacular houses of permanent construction differed from cotts in being built by paid labor using purchased materials rather than by the occupier using waste materials from manorial lands. Walls of materials more substantial than mud and clay could be higher, and therefore the house did not require a sunken floor in order to have a roof high enough to allow an open central hearth. Survivors of the Black Death were further able to accumulate land and to secure themselves advantageous terms for leases. The intensification of demesne farming reversed in the fourteenth century, and lands increasingly were rented to the exceptionally wealthy peasants in each village who had already accumulated enough land to provide the capital to make sizable leases profitable. These wealthier tenants could emulate the gentry's material standard of living, particularly as represented by the manorial hall. By the late fourteenth century the plan of open hall with crosswing(s) of chamber and/or service rooms at the end(s) was frequent among prosperous peasant households in southeastern England. These larger houses, apparently drawing on gentry models, were vernacular in the sense that in the fifteenth and early sixteenth centuries many thousands must have been built, since thousands survive today.[29]

Peasants' use of open central hearths survived their redesignings of construction, space, and function in housing. Indeed, the new priorities of design in these houses suited use of an open central hearth. The competency

of the householder with a longhouse was particularly manifest in his investment in crucks to support a high roof for a hall-like room. In the late fourteenth and fifteenth centuries many thousands of English peasant households distinguished themselves from their fellow villagers by investing in
cruck-built or timber-framed houses on stone foundations. These houses
usually had two or three bays consisting of an open-hearthed hall and one
or two chambers. In the North and Midlands houses were single-storied; in
East Anglia and Kent the combination of hall with second-story chambers
was more frequent. With its two-storied wings and jettied front reminiscent
of town houses, the Wealden house of the fifteenth- and the early-sixteenth-
century Southeast resembled the manor house rather than the longhouse,
even though the hall remained open to the roof and often had an open
hearth. An exception proving the more typical acceptance of the open central hearth was the preference for fire hoods in northern England as soon as
peasants there began to build large open halls. Lath and plaster fire hoods
there were of such size that they defined a room within the hall itself, and in
the middle of that subsidiary space was an open hearth around which members of the household gathered to sit on highbacked settles that further
enclosed the space.[30]

Vernacular emulation of architectural improvement perpetuated the open,
central hearth. Numerous proverbs from the fourteenth century through the
sixteenth century acknowledged the necessary coexistence of fire and smoke:

Make no fire, raise no smoke.

No fire, no smoke.

The smoke of a man's own house is better than the fire of another.

Among yeomen the open hearth suited an impressive cruck-built hall, just as
among more modest peasant households it allowed the extensive adoption
of the longhouse with byre. Longhouses coexisted with farmhouses having
detached barns and stables. In the medieval period these differences were
related more closely to relative wealth than to the evolution of design. Similarly, differences of wealth rather than evolution of design account more
strongly for the variations *among* longhouses. Elements of design evident by
the thirteenth century, such as three-room plans, partitions and walls between

spaces for humans and those for animals, separate entrances for humans and for animals, and hearths located so they could heat the inner chamber as well as the hall, continued for centuries to accommodate the open hearth.[31]

Chimneys and Privacy

Over the thirteenth and fourteenth centuries chimney fireplaces became frequent in English dwellings. Their adoption has seemed so natural to architectural historians and historians of material culture generally that it has largely gone uninvestigated. The chimney fireplace has become a marker of minimal civilized comfort. In fact, the chimney was not a precondition of medieval comfort generally. Use of the chimney fireplace in medieval England depended on particular circumstances—individual lodgings in corporate religious institutions, castles used as residences, and spatial protection for aristocratic women—that were compatible with continued use of the open central hearth in other social spaces.[32]

The origins of the chimney fireplace as a facility in English domestic heating are obscure. Chimneys were used in French domestic architecture earlier and more widely than in England. In twelfth-century France they were frequently used in houses other than castles, and "the chimney stack may have become universal at least a hundred years sooner than in England." The English term *chimney* derives closely from the French *cheminée*, whose etymology supposedly depends on the Latin *caminus*, relating to domestic and manufacturing furnaces. Another etymological candidate is *chemise*, referring to a cloth hanging from the mantle to keep smoke in the flue. French use of *cheminée* in its modern sense is documented from the twelfth century; English records begin to use *chimney* two centuries later. These differences of usage indicate both the French origins of the device and its relative infrequency in medieval England. Anglo-Saxon had no equivalent term; *fýr* signified both fire and hearth.[33]

The technology of a flue to convey smoke from an open fire—a chimney—is ancient, but it was not used for Roman domestic heating. Roman domestic architecture used completely open and completely enclosed fires for heating. Roman families took their meals in the atrium, a partially roofed court named from the blackening smoke (*ater* = gloomy black) given off by open fires and braziers. The flue (*evaporatio fumi* or *exitus fumi*) was used in antiquity as a means to exhaust smoke from bake ovens and the furnaces of hypocausts (ancient Roman central heating systems), as well as to increase the draft in furnaces for thermal processes such as metalworking and ceramics. The term *caminus* referred to the furnace whose smoke such flues exhausted; it did not have a domestic reference because there were no chimney fireplaces in Roman houses. Virtually all villas in Rome's transalpine provinces used hypocausts, in addition to the movable braziers and open hearths that usually heated villas in cisalpine Roman areas. Medieval Latin would use *caminus* to refer to the chimney fireplace, and the term *caminata*— from *camera caminata*—to refer to rooms that had chimney fireplaces.

ECCLESIASTICAL SOURCES OF DOMESTIC AMENITY

Plans from the 820s for the remodeling of the monastery of St. Gall in Switzerland provide an almost unique, and certainly the richest, early reference in medieval European records to the likely use of fireplaces with chimneys to heat living areas. The plan used various Roman heating technologies. Chimneyless stove ranges heated baths and provided fires for the kitchen. Hypocaust-like facilities heated the plan's infirmary and novitiate. But the plans also called for chimney fireplaces (*caminata*)—in the abbot's house, the guest house, the house for bloodletting, and the physician's house, all of which were relatively private spaces outside the claustral precinct. Most of the officers of the monastery had chimney fireplaces in their quarters, while none of the workmen or monks without office did.[34]

Where this design originated is still a matter of speculation. The expansion of monasticism in the fifth century could have provided a vector to northern Europe from Near Eastern sources, but what the sources there might have been is only a guess. Early chimneys invariably had ovenlike conical hoods over the hearth, and by inference from etymology as well as shape, ovens may have been the design source of the chimney fireplaces at St. Gall. The influence of St. Gall's chimney design on other monasteries, not to mention domestic spaces generally, is similarly hypothetical. After this early-ninth-century depiction there are no further illustrations of chimneys in northwestern European domestic spaces for several centuries. When records of chimney fireplaces became less rare, in eleventh-century France, the hypocaust had passed out of the northern European architectural vocabulary, though stoves had begun to be used in German areas from Alsace eastward. By then, monastic warming rooms in northwestern Europe were heated by braziers or open hearths. (Indeed, most of St. Gall's buildings with chimney fireplaces also had an open central hearth [*locus foci* = fireplace], with a central lantern [*testu*] overhead to vent smoke.) Thus, it is evident that the principle of flues for domestic hearths was known in the early Middle Ages from the technology of antiquity, and northern European building technology was compatible with the use of flues in houses, but apparently most medieval households resisted their adoption.[35]

Monastic institutions like St. Gall represented a rejection of traditional culture and everyday standards of living. In architecture this rationality articulated distinct spaces for different domestic activities—praying, eating (frater), sleeping (dormitory, or dorter), washing (*lavatorium*), even defecating (*reredorter*). This articulation of space contrasted sharply with the multipurpose use of space in secular dwellings. Even though monasteries too used hall-like spaces for most of their activities, the halls had specialized purposes. Similarly, the chambers that monasteries appropriated from secular architecture provided more intensive individual privacy than they did in familial households.[36]

The monastic articulation of accommodation provided models for lay people to copy. Parlors were initially simply passageways separating the claustral precincts from outside. The outer parlor connected the cellarer's range with outside supplies, while the inner parlor (locutorium or slype), at one end of the subdorter, enabled monks to communicate with outsiders while remaining cloistered. In the eleventh century, abbots and priors still slept in the dorter with the other monks, but they had a privileged location at one end, toward the parlor. Since they had to deal with outsiders, they increasingly sought alternative accommodation in the cellarer's range. By the end of the twelfth century, abbots and priors had moved out of the dorter and into separate lodgings that included hall, chamber, and chapel. Once the abbot's accommodation moved out of the dorter, his house took over the parlor's communicative function spatially, and the parlor became a ground-floor room with functions and facilities overlapping those of both the hall and the chamber in secular dwellings. It provided a space to receive visitors with more privacy than was available in the hall but with less intimacy than meeting in the chamber implied. This reception room for visitors to monastic houses apparently provided the model and name for the parlor in secular dwellings. Its defining feature was a decorated fireplace.[37]

With the rules and plans for monastic buildings so clear and purposeful in their austerity, exceptions and alternatives to ascetic standards were similarly self-conscious. Precisely because heating could not be taken for granted in monastic living spaces but was instead deliberately proscribed for both eating and sleeping spaces, more care was taken in its privileged use. In the eleventh century a new guest house was built at Cluny for noble visitors. It provided a model for individual physical amenity: each person had a separate bed and latrine, and there was a fireplace in their joint refectory. Early-thirteenth-century monastic architecture frequently introduced chimneys for heating spaces other than the warming room, such as monks' cells and guests' quarters. By the same period the higher secular clergy, such as bishops and deans, had chambers with chimneys, apparently borrowed from monastic examples.[38]

Lodgings for individuals without families or personal servants were more frequent in ecclesiastical institutions than in feudal households. Religious foundations such as chantries and university and cathedral colleges had to provide space for individual prayer and study as well as physical accommodation. These needs led to a more uniform standard of physical amenity there than in other residential architecture. Such lodgings accommodated more or less permanent occupation, in contrast to the transitory and flexible lodgings provided visitors in the hall, who might be bedded temporarily on the floor.[39]

The Carthusian order, which added over one hundred establishments throughout Europe during the fourteenth century, used cellular accommodation to allow a more solitary life. Carthusians prayed together daily, but took meals together in the refectory only on Sundays and feast days. On other days monks ate in their individual "cells," which were really small houses with ample space for one person. Their highly articulated facilities included a garden, a hall heated with a chimney fireplace, an oratory, a bedroom, and a latrine. The cells of the Carthusians reinforced the association between physical amenity and social withdrawal already implied by the contrast between the hall and the chamber in accommodation and social usage.[40]

Even in the more whole-heartedly communal orders, there was a tendency in the fourteenth and fifteenth centuries to compromise communal life for individual accommodation. From the late fourteenth century until the dissolution of the monasteries, remodelings of monks' accommodation often followed standards previously applicable to monks in need of medical treatment or recuperation. In many monasteries healthy monks increasingly took meals in the infirmary, the misericord, where the enhanced diet included meat. The insertion of new floor levels into refectory halls divided them into meatless fraters, where the order's rule could be followed, while providing equal space for nominal misericorda. In the more indulgent dining area, chimney fireplaces took the place of the refectory's pulpitum. The remodeling of the infirmary at Westminister Abbey in the 1360s added chambers and parlors. Although infirmaries were intended for the "transient sick," monks soon occupied them permanently and appointed them with cushions and curtains.[41]

Monks holding offices were entitled to exemptions from full compliance with the common life. Most monks with such privileges chose to live in private chambers, and many other monks found ways to follow their example. At any one time from the late fourteenth century through the dissolution of the monasteries, almost half the monks at Westminister Abbey lived in private chambers. Similarly, in a precocious example of a "grand country mansion," Durham priory built a subpriory at Finchale to provide three-week retreats for groups of four monks at a time. Visiting monks spent most of their time either in the prior's lodgings, which had a chimney, wainscoting, and bay and oriel windows, or else in the "Player Chamber," a heated parlor. At the end of the fourteenth century the monks at Durham priory itself rebuilt all of the conventual buildings except the refectory. The refectory's communal function ran against a new priority for individualized accommodation in the rest of the renovations. The new dormitory partitioned previously open sleeping areas into alcoves for individual study and sleeping. For such partitioned dormitories, the prior's parlor, which typically had feather beds, painted cloths, and silver candlesticks, provided a model for furnishings.[42]

A similar process of replacing communal living spaces with small residential units took place in nunneries in the fourteenth and fifteenth centuries. *Familiae,* small groups taking their meals together, effectively formed households within the larger nominal community. Sleeping accommodations became more private still, as separate spaces draped off within the dorter eventually were enclosed solidly as cells. These spaces allowed nuns to entertain visitors in quarters provided with fireplaces and windows, and furnished with wall hangings, chests, cupboards, and beds—just as the prioress had been accommodated all along.[43]

The system of corrodies (charitable grants entitling individuals to monastic accommodation) further associated monasteries with nontraditional definitions of standards of living. Corrodies (from *corrodere* = to gnaw away) provided lay people the domestic amenities of monastic establishments while requiring no obligation to their rules. Holders of corrodies included servants of the monastery, charitable cases, people able to buy one for themselves, and beneficiaries of royal or noble largesse. Corrodies were part of the late medieval shift in charitable priorities, from monasteries to secular church foundations, such as chantries, hospitals, almshouses, and colleges. The architecture of these secular institutions followed the principle of solitary accommodation. Fourteenth-century colleges typically provided two-story ranges of rooms, with several students occupying each room as a sleeping space and each having partitioned space for study. When heated, such rooms had chimneys, since the rooms' low ceilings precluded open hearths.[44]

Chimneys were especially likely to be used in the accommodation of respectable people who lived in small or solitary households, namely the clergy. Numerous houses were built for chantry priests in the fifteenth century. Some of them were collegiate in scale, others had only a few priests and were domestic in scale. The latter typically had a ceiled hall with a wall chimney, and the priests' individual chambers also had chimneys. Such chimneys did not necessarily convey higher status than central hearths. In the late fifteenth century small priests' houses lacked a parlor but were more likely than large ones to have a chimney fireplace, rather than an open hearth, in their hall.[45]

Use of chimneys in medieval accommodation corresponds in part with the clergy's increased preference for small, private spaces. This preference was most marked initially among the regular clergy, who already had a rationale for the importance of solitude, for prayer and study. In the twelfth and thirteenth centuries the higher secular clergy began to emulate monastic domestic accommodation and to preach their ideal of a more personal piety conducted in physical privacy. Such prayer called for special books—psalters and books of hours—and for a special place, the oratory, to read them. As oratories came into use for secular as well as pious activities, they became "closets"—eventually, in the seventeenth century, the focus of amenity in an aristocratic dwelling.[46]

THE CASTLE AND THE NEED FOR FIREPLACE CHIMNEYS

Besides their use in monasteries, chimney fireplaces also become numerous in castles built by the Anglo-Normans in the first half of the twelfth century.

The prestige of building a castle depended on building or supporting a monastery as well. Barons building castles in eleventh- and twelfth-century England supported the establishment of dozens of religious houses by Benedictines from Normandy. These connections in patronage allowed monastic architectural expertise from the Continent to be applied to the design of castles. The chimney entered Norman and English architectural vocabulary during a period of castle building.[47] Endemic warfare among French feudal lords, as they established seigneuries after the breakdown of the Carolingian principalities in the tenth century, required them to build fortresses to mark and maintain their dominion. From the late tenth century through the thirteenth century, castles were the most impressive, expensive, and sophisticated type of secular architecture. The donjon, or keep, a masonry tower capable of withstanding siege, developed as their crucial feature. These towers had no ground-level doors, and their external windows were minimal in size and number, in order to protect against missiles. In northwestern France, particularly in Normandy and along the Loire, the donjon was a place of refuge, perhaps with a solar, but not a residence. A walled area abutted the tower and enclosed service buildings, such as stables, and a hall in which the lord could entertain and live with his household in times of peace.

In structure (a tower) and function ("the personal defense of magnates against rivals or their own discontented peasants") the French castle represented a military and political revolution when it was imported to England. Though not necessarily a residence, the keep needed to have capability as domestic accommodation in order to fulfill its crucial military purpose, to withstand a siege. The initial Norman fortifications after the Conquest were motte-and-baileys, whose crucial feature was a steep artificial hill with a palisaded timber tower at its top. The motte was the dry moat and tower complex, the bailey an adjacent area of services, stores, and residences enclosed by a ditch. The small scale and timbered construction of the motte limited its domestic capacity to short periods, and over the course of the twelfth century mottes were usually replaced with larger structures of masonry. In resolving the difference between domestic and military functions, the keep became the barons' primary residence in Norman England. The White Tower at the Tower of London set a grand standard for the post-Conquest generation: a massive ground-floor wall with no external openings, a fortified second-story doorway reached by an external stairway and giving admission to a second-story hall, and upper stories with chambers.[48]

The distinctive feature of castles in England, the hall-keep, developed after the Conquest. Intended to overawe and dominate a conquered populace, the hall-keep had no equivalent on the Continent. Hall-keeps brought together the motte's combination of defensive and residential functions, the Continental preference to have second-story rather than ground-level halls, and the masonry construction techniques of the Norman gatehouse. Large masonry castles could not be built on artificial mounds, but they could provide their own defenses from height, and they could be built on a scale that allowed compartmentalization of domestic space in rooms set off from the hall.[49] Actually *living* in the keep encouraged innovations with the hall's arrangements for heat and light. These hybrid innovations inevitably required compromises between domestic and military imperatives. Window openings had to be kept small for defensive purposes, particularly on the lower stories, but to provide illumination they opened onto niches in the walls, even though such cavities compromised the tower's capacity to withstand shock missiles. Chambers to which the lord would withdraw from the hall could be stacked vertically over the hall or in towers, where their altitude then made larger windows less of a liability from missiles. When there were chambers above rather than alongside the hall, it was impossible to use smoke holes to exhaust smoke from an open hearth (Figure 1.5).

In the hall-keep, fireplaces were more necessary and possible than in the motte—more necessary because the incorporation of residential spaces meant that hall-keeps were likely to be multistoried and therefore relatively unsuited to an open central hearth, more possible because it was safer to build flues in masonry walls than in timber palisades. (What accommodation was like in the *timber* towers on mottes is obscure.) By 1200 hall-keeps often had chimney fireplaces in the hall. Flues for these early chimneys passed obliquely through the wall rather than rising vertically through the height of the building to the roofline (Figure 1.6). (Latrines in keeps were in design just inverted fireplaces, and were at least as numerous.) A vertical chimney flue would have provided a much more effective draft, but the flimsiness of the stack would have made it vulnerable to destruction by catapulted missiles, and a flue that passed vertically through the entire rise of the tower would have been equivalent to the besieger's tactic of undermining a wall. Architectural evidence for vertical chimney stacks does not become frequent until the thirteenth century, the same time illustrations of chimneys and fireplaces appeared in manuscript illuminations.[50]

Interior View.   *Section.*

Figure 1.5. Fireplaces in keep. Multilevel accommodation in castles precluded open central hearths. L. A. Shuffrey, *The English Fireplace* (London: B. T. Batsford, 1912), 16.

It cannot be assumed that the chimneys in castles represented improvements over open hearths in the exhausting of smoke. The short, oblique course of flues from fireplaces set into the walls of castles provided neither a vertical path for warm smoke nor a significant pressure differential between the fireplace and the outside air. The inefficiency of the chimneys in castles is suggested in the preference for having kitchens in the walled yard rather than in the keep, even though the location made service difficult. Outright improvements in physical amenity would have been, at best, a subsidiary imperative for the initial adoption of the chimney, since early castles were not primarily domestic spaces, and open hearths continued to be used in manors. There was always a tendency for domestic life to move out of the tower keep and into a hall in the bailey or castle yard. In the thirteenth century, as masonry walls provided castle yards in place of earthwork baileys, such halls became more secure and open hearths continued to be used in them.[51]

Indeed, from the early thirteenth century through the middle of the fourteenth century, English castle building moved the residential spaces of the hall, chamber, and chapel, out of the keep and encircled them with a defensive perimeter of curtain wall, towers, and gatehouse. When castles were remodeled along these lines, what had previously been second-story halls typically became solars. The new halls were built on the ground floor, with the result that halls once again had open hearths while solars now had chimney fireplaces. In the thirteenth century one castle might have several halls within its walls, each hall serving several noble households, and each household having its own chamber. The chambers were typically at second-story level, in towers and gatehouses, and accordingly had fireplaces and garderobes.[52]

The archetypal location of the chimney fireplace was in the chamber. The frequency of chimneys in aristocratic living spaces increased after Henry III adopted the chimney as a crucial feature of his remodelings of royal palaces

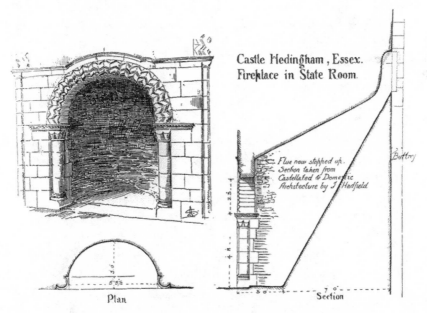

Figure 1.6. Castle chimney. In early chimneys smoke drifted horizontally as much as vertically through the wall. L. A. Shuffrey, *The English Fireplace* (London: B. T. Batsford, 1912), 15.

in the 1230s and later. Architectural historians often present Henry's remodelings as typifying designs of the mid-thirteenth century, but chronology suggests that they were innovative and trendsetting. These remodelings emphasized the importance of private chambers. Directions for building chambers for Prince Edward and for the "king's gentlemen-in-waiting" specified that each room have "fit windows and a privy chamber and a fireplace." These facilities set a new standard for respectable accommodation; virtually every reference to the construction or remodeling of a chamber at Henry's behest specified a fireplace.[53]

CHIMNEYS AND THE INCREASE
OF INDIVIDUAL ACCOMMODATION

M. W. Thompson has suggested that the castle in England, with its residential purposes, "may be viewed in some respects as an aberration of the hall culture": with the decline of castles in the fourteenth century came "the resurgence of the hall from its long confinement within castle walls." In the fourteenth century, castle planning more closely integrated domestic accommodations with fortifications by concentrating them in a roughly quadrangular plan. Rather than proliferating halls with satellite chambers, castles began to provide accommodation more precisely graded to rank and more carefully designed in relation to household composition. Within the same castle complex were a great hall, connected apartments of halls and chambers for households, and single-room lodgings. Chimneys became associated with solars, chambers, and parlors, but not exclusively. They were also found in other small rooms, garderobes, wardrobes, and lodgings for household officials and retainers.[54]

The rise of the chamber's importance over the long run is related to a decline in feudal military service. In the fourteenth century, knights with land frequently commuted their military obligation to their lord by a money payment, and magnates increasingly raised forces by hiring knights and then housing them. In parallel with the increase of corrodies in monasteries, there were more armed retainers in castles who could bargain the terms of their accommodation because their primary connection to the household was an economic contract rather than feudal allegiance. The protracted presence of such soldiers as outsiders to the familial household encouraged the construction of the household's lodgings apart from the hall, a marked trend in aristocratic building during the fourteenth and fifteenth centuries.[55]

Heightened military requirements incurred by dynastic and baronial wars in the fourteenth and fifteenth centuries further encouraged the lord's withdrawal from the hall. A great lord's mounted archers became as numerous as men-at-arms in the king's armies, so his household needed to maintain a large number of soldiers who had warhorses but were not of knightly status. Lodging them called for designs already used in corporate institutions, such as colleges and chantries, namely multistoried sets of rooms with chimneys. When lords had relied on their feudal tenants for defense, only a small number of them resided with the lord at any one time, and they could be put up rather casually in the towers of the castle or in the hall or in improvised accommodation.

As the number of hired retainers in a lord's following increased, the living spaces of the lord's household became increasingly separate, and the architecture of hospitality changed. Among both the Anglo-Saxons and the Anglo-Normans the hospitality of the hall had primarily provided food and drink rather than lodging. From the fourteenth century on, lords increasingly provided guests and staff separate lodgings in permanent buildings. The accommodations of these lodgings manifested a rough minimal standard of household amenity: "Such lodgings could contain a closet, an inner chamber, a wardrobe and at least one privy, in addition to the principal chamber," which almost invariably had a chimney fireplace. As the hall's role in accommodation declined, the increased number of lodgings and the concentration of chambers made residents proportionately more dependent on fireplaces. Private, second-story halls also became more fashionable among the aristocracy after the middle of the fourteenth century, and they usually had fireplaces as well (Figure 1.7).[56]

Literary articulations of discomfort with the hall's open hearth became more frequent as individual lodgings, with chimney fireplaces, increased. Chaucer's reference to a "smoky bower" in the "Nun's Priest's Tale" may be less significant as objective description than as an indication of newly critical awareness of a longstanding fact of life. Visual representations of chimney fireplaces became frequent in the fifteenth century, when French, Burgundian, and Flemish manuscript illustrations often showed aristocratic domestic spaces—usually chambers or studies—with glazed windows, fireplaces, and expensive fabrics draping walls and furniture. These illustrations are questionable regarding the social distribution of chimney fireplaces (many refer to chimney fireplaces in peasant dwellings, which archaeological evi-

Figure 1.7. Ornate stone chimneys. Late medieval chimneys borrowed their design and ornamentation from louvers. L. A. Shuffrey, *The English Fireplace* (London: B. T. Batsford, 1912), 33.

dence does not confirm), but they manifest a new attentiveness to facilities for warmth.[57] Contemporaneous guides to household management specified how a servant should use a fireplace to attend to his lord's needs:

at morne whan your soverayne will aryse, warme his serte by the fyre & se ye have a fote shete [footsheet] made in this maner. Fyrst set a chayre by the fyre with a cuysshe, an other under his fete / than sprede

a shete over the chayre, and se there be redy a kerchefe and a combe /
than warme his petycote, his doublet, and his stomachere / & than put
on his hosen & his shone or slyppers. . . .

[At night] loke there be a good fyre brennynge bryght & se the house
of hesement be swete & clene, and the prevy borde covered with a
grene clothe and a cuysshyn than se there be blanked, donne [down],
or cotton [for wiping], for your soverrayne & loke ye have basyn, &
ewer with water, & a towell for your soverayne than take off his gowne,
& brynge him a mantell to kepe hym fro colde / than brynge him to the
fyre, & take of his shone & his hosen; than take a fayre kercher of
reynes & kembe his heed, & put on his kercher and his bonet / than
sprede downe his bedde, lay the hede shete and the pyllowes / & whan
your soverayne is to bedde drawe the curtynes / than se there be morter
or waxe or perchores be redy / than dryve out dogge and catte, and
loke there be basin and urynall set nere your soverayne / than take your
leve manerly that your soverayne may take his rest meryly.[58]

The chimney's ability to reduce soot suited the premium that custom of the
time placed on clean textiles, which is evident in such directions.

During the fourteenth and fifteenth centuries *both* halls and chambers
became larger and their architecture more refined in designs for heating.
There was little reason for the hall to diminish in size simply because chambers increased in importance. The ritual significance of halls continued:
they were necessary for banquets, which required great space. The aristocracy's increased use of the hall as a specialized space for entertainment went
along with more elaborate provisions for feasts, especially for wines and
spices. But fifteenth-century books on courtesy also assumed that the king
and great lords would usually take their meals in their great chambers rather
than the hall. The chamber and parlor—and their chimneys—gained prestige in the fourteenth century (if sometimes grudgingly, as from Piers Plowman in the following quotation) as the destination for the lord and lady when
they withdrew from the hall for exclusive company in which to drink luxurious wine and dine on delicacies.

Wretched is the hall each day in the week,
Where the lord nor the lady liketh not to sit.
Now hath each rich man a rule to eat by himself

In a private parlour because of poor men,
Or in a chamber with a chimney, and leave the chief hall,
That was made for meals men to eat in;
And all to spare from spilling what spend shall another.

. . . .

When they had played in the hall
As long as their will them lasted
To chamber he can him call
And to the chimney they passed.[59]

Since open hearths continued to be used in medieval northern Europe after the chimney fireplace became a design alternative, the increased use of chimneys needs more than the triumph over ignorance as an explanation. Quite independently of priorities for physical amenity, certain types of spaces that precluded use of an open central hearth became more frequent—particularly the castle, the chamber, and lodgings. The technology of the chimney and fireplace had previously been available, but as long as the hall maintained its architectural priority the advantages of the chimney fireplace over the open hearth were not so compelling, or generic, as they seem in hindsight.[60]

The Option of Glazing in Medieval Architecture

The use of chimneys developed a close association with glazed windows, but, as was the use of chimneys, glazing was an option rather than a necessity throughout the medieval period. The glazed window allowed northern Europeans to overcome their preference for keeping window openings to a minimum. As sheer openings in walls, windows were traditionally viewed as liabilities to security and health. They gave entry to unwelcome intruders, they allowed the warmth of the house to escape, and at night they admitted the miasmic air. Mid-sixteenth-century medical wisdom advised: "In the nyght, let the wyndowes of your howse, specially of your chambre, be closed."[61] Windows had particular associations with illicit access to women, especially if the windows were large enough to allow entry as well as communication; windows to upstairs chambers were often barred. European vernacular housing traditions often limited openings in a wall to one—whether door, win-

dow, or chimney—and chimneyless designs often did without windows altogether, admitting light through the doorway.

Historians have typically viewed glazed windows as an unquestioned good,
because they reduced drafts and increased illumination: "It needs little imagination to realize what a contribution cheap glass was to human health and
happiness, making winter endurable for the aged and infirm, and prolong-
ing the lives of all. It must be reckoned the biggest single improvement in the
standard of living that has ever taken place." But in temperate climates there
is a trade-off between natural illumination and heat loss. As the number of
glazed windows increases, so does the loss of heat through radiation and
convection. Conversely, in subtropical and tropical environments glazed windows prevent cooling ventilation while allowing the entry of radiant heat.
And in medieval practice glazed windows were only a semipermanent improvement or feature of a house. In the fourteenth and fifteenth centuries
glazed windows migrated from house to house along with the other furnishings of itinerant aristocratic households, or else they were removed simply to
prevent damage. Panes and frames were so liable to breakage from wind that
they cost at least as much to maintain as to install.[62]

Because glazed windows depended on natural illumination, they could not
free domestic schedules from daily rhythms of light and dark. While glazed
windows allowed an artificial relationship with natural light—in the sense of
controlling the air that traditionally accompanied daylight—they also implied a passive acceptance of natural darkness. The priority of the bed in
early modern domestic consumption underlined this passivity, which manifested the weakness of cultural imperatives to redesign the domestic environment with a view toward its amenity.

Glass itself was ancient in its manufacturing technology. Glass resulted
from the fusion of alkalis and silica (usually from sand). Potash from wood
ashes or soda from the ashes of particular seaweeds provided the alkalis.
Lime was necessary to make the glass hard; though it was not recognized as
a separate ingredient, it was sufficiently present as an impurity in the ashes.
Color could be added, or subtracted, by mixing metallic oxides with the
sand and ashes. The simplest color of glass was green, from the iron oxides
naturally present in most sands. Conversely, the manganese oxides found in
the ashes of certain woods, especially beech, subtracted green and made
glass nearly colorless.[63]

Because the generic materials for glass were widely available and furnaces were small, semipermanent, and inexpensive, the manufacture of glass was mobile and potentially responsive to local demand. The scale of production was artisanal, with five or six people providing a sufficient workforce for a single glasshouse. The high demands for fuel in the heat processes for glass manufacture actually encouraged the migration of production on at least a regional scale. It was more efficient to move personnel and raw materials to fuel supplies in a region than to carry fuel from distant sources.

Glass could be made anywhere in medieval Europe, but there were distinct techniques used on either side of the Alps. Italian glassmakers used soda for their alkali and were capable of producing relatively clear glass. Transalpine glassmakers used potash, which produced a glass of varying greenishness depending on the concentration of iron oxide in the ashes. Both compositions produced a glass suitable for window glass.

Two different techniques produced the thin, flat glass suitable for window glazing. "Crown glass" resulted from spinning a piece of molten glass at the end of a rod. Centrifugal force extended a wide, thin disk from the rotating rod. The glass nearest the rod was thickest, since it spun more slowly, and that part of the disk left a "bulls-eye" after the thinner pieces had been cut into regular shapes. The second technique produced a rectangular sheet of "broad glass" by cutting open a cylinder of blown glass and then spreading it flat. Broad glass provided glazing panes more efficiently, because there was less waste from cutting and the panes were larger, but crown glass had superior qualities as a transparent glazing material. Because no foreign surface touched the glass while it was being spun, crown glass characteristically had a bright, smooth finish; broad glass had a duller and rougher finish, from contact with the flattening table and the smoothing instruments.

Villas and town houses throughout Roman Britain had glazed windows, but the Saxon invasions ended such use. The Romans had used the cylinder process to produce flat glass, and it remained the typical process in medieval northern Europe until the twelfth century, when the Crusades put Europeans in contact with the crown process, which had been used in the Near East since late antiquity. Europeans expanded upon the crown process by turning disks large enough to supply sections of flat glass, while Near Eastern traditions used the disk as a single pane. By the fourteenth century the crown process was closely associated with Norman glassmakers and the cylinder process with Lorrainers. Glassmakers in medieval England used both processes. The window glass produced by both processes had greenish tints from using wood ash, and hence they were known together as "forest glass."

Windows had a low architectural priority in early medieval housing. They were just openings other than a door. The large aisled longhouse of the Anglo-Saxon freeman (ten to twenty meters long and four to six meters wide) had only tiny windows ("eye holes") in their walls, which were made of wattle and turf. Light came through the door and the smoke hole over the open hearth. Anglo-Saxon terms for windows referred to seeing out and letting air in: *eág-þyrl* (eye hole), *eág-dúr* (eye door), and *wind-dúr* (wind door).[64] None of these terms suggested interior illumination; nor did they refer to the closure of an opening. On the contrary the window was closely associated with the element of air (and its attendant, smoke).

Bede provided the first record of glazing in Anglo-Saxon Britain when he recounted that, about 675, the Abbot of Monkwearmouth brought French glassmakers—"artificers hitherto unknown to the British, to glaze [literally 'to lattice'] the windows of the church and the galleries and upper rooms [refectories?]." (Lattices were installed diagonally to carry rain to the bottom of the window; their diamond pattern may have carried over to the one used for leaded windows.) Bede explained how glazing was superior to lattice since "the light shone within, yet the birds and rain could not penetrate." Early medieval British architecture used glazing only fitfully, in royal palaces and monasteries, and it was as likely to be produced by foreign workers on contract as by domestic craftsmen from monasteries.[65]

From the eleventh century on, window openings in major buildings— monasteries, churches, castles, and noblemen's houses—became larger, and there were more facilities to control the admission of light and air. Religious institutions apparently initiated the trend. William of Malmesbury, the twelfth-century chronicler, reported that glass windows, along with "thin linen cloths or a fretted slab," had been installed at a church in York late in the eleventh century. The glazing of church windows became frequent during the second quarter of the twelfth century. William also described the glazing of the cathedral choir at Canterbury, the earliest extant stained glass in an English church (1174), and emphasized its decorative effects: "nothing of the kind could be seen in England for its blaze of glass windows, for its glitter of marble paving, and its painting of many hues." Churches continued to be the site of innovations: wooden frames for glazed windows, with hinged shutters to regulate air and light, are first documented in England at Lincoln Cathedral in the thirteenth century.[66]

Sermons by the twelfth-century Cistercian, Bernard of Clairvaux, invoked light as a crucial religious metaphor, and the light he implicitly had in mind was that passing through glass. Cistercian churches had a strikingly bright and clear illumination that provided a deliberate contrast with the design of glazing in other twelfth-century religious buildings. The order's statutes of 1134, 1159, and 1182 forbade windows to have more than two colors or to have painted images at all: "Since only grisaille glass was permitted, its effect would have been of a dominant, clear, slightly green luminosity set off by lively geometrical patterns established by the varied designs of the leads."[67] Cistercian statutes, exceptionally, encouraged glazing for illumination rather than decoration.

Glazed windows figured prominently as features that brought architectural honor to a monastery. The chronicles of abbots and priors itemized how their building programs increased the prestige of their community by innovative designs. In the early twelfth century, Abbot William at St. Alban's "completed the stonework and glazing of very many others of the north and south aisles of the church; so that the church, illuminated with the gift of fresh light, seemed almost like new." William also improved the dormitory (*domilicium*) with glass windows "by which it is well lit." The building programs typically borrowed designs from the sacramental part of the monastery and used them for the enhancement of living areas. Abbot John de Brokehampton (1282–1316) of Evesham "worthily made the chapel of the Blessed Virgin Mary, with windows and handsome vaulting and gilded bosses; in which chapel were magnificently depicted the story of the Saviour and stories of various virgins. . . . He also made the chapter-house, ingeniously designed within and without, with excellent vaulting, without a central pillar ('base'), beautifully adorned with gilded bosses, and surrounded with glass windows. Which building on account of its spaciousness and beauty is held to be one of the chief of the chapter-houses of this realm."[68]

Chronology, design, and style suggest that the use of glazing in ecclesiastical buildings provided the model for secular architecture. Laymen had many opportunities to be impressed with the use of glass in ecclesiastical architecture. In making the comparison between sacred and secular architecture, Piers Plowman presented his visit to a monastery as an extraordinary architectural experience, particularly for the abundance of glass. There was a hall fit for a king, "with windowes of glas / wrought as a chirche," "and houses full noble, Chambers with chymneyes," "and iche hole y-glased." In England by the late fourteenth century, benefices, the vicarages that monasteries appropriated to parochial clergy, were likely to have numerous, large, and impressively ornamental windows. Windows built in the fourteenth century were likely to have two lights; those of the fifteenth century were typically larger and had more numerous lights. Vicarages in the fifteenth century often had two-story bay windows. A priest's house comparable to that of a prosperous yeoman would have, on opposite sides of the hall, two large windows with two rows of lights and traceried heads. The parlor, chamber, and service rooms might also have multipaned windows.[69]

Window glazing in medieval domestic architecture was exceptional before the mid-thirteenth century. The word for the windows in wood-framed Anglo-Norman manors in the twelfth and thirteenth centuries was simply *pertuis* (hole). The largest of these wall openings would be in the hall, and there would be a smaller one in the chamber. Others provided interior views between the chamber and the hall, and between the hall and the stable. A manor of the family with the largest seigneury in Cornwall, built around 1200, shows the potential for refinements in fenestration. There were round-headed, two-light windows in the north and south walls, with a total area of about two square yards, but there is no evidence of their being glazed. Instead, their mullions were carefully rabbeted for wooden shutters. The typical window in a late thirteenth-century large, stone-built town house (that of the Warden of Merton College, Oxford) was similar to that in a castle—a "tall two-light, transomed window" on each side of each bay in a hall with an open hearth. When thirteenth-century castle construction began to locate halls within perimeter walls rather than in tower keeps, the wall facing the castle yard could have large windows (though unglazed), and many did. The force of such examples is apparent in fortified manors built later in the thirteenth century and throughout the fourteenth century; they allowed large windows for the hall while surrounding the manor with a moat and guarding access to the second-story chamber.[70]

Glazed windows in secular dwellings begin to be frequently documented and archaeologically evident in the middle of the thirteenth century. In his directions for remodeling palaces, Henry III gave specific attention to windows' location, design, size, glazing, and illumination effects. Windows in the queen's chamber were to be extended with two marble columns, the window to be panelled ["lambruscari"] and closed with glass windows between the columns with panels which can be opened and closed and wooden shutters in one piece ["fenestras bordeas integras"] inside to close over the glass windows. And in the king's hall the upper window to the west near the dais to be closed with white glass windows, and in one half of the glass window a king sitting on a throne and in the other half a queen also sitting on a throne.[71]

Considerations of view as well as illumination apparently affected these re-modelings: windows were specified for rooms overlooking gardens.

Nobles' desire for more light became strongly evident in the late fourteenth and fifteenth centuries, when the aisles in halls were reduced and walls heightened in order to allow larger window openings and provide unobstructed light into the hall. These larger windows often took the form of a bay window illuminating the dais. As windows became larger they also became more elaborate in design, with trefoil, quatrefoil, and cinquefoil heads succeeding each other. The English word *story*, for a horizontal division of a building, derived from the Middle English term *storye*, which came from the Latin *historia* and referred to the story told by a horizontal series of illustrations on glazed windows. Chaucer expressed admiration for the many functions of window glazing when he described his chamber in *The Book of the Duchess:*

> . . . my chamber was Ful well depeynted, and with glas
> Were al the wyndowes wel yglased
> Ful clere, and nat an hoole ycrased,
> That to beholds hyt was gret joye.
> For hooly al the story of Troye
> Was in the glasynge ywroght thus,
> . . . .
> My wyndowes were shette echon,
> And throgh the glas the sonne shon
> Upon my bed with bryghte bemes,
> With many glade gilde stremes . . . .

Growing up in a London merchant's household and serving as an officer at the royal court had familiarized Chaucer with the most elaborate glazing to

Figure 1.8. Semiglazed windows. Late medieval windows combined fixed glazing with openings protected only by shutters. John Henry Parker, *Some Account of Domestic Architecture in England from Edward I to Richard II* (Oxford: John Henry Parker, 1853), facing 37.

be found in secular contexts. As his comparative self-satisfaction implied, glass covered only a part of most people's windows in late medieval northern towns. A fixed leaded frame of small panes was placed at the top of a window, and the lower unglazed opening had shutters of various sizes to control ventilation (Figure 1.8). As the Netherlander Erasmus explained in his criticism of English housing, an entirely glazed window had disadvantages for ventilation:

To begin with, they do not consider which quarter of the sky their windows or doors will face, and then their rooms are as a rule so planned as to make a through draught impossible, which Galen especially recommends. Then a great part of the walls consists of transparent glass panes which admit light in such a way as to exclude air, and yet admit through chinks what they call filtered air, which is considerably more unhealthy and stands there motionless for long periods.

Glazed windows, like chimney fireplaces, had their advantages, but not to the exclusive disadvantage of more traditional designs.[72]

Medieval concerns with physical amenity did not focus where we would expect them to have—on the elimination of the open central hearth and the extensive glazing of windows. In late medieval England and Wales there were alternatives to the hall and open central hearth practically unknown in the design of the pre-Conquest domestic environment, but the very fact of those alternatives makes the persistence of the hall/hearth complex a phenomenon in need of explanation. Rather than representing technological backwardness, it had a positive acceptability. The innovations in medieval architecture depended on particular changes in the requirements of hospitality for the ecclesiastical and aristocratic orders. As fewer clergy lived communally, they necessarily formed small households, whose resources and demands were accommodated more readily by fireplace chimneys than by halls with open hearths. Among the aristocracy, chimney fireplaces became more frequent as chambers gained priority over halls as the place for entertainment. What we might explain by the imperatives of privacy is more forcefully explained as the result of smaller scale, more socially exclusive conviviality. Though alternative spaces (the chamber) and facilities (the chimney fireplace) developed in medieval architecture and their priority in housing culture increased, they did not contradict the hall/hearth combination until the sixteenth century. Instead, both combinations—hall with open hearth and chamber with chimney fireplace—remained viable alternatives in designing the domestic environment in the late Middle Ages.

2

CIVIL COMFORT

Mansion Houses

AS THE TUDOR monarchy gained political dominance over the aristocracy in the late fifteenth century, the military function of aristocratic architecture became insignificant and even a political liability. Courtly styles of
manners and entertainment began to prevail over local ones. The hall was
increasingly designed to be an imposing entrance for visitors, whose social
destination was likely to be the great chamber. The great chamber largely
displaced the hall as the primary site of aristocratic social ritual: "Great
chambers were used for music, dancing and the putting on of plays and
masques; for the lying-in-state of corpses before funerals; for playing cards,
dice and backgammon in between meals; and for family prayers, especially
in houses that had no chapel."[1]

The structure of aristocratic households had remained basically the same
from the middle of the thirteenth century to the late sixteenth century, the
period of the hall's efflorescence. But with the increased political importance
of the Tudor court for aristocratic fortunes, the political importance of lesser
nobles' serving in the households of great lords diminished. The size of aristocratic households did not decline until the seventeenth century, but fewer

knights were serving in them. As household service became less politically deferential and more specifically organized for the domestic needs of the lords and their guests, household service changed in its composition and status as well as its size. Service in an aristocratic household was no longer the prerogative of gentlemen. The most apparent change was in the increase of women as servants for a wide range of domestic work previously performed by men. The shift in gender signified that the status of domestic work was in decline, and as servants lost status, they were increasingly accommodated in lodgings, often unheated, in gatehouses and in the dormers of stables.[2]

Extensive specialization of the residential spaces, a characteristic long nearly a monopoly of ecclesiastical buildings, now gained priority in secular architecture as well. The prestige in residential building lay with a combination of stylistic sophistication and innovative design. Renaissance styles introduced by palaces such as Somerset House in mid-sixteenth-century London moved rapidly into the countryside to houses like Longleat, where they provided examples of design (symmetry), material (brick and ashlar stone), and features (staircases and large glazed windows) that would be copied before long by gentry and even yeomen (Figure 2.1).[3]

Below the aristocracy most English rural houses in the early sixteenth century were still one- or two-roomed and single-storied, an arrangement suited to the use of a central open hearth. The chief improvement on such an open plan for prosperous yeomen and lesser gentry was to have a three-part plan of parlor, hall, and service wing, sometimes with a chamber over the ground-floor parlor and a loft over the service wing. An open hall usually separated the parlor and service wings, and it often had the only fire. An opening in the roof allowed smoke to escape and light to enter. Windows were seldom glazed, so covering them to cut off drafts from out-of-doors cut off daylight as well. Such a design perpetuated medieval housing patterns. Indeed, fifteenth- and early-sixteenth-century vernacular architecture in the south and east of England had manifested a resurgence of halls with open central hearths, as large numbers of vernacular houses were built of permanent construction. Yeomen were emulating the design of the gentry's manor houses, which in the fifteenth century had continued to have large halls with open central hearths. Houses of timber framing allowed the construction of service and chamber wings joined to the hall, but the hall's open central hearth was still usually the only fire in yeomen's houses; the hall remained a multipurpose space for cooking, eating, sleeping, and household production.

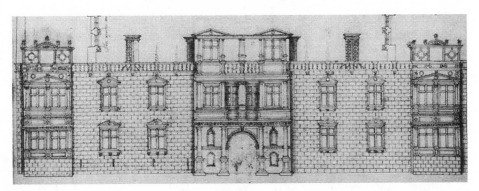

Figure 2.1. Renaissance civility. Protector Edward Seymour's highly influential palace on the Strand looked to French examples for classical correctness in symmetry, proportions, and architectural orders. John Thorp, *Elevation of Somerset House* (c. 1547). Courtesy of Sir John Soane's Museum, London.

In the middle of the fifteenth century, Henry VI's Lord Treasurer, Ralph Lord Cromwell, built a manor with the largest hall since Westminster. While giving priority to the accommodation of state visitors, it had an open central hearth (Figure 2.2).[4]

The hall accommodated an openness of household relations and hospitality that suited much of the yeomenry and lesser gentry long after the introduction of classical ideals in architecture. "Sumptuous" aristocratic architecture gained associations with public meanness and "private folly and vanity." Resistance to "polite" architecture (i.e., that which deferred to Renaissance imperatives of style) reinforced a different way of living from that dictated by the culture of gentility. Roger North, writing at the end of the seventeenth century, appreciated that adoption or resistance to polite architecture had corresponded to differences in how people wanted to live:

> In the ancient or Gothick times it was the mode for numerous familys to eat in the same room at severall tables and have few waiters; the butler for serving the master's table, and the porter the others (for the gates were all closed at that time) was sufficient. . . . But that way of a comon eating room made great halls open to the roof, with a lanthorne, to lett out smoak and stench, a laudable fashion, and consequently an indication of great dignity and plenty, and excuseth the unclenyness of it; but at present the way of the world is chang'd, and the eating is devided, many servants wait, and take their repast after the master, who is

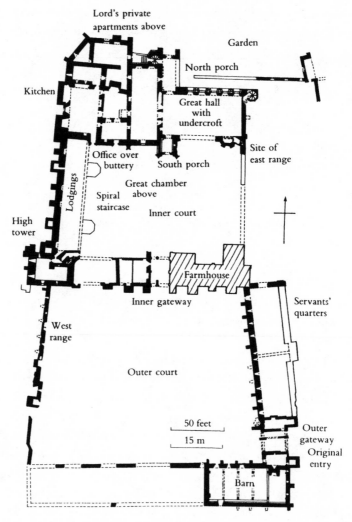

Figure 2.2. Late medieval hall and hearth. Ralph Lord Cromwell's manor, South Wingfield, had an open central hearth in the great hall and chimneys in the lodgings. M. W. Thompson, *The Decline of the Castle* (Cambridge: Cambridge University Press, 1988), 65. Reprinted by permission.

served at the table in a room layd out for that purpose. Therefore those wide halls are layd aside, and in the room of them comes the *grand salle,* which is a place to entertein persons coming to the house, and therefore ought to be well adorned, and neat. For the affectation of cleanness hath introduc't much variety of rooms, which the ancients had no occasion for, who cared not for exquisite neatness.[5]

Humanists, who typically had liminal social positions between the ecclesiastical and the secular, took the lead in presenting a contrast between vernacular and new polite standards of housing amenity. Erasmus, for example,
wrote to Cardinal Wolsey's physician, out of concern with the prevalence of
"sweating-sickness" in England, to complain about floors in English houses:
"generally spread with clay, and then with rushes from some marsh, which
are renewed from time to time but so as to leave a basic layer, sometimes for
twenty years, under which fester spittle, vomit, dogs' urine and men's too,
dregs of beer and cast-off bits of fish, and other unspeakable kinds of filth.
As the weather changes, this exhales a sort of miasma which in my opinion
is far from conducive to bodily health." Erasmus typified humanists, who
sought to distance themselves from the threateningly elemental qualities of
vernacular material culture. Thomas More contrasted the dwellings of contemporary Utopians—who inhabited structures resembling Renaissance palaces of "handsome appearance of three stories" and their walls "of stone
or cement or brick"— with early Utopians' houses, which were "low, mere
cabins and huts, haphazardly made with any wood to hand, with mud-
plastered walls. They had thatched the steeply sloping roofs with straw."
More was urging polite architecture upon the aristocracy, which whole-
heartedly took up the invitation. Italian architect Sebastiano Serlio, in his
influential 1537 treatise on Renaissance architecture, showed how to associate chimneys with civility, and how to dissociate their elemental function from
vernacular building—by building fireplaces in classical styles, even though
they had no cognate in the architecture of antiquity (Figure 2.3).[6] In a cou-
ple of generations a new vernacular English architecture would develop from
popular emulation of the aristocracy's imperative to refine its domestic environment.

The Hall-Parlor House

With Renaissance influences in architecture came an exclusive preference for
chimney fireplaces. In the second half of the sixteenth century, halls with
open central hearths became unacceptable to propertied people in the south
and east of England. Their houses became two-storied in the main block,
not just the wings, a design that precluded open hearths and encouraged use
of chimneys. These changes in housing standards motivated an extensive and

Figure 2.3. Renaissance chinmeypiece. Vignola [Giacomo Barozzio], *Regola delle Conque Ordini d'Architettura* . . . (Rome, 1563?), pl. 36. Courtesy of the Winterthur Library, Printed Book and Periodical Collection, Winterthur, Delaware.

protracted remodeling and renewal of English housing, labeled the Great Rebuilding in W. G. Hoskins's classic 1953 article. Remodelings and replacements of hall houses provided more privacy and separation from the elements, as the number of glazed windows, fireplaces, and specialized rooms increased and finer building materials, such as cut stone, were used. In the late sixteenth century in Kent, the county with the most-marked changes in rural housing, the number of rooms per house increased much more dramatically than the wealth per household. New imperatives applied to vernacular architecture—for parlors and staircases and for more chambers and service rooms. The number of rooms in larger houses increased from three–five to six or seven. This increase required ceiling over the hall, so that there could be bedrooms directly upstairs rather than in a wing. This ceiling required a chimney in the hall.[7]

Chimneys provided a fashionable way to represent status as well as to provide warmth. In the late Middle Ages (c. 1350–1500) prestigious chimneys were built of imported materials, usually bricks identified as "Flanders tiles." Such material provided an opportunity for luxurious display, in contrast to the plastered stonework or wattling that had previously been used in aristocratic houses and that continued to be used for chimneys and flues in vernacular houses. In the early fifteenth century, knights returning from campaigns on the Continent, where brick had prestigious associations with castle architecture, used the material to construct castles at home, particularly in East Anglia. Brick soon thereafter came into use in East Anglia as a material for chimneys in manor houses, replacing tile and stone for the construction of chimneys in architecturally pretentious houses. In the 1520s and 1530s, the use of brick for chimneys remained novel and prestigious. Some brick chimneys displayed elaborate ornamental shaping and patterning (Figure 2.4). Buckingham's Thornbury Castle has the earliest datable (1514) and most ornate brick chimneys in England.

William Harrison's *Description of England* (1577) provided the *locus classicus* of observations on architectural remodeling in the sixteenth century. No other comment on the English domestic environment has been quoted more often than this one by an Essex village rector:

> There are old men yet dwelling in the village where I remain, which have noted three things to be marvelously altered in England within their sound remembrance. . . . One is, the multitude of chimneys lately erected, whereas in their young days there were not above two or three, if so many, in most uplandish towns of the realm (the religious houses, and manor places of their lords always excepted, and peradventure some great personages) but each one made his fire against a reredos in the hall where he dined and dressed his meat.[8]

Figure 2.4. Ornamented brick chimneys. Early Tudor brick chimneys defied the constraints of their material in their sculptural variety and ostentation. L. A. Shuffrey, *The English Fireplace* (London: B. T. Batsford, 1912), 50.

In lowland England, for both symbolic and practical reasons, the axial chimney—one near the center of the house and aligned along the short axis of the house (see Figure 2.5)—came to define vernacular postmedieval design. Chimneys had been part of the English architectural repertoire for over three centuries, but now they became literally the central feature of houses, both spatially and structurally. In the last decades of the sixteenth century the typical location of fireplaces began to be between the hall and the parlor. They were built of brick and often provided fireplaces on both sides, for the parlor as well as the hall. This centrality was first a feature of yeomen's houses rather than the gentry's manors, which were more likely to have a chimney on the front wall in both the hall and the parlor.[9]

Much of the redefinition of household amenity focused on the parlor, where beds were in prominent display. Parlors marked a social watershed in taste: in sixteenth-century lowland England they became standard for gentry houses, and a desirable option for yeomen. The parlor redefined house plans by sharpening gendered differentiations of space. With their display of purchased fabrics and metals, parlors literally represented the household's material wealth, a husband's legal prerogative. Having a parlor sharpened the separation and distinctions among rooms in the house, particularly between rooms where domestic work took place—the women's realm of halls,

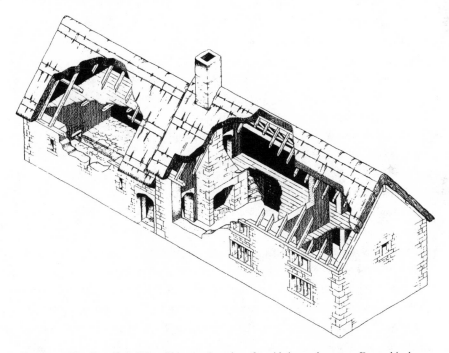

Figure 2.5. The Great Rebuilding. This reconstruction of a mid-sixteenth-century Devonshire long-house-with-byre illustrates the changes from medieval vernacular housing that marked the architectural design development called the Great Rebuilding: a chimney in place of a firehood or open central hearth, cut stone in place of dry-stone walls, mullions for glazed windows in place of shutters and bars, living areas storied throughout proscribing an open hall, upstairs chambers instead of a ladder to the loft. Eric Mercer, *English Vernacular Houses: A Study of Traditional Farmhouses and Cottages* (London: Her Majesty's Stationery Office, 1975), 40. Reprinted by permission.

kitchens, and service rooms—and rooms where people socialized or had privacy. Parlors were distinguished from the household's domestic economic activities: they did not contain tools nor store the results of household processing. Their location in the house tended to be toward the front and to be accessible from that side, while kitchens and other service rooms shifted toward the end or the back of the house, where strangers' access was less apparent. By the late seventeenth century in southeastern England, prosperous households with more than one parlor were likely to use one just for hospitality, not sleeping.[10]

The axial chimney represented a commitment to provide heat to the parlor. (In the Southeast if a house had more than one lateral chimney they were usually placed on the front of the house, apparently for ornamental purposes.) The most striking technical and architectural innovation in vernacular dwellings, an axial chimney built of brick, corresponded with a *reduced* need for a fire in the hall, because cooking was preferably done in a kitchen, and visitors were more likely to be taken into a heated parlor. Paradoxically, the axial chimney represented a *de*centralized design for domestic space, as the multiple functions of the hall dispersed to parlor, kitchen, and other service rooms, and staircases began to facilitate movement to and across the second story. To the extent that Renaissance criteria of balance and uniformity applied to vernacular architecture, the axial chimney responded to desires to have *some* feature at the center of the house.[11]

While the hall-parlor house conveyed more symbolic prestige to the male household head, it actually increased the *spatial* priority of areas used for female work; more money went into parlors, but service rooms added more space than parlors did. Houses that had more than the three rooms previously typical of rural architecture—hall, chamber, and buttery—had in addition specialized service rooms, which appeared at an even faster rate than parlors and chambers. As farmhouses in southeastern England became larger, in the sixteenth century, service rooms had at least as high priority as did enhancements of domestic space. A chamber over the heated hall was desirable not only to increase space for beds but to provide a dry storage place, and most houses in the Southeast, even of husbandmen and craftsmen, had a chamber on the second floor.[12]

Propertied households needed more storage space because they had more equipment for household production and thus more produce to store as well. The service rooms of the medieval three-part house had been the buttery for drinks and the pantry for bread and other foods. But the remodelings and new construction of farmhouses in the sixteenth-century South and Southeast readily added (in rough order of priority) milkhouses, backhouses (for malting and baking), kitchens, brewhouses, larders, and even apple houses. As the terms for several of these service rooms indicate, they represented a domestication of outbuildings. As service rooms became numerous, they were likely to be located in a wing to the rear of the house rather than off the hall. Indeed, their location defined the rear of a house, as opposed to its front, invariably the location of the hall and parlor. What had long been a convenience, a cross passage providing direct communication between the hall and the service rooms, was not adequate for the increased number of service rooms. Even though more rooms for services were under the same roof, their separation from the hall was apparently desirable as well.[13]

In the sixteenth and seventeenth centuries, "kitchens" became a crucial room within the house rather than a separate building. Rooms designated as kitchens were not necessarily for cooking. Some of them did not even have fireplaces. In the context of vernacular houses, the term *kitchen* initially referred to a multipurpose service area for the processing of foodstuffs, as by brewing or making cheese or salting meat, but not necessarily for cooking meals. In the second half of the seventeenth century, such kitchens were the most numerous service room in three- and four-roomed houses. Cooking might be done in the hall, since many houses still had only one chimney, which served the fireplaces of the hall and the parlor. In houses with two chimneys, the kitchen had priority over the parlor or sleeping chambers for having the second chimney. Apparently the use of heat to process materials had developed priority over sheer household warmth. With its own fireplace a kitchen could still have the desired separation of food preparation from hall and chambers.[14]

By the middle of the seventeenth century, there were new names for rooms, to take into account that the hall remained a room where cooking and eating took place while other rooms had taken on other of its functions—services, sleeping, and receiving guests. In the North and West, the *foreroom*, for receiving guests, was distinguished from the *backroom*, for services; in the South and Southeast, *kitchen* began to refer to the room for cooking rather than to an unspecialized service room. Cooking and eating were declining in architectural priority relative to sleeping or services or receiving guests; the preparation and consumption of food often moved into the space left over in the course of increased specialization. Most families continued to take their meals in the hall. For at least a century after parlors were introduced in the Southeast they were less likely than halls to be places to take meals.[15]

Despite the relocation and literal centrality of chimneys during the late sixteenth and seventeenth century, the number of hearths lagged behind the increased number of rooms. In Norwich, for example, during the period 1580–1730 one-fifth of the houses had three or fewer rooms and in those houses the mean number of hearths per house increased only from 1.1 to 1.3. Houses of four to six rooms, about two-fifths of the total, had only one more hearth than houses half their size; the average number of hearths among them increased only from 1.7 to 2.0 over the seventeenth century. Barely half of the parlors in early eighteenth-century Norwich had hearths, the same proportion as at the end of the sixteenth century. Fewer than half of all rooms had fireplaces with chimneys.[16]

Because domestic space was being divided up, even though they had more hearths in the house people were not necessarily warmer than they had been in an undifferentiated hall with one open central hearth. *Hearth* had been a synonym for *residence* in Anglo-Saxon and Norman tax levies, on the assumption that each household had only one hearth. But by the middle of the seventeenth century in England, because of the increased number of houses with multiple chimneys and of chimneys with more than one fireplace, chimneys had become such a readily apparent, though rough, index of household wealth that in 1662 the hearth tax replaced the poll tax. The act directed householders to enumerate their hearths. Royally appointed "chimneymen" had authority to enter houses lacking enumerations or seeming to have false returns. Chimneys could be counted from outside, and if there was more than one chimney, there was likely to be an above average number of hearths. The new tax was known colloquially as the "chimney-money." Having chimneys or multiple hearths was not regarded as necessary, and hearth taxes were really a tax on discretionary expenditure. As Sir William Petty wrote in "A Treatise of Taxes and Contributions" (1662), most chimneys were "useless and supernumerary."[17]

The hearth tax arose from the need for revenue with which to compensate the king for the loss of royal demesne and feudal income between the overthrow and restoration of the monarchy. The tax imposed an annual charge of 2s. on each domestic hearth. Households were excused if they were too poor to pay the assessed poor rates or church rates, or if they rented a house for less than £1 or had an annual income of less than £10. Objections to the tax arose from its regressive burden on modest households and on its intrusive manner of assessment. Chimneymen faced violent, and sometimes lethal, resistance to their efforts to collect distressed goods for defaulted taxes. In 1689 Parliament repealed the hearth tax on grounds that it encouraged violations of domestic space: "It is in itself, not only a great Oppression to the poorer Sort, but a Badge of Slavery upon the whole People, exposing every Man's House to be entered into and searched at Pleasure, by Persons unknown to him."[18]

Historians have studied hearth tax returns intensively for their demographic and economic information, but their information on the domestic environment has been a scholarly by-product of tabulating the social and geographic distribution of hearths. The evidence of the hearth tax records cuts both ways with regard to the amenities of the postmedieval domestic environment. On the one hand the high number of hearths in some houses marked the specialization and subdivision of space beyond the hall-and-parlor complex. On the other hand, despite the proliferation of chimneys, most people still lived in houses with only one hearth. Depending on the county and its subregions, about two-thirds to three-quarters of households had only one hearth, and only about half of such households were excused from the tax on grounds of poverty. About one-fifth of the population had two hearths. Counting hearths rather than households as the denominator, the unequal distribution of the tax burden is even more marked: fewer than one-fifth of the households, those with three or more hearths, could have over half of the hearths in a county. Some households had ten to twenty times as many hearths as most other dwellings.[19] Such distributions indicate the social basis for the apparent archaisms noticed over the course of three centuries as chimneys were introduced into vernacular designs.

Concerns for health did not compel households to add chimneys. Fires had implications for health as well as warmth. Medical learning taught that they were crucial for ventilation. Fires kept the air pure: "there must be a fire kept continually for a space to dry up the contagious moistures of the walls, & the savour of the lime and sand. . . . have a fire in your chamber, to waste and consume the evil vapours within the chamber, for the breath of man may putrefy the air within the chamber." But an open central hearth arguably met such requirements as well as or better than a chimney fireplace, so the former was not necessarily a retrograde facility. William Harrison did not take the adoption of chimneys for granted as an improvement in comfort, hygiene, or technology. Historians seldom note that Harrison thought the chimney was a step *backward* in household amenity:

> Now have we many chimneys, and yet our tenderlings complain of rheums, catarrhs, and poses [colds]. Then had we none but reredoses [stone or metal firebacks for open hearths], and our heads did never ache. For as the smoke in those days was supposed to be a sufficient hardening for the timber of the house, so it was reputed a far better medicine to keep the goodman and his family from the quack [hoarseness] or pose, wherewith as then very few were oft acquainted.[20]

Vernacular architecture manifested people's reluctance to add or to introduce chimneys. In the remodelings that created more rooms, additional chimneys were not necessarily added. Virtually all poor households had only one hearth, but not all households with only one hearth were poor: some belonged to propertied widows, artisans, husbandmen, and even yeomen. Many yeomen's households had only two hearths in an axial chimney between hall and parlor. The number of hearths correlated only weakly with either the number of rooms in a house or the wealth of its occupier. A proverb datable to the mid-seventeenth century expressed an ambivalence toward the desirability of numerous chimneys: "It is easier to build two chimneys, than to maintain one." In Cambridgeshire, for example, despite extensive rebuilding of houses, almost half of the houses still had only a single hearth, yet the size of such single-hearth houses could range from one to six rooms and the wealth of their occupier from £10 to £200. Houses with two hearths could have from two to ten rooms, and their occupier's wealth could range from £10 to £300.[21] Such weak correlations between the number of hearths and either the number of rooms to be heated or the wealth of the householder suggest that requirements for overall household warmth were not very strict and that individual preferences and needs varied widely. Even after the Great Rebuilding there were still many more unheated than heated rooms. The archetypal house resulting from the Great Rebuilding, with a chimney and ceiled-over hall, arguably had a lower proportion of heated domestic space than the late medieval hall house.

Simply having an axial chimney stack enabled a householder to make a sharp distinction in status from the single-hearth households of laborers and copyholders. Such a chimney implied a status comparable to lesser gentry, since an axial stack could accommodate flues for as many as four hearths in a two-storied house. But the status advantages of the axial chimney depended on the strength of vernacular designs among lesser gentry and yeomen. The period of the hearth tax coincided with the gentry's and merchants' giving up vernacular designs in favor of metropolitan standards of construction and plan—brick for the entire building, gable-end chimneys, kitchens devoted to cooking, and symmetrical elevations. At the vernacular level the use of brick in the construction of chimneys replaced combinations of wood framing and wattle and daub. Such flammable materials had been proscribed by building regulations in large towns since the early fourteenth century, but they continued to be used in the countryside in the seventeenth and eighteenth centuries.[22]

In England construction of the entire house in brick was by definition a break with vernacular traditions. In the Southeast the alternative of brick presented itself locally in the first half of the seventeenth century, as schools, almshouses, inns, and manor houses began to be built of the material. Dutch immigrants, who took brick construction for granted, had been numerous in many towns of the Southeast since the 1570s, but it was decades later before brick houses were often built for the households of the lesser merchants, craftsmen, or yeomen. In a carefully surveyed area of Hampshire, brick was found to be used in sixteenth-century farmhouses only for chimneys; not until the early eighteenth century was brick used often to build entire farmhouses there. In Midland villages, where there had been no brick farmhouses before 1680, by two decades later the material was frequent in new buildings. The antiquary Abraham de la Pryme described similar changes by the late seventeenth century in his history of Hatfield Chase, Yorkshire:

> The town itself, tho' it be but little yet tis very handsom & neat, the manner of the buildings that it formerly had were all of wood, clay and plaster, but now that way of building is quite left off, for every one now from the richest to the poorest will not build unless with bricks: so that now from about 80 years ago, (at which time bricks were first seen, used & made in this parish) they have been wholy used and now there scarce is one house in the town that does not if not wholy yet for the most part consist of that lasting & genteel sort of building.[23]

But until the second half of the eighteenth century, even in the southeast, the diversity of building materials—timber-frame, clay, flint and chalk, along with brick—belied these wishful expectations. As with so many antiquaries' observations on housing, Pryme's qualification really spoke to the wide variation in personal standards of amenity in the sixteenth and seventeenth centuries, despite humanists' and antiquaries' hopes for a uniform civility.

Sixteenth- and seventeenth-century antiquaries compared new, "civilized," designs for houses with older, vernacular features. Chimneys were undeniably cleaner than the open central hearth, and they put the element of fire in a more artificial and symbolically controlled space. Architectural historians have taken these reports at face value regarding innovations in particular areas. But since the designs reported as new were in fact alternatives that had been available for several centuries, the reports really indicate a new invidious sensitivity to the contrasts between standards that had previously coexisted. New designs for houses appeared to be superseding old ones because the construction history of most vernacular housing had been a succession of decay and renovation, while "civilized" houses put a premium on permanency.[24]

These antiquaries contrasted housing in their own time with their memories of the recent past, with such phrases as "in Times not past the remembrance of some yet living," "till of late yeares," and "since about 1616." They contrasted the newness of the changes with the supposed antiquity of the outmoded standards, as marked by phrases such as "the ancient manner of Cornish building," "in old time the houses of the Britons," and "the old maner of the Saxons." Antiquaries' archetypal archaism was the central, open hearth: "hearths in the midst of the room for chimneys, which vented the smoke at a louver in the top," "fyer in the middest of the howse against a hob of clay." But since these descriptions spanned more than a century, from the third quarter of the sixteenth century until late in the seventeenth, they really attest to the strength of vernacular alternatives to nominally civilized standards (Figure 2.6). The English antiquary John Aubrey, writing in the 1670s, described the houses of copyholders and other "ordinary" people as having "no chimneys but flues like louvre holes" before the Reformation; he claimed to have seen a few houses with such features when he was a boy. He also remembered when "copyholders and ordinary poor people" in Wiltshire lacked glazing in their windows but observed that "[now] the poorest

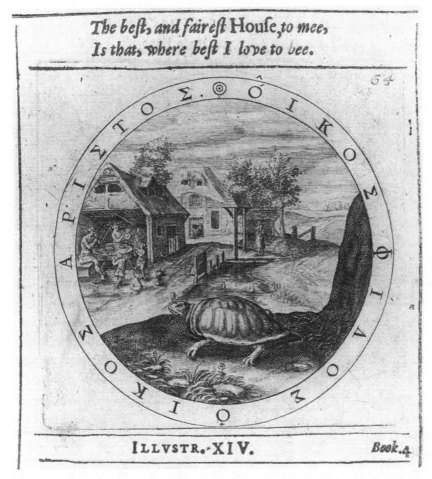

The best, and fairest House, to mee,
Is that, where best I love to bee.

ΑΡΙΣΤΟΣ · ΟΙΚΟΜ · ΟΚΟΙΟ · ΦΙΛΟΥΟ · ΟΙΚΟΜ

ILLVSTR. XIV.   Book.4

Figure 2.6. Peasant amenity. Humanists and antiquaries responded condescendingly to the barely furnished hall with open hearth and stairless loft. George Wither, *A Collection of Emblems, Ancient and Modern* (London: Augustine Matthews, 1635), 222. Courtesy of the Winterthur Library, Printed Book and Periodical Collection, Winterthur, Delaware.

people upon almes have it." A century earlier Richard Carew had collected remembrances of houses in Cornwall with "walls of earth, low thatched roofs, few partitions, no planchings or glass windows, and scarcely any chimneys, other than a hole in the wall to let out the smoke: their bed, straw and a blanket." In his own lifetime, he claimed, most of these "fashions" were "universally banished and the Cornish husbandman conformeth himself with a better supplied civilitie to the eastern patterne." But could such standards really have been universal in Cornwall in the middle of the sixteenth century, when at the turn of the eighteenth century Richard Gough recalled chimneyless cottages in the Shropshire parish of Myddle?[25]

Just as antiquaries used local memory, so other observers could make exotic comparisons with their localities to acknowledge and simultaneously to displace the coexistence of different standards. R. Plot compared the hovels in Staffordshire in 1680, "built only of turf in a conical manner," with "the houses of the Indians near the Straights [*sic*] of Magellan." William Harrison contrasted "the mansion howses" of the south of England, with "many places beyond the sea & some of the north parts of our country," where the dwellings had dairies and stables "under the same roof." For the mid-sixteenth-century physician Andrew Boorde the Scottish byre-house was physically near but culturally very distant: "The borders of Scotland toward England,—as they the which doeth dwell by Nycoll forest, and so upward to Barwyke, by-yonde the water of Twede,—lyveth in much povertie and penurye, havyinge no howses but suche as a man maye buylde within iii or iiii houres: he and his wyfe and his horse standeth all in one rome."[26] The phenomenon of such observations throughout the sixteenth and seventeenth century suggests continued coexistence of different standards of amenity rather than a revolution in comfort.

Domestication of the Glazed Window

Harrison's other metonym for new housing designs—besides the chimney— was the glazed window, considered a sign of "genteel" and civilized housing. But even as window openings in houses became larger, their glazing continued to be optional and temporary. In his Latin and English primer of 1519, William Horman explained glazing of windows, figuring that his readership would not necessarily be acquainted with it: "Glass windows let in the light and keep out the wind." In 1505 an English court still ruled that the window frames of a house (primarily its shutters) belonged to the heir as fixtures, while the glass should be distributed as personal property by the executors, on the principle that "the house is perfect without the glass." Well into the sixteenth century aristocratic households treated glass windows as a portable luxury rather than a fixture of the house. Until the end of the sixteenth century, glazed windows remained so particular, even in prosperous urban households, that they were recorded in decedents' inventories.[27]

Window glazing served a decorative as well as an illuminative function. Flat glass had been colored for medieval church decoration, and this decorative tradition was transferred to domestic use. Sixteenth-century windows had elaborate patterns of glass shapes and colors, and clear panes often had painted designs, such as coats of arms. In the sixteenth century, glaziers were expected to be able not only to install glass but to paint it—typically with heraldic devices, inspirational inscriptions, and figural ornaments. Until the middle of the seventeenth century most domestic window glass included the small circular panes with a large dimple remaining from the glassblowing. The distortions inevitable with such glass were acceptable because window glass was a component of domestic furnishing rather than just a medium for domestic light.[28]

Through the middle of the sixteenth century the demand for window glass in England was too small and sporadic to sustain a glass industry, so most window glass was imported. Glass from Norman, Flemish, and Burgundian sources was also of better quality and carried a lower price than that readily obtainable from English sources. Most of the glassmaking operations in medieval England had been temporary facilities built for specific building projects at monasteries, cathedrals, palaces, and castles. Only the Weald region to the south of London had an established industry producing glass, and it concentrated on inexpensive vessels rather than glazing. In the early sixteenth century the manufacture of flat glass in England was nearly moribund. If anything, the Reformation lessened demand for window glass, because there were fewer religious institutions requiring stained glass and looted monastic glazing provided a windfall supply. The demand for domestic window glass could not take up the slack: in the 1560s the total of all the window glass imported into England was less than the production of a single glasshouse.[29]

In the late 1560s immigrant glassmakers set up two glass furnaces, with the expectation that they were sufficient to meet all the demand in England. Only two decades later the production of window glass in England was equivalent to about seven glasshouses, or something in the range of one-half to one million square feet per year. After this rapid expansion in the first generation of a domestic window glass industry, production doubled between the 1590s and the 1630s. This growth in the glazing industry apparently met demand easily in the first half of the century, since prices did not rise with Sir Robert Mansell's monopoly of supply in the 1620s and 1630s, nor fall when he lost his monopoly.[30]

Because the industry was so small and unsophisticated, the immigration of a few Protestant refugee glassmakers in the 1560s could transform English glassmaking. They were pushed from the Continent by religious persecution and economic disruption rather than pulled to England by the attractiveness of its market for glass. But their relocation gave them an advantage in substituting domestic sources for disrupted foreign ones. Glassmakers from Antwerp, whose mirror industry competed with Venice's, brought skills to produce cristallo (an exceptionally clear glass) in addition to broad window glass. Emigrants from the Lorraine introduced improved techniques for broad glass.[31]

The chief innovation in the English glass industry was the use of coal as a heat source in place of wood. From the 1580s both Parliament and the crown had sought to reduce the apparent depletion of wood and timber supplies by prohibiting iron works and glasshouses from areas of intensive demand for fuel—especially along the Thames, in the Weald, and along the southern coast. Despite the supposed scarcity of fuel, however, the price of window glass remained relatively steady. Increases in production were apparently keeping up with demand, and importations of window glass virtually ceased, though there were no restrictions on them. In the late sixteenth century the wholesale price of window glass in London was about 3d. per foot for crown glass and about 2d. for broad. In the first half of the seventeenth century the price was usually less than 2d. for both types. The retail price of glass in London, including its installation, was 6–7d. per foot in the late sixteenth century and 4–5d. in the first half of the seventeenth century. Retail prices in the North were about a penny higher until the 1620s, when Newcastle developed as a glass center after the shift to coal.[32]

During the late sixteenth century glazing underwent the transition from a luxury to a decency as a matter of fashion, not cost. By the 1610s the successful substitution of coal as a fuel in glass furnaces removed a potential bottleneck to the expansion of production. But even after the manufacturers of coal-fueled glassmaking were granted a complicated series of monopolies for the production of all window glass, demand remained so moderate that prices largely held steady. Imports still dominated the market for mirrors, while they had become insignificant as a source of window glass. Indeed, Sir Robert Mansell gave priority to improving the quality and increasing the production of glass for the luxury trade in mirrors, while he simply leased out the privilege to produce window glass for the housing market. The production of glass by a coal-fired process encouraged the manufacture of a more transparent glass for window glazing. Mansell's efforts to duplicate cristallo required the development of sources for soda as an alkali, and the elimination of wood as a fuel reduced the ready availability of wood ashes (with their unintended greenish coloring agent of iron oxide).[33]

As the history of glass production suggests, glazed windows became an integral part of domestic material culture in the latter decades of the sixteenth century. In 1599 courts reversed their previous evaluation and ruled that window glazing could not be removed because "without glass it is no perfect house." John Aubrey asserted that glass windows had been rare except in churches and gentlemen's houses before the reign of Henry VIII, and he claimed to remember that as recently as the civil war copyholders and poor people in the remote west of England had not had any, implying that they now usually did.[34]

Glazing cost only pennies per square foot, and manor houses in the first half of the sixteenth century usually had only a few hundred square feet of glazing, yet not all of their windows would be glazed. In the second half of the century, though costs of glazing had increased a penny or so per foot, manor houses began to have over one thousand feet of glazing, and the greatest houses built in the latter decades of the sixteenth century had several times that amount of glazing. It cost £50.9.5 to glaze 1,700 feet at Middleton Hall; glazing at the royal palace at Nonsuch cost £348, for 8,000 square feet of windows. Buildings on the scale of Nonsuch had hundreds of windows, each of them taller than a person.[35]

The lavish use of window glazing in Elizabethan and Jacobean prodigy houses indicated the priority of decorative fashion, as opposed to practical needs for illumination, in creating demand for the use of glass. Robert Smythson, architect of Middleton Hall, Wollaton Hall, and Hardwick Hall, apparently introduced the use of larger, square panes with horizontal muntins of wood and stone. The fashion was to install glazed windows in every wall, in order to make a sheer display of glass to viewers outside. An account of the queen's visit to Kenilworth in 1575 responded appropriately: "a day tyme, on every syde so glittering by glass; a nights, by continual brightnesse of candel, fyre, and torch-light, transparent through the lyghtsome wyndz, az it wear the Egiptian Pharos relucent untoo all the Alexandrian coast." Such extravagant fenestration did not entirely suit interior arrangements, since it precluded placing large furniture against some walls and sometimes produced glare because of light coming from sources at right angles. The priority of impressing outsiders is most evident at Hardwick Hall. A sixteenth-century rhyme referred to "Hardwick Hall, more glass than wall," but in fact some of those windows were on solid walls and did not admit light into the interior or allow views out.[36] The social variation in the amount of glazing indicates that its adoption was first and foremost a matter of luxurious display and only secondarily an enhancement of domestic amenity. The Elizabethan aristocracy sought glazing on a scale previously found only in the greatest ecclesiastical buildings, while demand for glazing in the nation at large increased much more slowly even as the price of glazing declined with the readier availability from domestic sources.

Glazed windows in peasant houses were almost unknown until the late Middle Ages. Medieval longhouses with open hearths often did not have window openings at all. Instead light came through the opposing doors and through the smoke hole. If the terrain permitted the option, longhouses were often oriented with their long axis east-west, in order to maximize seasonal illumination through the north- and south-facing doors on the side walls. The opposed doors typical of longhouses manifested the trade-offs between illumination and ventilation. While admitting daylight, they could be opened or closed with respect to the direction of the wind and with the hearth's need for draft. The designs of longhouses often kept windows to a minimum in number and size, particularly when smoke holes or large flues for fire hoods or chimneys provided illumination from overhead. Glazing of windows in vernacular architecture began about the middle of the fifteenth century. Archaeologists have found evidence of glazing in late medieval peasant houses at Wharram Percy in Yorkshire, but the practice remained infrequent at the level of yeomen and lesser gentry until the second half of the sixteenth century.[37]

At the vernacular level, glazed windows first began to appear regularly in the houses of townspeople. Merchants in southern England led the way, in the 1560s, and by the latter decades of the century tradesmen in Midland and Home Counties towns began to have some of their windows glazed. In Midland villages glazed windows appeared in yeomen's houses in the last decades of the sixteenth century, and for decades they remained optional features of vernacular architecture. Designs of Midland farmhouses in the late sixteenth and early seventeenth centuries often provided one glazed window per room; some householders glazed only the hall windows. At the end of the seventeenth century yeomen's houses typically had three glazed windows per room, two at the front and one at the side or back.[38]

New England's vernacular housing typified how glazed windows became popular in rural areas, influenced, even from across the Atlantic, by the metropolis of London. Though glazing was almost from the start a standard component of framed houses in Massachusetts Bay, the distinction between glazed windows and the fabric of the house was still evident in some mid-seventeenth-century deeds from Plymouth Colony. They assured the buyer that the windows were a part of the deal and not something that would be moved out. For example, in 1645 Richard Chadwell of Sandwich, Plymouth Colony, deeded his glazed windows as part of the furniture when he sold his house to Edmond Freeman: "all that his dwelling house . . . with all the doors, locks, dressors, benches, glass, and glass windows, with the wooden shutters to them belonging and the bedstead matt and bedcord in the said house together with all lands to the said house belonging." In seventeenth-century Anglo-American vernacular architecture, front and gable walls had glazed windows, rear ones typically did not. In houses that faced southward, such a pattern would have protected the cold side of the house from drafts, but the look of the house's "face" apparently mattered at least as much as practical considerations. Houses with such status-conferring features as second stories and jettied overhangs had large glazed windows on the front elevation. Contracts typically called for a glazed window in each room on each floor, ones two to three feet high and three to five feet wide with two to five lights being typical. Windows on the front were usually of uniform size, and those on the gable were slightly smaller. Some of the lights were fixed—as apparently marked by the terms *clerestory* and *stool* (sill)—but most glazed windows included at least one vertically hinged casement.[39]

Building contracts in seventeenth-century Massachusetts suggest both pretension and restraint in the demand for window glazing. A 1637 letter from a gentry officeholder moving to Massachusetts Bay gave these directions regarding windows for his new house: "let them not be over large in any roome, and as few as conveniently may be," but no mention was made of glazing them. Some contracts specified "large casement windows"; others deferred to community standards and ordered "so many as in the judgment of men is needful." Still others played it safe with their pretensions by directing that "all the windows be of the bigness as they are generally made now to housing newly built here abouts in the neighbourhood, and . . . glaze all the windows."[40]

In seventeenth-century England glazed windows became so prevalent that in 1697 Parliament found a replacement for the hearth tax in a tax on windows. Although the tax, which funded the recoinage of clipped currency, covered all windows, not just glazed ones, it was glazing that allowed the proliferation of windows to the point of making them an appealing object of taxation. Households unable to pay poor or church rates were excused, but otherwise the house's occupant—not the owner—paid 2s. per year as "house duty." Those with ten to nineteen windows paid 4s. additional, and those with twenty or more paid an additional 8s. These rates were modified, invariably upward, several times during the eighteenth century.[41]

The cross window, of transom and mullion, with four lights was the respectable standard for much of the seventeenth century, until superseded by the sash window after 1690. The increased production of large, rectangular glass panes allowed the use of wooden frames strong enough to withstand frequent adjustments for ventilation. Sash windows were first used extensively at the court of Louis XIV; they were first reported in England at Windsor Castle in the late 1680s. The cross window did not necessarily imply glazing, since it could be shuttered closed, but the sash window only made sense when glazed. The sash window became a defining characteristic of gentry housing, one increasingly emulated in the eighteenth century by yeomen's and townsmen's households. Because sash windows were taller than they were wide, their use marked high ceilings in the rooms they illuminated, and relatively high ceilings became a differentiating characteristic of gentry houses.[42]

At the beginning of the eighteenth century a Boston merchant clearly implied the fashionability of window glazing when ordering materials from a commercial correspondent in London to renovate his house. He wanted "some curious clear glass if I mistake not it is called crown glass. . . . it seems to be such as that put before the dial plate of clocks. Mr. Eliakim Hutchinson hath glazed the front of his house with it and it looks exceeding well. I have a great mind to have one room or two glazed with that glass. . . . I have other glass enough for the back side of said house." He appreciated the technical advantages of the new type of glass, but what he really liked about it was the impression his new glazing would make on others. Initially, he planned to install the new type of glass in the now-traditional "iron case-ments[,] for tho Sash windows are the newest Fashion I don't so well fancy them as casements." Under the influence of his son, however, "who found fault with my directions . . . we now resolve for sash windows."[43]

Neat Furnishings

During the remodeling of the domestic environment in the sixteenth and seventeenth centuries, *comfort* still referred primarily to psychological and spiritual, not physical, circumstance. Take for example the diary of a minister, Ralph Josselin, the richest personal record available of daily life during seventeenth-century England. The word *comfort* appears at least every few days, but almost invariably in reference to providential blessings. The diary begins with his self-reassurances as his father was dying: "tis a [conti]nuall *comfort* to mee to thinke of my tender love to him"; he related a sermon to his father "with much joy and *comfort*." He regularly assessed his circumstances in reference to providential "*comforts*": his wife's pregnancy "proved indeed to our great joy and *comfort*"; God was "good to mee all the weeke last past, in my health, in my estate, *comforts*, friends: in my family my deare wife and babes, merciful in carrying mee on in my calling." The physical references for *comfort* applied to the weather, itself providential: "very faire and *comfortable* weather, fit for the harvest and plow, calling upon us to blesse god, who hath a regard unto us." When Josselin assessed his physical accommodation at home he used the terms *convenient* and *refreshment:* "went about the paire of stairs out of the hall into the chambers, sett up my skreene in the hall the weeke before, which we find very warm and convenient for us: tis of god we enjoy any refreshments that others want."[44]

Ease was the most frequent sixteenth- and seventeenth-century term to express appreciation of physical amenity. It implied the absence of distress or the relief of pain and annoyance and had strong connotations of restfulness. In the middle of the eighteenth century, Samuel Johnson still defined *ease* as "a neutral state between pain & pleasure." When *comfort* had a physical reference in seventeenth-century English, it too usually implied the relief of distress rather than the improvement of amenity. Seventeenth-century legal documents, such as wills, deeds, and statutes, used the term *comfortable* when referring to minimally adequate physical provision for people in needy circumstances. The laws of Plymouth colony authorized overseers in each town to take children of people too poor "to provide necessary and convenient food and clothing" and "despose of [them] . . . so as they may bee *comfortably* provided for." An "aged" man "not in a capassety to live and keep house of himselfe," "put his estate into the hands" of another man "that therby hee may have a *comfortable* livelyhood." In these maintenance contracts *convenient* meant "sutable" provision for generic needs: "Meat Drink apparil washing & lodging." "*Comfortable* subsistence" for a widow typically involved a child's obligation to allow her use of specified spaces in the house and yard—"sole and proper use of the parlor and chamber over it in my now dwelling house together with the free use of the garden out houses kitchings oven well seller and yeards as shee hath occasion"—provision of firewood and corn, pasturage of animals, access to orchard lands, and a money sum.[45] In its physical references *comfort* typically referred to the barest necessities.

The critical terms used most frequently in the early modern period to express admiration for houses referred to their appearance and their construction materials rather than to the physical experience of living in them. For example, take Adam Martindale, a schoolmaster and Quaker preacher who grew up in a yeoman household in the early seventeenth century. An eminent architectural historian cites Martindale's recollections of his father's remodelings as an example of a desire to have more "*comfort.*" But Martindale actually referred to his early homes as the new "pretty neat habitation" in which he was born and the "strong and large stonehouse" which his father later built. The design of houses for English freeholders in the seventeenth century involved an increase in the conceptual and spatial separation of the elemental from the domestic, as marked by such expressions as "genteel and lasting," "neat," "fair," "pretty," and "sure." Robert Blair St. George has shown how an increase in the separation of the spaces for humans, livestock, and raw materials marked the English yeoman's valuing of the "artificial" over the natural. There was "an overall tendency to push the service functions of the house toward the rear. Hiding the clutter of domestic process, the owner could now present a symmetrical product to his neighbors: the facade of his central-chimney house. Finally, as chimneys filled old smoke-holes, the open hall of the sixteenth-century house could be ceiled over to provide a second floor of chambers previously unavailable."[46] The central chimney symbolized control over the natural, human, and economic processes that produced a respectable way of life.

Physical amenity had a close association with cleanliness. Gervase Markham's directions to housewives for making cloth emphasized its propriety, not how it would feel: "she ought to cloathem [her family] outwardly & inwardly; outwardly for defence from the cold and comeliness to the person; and inwardly, for cleanliness and neatnesse of the skinne, whereby it may be kept from the filth of sweat, or vermine; the first consisting of woollen cloth, the latter of linnen." Filth caused discomfort:

> beware that you do not lye in olde chambres whiche be not occupyed, specyally such chambres as myse, rattes, and snayles resorteth unto. Lye not in suche chambres the which be depryved clene from the sonne and open ayre; nor lye in no lowe chambre except it be borded.
>
> Swepyng of howses and chambres ought not to be done as long as any honest man is within the precynct of the howse, for the dust doth putryfy the ayre, makynge it dence. Also, nygh to the place let nother flaxe nor hempe be watered; and beware of the snoffe of candelles, and of the savour of apples, for these thynges be contagyous and infectyve.

Pests were symptoms of dangerous hygiene, not just immediate irritants: "This impediment [lousiness] doth come by the corruption of hote humours with sweat, or els of rancknes of the body, or else by unclene kepynge, or lyenge with lousy persons, or els not chaungynge of a mannes sherte, or else lyenge in a lousy bedde."[47]

In its physical connotations, *comfort* still meant strengthening, and referred more readily to hygiene than to the furnishings of a house. To have a "commodious" house depended on its having fresh air: "if the air be fresh, pure, and clene, about the mansion or house, it doth conserve the life of man, it doth *comfort* the brain, and the power natural, animal, and spiritual, engendering and making good blood, in the which consisteth the life of man." Conversely, a weakening of the body implied *dis*comfort, which could be articulated most explicitly in reference to bad air. Keeping moisture from debilitating the air was a major consideration in the design of houses:

> And contraryly, evyl and corrupt ayres doth infecte the blode, and doth ingendre many corrupte humours, and doth putryfye the brayne, and doth corrupte the herte; and therefore it doth brede many dyseases and infyrmytes, thorowe the which, mans lyfe is abrevyated and shortned.

Many thynges doth infect, putryfye, and corrupteth the ayre, as the influence of sondry sterres, and standyng waters, stynkinng mystes, and marshes, caryn lyinge longe above the grounde, moche people in a smal rome lying unclenly, and being fylthe and sluttysshe; wherfore he that doth pretende to buylde his mansyon or house, he must provyde that he do nat cytuat his howse nyghe to any marsshe or marysshe grownde; that there by nat, nygh to the place, stynkynge and putryfyed standyng waters, pooles, pondes, nor myers [meers].

Vitruvius, the preeminent classical authority on architecture, taught English readers that the primary consideration in the "convenience" of buildings was their hygiene—that they provide occupants with "wholesome" air. Once such matters of siting had been settled, then rooms could be oriented to the sun and the prevailing winds in ways appropriate to their needs for warmth and light—libraries in the east, for example, so they "turned to the rising sun, because we generally study in the morning" and "for that the sone by natural heate at his rising draweth to him all corupte humors and evill vapors of the earth and quickeneth the spirittes of man."[48]

WHEN HARRISON referred to the chimney as a new facility in the houses of his own time, he parenthetically mentioned that it had appeared earlier in manors and religious houses. His qualification implied that the changes in standards of living were social and cultural as well as technological and economic. Norbert Elias's analysis of a "civilizing process" in manners during the Renaissance also applies to the domestic environment. This process of architectural refinement focused initially on the humanists' ideal domestic space, the study. Studies were synonymous with civility. In Renaissance palaces they received the sort of specialized attention to the design of the domestic environment previously characteristic of monastic establishments. As places for individual reading and thought on classical texts they elided the secular and the religious worlds. As spaces designed to store and display items carefully chosen for their style and their accommodation of an individual's highly self-conscious leisure—not just books but desks and chairs, glassware and mirrors, cushions and other textile amenities, facilities for artificial illumination, art objects—the Renaissance study was arguably the initial site of the early modern consumer revolution and of the expression of modern physical comfort. While reports of self-conscious satisfaction with

one's immediate domestic physical environment are generally scanty before
the eighteenth century, a large exception must be allowed for the innumerable happy comments about one's study. During the Renaissance, studies
became a trope for asserting one's success in rethinking domestic amenity.[49]

What the humanists made explicit regarding their studies, other households made implicit with their purchases of goods for their parlors and
chambers. Whole social levels in Harrison's era now valued amenities that
were previously the preserve of much smaller groups. From the yeomanry
up, there had been a redefinition of physical standards of living. At the level
of yeoman households, differences in wealth correlated more closely with
the quantity and quality of items than with the variety in *types* of consumer
durables. A relatively wealthy household used the same items as its less well
off neighbors to furnish its more numerous rooms; it just had more of them
and they were of a better quality. Most of a yeoman household's investments
in durable consumer goods were spent on bedding, chests, and pewter. Yeomen seldom owned such items as desks, nonreligious books, or upholstered
cushions and chairs, which were typical of gentry households, although they
were affordable. Because there was a social explanation for the changes in
consumption patterns, Harrison could analyze them by regional comparisons within England, where the changes in social relations of leaseholding
and land use varied regionally: "The furniture of our houses also exceedeth,
and is grown in manner even to passing delicacy: and herein I do not speak
of the nobility and gentry only, but likewise of the lowest sort in most places
of our South Country."[50] Households in the East Anglian fens, as well as
in the North and the West, perpetuated patterns of domestic furnishings
that had previously prevailed throughout England across much of the social
spectrum.

The architectural enhancement of domesticity corresponded with reorientation in household production and consumer spending. Households
apparently turned to or increased their production for the market in order
to have more income to spend on domestic furnishings. In the sixteenth and
seventeenth centuries these enhancements involved privacy, cleanliness, and
light. During this period pewter eating and drinking ware replaced wood,
beds became possessions of all propertied families, and rooms began to be
partitioned.

Changes in consumption developed by social emulation, which went
through two stages in the early modern period. The first began in the late

sixteenth century and ran through the first decades of the eighteenth. During that period increases in consumer spending went toward better bedding and eating ware. William Harrison's 1577 *Description of England* again provides the classic contemporary observation on new standards of accommodation: furniture of "passing delicacy," "neatness and curiosity"—tapestry, silver, pewter, brass, fine linen, "three or four feather beds, so many coverlets," and bedsteads made by joiners rather than carpenters—was now owned not only by nobles, gentry, and merchants, but also by "inferior artificers" and farmers with advantageous terms for leases. Harrison carefully explained how these new amenities resulted from changes in demand, not just wealth:

> Our fathers (yea and ourselves also) have lien full oft upon straw pallets, covered only with a sheet, under coverlets made of dagswain or hapharlots (I use their own terms), and a good round log under their heads instead of a bolster or pillow. If it were so that our fathers or the goodman of the house had within seven years after his marriage purchased a mattress or flock-bed, and thereto a sack of chaff to rest his head upon, he thought himself to be as well lodged as the lord of the town, that peradventure lay seldom in a bed of down or whole feathers, so well were they contented and [*sic*] with such base kind of furniture, which is also not very much amended as yet in some parts of Bedfordshire and elsewhere further off from our southern parts. Pillows (said they) were thought meet only for women in child bed. As for servants, if they had any sheet above them it was well, for seldom had they any under their bodies to keep them from the pricking straws that ran oft through the canvas of the pallet and rased their hardened hides.[51]

In the century after Harrison wrote, yeomen's wills became more specific and elaborate in identifying the bedding fabrics they bequeathed, with sheets of "Harden . . . canvas . . . hempen . . . Bockram . . . Holland . . . flaxen . . . linnen." Similar differentiations applied to the quality of mattress materials. Swan's down was the finest, then other feathers. A "flock" bed was filled with wool and could be found in servants' spaces. At Ham House in the 1650s, for example, flock beds were in the stables and outbuildings; servants inside the house in the garret rooms had bedsteads and feather beds. Well below flock in status was straw. A bedstead was optional for such a modest mattress, which might simply be placed on a sackcloth "bottom."[52]

Types of bedding materials marked status and wealth. Beds were center-pieces in the ceremonial rooms of seventeenth-century aristocratic houses, and their fittings were precisely scaled to the rank of their intended occupant. At Ham House in the 1650s the withdrawing room (to which guests moved after dining in the great dining room) had "a large French bedstead" with "a set of seat furniture [two armchairs and ten folding chairs] and a table-carpet all *en suite* with the rich bed-hangings of embroidered white satin." In an even grander house there would be a state bedroom. In these aristocratic settings, even the number of pillows marked gradations in status. A bed with just one pillow was likely to lack a headboard and to have only single valances of a modest fabric, like camolet. The ultimate in beds, and the ultimate source of much emulation, were those for royal visits. Besides plumes of feathers and bunches of artificial flowers above the posts, "the bed hangings comprised the maximum number of components possible at the time—six curtains (i.e., a pair to each of the three exposed sides of the bed), and narrow *cantonnières* (cantoons) to mask the joins at the head and corners will certainly have had both inner and outer valances between which the curtains ran round the edge of the tester."[53]

Royal beds were infinitely more costly than those of Harrison's archetypal yeoman—whose "course coverlids" could be filled acceptably with the "course lockes, pitch, brands, tarr'd lockes, and other feltrings" unsuited to spinning into yarn—yet both the aristocracy and the yeomanry had the same priority as to *types* of amenity. Proper sleeping was a major health consideration, and here, too, the word *comfort* had connotations of strengthening the body:

> Put your clothes in winter by the fire side: and cause your bed bee heated with a warming panne: unless your pretence bee to harden your members, and to apply your self unto militarie discipline. This outward heating doth wonderfully *comfort* the inward heat, it helpeth concoction, and consumeth moisture.

The mid-sixteenth-century physician Andrew Boorde explained the therapeutic physiology of sleep:

> Moderate slepe is moste praysed, for it doth make parfyte degestiyon; it doth nourysshe the blode, and doth qualyfye the heate of the lyver;

it doth acuate, quycken, and refressheth the memory; it doth restore nature, and doth quyet all the humours and pulses in man, and doth anymate and doth *comforte* all the naturall, and anymall, and spyrytuall powers of man. . . . I do advertyse you, for to cause to be made a good thycke quylt of cotton, or els of pure flockes, or of clene woull, and let the coverynge of it be of whyte fustyan, and laye it on the fether-beed that you do lye on; and in your beed lye not to hote or to colde, but in a temperaunce.

When Cotton Mather used the metaphor of a "*comfortable* chamber" in a sermon, the only furniture he mentioned was its bed.[54]

If beds and permanent houses were metonyms of "civility," then the "Wild Irish" who confronted their Tudor English colonizers were antonyms, beyond the pale in their proximity to the elemental. In their sufficiency without bedding or manufactured items for food storage, preparation, and serving, the Irish were a living repudiation of new vernacular standards for the English domestic environment:

That country is wylde, wast and vast, full of marcyces and mountayns, and lytle corne; but they have flesh sufficient, and little breat or none, and none ale. For the people there be slouthfull, not regarding to sow and tille theyr landes, nor caryng for ryches. For in many places they care not for pot, pan, kettyl, nor for mattrys, fether bed, nor such implementes of houshold. Wherfore it is presuppose that they lak maners and honesty, and be untaught and rude; the which rudeness, with thyr melancoly complexion, causeth them to be angry and testy without a cause. In those partyes they wyll eate theyr meat sytting on the ground or erth. And they wyl sethe thyr meat in a beastes skyn. And the skyn shall be set on manye stakes of wood, and than they wyll put in the water and the fleshe. And than they wil make a great fyre under the skyn betwyxt the stakes, and the skyn wyl not greatly bren. And whan the meate is eaten, they, for theyr dryke, wil drynk up the brothe. In such places men and women wyll ly to-gether in mantles and straw.

For a nomadic, herding people like the Irish, the mantle served as house and bed as well as clothing. These mantles were an English metonym for the wildness of the Irish, allowing them to live in the woods and to spend the night wherever they pleased: "it is his bed, yea and almost all his household stuff. For the wood is his house against all weathers, and his mantle his cave to sleep in." To Edmund Spenser, who knew the Irish as an official and planter in the 1580s, the mantle was an atavism that perpetuated an anomalous "Sythian" barbarity into the modern civilized era. Spenser recognized that the mantle perfectly met the "necessity" of Irish life—that was the problem.[55]

In the next century, Sir William Petty, the originator of "political arithmetic," could still use hearths to calculate the Irish population, since most people lived in chimneyless houses—"wretched nasty cabbins, without chimney, window, or door-shut, and worse than those of the savage Americans, and wholly unfit for the making of merchantable butter, cheese, or the manufactures of woollen, linen, or leather." By his reckoning most families in Ireland (one hundred sixty thousand of two hundred thousand) lived in "Cabins" with "no fix'd Hearth," and most of the rest (twenty-four thousand of forty thousand) had only one chimney. Most of the families with more than one chimney lived in cities and towns (ninety-four hundred of sixteen thousand). The occupants of such cabins "use few commodities; and those such as almost every one can make and produce." Their domestic economy and environment were antitypes to England's:

That is to say, men live in such cottages as themselves can make in 3 or 4 days; eat such food (tobacco excepted) as they buy not from others; wear such cloaths as the wool of their own sheep, spun into yarn by themselves, doth make. . . .

The cabins themselves prevented participation in the new consumer economy:

in which neither butter or cheese, nor linen, yarn nor worsted; and I think no other, can be made to the best advantage; chiefly by reason of the soot and smoaks annoying the same; as also for the narrowness and nastiness of the place; which cannot be kept clean nor safe from beasts and vermin, nor from damps and musty stenches, of which all the eggs laid or kept in those cabbins do partake. Wherefore to the advancement of trade, the reformation of these cabins is necessary.[56]

Petty's ethnocentrism led him to present English civility and Irish wildness as polar opposites architecturally. In fact, he wrote during a long period of regional *variation* in English housing design that had begun in the fifteenth century. Architectural historians characteristically see this diversity in evolutionary terms, so that areas not manifesting the stylistic changes characteristic of the South and East ("the classic norm") "lagged behind" or were "retarded" and where "progress was very slow." Besides the explicit teleology, such a view impedes understanding of either the new or the traditional, since the former can largely be taken for granted and the latter is important primarily for its impoverishment.[57] This invidious contrast between "civilized" and "backward" architecture has its origins in learned sixteenth-century commentary. The large hall, with its open hearth, came to be regarded as an archaism, as central chimneys and glazed windows became standard features of respectable housing among landholders in the South and East. But, as the architectural history of the American colonies would show, such respectability was still optional in English housing culture. Symbolically and economically, the chimney and the bed had priority in early modern English accommodation. They involved the greatest expense and they drew the most visual attention. Until the early eighteenth century almost any other expenditure on the domestic environment was optional.

COLONIAL COMFORT

Vernacular and Elegant Options

IN EARLY Anglo-American housing culture, people with the means to have ostensibly comfortable houses did not necessarily build them. When colonial governor William Bradford referred to the early houses of Plymouth Colony as "small cottages," he was employing a historical association of *cottage* with substandard housing. After all, these structures lacked foundations and had wooden chimneys, thatched roofs, earthen floors, unglazed or small-paned casement windows, and wattle-and-daub walls. But the term *cottage* nearly passed out of usage in colonial America, although most American households lived in houses that looked like cottages (see, for instance, Figure 3.1).[1] In contemporary England inhabiting a cottage marked people as lacking sufficient landholdings to support a household, but in early America there were many more cottages than cottagers. Most American households held sufficient land to provide livelihoods for their members, so they were not cottagers in the sense of living in a dwelling owned by someone else. Housing in late eighteenth-century America lacked the close architectural association with social standing that it had in Britain. Spending on fashionable architectural designs for heating, illumination, privacy, and

Figure 3.1. Vernacular housing. Cottagelike houses predominated along the Baltimore Road near York Town. *Columbian Magazine; or Monthly Miscellany*, 2 (Philadelphia: T. Seddon, July 1788), facing 357. Courtesy of the Winterthur Library, Printed Book and Periodical Collection, Winterthur, Delaware.

hygiene had a relatively low priority in colonial Anglo-America. It did not correlate so strongly with wealth as did consumer spending on stylish clothing, furniture, and ceramics.

When they built homes in the first generation overseas, English colonists demonstrated their recollections of supposedly archaic architecture. In both New England and Virginia they drew on traditions of "impermanent architecture" to build houses that were more finely crafted than huts but which employed materials requiring replacement at least generationally. These traditions predated the Great Rebuilding. They called for posts set in the ground and for hearths laid directly on the ground, and they made windows and chimneys optional. The continual arrival in the Chesapeake of immigrants from England kept such traditions of impermanent architecture alive throughout the seventeenth century. When Africans began arriving there in large numbers as slaves, toward the end of the century, they reinforced these vernacular traditions with new technical sophistication.[2] In New England, however, immigration was concentrated in the generation of the 1630s, and its social basis was largely of yeomen families from the south and east of England, just the group to extend the Great Rebuilding overseas.

Colonization of North America exaggerated the regional variation in early modern English housing culture, with its wide range in designs for household amenity. Colonization simultaneously reinvigorated archaic elements in English vernacular architecture and heightened awareness of these archaisms. English observers could make sense of the housing of the indigenous peoples by comparing it with earlier versions of housing back home. Thus the Jesuit missionary Andrew White made the housing of the Maryland Algonkians seem exotic by comparing it with a building, the longhouse, that supposedly existed only in memory in England:

> Their houses are built in an halfe ovall forme 20 foot long, and 9 or 10 foot high with a place open in the top, halfe a yard square, whereby they admit the light, and let forth the smoake, for they build their fire, after the manner of ancient halls of England, in the middle of the house, about which they lie to sleep upon mats, spread on a low scaffold hafe a yard from ground. In one of these houses we now doe celebrate [Mass], haveing it dressed a little better then by the Indians, till we get a better, which shall be shortly as may be.

White recognized the archaic quality of his hosts' houses while appreciating their amenities. Such housing arrangements, though "ancient," still had vernacular vitality in England. Colonists drew on these supposedly archaic traditions for their initial housing, using materials close at hand that could be quickly worked. A variety of materials and designs was used in the settlement of each colony: Indian longhouses, earthfast frames covered in riven clapboards, horizontal logs and vertical palings, wattling-and-mud walls with thatched roofs, and brick towers. From one colonial region to another there were marked differences in housing cultures, but within each region families with large differences in wealth and household size lived in similar domestic environments, and there was less diversity of plan, size, and construction materials than was true of the regions of Europe from which the colonists had come.[3]

Vernacular Alternatives in the Colonial South

The housing culture of the colonial Chesapeake bears comparison with that of upland England. In upland England—the Midlands, North, and along the limestone plateau running from northeast to southwest—far fewer buildings survive from the sixteenth and seventeenth centuries than is the case for the southern and eastern regions of England. Propertied households in upland regions tended to spend less on housing, both absolutely and relatively, than did ones in the lowland areas. Taxable wealth per household in England northwest of the Humber-Severn line was less than half that of southeastern England, and differences of wealth at the household level translated less directly into differences of accommodation. Most households slept only on the ground floor, and when parlors became more frequent after 1600 they were often unheated. Earthen floors were acceptable at virtually all levels of vernacular housing.

Late into the seventeenth century in much of upland England, in households of substantial as well as modest wealth the hall remained the most important domestic space for socializing and for domestic work. In late-seventeenth-century Devon, prosperous husbandmen usually had only a single service room, and wealthy yeomen had only two or three. Single-room houses remained acceptable for propertied households, and even prosperous farming households were more likely to locate chimneys on gable ends or on the cross passage rather than have an axial chimney between hall and parlor. In late-seventeenth-century Yorkshire, parlors were rooms for sleeping, and many of them remained unheated. Yeoman households there combined domestic and agricultural purposes in one space, as in the storage of crops and tools in chambers. Most domestic life took place in a single space, still usually called the "house." Since the parlor had low priority as a room for leisure and receiving guests, when two-story farmhouses were built in the late seventeenth century they lacked a parlor and had sleeping chambers on the second floor. On substantial farms in early-seventeenth-century West Yorkshire and Lancashire, those with barns and hayhouses, dwellings were often referred to as "firehouses," because they had no kitchens, only the hall, where the fire was. Even when houses there had wainscoting, glazing, and wooden parlor floors, they often had a fireplace only in the hall.[4]

The continued importance of cattle raising in the west and north of Eng-

land apparently made farmers reluctant to give up the cross passage's convenient access to the byre and dairy. Longhouses with byres continued to be built
by cattle-raising yeoman households in poor areas of the West and North
(Devonshire, Herefordshire, Lake District, and Yorkshire) into the middle of
the seventeenth century. How the buildings were used depended on the occupants' type of agricultural enterprise (pasture rather than arable), not poverty.
When households separated the byre from the house, they retained a "lower"
end of the house for storage and general service purposes. In regions where
the longhouse was a viable plan, prosperous farmers who added parlors and
service rooms typically placed them along the same facade, rather than rel-
egating the service rooms to the rear and then putting the parlor in front, as
in the South and Southeast. The influence of longhouse traditions is also
apparent in the use of firehoods in place of chimneys in the North.[5]

IN SEVENTEENTH-CENTURY Virginia, as in the upland regions of England, variations in wealth were wider than variations in the quality of vernacular housing. Substantial planters lived in post-in-ground "Virginia
houses" that followed the hall-chamber-kitchen pattern. Planters in the seventeenth-century Chesapeake *chose* not to build the "substantial" or "fair"
houses preferred by husbandmen and yeomen in lowland England. Until at
least the middle of the eighteenth century, vernacular housing in the Chesapeake conformed to the building standards of the first generation of settlers.[6]

Historical archaeologists have found that "earthfast" construction characterized early Chesapeake houses. Colonists used construction methods that
in England had begun to be superseded in the thirteenth century by buildings using stone footings or foundations for their frames. Colonial Chesapeake building practice demonstrates that earthfast construction remained a
part of the English architectural repertoire at that time. In England, as the
priority for investment in housing increased, it was cases of meager means
that dictated such construction methods, but in the Chesapeake, investment
in the minima of the Great Rebuilding—chimneys, ceilings, and wooden
floors—was apparently optional regardless of means. Earthfast houses in
Virginia were built with care, particularly in the choice of woods that could
endure as posts in the ground. Europeans in the nonplantation colonies further north used the same construction techniques, but they employed them
for transitional housing, until houses of permanent construction could be
afforded. From the beginnings of colonization in the north, architectural

permanency, as marked particularly by brick foundations and brick chimneys, apparently had a symbolic as well as practical importance that it lacked in plantation societies.[7]

Clifts, a "manner house" built in Westmoreland County, Virginia, about 1670, represents the architectural ambition of a substantial planter. For his prosperous, servant-holding tenants, the owner built a framed cross-passage house with vertical supports set in post holes, with its clapboard sheathing coated in tar. An open central hearth heated the hall and chamber. The hearth itself had a stone surface set into clay, with a wattle-and-daub firehood. Archaic as such a hearth would have been in much of southern England, it represented much more care with heating than the owner took with the servants' quarters, where the only arrangement for the fire was a hole in the ground. Both buildings had earthen floors. When the servants' quarters were replaced about 1700, the new building had an exterior chimney made of wood covered with clay. The master's house had a central hearth and firehood. These construction techniques, particularly the designs for heating, were typical of many prosperous and most modestly propertied families in the Chesapeake during the last third of the seventeenth century and into the first third of the eighteenth century.[8]

Around 1730 Clifts was torn down and replaced with a brick mansion, named Stratford Hall. Over the previous two decades wealthy planters had ceased to use hole-set posts for their houses and started using brick extensively for foundations, chimneys, and sometimes walls. Use of brick for a manor house marked the completion of a series of separations between the household economy and the domestic functions of the manor house. As Robert Beverley said of the process early in the eighteenth century, "All their Drudgeries of Cookery, washing, Daries, &c. are perform'd in Offices detacht from their Dwelling-Houses, which by this means are kept more cool and Sweet."[9] At Clifts, for example, over the preceding half-century the cross passage had been blocked up, so that access to the hall was buffered by a porch entry; separate buildings had been constructed to provide space for kitchen and dairy work that had previously been done in the master's house; and an open work shed at the rear of the cross passage had been removed. Meanwhile, the hall had become a space with facilities for entertaining—appointed with prints and portraits, tables and chairs, and mirrors—and the chamber had been enlarged to provide fuller retreat from the hall, serving as a sitting room as well as an area for sleeping.

Planters built such small, well-finished, hall-and-parlor houses as this one from the 1710s through the rest of the colonial period. The frame construction and single-pile (one room deep), story-and-a-half plan and elevation characteristic of earthfast housing continued through this transition from farmhouse to mansion, as did the ready use of outbuildings for domestic service functions. Less wealthy planters built on a modest scale in a modulated emulation of the pretentious brick mansions simultaneously being built by the wealthiest planters. Many of these smaller mansions met Georgian standards of external symmetry, with gable-end chimneys, balanced window bays, and central entrances, even if the rooms and fireplaces within were of different sizes.[10]

Among houses advertised for sale in the *Virginia Gazette* from 1736 to 1780, a group presumably biased upward in quality and toward long-settled areas, over two-thirds had only one or two rooms. Most of their owners had chosen to live in well-finished small houses with several outbuildings rather than in larger ones with more specialized rooms. And many propertied families compromised the quality of finish in one respect or another—tar-covered siding, shutters rather than glazed windows, wooden rather than brick foundations, or chimneys of wood and clay rather than brick. If their circumstances improved, any increased investment in housing went into quality of finish and permanency of construction, not scale.[11]

Investment in architectural scale in the eighteenth-century Chesapeake went into outbuildings. As with earthfast construction in the seventeenth century, this development in Virginia architecture represented an atavism. During the Great Rebuilding in England service rooms within the dwelling had multiplied and/or, as with kitchens, been moved into the house. In Virginia there was a strong imperative to move the kitchen out of the house. In a long-settled area of Virginia in the 1760s a planter with a separate kitchen and a tobacco house on his plantation of several hundred acres might well live in a one-room house that in size came somewhere between the two outbuildings. After kitchens and tobacco houses, in rough priority of necessity, came barns, dairies, smokehouses, corn cribs, and stables.[12]

Despite its rapid economic growth, the Chesapeake lagged behind more town-oriented regions of the colonies and England. In tracing the first phase of Chesapeake households' participation in the preindustrial consumer revolution, Lois Carr, Gloria Main, and Carole Shammas have shown that what were frequent household possessions elsewhere by the middle of the eighteenth century—"coarse ceramics, bed and table linen, chamber pots, warming pans, and some means of interior lighting"—had been found in fewer than one in three Chesapeake homes as late as the 1720s. Until the 1720s such items were only owned by some of the rich, even though they were not very expensive. Most households in the Chesapeake lived with the same items of material amenity, despite their differences in wealth. Differences in wealth corresponded to a household's having greater or lesser amounts of the same *types* of possessions as neighboring households, namely land, buildings, servile labor, and livestock.[13]

Until the 1720s Chesapeake planters used architecture to indicate economic success simply by having more buildings, but in that decade a few dozen rich planters began to build symmetrical, large, and permanent brick houses that incorporated a distinctive redesign of the traditional hall. It was no longer a multipurpose living area with direct access from the out-of-doors. Instead, the entrance became a separate hallway that ran through the center of the house and provided an area for meeting outsiders. Off this hallway, the successor to the great hall became a parlorlike room for entertainment. The domestic areas of such houses became more specialized. Most rooms had at least two large, glazed windows, and access to these rooms required passage through the hallway (accordingly now named the "passage"). Virtually all mansions in eighteenth-century Virginia had central passages, and most of them unabashedly announced their double-pile plan by having double chimneys.

Even though most rich planters adopted the passage, the development of the "dining room" in the first half of the eighteenth century continued traditions of domestic informality. *Dining room* referred to a first-story, multipurpose domestic space for storage, eating, and sleeping once the "hall" became a room to meet outsiders. *Dining room* was something of a misnomer, since the room took over several functions in addition to being the space for dining. Besides having tables and chairs for use during meals, dining rooms could house beds, store tools, and provide access to the house from the kitchen in the yard. Houses with dining rooms typically had a chamber as well, which was the most private part of the house and had access only from the dining room. As Dell Upton has written, "the dining room was the heart of the family's house, as opposed to the hall which was the center of the family's social landscape."[14]

Numerous visitors to Virginia mansions from the 1720s onward noted admiringly how the central passage, with its doorways on opposite sides of the house, encouraged cooling breezes through the house and provided a shady refuge from the sun. They reported how seating furniture, and even beds, were brought there in summer. But through the middle of the eighteenth century only a minority of houses in Virginia had more than one room, and among them fewer than one-fifth had a through passage; this proportion increased to two-fifths of multiroomed houses by the end of the colonial period. Houses that did have cross passages frequently compromised cross ventilation in the hall and dining room by having chambers or closets that made them double-pile. Though houses with central passages gave a high priority to the ornamental function of the chimneypiece, the central passage actually lessened heating efficiency, since it inserted a large, unheated volume into the middle of the house. Central passages usually had open stairs, which further reduced the effectiveness of the multiple fireplaces.[15]

Despite the introduction of the central passage, the hall-and-parlor plan continued to mark wealth in Virginia, even though such houses were much more modest than the grand mansions that began to be built in the early eighteenth century and that have been the stereotype of plantation architecture. At the end of the eighteenth century planters still typically built houses of one and two rooms. Most of the propertied population did not repudiate vernacular architecture; instead they incorporated into it elements of genteel design, such as brick foundations and chimneys, plastered ceilings, and some specialized rooms for entertainment. Most of the free population in eighteenth-century Virginia lived in lofted single-room houses, with entrance directly from outside and only a single window. When in 1785 Thomas Jefferson said of Virginians' houses that it was "impossible to devise things more ugly, *uncomfortable*, and happily more perishable," he was applying a set of values that his compatriots had knowingly resisted.

Slave Housing

Virtually all houses that have survived from the colonial South belonged to slave owners. Almost none of the houses occupied by the slaves themselves survive from the colonial period. In Virginia, slaves had been housed from the start in accordance with very minimal standards for Anglo-Americans, since they shared accommodation with indentured servants from the British

Isles. Beginning in the third quarter of the seventeenth century, masters housed their unfree laborers, indentured and enslaved, in separate quarters, typically of deliberately impermanent construction, with clapboarded frames supported vertically by posts set in the ground. Over the next half-century, as enslaved Africans came to predominate as the unfree labor force, their accommodation became segregated from that of European laborers, who were never enslaved. During this transition much of the free population, including people with the economic means to build otherwise, continued to be housed in earthfast buildings. But during the later colonial period such houses became a mark of poverty, as even modestly propertied households began to have houses with one or more of the following features: brick foundations, board floors, glazed windows, plastered walls and ceilings, stairs, and brick chimneys.[16]

By the late colonial period the minimum standard of accommodation likely to be desired by people in a position to have discretion in their standard of accommodation, such as overseers, included walls that were raised off the ground and plastered, board floors, and a brick chimney serving every room. In the eighteenth century, framed houses were more likely than ones built of logs to be finished inside, to have glazed windows, to have brick chimneys, and to have board floors. At any one time a sizable proportion of the free population lived in accommodation below this standard and closer to that of slave families—for example, some log houses lacked windows altogether—but members of such households usually expected to meet this standard eventually. In the Chesapeake during the late eighteenth and early nineteenth centuries, log houses were not necessarily a mark of low social status among tenants or small landowners, even though the large majority of slaves lived in them and framed houses were clearly preferable among the free population. Finish, not type of construction, marked status: in the middle of the eighteenth century a minimally finished house for a tenant family cost six to seven times as much as a house for an enslaved family, and provided about twice as much space. Brick chimneys and glazed windows were slightly above the minimal standard for free people's housing; some very modest houses had them, most did not. Brick was the distinguishing material: in the early nineteenth century very few slave families lived in brick houses, and few of them had brick chimneys or brick footings for their walls.[17]

Just as some poor free people had accommodation of a standard comparable with that of most enslaved people, so some few slaves lived in buildings of a standard associated with wealth. During the colonial period, slaves' accommodation varied in accordance with the resources and structures of their particular plantations. Some had no domestic space of their own and slept in basements or attics in the owner's house, or in areas where they worked during the day, such as stair landings and chambers, or in the kitchen and stables. Since such "offices," spaces in which household or farm work was performed, were sometimes architectural showpieces, they provided a paradoxical combination of high-status levels of construction—brick foundations and chimneys, stairways, glazed windows—with barrackslike accommodation. Conversely, people working at tobacco "quarters" remote from the main plantation were likely to share accommodation with people not related to them as well as with kin, in gangs of ten to twenty, and the construction of such quarters hearkened back to seventeenth-century standards. By the middle of the eighteenth century a separate house for individual slave families was an identifiable type of dwelling, but its proportion among all slave housing was low in comparison with haphazard and barrackslike accommodation. By early in the nineteenth century it would be the norm.[18]

Since slaves built the houses of plantation owners, and some of them often worked in those houses once completed, they were well aware of the highest standards of taste and design that lesser planters were emulating, but they did not see much of it in their own housing. When slaves had separate accommodation, it was likely to include, at best, a pot and blanket, a ground-level frame for bedding, shelves resting on pegs driven into walls, hooks from rafters, and board-lined storage cellars. Slaves' bedding was distinctly substandard by comparison with that used in propertied Anglo-American households since the early seventeenth century: most slept on straw; a minority had "beds" in the sense of bedding (a tick filled with straw); bed frames were rare, though a minority had boards pegged or dovetailed to form a frame on the floor. Stools, tables, chairs, and benches were unusual. Slaves' earthfast houses continued to have open central hearths in the eighteenth century, when the minimal housing of the free population required at least a log and clay chimney.[19]

It would be inappropriate to extol the virtues of simplicity in the accommodation of a captive population, but it is arguable that some of the features of slave housing most disagreeable from a modern North American perspective were functional and sophisticated in a preindustrial context. The most apparently elemental feature of the archtypal slave house, its dirt floor, was typically a carefully prepared surface designed for functionality. Earthen floors were "artificial." They provided a hard, smooth surface that was easily cleaned and was graded for drainage. Their surface was a mixture of particular grades of clay, to which further materials, such as oxblood, ashes, and lime, were sometimes added, and the whole mixture was heated before application. The floor received further attention in the construction of storage pits, which apparently had a higher priority among African Americans than among European Americans in the Chesapeake. Such pits were carefully lined and compartmentalized with boards. Similar sophistication went into the design of the slave house's most noticeable designator of status, its log and clay chimney, which gave the appearance of sloppiness. The chimney above the fireplace typically leaned away from the wall of the house at such a precarious angle that it was often supported by angled braces set in the ground. In the event of chimney fire, however, the functionality came into play, as the chimney was pushed over away from the house. Such a chimney could be rebuilt the next day, mostly from the same materials.[20]

If a plantation had more than one slave quarter, slave accommodation was likely to be dispersed about the plantation. In the eighteenth century slaveowners preferred to keep even the nearby quarters just out of sight, though carefully oriented to the main house, while in the nineteenth century a row of slavehouses was often a showpiece along the main approach to the plantation. The area between buildings was effectively part of slave accommodation. House yards provided space for vegetable gardens and poultry pens. Work areas, such as kitchens, stables, and carpenters' and blacksmiths' shops, were also customary social spaces for slaves. And family gatherings often drew slaves away from their immediate domestic setting, since spouses, parents, and children were so likely to be forced to live apart but on nearby plantations.[21]

This domestication of the space between buildings corresponds with contemporaneous practices throughout much of West Africa. There separate buildings served particular activities such as sleeping and storage, while most cooking, eating, and socializing took place out of doors. Groupings by age, gender, marital status, and lineage often required siblings, parents and children, and some spouses, to sleep apart. Only the compound, rather than a single building, could organize all these domestic relations spatially. Anglo-American historians are extraordinarily fortunate to have the observations of an Igbo, Olaudah Equiano, from the Ika region on the Niger River, who published his abolitionist autobiography in 1789 after having spent his youth enslaved in Virginia and the West Indies. Equiano implicitly compared the indigenous architecture of his homeland with the buildings he had known while enslaved in Virginia in the middle of the eighteenth century:

> In our buildings [in Africa] we study convenience rather than ornament [as in Virginia]. Each master of [an Igbo] family has a large square piece of ground, surrounded with a moat or fence, or inclosed with a wall made of red earth tempered, which, when dry, is as hard as brick. Within this are his houses to accommodate his family and slaves; which, if numerous, frequently present the appearance of a village. In the middle stands the principal building, appropriated to the sole use of the master, and consisting of two apartments; in one of which he sits in the day with his family, the other is left apart for the reception of his friends. He has besides these a distinct apartment, in which he sleeps, together with his male children. On each side are the apartments of his wives, who have also their separate day and night houses. The habitations of the slaves and their families are distributed throughout the rest of the inclosure.[22]

Given the continentwide reach of the African slave trade, people arrived in the North American colonies from societies with a wide variety of architectural traditions. Africans from different regions built in wood, thatch, stone, bricks both sun- and kiln-dried, wattle and daub, and clay. Skills with most of these materials meshed with Anglo-American construction techniques and materials. Again, Olaudah Equiano provides extraordinary detail:

> These houses never exceed one story in height; they are always built of wood, or stakes driven into the ground, crossed with wattles, and neatly plastered within and without. The roof is thatched with reeds. Our day houses are left open at the sides; but those in which we sleep are always covered, and plastered in the inside with a composition mixed with cow dung, to keep off the different insects which annoy us during the night. The walls and floors also of these are generally covered with mats. Our beds consist of a platform, raised three or four feet from the ground, on which are laid skins, and different parts of a spungy tree called plantain. Our covering is calico or muslin, the same as our dress. The usual

seats are a few logs of wood; but we have benches, which are generally perfumed, to accommodate strangers: those compose the greater part of our household furniture. Houses so constructed and furnished require but little skill to erect them. Every man is a sufficient architect for the purpose. The whole neighbourhood afford their unanimous assistance in building them, and in return receive and expect no other recompense than a feast.[23]

Archaeology has revealed a decidedly more African component to slaves' housing in early South Carolina than has been found in Virginia. Through the first three-quarters of the eighteenth century, slaves in South Carolina built fundamentally different houses from those of European settlers and colonists. They had thick clay walls set in trenches with posts providing internal support to the wall. The houses often contained two rooms with a solid wall between them. Such houses sometimes had doors in each gable, a very unusual plan for Anglo-Americans. These doors provided the only opening for light as well as access. Palmetto leaves covered the narrow gable roofs. The yard was part of the domestic space and was used not only for the garden but for the cooking fire. Meals were taken in the yard, seated on the ground or on pieces of wood. Small houses primarily for sleeping and storage complemented use of the yard, where most daytime domestic activities were conducted. These early slave houses in South Carolina were smaller than ones in Virginia, averaging just over two hundred square feet per room, whereas those in Virginia had over three hundred fifty square feet. Such small, relatively massive houses had features that moderated climatic extremes of heat and cold. The solid walls provided insulation from daily thermal fluctuations. The earthen floor stayed cool in an interior fully shaded from the sun. When there was a hearth at all, it was chimneyless and lacked permanent location. Its primary purpose was heating, but when poor weather forced people inside it was used for cooking too. This chimneyless hearth dried the house and maximized the fire's output of heat; its smoke acted as a smudge against insects.[24]

In the latter decades of the eighteenth century slave housing in lowcountry South Carolina gradually conformed to the standard developing in the Chesapeake: roughly twenty foot–by–fifteen foot log houses with chimneys. At such house sites most cooking was done on the interior hearth rather than out-of-doors as earlier. During the early stages of the transition, chimneys

were combined with clay-walled houses and with wattle-and-daub walls supported by earthfast posts. Slaves' houses in lowcountry South Carolina continued to be distinctive in their tendency to be smaller than ones north and
westward, in their restrictiveness in allowing openings in the walls, and in
their occasional continued use of open central hearths.[25]

Nearly all surviving slave housing in the United States dates from the nineteenth century and is of a type found throughout the South: framed duplexes
with brick foundations and brick chimneys. Such houses are even more
exceptional than is usually the case with survivals. They were intended from
the start to be showpieces; they usually have uniform frontages, are aligned
orthogonally with the slaveowner's house, and often are visible from it and
from the plantation's main approaches. Such presentable houses might have
beaded weather boards, molded trim around the windows facing the owner's
house, and be whitewashed. They sometimes had board floors, with brick or
log piers keeping their walls off the ground.[26]

From the late eighteenth century through the Civil War most slaves in the
United States lived in single-household gable-roofed log houses with one
room and a loft reached by ladder. The most prominent architectural feature was an external gable-end chimney made of the same materials as the
shell of the house, but the chimney's crib of logs was of lighter wood and the
daubing of clay covered the entire inside of the flue. Packed clay also composed the floor. Doors were expected to provide light as well as access, so that
a wall with a door would not have a window, and if there were a window on
the facing wall then there would not be a back door. Slave dwellings might
have no window at all; few had more than one, which would be shuttered
rather than glazed. Such windows seldom had an opening larger than three
square feet, and two square feet was more typical. Ceilings and interior walls
lacked either plaster or wainscoting.[27]

Late-eighteenth-century slave houses were distinguished by their location,
their uniformly unornamented level of finish, and their small likelihood of
being remodeled or expanded. But in design and construction they resembled what had been the housing of poor people or settlers among the free
population. Tenant housing in the mid-eighteenth-century Chesapeake had
usually been built of logs, roughly twenty by sixteen feet, with wooden floors,
and a chimney usually of wood but sometimes brick. Tenants typically had a
separate kitchen and other outbuildings, such as a corncrib. Such houses had
clapboard roofing rather than shingling, were seldom plastered, and often

lacked glazing. The two markers of improved housing, glazing and brick, were marginal.[28]

From the 1780s onward slave owners were increasingly likely to provide slaves with housing that measured up to, and largely defined, minimal standards of comfortable accommodation. Barns and barracks would not do, at least for housing families. This concern of some slave owners with the standards of their slaves' housing was part of the broader humanitarian definition of comfort in the second half of the eighteenth century. But their use of those standards met a more pressing need to apologize for their treatment of their human chattels in the face of nascent antislavery developments throughout the European Atlantic culture. By the early decades of the nineteenth century slaveowners were applying (minimal) European standards to their slaves' accommodation. One apologist for the treatment of slaves tried to have it both ways:

> Their dwellings consist of good clay cabins, with clay chimneys, but so much attention has been paid of late years to their *comfort* in this particular, that it is now very common, particularly on the Sea Islands, to give them substantial frame houses on brick foundations and with brick chimneys. Many are of opinion that they enjoy more health in open temporary cabins with ground or dirt floors. But this does not correspond with the experience of those who willingly incur the expense of better buildings.

As explained in a later chapter, *comfort* emerged as a term in denunciatory descriptions of slaves' living conditions just as a conscientious movement developed among slave owners to build accommodation that met minimal standards for decent living, as measured by how poor European Americans lived.[29]

Continental European Vernaculars in the Colonies

Besides Africans, the other large groups diversifying vernacular architecture in the British colonies came from Dutch and German areas of continental Europe. They too had designs for elementary comforts of heating and illumination that were different from those of early modern Anglo-Americans.

In early-eighteenth-century Albany, for example, large houses had windows whose design left part of the opening shuttered but unglazed, to provide ventilation, and the other part fitted with fixed or casement leaded-glass. And Dutch fireplaces were really open hearths with a firehood, located against a wall. The mantles projected so far into the room, five or six feet being frequent, that it was easy for people to gather virtually around the fire. These unjambed fireplaces attracted the attention of English observers.

> The fire places have no Jambs (as ours have) But the Backs run flush with the walls, and the Hearth is of Tyles and is as farr out into the room at the Ends as before the which is Generally Five foot in the Low'r rooms, and the peice over where the mantle tree should be is made as ours with Joyners work, and as I supose is fastn'd to iron rodds inside.

Such fireplaces indicated a priority for close proximity to a fire, much as did an open central hearth. The Dutch use of stoves indicates a similar desire for proximity to the source of heat. The chimneyhood was part of the workspace and provided space to smoke meats. Chimneyhoods were not a feature of impermanent architecture. They were built of brick and required careful construction to support the projecting weight.[30]

When vernacular houses in England were introducing chimneys into halls and chambers in the sixteenth and seventeenth century, German farmhouses were isolating domestic spaces from direct exposure to the hall's fire. The *Stube* developed as an enclosed living area heated by a stove. Entry into the *Stube* was from the *Lucht,* a space within the hall house providing direct access to the farm animals and agricultural storage. The basic element in early modern house plans in middle and southern Germany (from which came most German emigration to Pennsylvania) was the combination *Küche* and *Stube.* The *Küche,* or hall, of the German house had a chimney fireplace, while the *Stube,* the parlor, had a five-plate jamb stove, heated by coals pushed through from the *Küche*'s fireplace on the other side of a common wall. From the Middle Ages the *Stube* had high status associations from its use in castles and monasteries, where the wood-lined *Stube* formed the core of the residential space. The *Stube* became part of German vernacular architecture in the late Middle Ages, as space for it was partitioned off from the *Küche.*[31]

Snugness and smoke-free cleanliness became a standard in German domestic accommodation. Since the heat source for the jamb stove did not draw air from the room it heated, the *Stube* could be much tighter and more draft free than a room with an open fire. (An upstairs chamber would be heated by a jamb stove fed by a small fireplace whose main purpose was to provide the needed coals, rather than to heat its own room.) Because the *Stube*'s heat depended on coals from an open hearth in another room, chimneyhoods in German houses, just as in Dutch houses, were not necessarily an indication of shortcomings in wealth or architectural resources. Indeed, *Rauchkammer* (smoke chambers for smoking meats above the *Küche*'s hearth) manifested prosperity. Chimneys, on the other hand, did have status associations, at least among those able to afford roofing tiles. Less well off German peasants viewed stone chimneys as fire hazards, because they passed sparks too readily up onto thatched roofs.[32]

In eighteenth-century Pennsylvania, German house plans retained a central chimney, but much more often than in Germany itself they had the three-room plan of the *Flurküchenhaus*, with a narrow *Küche* running through the house from front to back. With two doors opening directly from the outside into the most active space, the house plan gave ready accessibility to outsiders, and there was a social imperative to leave a door open during daylight. In addition, these German settlers had a period of ritual sociability in the evening when they sat outside their houses. For full separation from the outside there were the *Stube*, accessible from the *Küche*, and the *Kammer*, reached from the *Stube*. In the second half of the eighteenth century quasi-symmetrical Georgian facades, with balanced numbers of windows and sometimes two doors, masked the continuation of this house plan, but the location of the chimney on the gable often required giving up the *Stube*'s stove.[33]

The Great Rebuilding in New England

In seventeenth-century New England colonists distinguished sharply between archaic and vernacular styles. Most houses built in Plymouth Colony in the first two decades of settlement had wooden chimneys, thatched roofs, wattle-and-daub walls, and unglazed windows. Some of them were framed, others had "palisaded" walls of closely set log studs. Some were earthfast; others had ground-set sills. Such heterogeneity apparently resulted from the recruitment of immigrants in different regions of England and the options available to them for both up-to-date and archaic designs. About 60 percent of these settlers were from the south and east of England, 30 percent from the west, and 10 percent from the north. In 1637 Samuel Symonds wrote from Ipswich in Norfolk to John Winthrop, Jr., about having a house built for his arrival in Massachusetts Bay. Symonds was gentry, not yeoman, yet he wanted to build an archaic house, one with a big hall, over thirty feet long and sixteen feet wide. He wanted wooden chimneys at both ends, but they would be nearly open hearths, since his chimneys were really firehoods and might have run the entire width of the house. He gave no directions for partitioning the first floor, and he did not care whether or not the second floor was partitioned either. Here was someone who had been exposed to the Great Rebuilding, but who deliberately chose a contrary design. Most telling were his directions for windows: "for windows, let them not be over large in any roome, and as few as conveniently may be." There were no directions for glazing them.[34] This was not backwardness so much as a set of alternative standards that are difficult to fit into a linear model of modernization.

But within a generation of colonization most vernacular architecture in New England, particularly Massachusetts Bay and the Connecticut colonies, demonstrated the same desire to be up-to-date and innovative that William Harrison had described as characteristic of builders in lowland England from the yeomanry up. (In Maine and New Hampshire, colonists from the west of England predominated, and seventeenth-century houses there often joined one large room with a chimney to one or more unheated rooms. Houses there also perpetuated the linear three-part plan of chamber-hall-service rooms, rather than shifting the service areas to the rear of the house.) Most colonists in seventeenth-century New England built houses that resembled the two-roomed houses of laborers in southeastern England, with a hall used for cooking, eating, and sleeping, and a second room either for sleeping or services and storage. These colonists improved their houses in the idiom of the Southeast, with parlors, additional service rooms, and axial brick chimneys: "the lord hath been pleased to turn all the wigwams, huts and hovels the English dwelt in at their first coming into orderly, fair, and well-built houses, well furnished many of them, together with Orchards filled with goodly fruit trees and gardens with variety of flowers." According to William Bradford this second generation of colonists in Plymouth wanted to have "good and fair houses." "Fair" implied framed.[35]

Building contracts written in New England itself usually took massive stone chimneys for granted, and in this respect they fully shared in the standards of the Great Rebuilding. The features of the house designs adopted by English freeholders in the late sixteenth century involved an increase in the spatial separation of the elemental from the domestic. They were most comprehensively evident in New England, where all of the European housing was new in the seventeenth century and most of the population lived in the households of yeomen. Evidence for brick foundations in Massachusetts Bay Colony first appears in the 1650s, as do hall-and-parlor plans with axial chimneys. Expansion of this plan involved a lean-to at the back, usually for a kitchen and dairy, but not necessarily with a hearth. Sleeping and eating had specialized furniture and equipment, but not separate rooms. Beds could be located in any ground-floor rooms as well in the chambers above, and conversely the chambers provided work space and storage as well as sleeping accommodation. The family's daily meals would be taken in either the kitchen or hall, while meals with outsiders could be in a chamber or in the parlor.[36]

Most houses in Plymouth Colony and Rhode Island differed in scale and plan from those nearby in Massachusetts Bay. In southeastern New England after the middle of the seventeenth century, houses of different size and plan—two- as well as single-storied, with central as well as gable-end chimneys—coexisted, but the modal house was single-celled, a story and a half tall, and had a large (at least eight feet wide and five feet high) stone fireplace at a gable end. But houses in the two smaller colonies also belonged to the Great Rebuilding. From the 1640s on there are references to brick chimneys and to glazed casements. Wooden floors became frequent at least as early; in England they were much less common in houses of comparable size or households of comparable status. Expansion usually took place by extension along the gable end, by placing another chimneyed one-room cell next to the first. In the early eighteenth century such asymmetrical houses in Rhode Island and the former Plymouth Colony were often remodeled or replaced by ones approximating the standard of seventeenth-century Massachusetts Bay, sometimes two-storied but usually with rooms on either side of a central brick chimney.[37]

Buildings may not provide historical evidence as explicitly as written documents, such as building contracts, do, but physical remains have their own stories to tell. The archaeology of the Mott House in Rhode Island serves as a caution against the architectural Whiggism so often apparent in preoccupations with stylistic change. Analysis of the remodelings of a single house has the virtue of showing real evolution, and continuity, in style and design, and avoids the creation of a single stylistic narrative from a succession of floor plans from different houses. The Mott house, built sometime before 1680, began as a one-room building, sixteen feet square, with a chimney in the southwest corner. About 1680 a two-story, single-cell addition was built out from the south wall. It, too, had an end chimney. (See Figure 3.2 A and B.) Mott constructed a second house, a bigger and better-built version of the initial house. In both, he had ignored the symmetrical style of the yeoman's "Cape-Cod House," with its central chimney and five-bay front (each window or door is counted as a bay, or opening). When compared with the central, lobby entry of the Cape Cod House, the Mott house showed a readier acceptance of elemental conditions. The only entry in both versions of Mott's house was directly from the out-of-doors to the hall, the main domestic space, where the doorway admitted daylight from the southern exposure (thus providing the maximum of natural illumination in winter, when it was most scarce) and where the large central fireplace was the center of activity. Heat and light had a naturally reciprocal relationship in this house. The hearth and the doorway were the main sources of light, and windows were relatively unimportant.[38]

In the late 1720s Mott's son completely altered the building (see Figure 3.2 C). He tore down the original part of the house (largely leaving the walls of the 1680 addition in place) and replaced it with a two-story, single-room ell, and he added a kitchen lean-to at the back. He also tore down the enormous fireplace on the west wall of the first remodeling (of 1680) and used the base of the chimney of the original house to provide a fireplace for the 1680 hall and the new parlor. He also built a fireplace for the kitchen lean-to. Now he had a house that *looked* up-to-date because it had a central chimney. This remodeling reoriented the house in regard to the natural elements, especially light. The house no longer faced south, and light no longer directly entered the kitchen hearth area. Instead the main entrance was a lobby that provided a buffer zone between the living space and the out-of-doors. Sometime in the next fifty years the Mott house was remodeled again, this time by removing the kitchen lean-to, by putting a two-story addition across the rear, and by adding a hipped roof. Now there was "the novel plan and fashionable facade of the eighteenth-century New England Georgian house."[39]

In the 1690s urban colonists had begun to build houses that were cos-

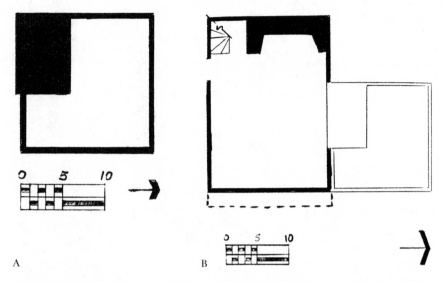

Figure 3.2. Vernacular and genteel remodelings. Mott house: (*A*) First stage, before c. 1680; (*B*) c. 1680; (*C*) Jacob Mott II's house, c. 1775. Dell Upton, "Architectural Change in Colonial Rhode Island: The Mott House as a Case Study," *Old-Time New England* 69, nos. 3, 4 (January–June 1979): 18–33; drawings by author. Reprinted by permission of the author.

mopolitan alternatives to New England's vernacular architecture. Among the artisans immigrating to New England had been "carpenters, masons, brick-layers, joiners, plasterers, carvers, and painters" familiar with the baroque Anglo-Dutch architectural styles that had been fashionable in London since the 1660s. The presence in the colonies of royal governing officials after 1686 and of Anglican churchmen after 1692 reinforced creole taste for classical styles. Besides their classically derived ornament, the cosmopolitan tastes introduced new designs for heating and lighting: brick walls with paneled chimneys in the gable ends, central staircases, bolection frames (i.e., with molding) for fireplaces, sash windows, and three-story symmetrical eleva-tions. In Boston, after the fire of 1711 required extensive rebuilding, some arti-sans' houses boasted such features of "mansion" architecture.[40]

By the middle of the eighteenth century the elite of the Connecticut River Valley were building houses according to these metropolitan standards for heating and illumination. In the countryside their houses were innovative in their thorough symmetry, classical ornamentation, and specialization of domestic space. Earlier houses of wealthy Valley families had been distinc-tive mainly in their size; in the late seventeenth century, "the massive central

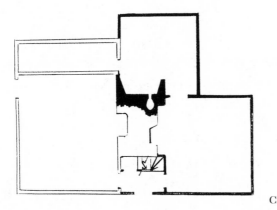

C

chimney, the steeply pitched roof, the single-pile (single-room-deep) two-story, hall-and-parlor plan, the unpainted, clapboarded facade, the hewn over-hang, and the corner door on the gable end could be found in many houses in that region." The new house design directed innovations toward changes in the quality and quantity of domestic illumination. New Englanders had earlier disdained a formal central entrance, and glazed windows had carried suspicious connotations of luxury. Given this aversion to glazing and the consequent need to limit the number of windows, in order to provide natural illumination, the traditional design had been asymmetrical, with a door on the southern gable end that admitted daylight into the main family room, where, as in Mott's house, the large fireplace was the center of activity.[41]

The new mansion style put domestic life at a further remove from the out-of-doors. It eliminated the gable-end door and used a gambrel roof to add windows on the upper stories. The new design replaced the massive traditional central chimney with smaller fireplaces at each gable end. Rooms became smaller and more numerous in order to accommodate more frequent, but smaller-scale, entertainment such as daily tea and small dinners. The spaces for socializing became decorated with "elaborate jointery work such as fielded paneling, scalloped cupboards, pedimented doorways, window caps," decorations whose genteel formality and classicism marked them off from the elemental worlds of the kitchen and the out-of-doors.[42]

The replacement of the gable-end door with a central doorway and lobby entrance was the most widely emulated feature of genteel house design.

Three-quarters of the houses in the Valley continued to be single-storied and to have central chimneys, while two-thirds of the houses in towns had two stories by the 1770s. What had begun as an architectural assertion of wealth, power, and civility by a rural elite had become a manifestation of popular identifications with urban culture. With two stories on a double-pile plan and chimneys on opposing gables, the mansion house was the alternative to the hall-and-parlor, central-chimney rural house. Where the central chimney of the hall-and-parlor house had symbolized the importance of being inside, the mansion house's central passage and elaborate doorways emphasized the importance of gaining admission.[43]

Elegant Housing

During the first three-quarters of the eighteenth century only a small proportion of northern households categorically differentiated their dwellings from the general housing stock. Carole Shammas has calculated that in the 1770s only the wealthiest 10 percent of households

> emptied one or both of their two front rooms of beds and household production materials, and proceeded to decorate their homes with fine wood pieces, upholstered leather chairs, window curtains, and even floor coverings. The vast majority of owners of rural English and American houses, even those who were relatively affluent, just did not decorate rooms. Early modern men and women decorated moveables, specifically their beds and their tables. Perhaps there was a special chair for the head of the household, more and more frequently rush or cane seats for others, and a picture or wall hanging, but not cabinetry, stuffed chairs, wallpaper, floor carpets, or sufficient lighting for night-time entertainment.

For most of the households in New England the standards of accommodation—objectively, and perhaps subjectively as well—did not change markedly during the eighteenth century. The hall-and-parlor plan with axial chimney prevailed in the countryside; single-story houses were seven times more frequent than double-pile, two-story "mansion" houses. For example, in central Massachusetts (Worcester County) at the end of the eighteenth century most houses were small, having floor plans of less than 850 square feet, and two-thirds were single-storied. In late-eighteenth-century Massachusetts two-story houses predominated only in highly commercialized coastal Essex County, where they made up over three-quarters of the housing stock.[44]

Most differentiation occurred in an urban context. There tradesmen lived in multistory and multiroomed brick houses. These buildings had costly levels of finish, with "sawn and beaded siding, large sliding sash windows, decorative modillion cornices, and a variety of carefully plastered and trimmed rooms." Tradesmen, most of whom rented housing, used their front room for making a livelihood rather than for entertaining. They enhanced their accommodation by having chambers rather than sleeping in the attic and by having a separate kitchen at the back. They showed their architectural taste in the room designed primarily for entertaining, the parlor and sometimes the chamber, particularly focusing on fireplaces and mantels (Figure 3.3). Otherwise their architectural investment was modest. Outside the large commercial towns, people of comparable means largely disregarded such details, despite exposure to urban architectural standards.[45]

EARLY AMERICAN housing had an enormous variation in value. Investment in housing was more of a luxury than it is today. According to the 1798 Direct Tax Assessments the most valuable 1 percent of houses were worth as much as the least valuable 40 percent. This distribution did not correspond so directly with the distribution of wealth as it did in England and Wales, where the median wealth was lower than that of the free population in America. But in both Britain and America, the extent of window glazing was the most direct measure of a house's value. The median number of windows in houses in England and Wales in 1759 was between six and nine; even forty years later in the United States the median number of windows was less than three, with fewer than twenty panes of glass in all.[46]

Much of the history of polite Anglo-American architecture in the eighteenth century involves the increased priority and stylization of window glazing. But most vernacular American architecture before the nineteenth century gave a low priority to window glazing. Domestic illumination was a marginal consideration. Windows were optional. A large minority of houses used doors as the sole opening for natural light. About half had either no window or only one window with one pane of glass. Among houses with any windows all, half had only one window, with fewer than ten panes of glass

Figure 3.3. Differentiation of space. The small fireplace and fine molding of chimneypieces symbolized genteel distancing of social activity from the everyday necessities of cooking and heating. Thomas Milton, John Crundon, and Placido Columbani, *The Chimney-piece-maker's Daily Assistant* . . . (London: Henry Webley, 1766), frontispiece to vol. 1. Courtesy of the Winterthur Library, Printed Book and Periodical Collection, Winterthur, Delaware.

for the whole house, while the most valuable 20 percent of houses had eight or more windows, each having nine or more panes of glass. The dispensability of glazing was less apparent in towns, where houses with low assessments had more windows and panes of glass than ones of comparable value in the countryside.[47]

The 1798 federal tax assessed houses according to their "elegance." Congressional debates on the tax defined two categories of houses: those of farmers and laborers with little discretionary spending on their design and decoration (all of their spending on housing was "necessary") and ones in towns (synonymous with "elegance"): "Houses are articles of expense, and produce nothing. They are merely instrumental (and when they do not exceed the measure of convenience they are necessary) to our enjoying other *comforts*." The act directed that assessments of houses take into account "their situation, their dimensions or area, their number of stories, the number and dimensions of their windows, the materials whereof they are built, whether wood, brick, or stone, the number, description, and dimensions of the outhouses appurtenant to them." (See Figure 3.4.) The median *assessed* value of urban houses was almost ten times that of rural houses—$614 versus $77— a much greater disparity in tax liability than in incomes or wealth (if land were included).

> A good house, though in itself unproductive, is more frequently an indication of the wealth of the occupant, than even a valuable and productive farm. For a man, consistently with public economy, may live on a farm, though he may be embarrassed in his circumstances, and though the farm itself may be mortgaged. If it produces any surplus beyond the interest which he pays, he may as well cultivate that farm as another, but in no case is an embarrassed or a poor man justifiable in holding a valuable house. It must add to his difficulties. He ought to sell it and pay his debts, or let it, and save the difference of rent. If he will do neither, let him pay for indulging his vanity or his folly.

The tax was levied on houses and on houselots up to two acres. Since houses were "unproductive objects, and, in a fiscal view, mere indices of expence," the tax could be framed as a progressive tax on a luxury, with rates rising with the assessed value. Building materials entered into the evaluations because they implied priorities of permanence, but they mattered less than elegance,

Figure 3.4. Elegance. The picket fence encloses a carefully refined housescape, with pedimented portico, classical orders in the trim, a summerhouse, and a painted barn. Ralph Earl, *House Fronting New Milford Green* (1795–96). Courtesy of Wadsworth Atheneum, Hartford, Connecticut and the Dorothy Clark Archibald and Thomas L. Archibald Fund.

as measured by the number of glazed windows—hence the phenomenon of 40 percent of those houses in Mifflin County, in central Pennsylvania, falling into the assessment category of $500–999 (putting them in the top 13% nationwide and the top 9% in rural districts) despite their being built of logs.[48]

Alexander Hamilton recommended to Oliver Wolcott, Secretary of the Treasury, a more elaborate itemization of decor than was eventually enacted in the tax statute, but his categories suggest how certain elements of housing constituted luxuries. Hamilton wanted to preclude subjective valuations by having specific criteria for assessment. In construction materials, he only distinguished between log houses and others. Log houses he would assess at twenty cents per room. Other houses would be assessed at higher rates per room, depending on the number of rooms in the house: twenty-five cents per room for two-room houses; thirty-three and one-third cents per room for three-room houses; up to one dollar per room for houses with seven or more rooms. Each room painted *inside* he would tax an additional twenty-five cents; each room papered, fifty cents; tile or stone chimneys, fifty cents, chimneys with a marble face, one dollar; staircases of cedar or ebony, fifty cents, ones of mahogany, one dollar; stucco cornices, one dollar, stucco ceilings, two dollars. "Pillars or pilasters outside in front" would have increased assessments by one dollar, while any marble facing would have raised them by two dollars. Thus, almost any decoration of any room or the exterior would result in an assessment equivalent to most log houses when undecorated.[49]

At any one time in the late eighteenth century, a large proportion of the American population (outside New England) lived in houses built of quickly worked local materials, usually logs. In newly settled areas, as many as 90 percent of the houses were of log construction. Two people could build a house of logs in less than a week. According to the 1798 Direct Tax Assessments, windows, and even more so window panes, were the chief architectural improvements, adding more value than material of construction, floor area, or number of stories. In the countryside, glazed windows were a luxury, but living in a house built of logs did not preclude such refinement, nor was sheer affordability the main constraint. The plans, amenities, and finish of the houses in which most Americans still lived at the end of the eighteenth century—room-and-loft house plans, wood and clay chimneys, few and small windows, and construction from local raw materials—would have earned them the derogatory designation "cottages" in England.

PART TWO

From Luxury to Comfort

DECENT COMFORT

Candles and Mirrors

PEOPLE IN different societies have used a nearly infinite variety of fuel sources and appliances for lighting: wooden splinters, pitchpine candles, lamps with floating wicks, lamps with spouts for wicks. There is a whole zoo of illuminant animals: in Denmark penguins with moss wicks in their stomachs, dogfish tails in Newfoundland, candlefish in northwestern North America. Few illustrated histories of lighting forgo a picture of a forlorn stormy petrel being burned whole, with a wick threaded through the carcass, by Shetland Islanders using it as a candle.[1] But by concentrating on appliances, the history of lighting has neglected questions about its use, distribution, and social significance.

The history of artificial illumination in preindustrial Europe is obscure. Even Fernand Braudel in the first volume of his great trilogy on material culture devoted only a few sentences to lighting: he said it was "almost nonexistent" except as "an object of pride and even ostentation." Braudel could ignore the topic of artificial illumination because he knew that its technology was virtually unchanged since antiquity. Romans had used lamps for both religious observance and domestic illumination from their city's begin-

ning; illumination from solid fuel, in the form of candles, was an early imperial borrowing from the Near East.[2] Roman trade in both oil and wax was
more highly developed than it would be again in Europe until the sixteenth
century. The lamps common in Roman homes in the first century A.D. gave
better light to more people than would be the case again until the eighteenth
century, when whale oil and spermaceti wax provided well-off Europeans
with cleaner and more reliable versions of traditional illuminants.

The Technology of Artificial Illumination

Until the use of coal gas in the early nineteenth century, the basic technology of lighting had remained the same from thousands of years before classical antiquity. Flames from the incomplete combustion of organic materials
provided light. Besides the open fire, the most frequent and ancient appliance
for such combustion was the lamp. Lamps used a wick to burn animal and
vegetable oils. Paleolithic cultures had grease-burning lamps made from hol-
lowed stones, such as those used over fifteen thousand years ago to illuminate paintings in the cave at Lascaux. At the beginnings of imperial civiliza-
tions five thousand years ago, artisans were making ceramic and metal lamps
to burn oil processed from animal fats. Subsequent preindustrial appliances
did not provide significantly superior light, but they allowed more control
over the wick and more protection of the oil supply from contamination and
spilling. A candle really burned as a miniature lamp: the heat of the flame
melted the wax or congealed animal fats encasing the wick, which then
burned as a lamp.[3]

The preindustrial technology of illumination dictated that lighting could
be only occasional for most people most of the time. The wicks of oil lamps
and tallow candles required trimming every fifteen minutes or so. The need
for trimming inhibited general illumination, because as few as ten lamps
or candles required one person's constant attention. Without trimming, oil
lamps would flicker as the wick drowned in the oil and candles would "gutter" as burning wick fell upon the unmelted tallow. The flame of these illumination sources was inevitably sooty and a menace to respiratory health
even before they began to exhaust a room's oxygen. Both oil lamps and tallow candles burned edible fats, and the protein impurities in animal fuels
such as tallow and fish oil became rancid and gave off obnoxious odors when

burning. And both tallow and natural oils were environmentally unstable: tallow candles melted at 122°F, which meant they melted themselves away prematurely in hot weather; lamp oil congealed in northern winters. Lamps had the advantage over candles of burning many hours on small amounts of fuel. In principle a pint of lamp oil could easily provide light for an entire day. Roman religious beliefs forbade extinguishing a flame, but constantly burning lamps also gave off so much soot that the Latin word for the main living area in a house, *atrium*, referred to blackening smoke.[4]

Beeswax candles were the luxurious exception in European illumination. They had little offensive smell, and their wicks required less trimming because of their higher combustion temperature. Properly made wax candles could burn unattended for hours. The ratio in thickness between wick and wax was the critical factor in their performance: if the wick was thick for the size of the candle, it gave off smoke by burning faster than it could melt the wax; too narrow a wick allowed the wax to melt so fast that it wastefully ran down the sides of the candle before the wick could burn it.[5]

On the Continent illumination needs competed directly with food demands in vegetable oils, especially olive oil. With its flocks of sheep providing tallow as a by-product of the wool industry, England was a candle, not a lamp, culture. Tallow candles varied greatly in quality. Molded ones approached the hardness and smoothness obtained in wax candles. Rushlights, too, used grease as a fuel. For sheer illumination they were a satisfactory alternative to tallow candles, but they were unacceptable in households with any pretension to refinement, and even in modest households their usage was infrequent. Their light was equivalent to a candle, but they burned at a near horizontal angle and consequently dripped grease in a line across the floor. Though the American historical society for artificial illumination named its journal *The Rushlight*, there is virtually no evidence for the use of rushlights in seventeenth- or eighteenth-century Anglo-America.[6]

Nearly all existing studies of lighting conclude that it was wretched in the early modern period. This conclusion begs the question that better lighting was desired but technologically unobtainable. An alternative perspective would be that artificial illumination was usually either sacred or a luxury and simply not a critical part of most people's daily lives. Ecclesiastical and aristocratic use of candlelight after dark conflicted with vernacular reliance on natural illumination for activities. This reliance was as much moral as practical: artificial illumination implied a neglect of responsibilities. A sixteenth-century manual on household management gave such a "lesson for the husband" by pointing out the trade-off between prudent household economy and the use of candles:

> One thinge I wyl advise the to remember, and specially in wynter-tyme, whan thou sytteste by the fyre, and hast supped, to consyder in thy mynde, whether the warkes, that thou, thy wyfe, & the servauntes shall do, be more avauntage to the than they fyre, and candell-lyghte, meate and drynke that thou shall spende, and if it be more avantage, than syt styll: and if it be not, than go to thy bedde and slepe, and be uppe betyme, and breake thy faste before day, that thou mayste be all the shorte wynters day about thy busynes.

Under "afternoon matters" for housekeeping, another manual advised:

> The day willeth done whatsoever ye bid,
> the night is a theefe, if ye take not good bid.
> Wash dishes, lay leavens, save fire and away,
> locke doors and to bed, a good huswife will say.
> In winter at nine, and in summer at ten,
> to bed after supper both maidens and men.
> In winter at five a clock, servant arise,
> in sommer at foure is verie good guise.

When in 1630 the Reverend Francis Higginson, recently settled in Salem, Massachusetts Bay, drew up a list of "needful things" for settlers, he itemized food for a year, weapons and armor, clothing, tools, and spices, but he included no facilities for artificial illumination among the recommended housewares. Nor was candlemaking a regular part of traditional domestic economy. Thomas Tusser's *Five Hundred Points of Good Husbandrie* (1580) has instructions for brewing, baking, cooking, dairying, scouring, washing, and malting—but not for candlemaking. Surveys of early-eighteenth-century inventories for references to tools and materials for household manufactures have found that over half the households had spinning wheels and two-fifths had some indication of other home manufactures, but the simple tools and readily available materials for making candles were almost unrecorded. When found at all, candlemaking equipment was most likely to be in wealthy

households. Only in the nineteenth century, when artificial illumination became a more regular component of domestic activity, did candlemaking become a regular part of housework.[7]

Candles *could* be used intensively for practical purposes, such as to extend
the period for activities usually requiring daylight. In the seventeenth century highly educated people sometimes expressed a self-consciousness about
reading after dark, as something that they might and should be doing. John
Aubrey wrote of the mathematician William Oughtred that "his wife was
a penurious woman and would not allow him to burn candle after supper,
by which means many a good notion is lost." Ralph Josselin several times
recorded renewed resolves to use candlelight for improving reading.

We begun this morning to rise early, and to spend some time by fire and
candle, I intend in morning to read over the liberall arts.

This night I began by candle light to read the ecclesiastical history,
called the Centuries of Magdeb.

While under Samuel Pepys' direction during the wars of the 1690s, the Navy
Board had seventy-five people working after dark, which consumed about a
gross of candles each night. Over that decade, officials calculated, the board
consumed more than sixty thousand candles, at a cost of over £1500 for
nearly 2,500 person/nights. But these exceptions, by showing the technical
possibility of greater use of artificial illumination, prove the rule that most
people did not take candlelight for granted as a way to extend the day in
everyday life. A study of the material culture of seventeenth-century rural
England and the Chesapeake found that lighting was considered optional
rather than a necessity. Fewer than one-third of modestly propertied households (with possessions worth £10–50) had furniture items for lighting. More
than half, but fewer than two-thirds, of substantially propertied families
(£50–250) had such furniture. Even among wealthy households, rates of ownership in different areas varied from one-half to four-fifths.[8] Artificial illumination was an optional rather than a crucial part of people's daily lives.

The Ritual Use of Candles

Europeans' most frequent familiarity with artificial lighting was in church. Though early Christians resisted the ritual use of lamps and candles as pagan and Jewish, the Church transmitted the culture and technology of artificial illumination from antiquity to medieval Europe. Wax candles and oil lamps were fixtures of church furnishings long before they were regular parts of everyday living. As Bishop of Nola at the beginning of the fifth century, St. Paulinus described how to use a perpetual lamp as a fixture in sacristies, thereby carrying into the church a practice that had been customary at Roman household shrines. Later in the century Pope Zosimus (417–18) began the practice of burning a lamp over the altar from Easter Sunday to Ascension Day; elaborate Paschal candelabra developed for the observance. By the eighth century St. Peter's Basilica in Rome reportedly had a sanctuary lamp with more than thirteen hundred wicks floating in pools of oil. In the tenth century candles began to be placed on the altars of Roman Catholic churches during Mass; previously they had been held by the priest's servers or placed on adjacent tables. (The Cistercians' resistance to the burning of candles in church derived from the popularity of the use of candles, just as their simultaneous resistance to the ornamentation of churches with stained glass was prompted by its popular use.)[9]

The medieval terms for household candles referred to types used in church and for religious observance.

> The curteyns let draw them the bed round about;
> se his morter with wax or perchere that it go not owt.

Morters were lamps or wax tapers "set in churches, to burn over the graves and shrines of the dead"; *percheres* were large wax candles "commonly set upon altars." Church candles defined the highest quality. They were pure beeswax and bleached white. Pope Gelasius (492–96) introduced Candlemas, a day for blessing candles, on February 2, thereby superseding a Roman fertility festival, Lupercalia, held on that day. The Christian festival celebrated the presentation of Christ, "the true light to lighten the Gentiles," in the Temple and the purification of his mother. The connection between the latter and candles was made using the confused symbolism of the supposedly vir-gin bee. According to Roman folklore, the mother bee gave virgin birth and produced the wax. The drones were analogous to the religious serving Christ. Much Christian symbolism was applied to candles. The wick in the candle could be compared with the soul of Christians, alight with grace. Corre-spondingly, the penance for sinners (including those condemned to an auto-da-fé) often called for them to appear publicly with an unlit wax candle, which served as a fine for their sins and a symbol of their need for grace. Bequests of candlesticks and the endowment of sanctuary lights were some of the most common provisions of medieval wills. In aristocratic households that had chapels, typically one-third of the candles consumed would be devoted to religious observance. At Ham House in the 1670s, furniture for artificial illu-mination was still extensive only in the chapel, which had ten sconces and eight candlesticks. This use of candles for domestic religious observance con-tinued in the late eighteenth century; it was recorded in the diary of the stereotypical Reverend James Woodforde, that he had a large wax candle that he burned only at Christmas.[10]

Throughout the medieval and early modern period, the daily use of can-dles in most secular households was for retirement to the chamber. Anglo-Norman schedules, as represented in the fabliaux, were not very different from Anglo-Saxon. The daily routine of eating in the thirteenth and four-teenth centuries did not require artificial illumination. People usually ex-pected to go to bed right after supper and to rise at daybreak. Breakfast, just bread and a drink, was taken casually according to individual schedules. The large and formal meal was a dinner in the late morning, about the fifth hour of the seasonally varying twelve hours of daylight. Supper was at dusk. There are some medieval illustrations of eating and other activities taking place by candlelight, but they are few.[11]

Candles were associated primarily with going to bed and with sleeping, not with activity after dark. They indicated wealth and status, because only expensive wax candles could burn all night, and such use implied the pres-ence of a servant, who carried the candle while leading the household's mas-ter and mistress to bed and then looked after the candle through the night. Fifteenth-century guides for household management directed that candles burn all night beside the bed of the household's lord. The usher was respon-sible for candles because they came from the pantry:

A morter of wax thet wille he bryng,

From Chambur, syr, with-out lesyng;

That all nyght brennes in bassyn clere,

To save the chambur on nyght for fyre.

Then yeomen of chambur shynne voyde with ryme [clear torches]

The torches han holden wele that tyme.

The chambur dore stekes the ussher thenne,

With preket and tortes that conne brenne.

These night candles posed a risk of fire. Most of the references to candles in early modern diaries are to their starting fires. Samuel Sewall, for example, thought a fire in his house might have been the result of a mouse "tak[ing] our lighted Candle out of the Candlestick on the hearth and dragg[ing] it under my closet-door."[12]

A major reason for retiring at darkness was the expense of candles, which were treated as luxuries and emblems of status. Candles were a clearly ranked component in the daily allowances ("messe") for household officers, along with their rations of bread and ale.

In chambur no light there shall be brent,

Bot of wax, ther-in that all men kenne;

Iche messe a candelle fro alhalawghe [All Saints'] day

To candelmesse, as I thou say;

Of candel liveray squiyers schalle have,

So long, if hit is mon wille krave.

Of brede and ale also the boteler

Schalle make lyvere thurgh-out the yere

To squyers, and also wyn to knyght,

Or ellys he dose not his ofict ryght.

In the few corrodies at Westminister Abbey that included candles, the allotment was on the order of twenty-five pounds or so per year, or one candle per night. People went to bed taking a candle from the fireplace to the chamber. Medieval candlesticks were heavy, solid iron and brass, and not meant to be moved about, so candles were removed from them and carried by hand to the desired location and then stuck on or in another candlestick.[13]

Venice, the source of most luxury goods in the late Middle Ages, was the chief supplier of wax candles and of new designs for candlesticks. Most of Venice's wax came from the East, and European usage of socketed candlesticks apparently derived from Persian examples there. Medieval candlesticks were initially of the pricket type; candles were stuck on a spike atop the candlestick. The simplest type was a tripod, one leg of which was extended to provide the spike. With its stability on irregular surfaces, the tripod base allowed flexibility in placement. Socketed candlesticks began to be used in households in the fourteenth century, about the same time that enlargement of windows increased the natural illumination in manorial halls and glazing reduced flickering of candle flames from drafts. Socketed candlesticks initially had tripod bases, too, but a flat base became standard in the late fifteenth century as furniture and interior finishing provided more level surfaces. Most of these early socket candlesticks had massive bases, like their Persian predecessors, but lighter, more portable ones became available in the fifteenth century. From the fourteenth century through the late seventeenth century metal candlesticks were usually made of solid metal—bell metal, pewter, or brass—which was cast and then smoothed on a lathe. Their design chiefly dealt with control of the melted tallow and wax. Long stems with a variety of lathe-turned moldings allowed the melted fuel to cool before it reached a saucerlike pan near the base. For most of the early modern period, candles and candlesticks were luxury items supplied by manufacturers who had initially served ecclesiastical demand.[14]

A repertoire of emblems, both religious and secular, exploited candles' rich symbolic potential. Before Dutch genre painting of the seventeenth century, candles were most likely to be represented according to the iconography of a few religious scenes, notably St. Jerome in his study and the Annunciation. But Dutch genre painters partook of the Christian and philosophical symbolism of candlelight as a reference to apparent versus true illumination, false versus true wisdom, and to divine grace. Seventeenth-century emblem books used candles to illustrate a variety of moral teachings:

Those Fooles whom Beauties Flamt doth Blinde,
Feele Death, where Life they thought to finde.
. . . .

My Substance, and My Light, are spent,
In seeking other mens content.

A burning candle in a scene with a public figure reminded viewers of altruism—"I am consumed in the service of others." The owl, which could not see in broad daylight, represented false wisdom when surrounded by lit candles:

> Hee that is Blind, will nothing see,
> What light soe're about him bee.

Candles could have such symbolic force because they marked stark differences in everyday life—light from darkness, wakefulness from sleep, the solemn from the everyday.[15]

BAROQUE COURTLY life used illumination at literally spectacular levels of luxury, largely following examples in the theater. Through the sixteenth century, theater was performed out of doors, in order to take advantage of natural illumination. Lamps and candles on stage, along with fireworks, were employed primarily to create special effects. In the seventeenth century theater moved indoors, as courts became the primary audience and setting for performances. In the eighteenth century theaters still began their performances in the afternoon, but they often ended after dark. More than three hundred candles illuminated performances in the opera house at Versailles, where lighting cost more than the musicians and performers and involved as many people, since one person could tend only ten or so candles. Illuminated *fêtes champêtres*, garden parties, at Versailles used thousands of lamps. Such stylized use of the night heightened distinctions between metropolitan and provincial cultures, as well as between luxury and frugality. The domestic use of more than one candle remained a mark of extravagance, while at Versailles candles were never relit. Nobles in service at the court collected the unburnt portions for their own use or to give away or sell. Sometimes these nobles were expected to act as human candlestands and to trim the candles they held.[16]

Following the example of the court at Versailles, noble palaces increased their furniture for lighting. In 1654 at Ham House, the most influential house for interior decoration in late-seventeenth-century England, the inventory had listed neither candlesticks nor candlestands outside the kitchen. A visit to Paris in 1670 apparently influenced Elizabeth Dysart's taste in favor of French interior design and encouraged her to apply it at Ham House after

Figure 4.1. Owl's blindness despite illumination. George Wither, *A Collection of Emblems, Ancient and Modern* (London: A.M., 1635), 253. Courtesy of the Winterthur Library: Printed Book and Periodical Collection, Winterthur, Delaware.

she married the Duke of Lauderdale in 1672. In the household's inventories for 1677, 1679, and 1683 there are numerous candlestands, some of them with candlesticks listed as well. The example of Versailles also influenced English use of mirrors. As artificial illumination became a mark of refined entertainment, mirrors developed a close association with candles, and inventories invariably listed candlestands in conjunction with looking glasses. Together they formed the "ensemble" that came to be dictated by fashion in interior decoration. The ensemble of pier glass (see Figure 4.2) and a pair of candlestands handsomely complemented chimneypieces in the same room.[17]

The Looking Glass: From Aristocratic to Popular Luxury

Ownership of looking glasses marked a new popular demand for artificial illumination. In less than a century looking glasses went from being an aristocratic luxury to a vernacular decency. In 1675 fewer than 10 percent of a sample of English household inventories outside London and the Home Counties recorded them. In London itself they were found in only one-third of inventoried households. Fifty years later they were the most frequently listed item of furnishing besides beds, chairs, and tables.[18]

From antiquity through the Middle Ages, mirrors had figured as importantly in religion and philosophy as in daily life. Egyptians invented the mirror of polished bronze, and many Etruscan and Greek examples survive. Numerous mythological scenes in Greek art illustrate the use of mirrors in grooming, and Greek philosophers referred to mirrors' reflections when explaining geometric phenomena. Mirrors also figured powerfully as multivalent metaphors in ethics and metaphysics. They provided a means to self-knowledge, and they marked an irrational vanity. The ambiguity of the mirror's imagery corresponded with the fact that polished metal disks could not provide a perfect reflection of what could be seen directly. The metaphysical significance of the mirrored view as an imperfect one depended on reflections' being *empirically* imperfect. Plato repeatedly referred to the view provided by a mirror, rather than by direct sight, to make his contrast between ideal forms and the perception we have of them. Similarly, when Paul wrote the Christians at Corinth about the difference between earthly life and that with God—"Now we see only puzzling reflections in a mirror, but then we shall see face to face"—he expected the Corinthians to see the first half of the analogy for themselves.[19] After all, Corinth had a major mirror industry.

The technology to produce mirrors changed little between antiquity and the twelfth century, when German and Netherlandish glassmakers began to make mirrors by coating the inside of glass spheres with a mixture of tin and antimony bound by resin. When cut into lenses they sold for pennies apiece

Figure 4.2. Pier glass and girandole. Thomas Chippendale, *The Gentleman and Cabinet-Maker's Director* (London, 1754), pl. 142. Courtesy of the Winterthur Library, Printed Book and Periodical Collection, Winterthur, Delaware.

when imported to late-medieval England. Given the dullness of the lead and the heavily greenish hue of nominally clear glass, such mirrors often illustrated little more than the notion of reflection. Simultaneously, in order to encourage hope in a perfection not of this world, medieval Christian teachings revived classical themes of mirrors' technological inadequacies. From the twelfth century to the sixteenth century, the Virgin's purity was that of a "spotless mirror," precisely because no human could make one. Mirrors of polished steel provided the highest quality reflections, and they were suscep-tible to spots of rust.[20]

The more familiar King James translation (1611) of Paul's letter to the Corinthians, "For now we see through a glass, darkly," is an anachronism arising from the post-antique development of glass mirrors. The choice of preposition, *through*, indicates that the translators really found glazed win-dows (with their greenish tint and optical distortions) rather than mirrors to be the apposite analogy. During the Renaissance, mirrored images *had* be-come nearly perfect reflections of perceived reality. Demand for mirrors was high in Italy, where they were favorite items to furnish Renaissance studies: flat mirrors brought extra illumination to the page, while convex mirrors could magnify text, and looking at any mirror was believed to relieve eye-strain from reading. In the late fifteenth century, Venetian glassmakers, using soda as their alkali, had developed a clear, virtually colorless glass, *cristallo*. It had high value because of its resemblance, as the name suggests, to rock crystal. As a precious material, rock crystal was used for decoration and ves-sels rather than glazing, but in the sixteenth century, Venetian mirror mak-ers began to use flat cristallo in mirrors. To polished sheets of this glass, they applied a highly reflective backing of a mercury-tin amalgam that Flemish mirror makers had recently developed. With this combination in the early sixteenth century, Venetian mirror makers began a prosperous dominance of the luxury mirror market, which they maintained for the next one hundred fifty years.[21] *Looking glasses* became the generic term in English for mirrors.

Until the middle of the seventeenth century Venetian glassmakers had a monopoly in the luxury mirror market. In the 1660s both the English and French governments began to encourage domestic producers, and they lured Venetian glassmasters by granting patents and other privileges. Venetian manufacturers had produced mirrors from cylinder-blown glass, but French mirror makers soon produced a superior mirror glass by a casting process that produced larger, flatter pieces.

BAROQUE INTERIOR design concentrated on the arrangement of win-dows, mirrors, and fireplaces. Both fireplaces and windows became more numerous, but while windows increased in size, fireplaces became smaller. The increase in light from windows made mirrors more effective. In a prece-dent established by a series of rich seventeenth-century French interiors, the looking glass became inextricably linked with the ornamented fireplace as the stylistic test of a family's respectability. Beginning in the 1620s, a "national style of aristocratic interior decoration," developed in Parisian mansions, and after 1660 it became an international standard, practiced by fashionable Dutch and English notables as well. The first mansion to display the style was the house of Catherine de Vivonne, Marquise de Rambouillet. Her architects self-consciously sought to apply Italian Renaissance standards for architectural harmony and regularity to the *interior* of a *private* building. Two tests of success in interior design became consistency (*ameublement*) in the upholstered furnishings of a room and an ornamental chimneypiece incorporating a looking glass. To achieve decorative balance between the chimney and the looking glass, the mantle had to be lowered and the face of the hearth reduced. The resulting fireplace was smaller, cleaner, and more removed from social activities, which were now illuminated by diffuse reflection from the looking glass.[22]

Because Mme. de Rambouillet maintained the most distinguished salon in Paris, her urban palace literally set the style for the rest of the kingdom. As the daughter of a French ambassador, she had grown up in Rome and easily claimed authority on Italian design when, newly married, she moved back to Paris and began to remodel her house. Coincidentally, the Luxembourg Palace was under construction for the Regent, Marie de' Medici, who sent her decorators to Mme. de Rambouillet's house for ideas. To capitalize on the instant fashionability of the new decorative style in domestic architecture, lavishly illustrated design guides appeared with titles like Pierre Le Muet's *La manière de bien batir pour touttes sortes de personnes* (1623) and Louis Savot's *L'Architecture françoise des bastimens particuliers* (1624).

The designs in pattern books of interior architecture invariably focused attention on the chimneypiece, making it the most prominent feature of a room. The chimneypiece was also the greatest technical challenge for decoration, because the chimney had certain functional requirements as well. This focus on the chimneypiece as the test of interior design continued at least until the 1720s in France and past the middle of the eighteenth century in England. English visitors to stylish French mansions in the seventeenth century expressed their admiration of interior design with such comments as "most precious moveables," "*luxe* and excesse Italy," "small but extremely neat," "soe fine and magnificent." Unlike twentieth-century historians, these observers did not explicitly equate luxury with physical comfort.[23]

Sir Henry Wotton's *Elements of Architecture* (1624) promptly introduced the new style to England and the Netherlands. As a friend of Francis Bacon, John Donne, and Constantyn Huygens, and ambassador to Venice for two decades, Wotton served as the perfect agent for introducing northwestern Europeans to a French decorative innovation deriving from Italian architectural design. Huygens shared Wotton's ambition to popularize a style combining Italian regularity and order with French convenience (*commodité*). In another one of his roles, secretary to the stadholder of the Netherlands, who was pro-French, he assisted in a Dutch translation of the *Elements*.[24] Inigo Jones may first have applied these lessons in the English architectural context, when in 1636 he borrowed from a French book of chimneypiece designs to redecorate rooms for Queen Henrietta Maria, the daughter of Marie de' Medici.

The political associations of such designs delayed the English aristocracy's whole-hearted adoption of the new domestic interior until the Restoration. Shortly thereafter, the London fire of 1666 provided a coincidental imperative for new construction, and the number of small fireplaces greatly increased during the city's rebuilding. They accorded with cosmopolitan style and suited the increased use of coal for heating. The colossal enterprise at Versailles was making an unquestionable standard of what had hitherto been the fashionably innovative design of mirrored chimneypiece and small fireplace. Ironically, the gigantic scale and cold formality of the French court reinforced the trend toward equating domestic amenity with small, elegantly designed chimneypieces. A new room, the closet, developed as a truly private space literally behind the scenes of the court. In this privileged but necessarily small room, a modestly scaled but exquisitely designed combination of chimney and looking glass identified the ideal personal space.[25] Smaller fireplaces necessitated more fireplaces, which meant more chimneypieces; with more chimneypieces came more looking glasses.

With so much foreign demand, the Most Serene Republic relentlessly enforced its monopoly of the transalpine luxury market through exclusive manufacturing privileges and terroristic punishment for industrial espionage. Effective competition developed only in the 1660s and 1670s, and then only with assistance from the governments of France and England. Jean Baptiste Colbert, minister of the navy and commerce, had the French ambassador to Italy smuggle mirror makers from Venice, paid them royal pensions, arranged for their wives to join them, and established them in a royal manufactory with the intent of training French artisans for a domestic mirror industry. Capital for the enterprise came from royal loans owed the councilors and tax receivers who directed the company and were guaranteed orders for the royal palaces. Meanwhile, suspiciously high numbers of Venetian mirror makers working in France died unexpectedly, apparently at the hands of Venetian secret agents. Within a decade, however, fine French looking glasses were competing effectively with the quality, if not the price, of ones from Venice. In 1672 the king bought seven hundred looking glasses from the royal manufactory, and thereafter ceased to buy any from Venice. In the 1680s French mirror makers developed a process for making large flat pieces of glass by casting rather than from blown cylinders, and for the next century the best large looking glasses came from the French royal manufactory.[26]

At the same time that Colbert sponsored the nascent French mirror industry, George Villiers, the second Duke of Buckingham, played a similar, but more directly entrepreneurial, role in England. Having secured his own patent to make glass and bought the patents of others, the duke formed the Worshipful Company of Glass-sellers and Looking Glass Makers and founded a glassworks at Vauxhall. He, too, recruited Venetian mirror makers to begin operations, and the quality of English mirrors soon rivaled that of all but the largest French looking glasses.[27]

With the reflective accuracy of looking glasses taken for granted, fashion focused on their scale and style. In 1698, during one of her inquisitive journeys to "form an Idea of England," Celia Fiennes commented on the expanse of looking glass at Chippenham Park in Cambridgeshire, the house of Admiral Edward Russell. Made Lord Orford just the year before, Russell could study his now lordly image in a full-length looking glass and juxtapose it with his "pictures at full proportion of the Royal family." Fiennes appreciated the newness of the opportunity:

In the best drawing room . . . was no looking-glass but on the chimney-piece and just opposite in the place a looking glass used to be was 4 panels of glass in length and 3 in breadth set together in the wainscot; the dining room had this looking glass on the two piers between the three windows. It was from the top to the bottom 2 panels in breadth and 7 in length, so it shows one from top to toe. . . . the chimney pieces and the sconces stand on each side the chimneys and the glasses in those

chambers where were loose looking-glasses, which were with fine carved
head and frames some of them natural woods others gilt, but they were
the largest looking-glasses I ever saw. . . . the great curiosity of this wood
carving about the doors, chimneys, and sconces, together with the great
looking glass panels is much talked of and is the finest and most in quantity and numbers that's to be seen any where.[28]

As Fiennes noted, in fashionable interiors pier tables and sconces provided
illumination for mirrors from both sides by holding pairs of candles to
brighten the reflections.

As ownership of looking glasses ceased to be a rarity, variations in their
ownership depended less on wealth and more on connection with cosmopolitan ways. Though looking glasses were a new item for popular consumption, deep potential demand developed immediately, and production rapidly
increased in the last quarter of the seventeenth century. By 1695 over one
thousand people worked in London's twenty-four glasshouses, most of them
producing looking glasses along with drinking ware and window glass. In the
rest of the country there were at least twice as many glasshouses but less specialization in looking glasses. By the early eighteenth century modestly propertied English households could afford looking glasses. Looking glasses cost
as little as one shilling, and most cost less than twenty-five shillings. They
could be found in nearly one-third of the households with goods valued at
£11–15 and over three-fifths of those valued at £26–100, when the median
value of household goods was about £25.[29]

Owning a looking glass gave a person a self-evident claim to gentility.
Over the period 1675–1725, approximately three-quarters of London's propertied households had looking glasses, compared with one-half of the households in provincial and lesser towns and only one-fifth in villages. Tradesmen, other than those of low occupational status, were as likely as gentry
to own mirrors, and even tradesmen of low status were twice as likely as
yeomen to have them. Variations among commercial households of similar
wealth depended on the relative respectability of their livelihoods: "cheese-
mongers, coalmongers, soapmakers" were less likely than "merchants, mer-
cers, and drapers" to spend money on items for household display.[30]

Colonial American ownership of looking glasses illustrates their extensive
demand and ready availability. For example, in the commercial farming town
of Wethersfield, Connecticut, before 1670 only the inventories of the town's

richest inhabitant and the schoolmaster (from a Hartford merchant family) recorded looking glasses. During the next half-century they became posses- sions of over half the town's households, but the wealthiest quarter of house- holds owned two-thirds of the looking glasses, even though their average value was only five shillings. Just as in the metropolis, variations in owner- ship depended more on exposure to urban fashions than on sheer wealth. In Essex County, Massachusetts, for example, 35 percent of the county's in- ventoried households owned looking glasses in 1700, compared with 75 per- cent of households in the county's commercial town of Salem. Ownership of looking glasses in Wethersfield, with its predominantly rural population, reached this level (75%) only in the middle of the eighteenth century, and thereafter the proportion did not increase. In Pennsylvania there was a pro- nounced difference between urban and rural patterns of ownership: half of the urban inventories dated between 1705 and 1735 recorded mirrors, com- pared with fewer than a quarter of those from the whole region of south- eastern Pennsylvania. Sooner or later, however, depending on locale, look- ing glasses became a typical household possession. With the establishment of this consumption pattern as conventional, fashionable demand shifted to- ward having more numerous and more elaborate looking glasses. The larger looking glasses of the rich, when placed in carved and/or gilded frames, could cost £2–5, ten to twenty times above the average. Less wealthy households began to own more than one of the simple looking glasses.[31]

In the eighteenth century, looking glasses became the most specialized type of furniture in rooms intended to receive outsiders. The ideal location for a looking glasses was in axial orientation to a fireplace, either above it as a chimney glass or opposite as a pier glass. Such arrangements were too expensive for most propertied households, however, because of the expo- nential increase in price for large mirror glasses and the expensive paneling and woodcarving required to set the glass properly. Such an arrangement could cost tens of pounds, equivalent to the annual household budget of a middling tradesman's family. Most households that had looking glasses used them as pieces of furniture in locations chosen for display, rather than for personal grooming—in parlors rather than chambers. The conjunction of mirrors and candlelight accorded with a desirability for sheen and luster in interior decoration, whether in paintings, metals, fabrics, or furniture finish. Contributing to the lustrous surfaces in a room was the window glass. The improved technology and availability of plate glass for mirrors were applied to window glass as well. As window glazing, plate glass was a luxury that set the standard for other types of glass to achieve more cheaply.[32]

From Luxurious to Decent Lighting

In the late seventeenth century, the examples of the court and the aristocracy made the choice of after-dark and later hours for socializing increasingly fashionable. Lavish use of lighting for festive occasions increased further in the eighteenth century (Figure 4.3). Over the course of the eighteenth century, chandeliers went from being a rarity that might be found only at a state dinner of Charles II to being routine features in churches and theaters. Sir Robert Walpole used one hundred thirty wax candles to illuminate the hall at Houghton when he entertained the Duke of Lorraine in 1731. At the coronations of both George II and George III several thousand candles were lit in less than a minute, instantaneously transforming the interior of Westminster Abbey from gloom to brightness. Major John André sent *Gentleman's Magazine* an account of a similarly "superb entertainment" in Philadelphia in May 1778, at a hall specially built for the occasion of Sir William Howe's resignation of his command. Supper was served

> in a magnificent saloon . . . [with] fifty-six large pier glasses, ornamented with green silk artificial flowers and ribbands: 100 branches with three lights in each, trimmed in the same manner as the [eighty-five] mirrours ['decked with rose-pink silk ribbands, and artificial flowers']; 18 lustres each, with 24 lights, suspended from the ceiling, and ornamented as the branches; 300 wax-tapers, disposed along the supper tables. . . . All these, forming together the most brilliant assemblage of gay objects, and appearing at once as we entered by an easy descent, exhibiting a *coup d'oeil* beyond description magnificent.[33]

The commercialization of leisure had accustomed the propertied populace to artificial illumination in public buildings that was on a scale far beyond what they knew at home. London masquerades used the lighting facilities of theaters and supplemented them with dozens of additional lights. At Vauxhall Gardens, using the trappings of celebration for everyday entertainment, overhead lamps illuminated the bandstand and walkways. From their expe-

Figure 4.3. Festive illumination. William Hogarth, *Analysis of Beauty* (London, 1733), pl. 2. Courtesy of the Lewis Walpole Library, Print Collection, Yale University.

riences at the pleasure gardens of Vauxhall and Ranelagh the metropolitan public associated fashionable leisure with large-scale illumination, and with staying out later as well. In addition to theaters and opera houses, other places of commercial leisure, such as coffee houses, clubs, cockpits, and assemblies, drew customers with the promise of nighttime illumination.[34]

During the great era for the manufacture and use of candlesticks, from the middle of the seventeenth century through the eighteenth century, the types of lighting furniture proliferated. The use of candles in pairs increased, as did the variety of their designs. Chandeliers, girandoles, and sconces that held two or more candles provided illumination from more than one point, in contrast to the vernacular use of a single candle, moved from one location to another where illumination was needed. Furniture needing good lighting—card tables, dressing tables, writing tables—gained specialized supports for candlesticks. Candlesticks holding a single candle were infrequent in comparison with more expensive furniture for lighting.[35]

In the late seventeenth century, candlesticks became more luxurious, but also more affordable, because brass and silver candlesticks began to be cast, in two hollow halves braised together, rather than being turned from a solid piece. The new process provided candlesticks that were lighter and cheaper, and they were easier to use, because the hollow stem made it possible to clean out the socket by means of a plunger. In the 1780s, hollow casting of both silver and brass candlesticks was replaced by solid casting, a simpler process, further reducing costs of production. The manufacture of Sheffield plate (silver on copper) began in the 1760s and 1770s; the technique suited the finer detail of the newly fashionable neoclassical designs, which derived from cosmopolitan lighting practices. Brass did not lend itself to the delicacy called for by neoclassical ornament, but since Sheffield plate was almost as inexpensive, brass was losing its popularity as a material for candlesticks anyway. Meanwhile, glass was increasingly used for candlesticks, presumably for its glittering reflections.[36]

Ownership of lighting facilities began to increase in the late seventeenth century as new consumption patterns spread rapidly among modestly propertied as well as rich households. Demand for what eighteenth-century usage referred to as "decencies" shifted from the province of the cultivated aristocracy to the propertied populace. These decencies enhanced the style of the domestic environment and provided specialized furniture for entertaining at teas and small dinners. In the middle of the eighteenth century newspaper advertisements for the furniture of artificial illumination began to emphasize fashion and taste, by using terms such as "carved and gilt" and "newest patterns," or by identifying elaborate materials such as "walnut frames with gild edges . . . sconces in burnished gold, glass bordered, mahogany and black walnut frames, with gild ornaments of all sizes," or by introducing completely new types such as "some curious four armed cut glass candlesticks ornamented with stars and drops, properly called girandoles."[37]

The need for natural light had meant that fashionable society, not just rural households, had traditionally taken their main meal in the middle of the day, but in families with genteel leisure, the dinner hour became later over the course of the eighteenth century. It was typically 2 P.M. in the early eighteenth century and 3 P.M. by the 1730s. By the 1780s it was 4 P.M. Tea, not yet a regularly scheduled meal, would occur late in the day. Supper was taken before bed, and it was a perfunctory serving of leftovers, not a prepared meal. Tea and supper were meals of prosperous respectability, but their food preparation requirements and social aspects suited conditions of low illumination.[38] Possessing candlesticks symbolized that a family could entertain after dark, even if it seldom did.

William Hogarth's prints study the increased popularity of artificial illu-mination in the eighteenth century. The details of scenes in Hogarth's best-known series—*The Idle and Industrious Apprentices, The Harlot's Progress,* and *The Rake's Progress*—show a precise correspondence between social status and lighting. At the bottom of society there is virtually no artificial lighting. The Idle Prentice habituates rooms whose furnishings are meager, broken, and either unlit or lit by sources over which the residents have no control (the watch's lamp, the fire). The room he shares with a prostitute has no lighting whatsoever—neither window nor flame—their bed is broken, and their only furnishings are broken crockery (Figure 4.4). The illegal tavern in which he is arrested has lighting, but only by means of a fire. The Harlot is a solid notch better off than the Idle Prentice. She has decorated chairs, fireplace apparatus, and decent bedding. She has a corresponding level of lighting—most of her light comes from the hearth, but tallow candles hang by the door. Earlier in her career the Harlot was on the verge of respectability. Her room then was much more comfortably furnished, with a chair and table, full bedding, prints, and pewter mugs. She could entertain at home, where she had the lighting of the modestly propertied: leaded windows and a sin-gle wax candle. A comparable but slightly shabby and irresolute respectabil-ity is found in the Distress'd Poet's garret, where the level of lighting is the same as the Harlot's—a window and a wax candle. This level of accommo-dation lay on the social dividing line where artificial illumination would be taken for granted.

The third series, *The Rake's Progress,* illustrates a level of consumer spend-ing that has crossed the threshold from "decency" to elegance. In a picture that compares his father's spending habits with the Rake's (Figure 4.5), the deceased father's miserly way of life is represented by a modest pricket can-dlestick and save-all for candles on the mantle. The Rake, of course, is try-ing to make the transition from trade to gentility. His concern with illumi-nation has shifted from household economy to deciding how to spend his money for most conspicuous effect. As a mark of gentility there is a wall sconce with a mirror on his side of the room. Once the Rake moves into soci-ety he is in an even more highly illuminated environment. There are large-paned windows reaching to the ceiling and between them is a large mirror—

Figure 4.4. Absence of artificial illumination. William Hogarth, *The Idle and Industrious Apprentices*, (London, 1747), pl. 7. Courtesy of the Lewis Walpole Library, Print Collection, Yale University.

the inescapable accompaniment of leisured artificial illumination. By the third scene of the Rake's progress, the leisure has become a bit out of hand (Figure 4.6). The scene is a tavern on Drury Lane. Domesticity has been overturned: it is 3 A.M., and the Rake has been in a fight with the watch. There is a mirror with two candles, but the mirror itself is broken. In this context the candle and artificial illumination have destructively licentious connotations: the maid burns the map with a candle, and the porter carries a platter on which the "posture" dancer in the foreground will dance. There is a similar association of lighting and vice in the scene of the Rake in a gambling house. The croupier is holding a pair of candles, while two more light the work of a loanshark and an advertisement for marked cards. In Hogarth's *Midnight Modern Conversation*, the hour is actually 4 A.M., but the setting is slightly more respectable than the Rake's world. It is a coffee house with a fine clock, carved furniture, and paneled walls; the occupants are tradesmen trying to pass as gentlemen but betraying themselves in drunkenness. Hogarth portrays the luxurious use of candles as having an association with stay-

ing up too late and getting into trouble. The association of artificial illumination and vice is heavily symbolized in *Masquerade Ticket*, showing a royal
masquerade to mark Johann Jacob Heidigger's appointment as Master of the
Revels for George II. It features two altars, for Venus and Priapus. Three sets
of suspended candles light the scene.

Such prints imply an uncertainty toward artificial lighting among the
middling sorts. Any popularization of artificial illumination needed to overcome this uneasiness. Since lighting was traditionally used for display at least
as much as for illumination, an excess of it had aristocratic connotations. In
the world of elegance, lighting was a forthright luxury, to be consumed in an
extravagant manner. The ballroom scene in the *Analysis of Beauty* (Figure 4.3)
is brightly lit, with a candelabrum and seven wall sconces illuminating dance
postures that reveal a hierarchy of refinement. Such elaborate lighting
inevitably had associations with pretense and mannered immorality. But in

Figure 4.5. Contrast of the father's frugal and the Rake's genteel artificial illumination. William
Hogarth, *A Rake's Progress* (London, 1735), pl. 1. Courtesy of the Lewis Walpole Library, Print Collection, Yale University.

Figure 4.6. Artificial illumination for debauchery. William Hogarth, *A Rake's Progress* (London, 1735), pl. 3. Courtesy of the Lewis Walpole Library, Print Collection, Yale University.

Hogarth's England of the 1730s and 1740s, an inadequacy of artificial illumination carried shameful social associations as well. Taken altogether, Hogarth's representation of lighting is a contradictory one that corresponds to broader tensions that developed in the culture of artificial illumination during the eighteenth century. On the one hand the details of his prints imply that artificial lighting was present in virtually any respectable household; its inadequacy was a mark of viciousness and crime. But lighting was not a necessity; it was a fashionable want.[39]

During the eighteenth century, a modest use of candles became a decency for people aspiring to cosmopolitan refinement without extending into luxury and its negative connotations. For "a family of but Middling Figure," at a rate of three candles per night, "Summer and Winter, for ordinary and extraordinary Occasions," the annual cost would be at least £7 at 5d. per night—more than sugar and laundry, less than butter and shoes. Candles were sold or allotted by the pound, with the count of candles per pound identifying their size. The usual range was from four to twenty-four candles per

pound. In the Anglo-American colonies in the eighteenth century, dipped
tallow candles cost about 9d. per pound; molded tallow candles about 11d.
Beeswax candles cost about 13d., and spermaceti about three times that.
Demand for candles increased over the eighteenth century, even though their
cost did not go down and they had already been as affordable as everyday
necessities. British demand for tallow candles doubled in the second half of
the eighteenth century. When in 1784 William Pitt proposed to raise the tax
on candles by a half-penny per pound, he calculated that even poor families
consumed ten pounds per year. He estimated average consumption in the
population at large to be about thirty pounds per family.[40]

In *The Wealth of Nations* Adam Smith identified candles as one of the "necessaries" of life, by which he meant "not only those things which nature, but
those things which the established rules of decency have rendered necessary
to the lowest rank of people." Considering candles a necessity was new. In
seventeenth-century Essex County, Massachusetts, which included Boston,
fewer than half the estates with itemized inventories had specialized equipment for lighting: 37 percent (193 of 520) had candlesticks; 10 percent (51 of
520) had lamps. In early-eighteenth-century Pennsylvania, a large proportion of the population who could afford to have candlesticks chose not to
have them. Ownership there was only slightly a function of wealth. One-fifth
of the least wealthy propertied families, those with personal wealth of less
than £100, owned candlesticks. But the frequency of ownership barely increased in estates under £400; only about one-quarter had them. Even in
the wealthiest estates, those over £400, only a minority, two-fifths, owned
candlesticks. Yet candlesticks were not luxuries in expense. Mid-eighteenth-
century colonial newspapers advertised brass and iron candlesticks costing
22s., 18s. 6d., and 16s. a pair, a fraction of the cost of silver candlesticks, which
were worth their weight in money.[41]

By the 1770s almost three-quarters of a sample of inventoried estates in
the thirteen colonies had candlesticks; by colony, the proportion of owners
ranged from two-thirds in South Carolina and Virginia to four-fifths in New
York and Massachusetts. In northern commercial cities the rate was even
higher—almost 90 percent in Boston. By the late colonial period rates of
owning candlesticks varied with wealth, from 90 percent for estates inventoried at over £300 to 50 percent for those worth less than £49 (approx. 80%
for £100–299, 60% for £50–99). Just how rich the material culture of lighting could be is shown by the 1770 postmortem inventory of the estate of

Lord Botetourt, governor of Virginia, with its "31 snuffers and extinguishers, 114 lighting devices and 952 illuminants."[42]

A comparison of artificial illumination in the households of Landon Carter of Sabine Hall and his nephew, Robert Carter III of Nomini Hall, shows how, even among the wealthiest Virginia gentry, there was a difference between urban and rural uses of domestic lighting. On his plantation, Landon Carter's day was that of a farmer. A cantankerous widower, he had little time for gentility, and he usually went to bed at nightfall. Artificial illumination was problematic and somewhat unfamiliar to him. He had difficulty obtaining a reliable supply of candles on the local market. He complained of shopkeepers who sent him candles of myrtle wax rather than beeswax, and of a tallow chandler in Norfolk who neglected to fill his orders. Since he had trouble buying candles, he had to borrow them from other planters, and he in turn grudgingly loaned candles to them.[43]

Inadequate as his commercial supplies of candles were, it was not until the Revolutionary War interrupted them that Landon Carter began to produce his own candles on a significant scale. In the spring of 1777 he reported that one of his female slaves had molded almost three gross of tallow candles, but he did not understand the process she used. Though he prided himself on his expertise in all aspects of plantation management, he was quite ignorant of candlemaking. He was unsure how much tallow might be rendered from beef fat, and he wondered if he should copy other people who "pare their fat from their pieces for table and join that to their tallow."[44] To be self-sufficient in candles, he would have had to restrict his consumption to fewer than two per day.

To the extent that Landon Carter was familiar with artificial illumination, he was suspicious of its associations. His diary makes few references to activities that took place after dark, and most such comments were disapproving. He associated nighttime leisure with the dissoluteness of his coresident adult son, whom he faulted for "worshiping the rising sun and disregarding the setting." He hated his son's gambling more than any other of his vices, and noted that the young man and his friends "play to bedtime and that to very late hours." It puzzled and distressed him that they could play cards in disregard of the way daylight naturally defined the day; instead, they played "from after breakfast until late bedtime."[45]

In contrast to his uncle's household, that of Robert Carter had a strict schedule that delineated daytime from nighttime activities. The children's lessons with their tutor, held during the morning, began and ended with a bell at regular hours. Dinner, the main meal, was regularly at three o'clock. Supper was about nine o'clock, and people usually retired between ten and eleven. In Robert Carter's household, there were precise divisions between activities using natural and artificial light. Daylight was necessary for dinner, the family's most important time for taking their leisure together. "Evening" was defined as "the time between Dinner and day-light-End," to be used for sociable leisure, such as dancing, family walks about the plantation, riding to neighboring plantations, and entertaining casual visitors. The time after dark was usually for more intimate leisure that required some but not much illumination. "Candlelight" was one of the chronological demarcations of the day, like "dinner," "evening," and "supper." After candlelight individuals might read by candlelight, but it was more usual for them to gather by a fire for activities requiring less light, such as conversation or music. "Supper" brought ordinary days to a close; it was a time of nutritional refreshment rather than leisure.[46]

Higher levels of illumination implied festivity. At such times, Philip Vickers Fithian, the Presbyterian tutor from New Jersey whose journal describes the Robert Carter household, would note the exceptional use of candles for general illumination. He also counted them: "The room looked luminous and splendid; four very large candles burning on the table where we supp'd, three others in different parts of the room; a gay sociable Assembly, & four well instructed waiters!" This may have seemed extravagant to someone aspiring to a career as a Presbyterian minister, but the actual amount of artificial illumination used even on festive occasions was modest. In this instance, a group of at least seven adults, some children, and four servants had seven candles at a supper lasting about an hour: by ten o'clock people had retired for the night. While toasting at a dance might go on 'til midnight, the dancing, which began at candlelight, was over by supper. After supper the company would gather around a fire to play games and make toasts.[47]

At Nomini Hall candles symbolized the routine of refined domestic leisure. Carter expressed his appreciation to Fithian by sending "large clear, & very elegant Spermaceti Candles" to him on Christmas eve and Christmas night, and Fithian was duly impressed. But in fact daylight and firelight provided the regular illumination. Even in this genteel and wealthy household, the fireplace was still the chief gathering place for the family and determined that nighttime leisure would be informal and conversational.[48]

Artificial lighting symbolized an environment in which some domestic activities could take place with fewer of their traditional elemental constraints. The genteel style of life in the eighteenth century asserted this independence from elemental processes and constraints by stylizing artificial illumination in the architecture, furniture, and interior design of domestic life. It was an urbane style that marked households' identification with cosmopolitan life. Most of the rural population continued to live in houses suited to a domestic schedule determined by the availability of natural light.

5

CONVENIENT COMFORT

Political Economy

DURING THE eighteenth century Anglo-Americans increasingly used the word *comfort* to indicate satisfaction and enjoyment of immediate physical circumstances. In November 1795, upon returning to his Norfolk (England) home from London, the Reverend James Woodforde noted: "We drank tea, supped and slept at our *comfortable* quiet, happy, thatched dwelling." Over the forty-five years during which he kept his diary, from 1758 to 1802, Woodforde carefully analyzed his physical comforts and discomforts. He assessed, for example, the quality of his sleep: "Very ill indeed today having had a very indifferent night of rest last night, owing to the night candle filling the room in being so long going out with intolerable smoke and stink." He not only recorded when he was too hot or too cold, but verified his subjective impressions with thermometer readings. He noted when he used bed warmers. The minutiae of his reporting on comfort included his use of an umbrella on numerous rainy days.[1]

The Reverend Mr. Woodforde's attention to comfort poses a historical problem precisely because his standards seem so similar to those of Anglo-Americans since his time. The notion of comfort as physical comfort—self-conscious satisfaction with the relationship between one's body and its immediate physical environment—was an innovation of Anglo-American culture. This usage indicated a disposition to criticize traditional material culture and to improve upon it. Thomas Jefferson criticized most Virginians' housing as "*uncomfortable*." Jefferson's former compatriot, Benjamin Thompson, Count Rumford, recommended the technical virtues of his design for chimney fireplaces by appealing to "those who *know what comfort is,* and consequently are worthy of the enjoyments of a *clean hearth* and *cheerful fire*."[2] Jefferson and Rumford used *comfort* in a new way, to anticipate a new world.

Earlier in the century each of Woodforde's concerns—ample ventilation of sleeping quarters, the elimination of smoky chimneys, umbrellas for rainy weather, furnishing homes for domestic leisure—had drawn the attention of Anglo-American political economists, moral philosophers, scientists, humanitarian reformers, even novelists. These commentators sought to evaluate the relations of body, material culture, and environment in the name of physical comfort. As they reconceptualized values, redesigned material environments, and urged the relearning of behaviors, they gave the term *comfort* a new, physical emphasis, changing its centuries-old reference to moral, emotional, spiritual, and political support in difficult circumstances. To be "comfortless" had meant being "without anything to allay misfortune," and "discomfort" involved feelings of "sorrow," "melancholy," and "gloom" rather than physical irritability.[3]

Comfort in the Consumer Revolution

Language and concepts emphasizing a physical meaning of comfort developed initially in the nascent philosophy of political economy, around 1700, as it analyzed the differences between luxury and necessity. Luxury had long been the subject of political and social thought, but its defining antonym, *necessity,* had been taken for granted as having a natural definition. When eighteenth-century political economists began to analyze necessity in relation to the market, they effectively deconstructed luxury, by showing how things regarded as luxuries in one context could be considered necessities in another. They saw the meeting of human needs as a cultural, rather than natural, process, and pointed out that the standards by which basic human needs were met could be improved. The term *comfort* increasingly applied to those standards and assessed their fulfillment.

This new emphasis on physical comfort was manifested in the eighteenth-century consumer revolution, but it cannot be taken for granted that comfort was a natural motive or the only motive for new consumption patterns. Items that people might have wanted "for their comfort" were explicitly desirable for other reasons, especially concerns about gentility and health. Theories of political economy in the first half of the eighteenth century made comfort a legitimizing motive for popular consumption patterns. By the middle of the eighteenth century the imperatives of physical comfort had focused scientific and technological expertise on more amenable designs of the domestic environment. And by the last decades of the eighteenth century the ideal of physical comfort had gained sufficient ideological force that humanitarians incorporated it in their appeals for social justice toward the poor, the incarcerated, and the enslaved, groups whose lack of comfort they felt crucially needed to be remedied. At the end of the eighteenth century physical comfort could be asserted as a right of the unprivileged and a humanitarian responsibility of the propertied.

The language of comfort gave meaning to a consumer revolution in Anglo-American society, as more people had more money to spend on more goods. In addition, fashion increasingly shaped demand. The propertied populace began to buy goods previously the exclusive province of the wealthy. People referred to their new consumer preferences as "conveniences" and "decencies"—amenities somewhere between necessity and luxury in the scale of wants and needs. Matching chairs and tables of carved walnut and other fine woods provided specialized furniture for socializing. The new drinks of tea, coffee, and chocolate required specific wares of glass and ceramics for preparation and serving. Looking glasses and clocks allowed luxurious display of technology. Tea and small dinners for guests became feasible domestic leisure activities.[4]

Clothes were the most popular object of fashionable spending. Seventeenth-century French courtiers introduced Europeans to a style of informality by replacing women's bodices and men's doublets with gowns and coats respectively. They preferred highly patterned clothes of silk and cotton over heavy, stiff materials of velvet, satin, brocaded silks, and embroidered wool. Relatively inexpensive printed and painted cottons, initially from the

East Indies, enabled a larger proportion of the population to dress in clothes with the smooth surfaces, bright colors, and exotic ornament long associated with silk. People could dress in cleaner clothes because cotton could be washed more readily than wool or silk. The lightness of cotton—in fabrics such as calico, chintz, and muslin—leant it well to a proliferation of accessories and types of garments, such as petticoats, gowns, cravats, and handkerchiefs.[5]

Commentators attributed the appeal of the new styles and fabrics to their greater ornamentation, not their easier wear. Men's and women's dress became more highly gendered in structure and fabric, as the bodiced gown was replaced by the mantua, a loose gown of light fabric, worn over a stay fashioned of stiffly resilient materials such as starched canvas, leather, whale bone, and steel. For the first time women could legally make women's clothes for sale, but only the mantua; male tailors maintained their privileges by making stays. Stays wrapped a woman's torso from her bust to below her waist. To our modern, post-corset, imagination, stays seem inherently uncomfortable, yet before the second half of the eighteenth century people did not often record complaints about the discomfort of stays. All women were expected to wear them. They maintained respectability and ideal body shape; loose stays signified impropriety. Stays provided Hogarth his best example from everyday life to illustrate "the line of beauty," not "bulging too much in their curvature" as to become "gross and clumsy," nor so "straighten" as to be "mean and poor." Although eighteenth-century medical experts condemned stays because of women's tendency to lace them too tightly in order to achieve a slender waist (Figure 5.1), they were thought, when properly used, to provide support for people supposed to have inherently weak skeletons, namely women and young children. The garments actually caused the condition they were thought to alleviate, since they allowed stomach muscles to atrophy from disuse, diminishing their capacity to support the spine. Children's use of stays relaxed after mid-century, in response to Lockean and Rousseauist ideologies of childrearing; and women's use eased in the 1780s, when an avant-garde fashion dictated abandoning them in the name of neoclassical simplicity. In the 1770s and 1780s, informal "undress" became fashionable as "natural elegance, in which the body is left to that freedom so congenial to common sense."[6]

Just as stays were not necessarily synonymous with discomfort, items that we now associate with comfort may not have been designed with that intent.

Figure 5.1. Fashion. A husband tightens his wife's stays before they go out in Macaroni outfits. Published by Bowles and Carver, after John Collet, *Tight Lacing, or Fashion before Ease* (London, 1770–75). Courtesy of the Lewis Walpole Library, Print Collection, Yale University.

Easy chairs, for example, were not for everyone's comfortable seating; rather they were designed for people who could not move easily on their own—chronic invalids, women in the late stages of pregnancy or recovering from childbirth, and men with gout (Figure 5.2). Their recommended virtues were ease and warmth; their upholstery allowed long periods of sitting and pro-

Figure 5.2. Hygiene. A man with gout sits in an easy chair, while others sit more upright in less upholstered chairs. Thomas Rowlandson, *The Comforts of Bath* (London, 1798), pl. 1. Courtesy of the Houghton Library, Harry Elkins Widener Collection, Harvard University.

vided insulation as well. Reclining backs and adjustable leg supports facilitated sleeping. These adjustable backs and leg supports derived from the sleeping chairs that had been used in aristocratic "closets" since the seventeenth century, but for most of the eighteenth century these apparent anticipations of La-Z-Boy chairs remained unused for general seating. They were not used in parlors, where they would have been available for general choice as sitting; instead they were found in bedrooms and chambers, usually upstairs. Many of them had "close stools" (fitted chamber pots). Medical hygiene shaped the design of easy chairs, not physical comfort for everyone. Similarly, "go-chairs" for invalids provided "ease and *comfort*," and "hollow-seated chairs" made "sitting easy beyond expression." Eighteenth-century chairs were not designed primarily for ease and comfort; they were supposed to aid sitting with properly respectful and refined posture and to fit the clothes and wig of the sitter. Seating furniture provided a prop for the ordering of social status.[7]

The primary purpose of furniture was to express genteel taste. George

Hepplewhite's favorable terms when recommending his designs included "elegant," "rich and splendid appearance," "pleasing and striking effect to the eye," "newest fashion," "grandeur of ornament and gravity of appearance," "lightness of appearance," as well as "great utility," "conveniencies," and "universal utility," but not "*comfort*." In promoting his furniture, Thomas Chippendale used the evaluative terms "magnificence, proportion, and harmony," "look very grand," "will have a very good effect," "will look extremely neat," "an exceeding genteel and grand appearance," "handsome and elegant."[8] As these terms suggest, much of the spending during the consumer revolution attempted to express gentility, an explicit ideal of taste and behavior that had existed since the Renaissance—as marked by its many cognates: *gentilezza, civilité, civilitas, civility, refinement,* among others. Gentility was a specific set of manners that placed a premium on pleasing others in appearance, conversation, and social interaction. Its codes of graceful behavior found expression throughout material culture—in dress, in dining, in music and dance, in architecture and interior decoration. By using bodily restraint to establish social boundaries, persons of all social conditions could (in principle) learn gentility, and then apply it to their social situations. By the eighteenth century, gentility had been illustrated in highly didactic representations in print, visual culture, the theater, and everyday example (Figure 5.3). There were guidebooks to *The Rudiments of Genteel Behavior,* with illustrations of the correct postures in which women and men were to stand, walk, give and receive gifts, and dance, in order to "be, and appear, easy, amiable, genteel and free in their person, mien, air and motions, [rather] than stiff, awkward, deform'd, and consequently, disagreeable."[9]

People acquired goods more often to display such gentility than they did for purposes of personal comfort. To facilitate comparisons of current and colonial-period consumption, two historians devised an index of "ten items that most westerners now consider the basic household equipment needed to ensure a minimum of *comfort* and cleanliness: a mattress, a bedstead, some bed linen, a table, one or more chairs, pots for boiling food, other utensils for food preparation, some coarse ceramics, table forks, and some means of interior lighting." In the seventeenth century ownership of these goods varied with wealth—as though they were luxuries—even though there were inexpensive versions of each item. Even among the wealthy they were not considered necessities: many families who could easily afford to buy these items did without some of them. In the eighteenth century ownership of

Figure 5.3. Gentility. Having just inherited the wealth his father made in commerce, the Rake is instructed in the manners and skills of a gentleman by a dancing master, a fencing master, and a landscape gardener, while a poet, tailor, harpsichordist, and jockey attend him. William Hogarth, *A Rake's Progress* (London, 1735), pl. 2. Courtesy of the Lewis Walpole Library, Print Collection, Yale University.

these goods became more general, but more people bought more goods associated with elegance and gentility—notably fashionable clothing, tea ware, table knives and forks, glassware, and mirrors—than they did goods assumed to increase comfort.[10] Most of the goods featured in the consumer revolution had crucial functions in sociability, most obviously with clothing, but also with items used in domestic settings, such as tableware, tea ware, seating furniture, and even bedding. Personal needs for comfort were apparently subordinate; even spending on food went disproportionately toward entertainment and genteel ritual. Comfort, like gentility, was something to be learned and expressed, but most of the Anglo-American population initially found it more desirable to enhance gentility than comfort. At the beginning of the eighteenth century they made gentility much more explicit than comfort as an imperative in material culture.

The Relativity of Luxury and Necessity

Premodern religious, moral, political, social, and economic commentators ignored what we understand as comfort as a regular subject of analysis. Prior to the late seventeenth century, moral philosophy on consumption patterns was interested in luxury. Neither classical nor Christian philosophers could say anything good about "luxury," because it referred to behavior that violated a sanctioned order, whether divine or social. Material manifestations of luxury were symptomatic of corruptions of character: men's commitments to public virtue weakened as they succumbed to the effeminate softness synonymous with a luxurious material culture. Christian preoccupations with individual sin reinforced the classical moral associations of luxury and made it a threat to all individuals regardless of social and political status. But early modern economic and social thought, especially in commercial and sumptuary legislation, had allowed aristocratic privileges of luxury. What might be disapproved as luxury for commoners was for nobles considered a means to uphold rank and thereby the social order. By the eighteenth century, as more people's consumption of goods emulated that of the aristocracy, luxury's antonym, *necessity*, became associated with poverty and death.[11] Although eighteenth-century usage still contrasted luxury with necessity, *comfort* increasingly applied to a middle ground between necessity and luxury. This development required people to rethink both necessity and luxury. Prior to the eighteenth century no one thought that luxuries could be specified objectively; instead they manifested idiosyncrasy and mindless social aping. Conversely, necessities had objective definition by the supposed requirements of subsistence.

The relativity of necessity and the acceptability of luxury became apparent in apologies for consumption in England's domestic economy. Sustained criticism of the priority of production in England's political economy flourished in the 1690s. This priority had depended on the assumption that England's wealth came from the export of manufactures, particularly cloth. Consumption of foreign goods supposedly lessened national wealth. In this context consumption of England's domestic production was largely a matter of indifference, because according to theory it neither increased nor diminished the total wealth of the nation. These assumptions broke down in the latter decades of the seventeenth century: "Every index of economic growth showed an advance: agricultural output, capital investment, imports from the Indies and the New World, the range and quantity of home manufacturing. Most striking was the abounding evidence of a rise in the level of domestic consumption." Most economic rethinking in this period repudiated simplistic models of the balance of trade as a zero-sum game and argued instead that protectionist measures could be self-defeating if they reduced other countries' capacity to consume England's exports. Nascent political economists also rethought the psychological dynamics and social implications of consumption at the micro level, as the consumption of Indian fabrics became a synecdoche of economic change—the substitution of newly fashionable goods for traditional ones, the popularization of luxury beyond the aristocracy, and the simultaneous expansion of domestic and foreign markets. Traditional interpretations of luxury could readily account for both increase and diversification in consumption patterns, but only in negative terms of sin and social disorder. New arguments interpreted these patterns as social goods, whatever they revealed about people's psychology.[12]

Nicholas Barbon, a physician interested in London real estate development, presented the most forthright among these early analyses of people's potential to consume material goods. He minimized the natural basis of needs: "if strictly Examined, nothing is absolutely necessary to support Life, but Food; for a great part of Mankind go Naked, and lye in Huts and Caves." History showed that the cultural construction of needs had no limits: "The Wants of the Mind are infinite, Man naturally Aspires, and as his Mind is elevated, his Senses grow more refined, and more capable of Delight; his Desires are inlarged and his Wants increase with his Wishes, which is for everything that is rare, can gratifie his Senses, adorn his Body, and promote the Ease, Pleasure and Pomp of Life." Several of these reasons why people consumed, including the strongest—the desires for rarity, adornment, and pomp—were not identical with physical comfort, but "ease" was closely similar. Barbon listed "Shoomakers, Sadlers, Couch, and Chair-Makers" as occupations serving the "Ease of Life." But historical comparisons revealed no objective standard for convenience: "every Old Fashion was once New. . . . And therefore since all Habits are equally handsome, and hard to know which is most Convenient: The Promoting of New Fashions, ought to be

Encouraged, because it provides a Livelihood for a great Part of Mankind."
In place of a classical model that discussed consumer behavior in moral and
political terms—making luxury virtually by definition acceptable only as a
privilege of the aristocracy—a psychological model of consumer behavior
accounted for everyone the same way, for better or worse, and justified consumption as providing remunerative work for others. John Locke, another
physician writing at the same time as Barbon, identified "civil interests" with
"life, liberty, health, and indolency of body; and the possession of outward
things, such as money, lands, houses, furniture, and the like." Such possessions, said Locke, were a major good in any "society of men," since governments existed only "for the procuring, preserving, and advancing of their
own civil interests."[13]

Eighteenth-century English writers initially used *convenience* to describe
people's physical satisfaction with their immediate material culture. In the
fifteenth and sixteenth centuries *convenience* (more frequently, *conveniency*) had
strong connotations of harmony and conformity to a given order, as in
"congruity of form, quality, or nature." But during the seventeenth century
this meaning became obsolete, as *convenience* increasingly referred to open-
ended suitability "to the performance of some action or to the satisfying of
requirements." For example, a defender of the East India Company's expor-
tation of bullion used the term to justify the importation of Indian manufactures simply on the basis that people wanted them: "The true and principal Riches, whether of private Persons, or of whole Nations, are Meat, and
Bread, and Cloaths, and Houses, the *Conveniences* as well as Necessaries of
Life." A 1730s guide to manners echoed the old definition of convenience as
harmony while, without apparent irony, applying it to the most arbitrarily
fashionable and rapidly changing sphere of material culture, namely clothing: "[Propriety], I call a certain Suitableness and *Convenience* betwixt the
Cloaths and the Person, as Courtesy is the framing and adapting our Actions, to the Satisfaction of other People; and if we desire to be exact, we
must proportion them to our Shape, our Condition, and our Age." As a predecessor for what would eventually be known as *comfort* regarding possessions
in a consumer society, *convenience* had two advantages: it measured usefulness
according to "any purpose," and it left the purposes themselves morally neutral and open-ended. Under the rubric "conveniences," a 1786 guide to living in London discussed hiring carriages, buying wine, borrowing books,
finding card players, discussing improving topics, hearing parliamentary and

other debates, attending musical concerts, and taking hot, cold, and fresh water baths.[14]

Luxury did not lose its iniquitous connotations once liberal political economy developed, but application of the term to specific consumption patterns often carried less calamitous implications than previously. With respect to material—as opposed to political—culture, in the early eighteenth century, references to luxury became increasingly satirical rather than wholeheartedly condemnatory.[15] Satire carried much of the argument of Bernard Mandeville, yet another physician among the liberal revisionists, on the propriety of material consumption—"what we call the *Comforts* of Life." In *The Grumbling Hive* (1705) Mandeville scandalously disregarded the association of luxury with the vices of avarice, envy, pride, and vanity, and argued instead that they all contributed indispensably to public and private prosperity.

> The Root of Evil, Avarice,
> That damn'd ill-natur'd baneful Vice,
> Was Slave to Prodigality,
> That noble Sin; whilst Luxury
> Employ'd a Million of the Poor,
> And odious Pride a Million more:
> Envy it self, and Vanity,
> Were ministers of Industry;
> Their darling Folly, Fickleness,
> In Diet, Furniture and Dress,
> That strange ridic'lous Vice, was made
> The very Wheel that turn'd the Trade. . . .
> Thus Vice nurs'd Ingenuity,
> Which join'd with Time and Industry,
> Had carry'd Life's Conveniencies,
> It's real Pleasures, *Comforts,* Ease,
> To such a Height, the very Poor
> Liv'd better than the Rich before,
> And nothing could be added more.

In *The Grumbling Hive*'s notorious prose commentary, *The Fable of the Bees* (1714), Mandeville not only defended luxury for its unintended social benefits, he deconstructed the distinction between necessity and luxury to show that *all* supposed "necessities" were social constructions and therefore "luxuries." It made no difference whether a material item was considered a luxury or a necessity, since the distinction between them broke down when applied to specific items in specific societies: "The *Comforts* of Life are likewise so various and extensive, that no body can tell what People mean by them, except he knows what sort of Life they lead. The same obscurity I observe in the words Decency and Conveniency, and I never understand them unless I am acquainted with the Quality of the Persons that make use of them. . . . People may go to Church together, and be all of one Mind as much as they please, I am apt to believe that when they pray for their daily Bread, the Bishop includes several things in that Petition which the Sexton does not think on." (See Figures 5.4 and 5.5.) "Luxury" simply measured the extent to which "Thought, Experience, and some Labour" had made "Life more *comfortable*" than an animal-like "primitive Simplicity."[16]

The development of political economy in the eighteenth century made it possible for both *luxury* and *necessity* to become morally neutral terms. Both of them became associated at least as much with physical well-being as with morality and mortality. Mandeville had set the agenda for political economists' analysis of how demand shaped economic development. He cleared the way for standard of living to be a problem in its own right. The extent and degree of convenience and comfort among the populace became measures of northwestern Europe's progress from barbarism to civilization. Yet these measures had no standard scale or absolute morality. If luxury was everything "not immediately necessary to make Man subsist as he is a living Creature," then all material goods, even those of "naked Savages," were luxuries. Peoples in every society "had made some Improvements upon their former manner of Living; . . . in the Preparation of their Eatables, the ordering of their Huts." In assessing what was a luxury, "Our Admiration is extended no farther than to what is new to us, and we all overlook the Excellency of Things we are used to, be they never so curious." For Mandeville *comfort* meant desirable physical circumstances: "convenient Houses, handsome Furniture, good Fires in Winter, pleasant Gardens in Summer, neat Clothes, and Money enough to bring up their Children. . . . These I have named are the necessary *comforts* of Life, which the most Modest are not asham'd to claim, and which they are very uneasy without."[17]

Robinson Crusoe, published five years after *The Fable of the Bees*, romanticized this new notion of comfort. Crusoe, confronted with providing for himself

A MASTER PARSON with a GOOD LIVING.

Figure 5.4. Relativity of luxury and necessity. These depictions of the life of the master parson and the journeyman parson (Figure 5.5) offer a series of precise contrasts. Carington Bowles, after Robert Dighton, *A Master Parson with a Good Living* (London, 1782). Courtesy of the Lewis Walpole Library, Print Collection, Yale University.

from scratch, demonstrates in detail what it meant to be comfortable in early modern England. The chief importance of these details for the invention of comfort is their sheer existence in "the first fictional narrative in which an ordinary person's daily activities are the center of continuous literary attention." Much of that narrative focused on a problem just becoming culturally explicit, the achievement of physical comfort. Defoe's novel revealed both

A JOURNEYMAN PARSON with a BARE EXISTENCE.

Figure 5.5. *A Journeyman Parson with a Bare Existence* (London, 1782). Courtesy of the Lewis Walpole Library, Print Collection, Yale University.

symptom and cause of the issues arising from that explicitness, and he explored both by juxtaposing the emotional and physical aspects of comfort. When Crusoe had safely landed on shore after his ship's wreck, he "solaced [his] mind with the *comfortable* part of [his] condition." Then he evaluated his physical circumstances: "I was wet, with no clothes to shift me, nor any thing either to eat or drink to *comfort* me." His immediate recourse was animal-like, to climb a tree for protection; there he slept "*comfortably*." The next day, "destitute of all *comfort* and company," he began to reestablish a familiar material culture by looting the wrecked ship and fashioning what he desired from the island's natural resources.[18]

Crusoe's situation starkly tested Mandeville's cultural definition of a continuum of material needs from necessity to luxury. His strategy implied the priority among his physical needs. From the ship he took food and drink, bedding, clothes, carpentry tools and supplies, and weapons. Aside from his bed, most of Crusoe's initial material comforts came from items that would be ingested—refined foods, alcoholic drinks, and tobacco. Among consumer durables they were mostly metal items—razors, scissors, knives and forks, and some money, the uselessness of which he appreciated but "upon second thoughts, I took it away." His most valued consumer goods were ones of literary culture—"pens, ink, and paper," and books, particularly religious ones. Among his deprivations Crusoe most missed candles for artificial illumination. He improved on his housing by building a wall and a thatched roof over the cave opening behind his tent. The cave room was a multipurpose space, "a warehouse or magazin, a kitchen, a dining room, and a cellar." Eventually he replaced the tent with a raftered shelter for better protection against rain. Crusoe had built himself a hall-and-parlor house. Once he had rooms, he built furniture: "I began to apply myself to such necessary things as I found I most wanted, as particularly a chair and a table; for without these I was not able to enjoy the *comforts* I had in the world; I could not write, or eat, or do several things with so much pleasure without a table."[19] His needs would not have been out of place for the third quarter of the seventeenth century, and indeed Defoe set the novel in that period.

Once Crusoe had satisfactorily accommodated himself, he began to explore the interior of the island. One "delicious vale" particularly appealed to him. With conscious irony, he built himself a rural retreat—"a little kind of bower"—on his deserted island. Crusoe claimed that this bower marked his achievement of comfort. Having spent most of the narrative up to that point in dealing expansively with his material needs, he now extolled his physical contentedness with his new home:

> I cannot express what a satisfaction it was to me, to come into my old
> hutch, and lye down in my hamock-bed. This little wandring journey,
> without settled place of abode, had been so unpleasant to me, that my

own house, as I called it to my self, was a perfect settlement to me, compared to that; and it rendred every thing about me so *comfortable*, that I
resolved I would never go a great way from it again, while it should be
my lot to stay on the island.

Yet two major increments in his physical comfort were still to come—
freshly baked bread and an umbrella. In principle comfort implicitly involved knowing what amenities one really needed, having them, and de-
siring no more. But Crusoe repeatedly contradicted a simple equation of
comfort with the satisfaction of sheer necessities. When he later discovered
a wrecked Spanish ship his needs expanded again: "I took a fire shovel and
tongs, which I wanted extremely; as also two little brass kettles, a copper pot
to make chocolate, and a gridiron." As Mandeville had argued, there was no
objective basis for distinguishing Crusoe's comforts from luxuries. Isolation
on the island had led Crusoe to learn the Mandevillian lesson that he had
come to take his physical comforts for granted as natural, when in fact they
were deeply historical. A few years later in *The Complete English Tradesman*
Defoe would urge that the history of physical comfort in England be a
source of national pride:

> The same trade that keeps our people at home, is the cause of the well
> living of the people here; for as frugality is not the national virtue of
> *England,* so the people that get much, spend much; and as they work
> hard, so they live well, eat and drink well, cloath warm, and lodge soft!
> in a word, the working manufacturing people of *England* eat the fat,
> drink the sweet, live better, and fare better, than the working poor of
> any other nation in *Europe.*[20]

(See Figure 5.6.)

As the examples of Mandeville and Defoe indicate, development of a
popular culture of fashionable consumption in the eighteenth century coincided with a new language to describe the physical basis of material need.
David Hume gave philosophical respectability to the new revisionist and rel-
ativistic view of luxury. (Indeed, when in 1760 he republished his 1752 essay
"Of Luxury," he retitled it "Of Refinement in the Arts.") Luxury meant
"great refinement in the gratification of the senses; and any degree of it may
be innocent or blameable, according to the age, or country, or condition of

Figure 5.6. Prosperity. On Beer Street, consumption of the "balmy juice" accompanies trade in meat, drink, fish, clothing, shoes, books, even art. William Hogarth, *Beer Street and Gin Lane* (London, 1751). Courtesy of the Lewis Walpole Library, Print Collection, Yale University.

the person." Hume reminded his readers of "philosophers'" efforts "to render happiness entirely independent of every thing external," but he considered "that degree of perfection is impossible to be attained." Other Scottish moral philosophers, notably Francis Hutcheson and Adam Ferguson, gave similarly measured interpretations of the historical and social relativity of luxury. Their interpretations used the uncertainty implicit in traditional notions of luxury (as conditions in excess of what necessity required) to show that improved standards of living did not necessarily pose a liability to public virtue. Ferguson pointed out that one might

> propose to stop the advancement of arts at any stage of their progress, and still incur the censure of luxury from those who have not advanced so far. . . . if the dispute were to turn on the knowledge of what is physically necessary for the preservation of human life, as the standard of what is morally lawful, the faculties of physic, as well as of morality, would probably divide on the subject, and leave every individual, as at present, to find some rule for himself.

Luxury now referred neutrally to desirable possessions, "that complicated apparatus which mankind devise for the ease and convenience of life. Their buildings, furniture, equipage, cloathing, train of domestics, refinement of the table, and, in general, all that assemblage which is intended rather to please the fancy, than to obviate real wants, and which is rather ornamental than useful."[21]

Standards of Living

What was previously an oxymoron, Hume's "innocent" luxury, became a topic for analysis by political economists, social commentators, and scientists. As one of the advocates of paper money wrote during a fiscal controversy in Massachusetts in the early 1750s, "Every man has a *natural Right* to enjoy the fruit of his own Labour, both as to the *Conveniencies*, and *Comforts*, as well as the *Necessaries* of Life, *natural Liberty* is the same with one Man, as another; and unless in the Enjoyment of these Things they hurt the Community, the Poor ought to be *allow'd* to use them as freely as the Rich." After the Seven Years War, Britain's commercial expansion and popular prosperity became less ambivalently associated with national pride and identity. When *luxury* referred to political corruption it continued to have condemnatory power, but the term lost much of its moral force when referring solely to consumption patterns. In his *Letters from a Farmer in Pennsylvania to the Inhabitants of the British Colonies,* John Dickinson attacked the Townsend duties because they fell on "absolute *necessaries or conveniences*," such as paper and glass, "which use and custom have made requisite to the *comfort* of life." Dickinson ridiculed the primitivist opportunity presented by Parliament's taxes: "Some perhaps, who think mankind grew wicked and luxurious, as soon as they found out another way of communicating their sentiments than by speech, and another way of dwelling than in caves, may advance so whimsical an opinion. But I presume no body will take the unnecessary trouble of refuting them."[22]

As Dickinson's loftiness implied, classical republicanism and other ascetic strains in British radical and opposition political thought provided an ideological counterpoint to emergent liberal political economy. Use of this ideology (in both Britain and America) in support of American political resistance to imperial reform gave renewed relevance to the classical critique of luxury. Prevailing consumption patterns were interpreted to be causes as well as symptoms of weak public virtue and liability to political corruption. John Adams blamed "the late ministerial Measures" on "the universal Spirit of Debauchery, Dissipation, Luxury, Effeminacy and Gaming": he saw the "Prodigality, in Furniture, Equipage, Apparell and Diet," as "drawing down the Judgments of Heaven" in those same tyrannous acts. But calls for the restoration of civic virtue through "Frugality, Œconomy, [and] Parcimony" seldom provided a positive definition of desirable consumption patterns. Instead they expressed primitivist fantasies: "Let us Eat Potatoes and drink Water. Let us Wear Canvass, and undressed Sheepskins, rather than submit to the unrighteous, and ignominious Domination that is prepared for Us." When Abigail Adams urged that their family "return a little more to the primitive Simplicity of Manners [of our Fathers], and not sink into inglorious ease," John responded by recommending that she remove the coat of arms from the family's carriage, but he kept the carriage itself.[23]

Appeals to "primitive simplicity" contributed to nascent republicanism at the same time that British political economists began to use the improvement of standards of living as a measure of the progress of civilization. Adam Smith put the problem of consumption—"what are the naturall wants and demands of mankind"—at the heart of understanding the human condition. Humans differed from animals by their inability to live naturally in nature.

Man has received from the bounty of nature reason and ingenuity, art, contrivance, and capacity of improvement far superior to that which she has bestowed on any of the other animalls, but is at the same time in a much more helpless and destitute condition with regard to the support and *comfort* of his life.

Precisely because humans needed technology to survive in nature, all of their encounters with nature held out the possibility of improving their condition. But such improvements could not be measured against an absolute objective standard:

> The same temper and inclinations which prompted him to make these improvements [cooked food, clothes, housing] push him to still greater refinements. This way of life appears rude and slovenly and can no longer satisfy him; he seeks after more elegant nicities and refinement. Man alone of all animalls on this globe is the only one who regards the differences of things which no way affect their real substance or give them no superior advantage in supplying the wants of nature.

Indeed, the desire for "frivolous distinctions and preferences in things otherwise equall" largely shaped mankind's "distress and uneasieness" to improve standards of living. Most of the human story resulted from these artificial needs:

> all the arts, the sciences, law and government, wisdom, and even virtue itself tend all to this one thing, the providing meat, drink, rayment, and lodging for men, which are commonly reckoned the meanest of employments and fit for the pursuit of none but the lowest and meanest of the people. All the several arts and businesses of life tend to render the conveniencies and necessaries of life more attainable.

The technology and social organizations of civilization developed for purposes of consumption.[24]

Josiah Tucker, Adam Smith's shrewd though less systematic contemporary in political economy (and tutor to the Prince of Wales on the subject), favorably compared English consumption patterns with those of other countries and forthrightly analyzed the emulative motivations shaping them. English manufactures, he argued, are more adapted for the Demands of Peasants and Mechanics, in order to appear in warm circumstances; for Farmers, Freeholders, Tradesmen and Manufacturers in middling Life; and for wholesale Dealers, Merchants, and all persons of Landed Estates, to appear in genteel life; than for the Magnificence of Palaces or the Cabinets of Princes. Thus it is . . . that the *English* of those several denominations have better Conveniencies in their Houses, and affect to have more in Quantity of Clean, neat Furniture, and a greater Variety, such as Carpets, Screens, Window Curtains, Chamber Bells, polished Brass Locks, Fenders etc. (Things hardly known Abroad among Persons of such a Rank) than are to be found in any other country in *Europe, Holland* excepted.

Adam Smith explained motivations in a consumer society with a similarly detailed analysis of standards of living and determined that people's desire for convenience manifested an optimism that technology could provide happiness. He defined "conveniency" tautologically as "the fitness of any system or machine to produce the end for which it was intended." This "conveniency" translated into economic demand because the rich had more of it and others wished to emulate the physical world of the rich: "The palaces, the gardens, the equipage, the retinue of the great are objects of which the obvious conveniency strikes every body." However, items such as toothpicks, ear pickers, and nail clippers had no particular desirability except by association with an "ease" experienced only by the rich: "If we consider the real satisfaction which all these things are capable of affording, by itself and separated from the beauty of that arrangement which is fitted to promote it, it will always appear in the highest degree contemptible and trifling. But we rarely view it in this abstract and philosophical light." The real needs of the rich and the poor for "ease of body and peace of mind" were the same regardless of social status. Yet the false "pleasures of wealth and greatness" provided the "deception which rouses and keeps in continual motion the industry of mankind."[25]

English adoption of the umbrella provides a parable of Smith's argument that the culture of comfort could endow a symbolically prestigious object with new meaning on the basis of its everyday advantages for everyone. Since antiquity—in Egypt, China, India, Greece, and the Vatican—use of the umbrella as protection from the elements (particularly the sun) had been a matter of strict privilege and often of religious ritual. Apparently borrowed from Chinese examples, umbrellas became fashionable among women at the French court in the seventeenth century, where attendants could be counted on to deal with their unwieldy weight. The umbrella began its career as an item of Parisian consumption when, in the early eighteenth century, a purse maker adapted his trade's technology to make a lightweight, collapsible umbrella that provided protection from the rain as well as the sun. By the middle of the eighteenth century this device had come into popular use in Paris, by men as well as women: it satisfied desires for courtly associations as well as environmental protection. Satire soon marked the fashion's spread to England, while reinforcing the umbrella's female associations.[26]

The English climate had been rainy for a long time, but only in the last decades of the eighteenth century did umbrellas come into general use. They had earlier caught the admiring interest of British travelers such as the military officer James Wolfe and the humanitarian James Hanway, and in the 1760s and 1770s imported ones were advertised as fashion novelties. But French associations frequently made their venturesome users liable to public abuse, especially in the name of hackney coachmen whose livelihoods depended in part on providing protection from the rain. Horace Walpole noted contemptuously of the French: "They walk about the streets in the rain with umbrellas to avoid putting on their hats." As Walpole indicated, English observers initially thought the French carried the "new and most troublesome invention to save the beauty of their head dress," not to stay dry. Yet in the 1780s umbrellas became fashionable for English men as well as women, in counterpoint to the decline in carrying swords. Guides to "Walking London Streets" explained the prudent way to carry the newly popular device, and satirists described the mayhem from opening umbrellas when a shower fell on the Sunday promenade in London's Mall (Figure 5.7). Now British manufacturers advertised "much approved pocket and portable umbrellas, which for lightness, elegance and strength, far exceed anything of the kind ever imported or manufactured in this kingdom." The Reverend James Woodforde must have officiated at many rainy graveside services before he began recording his use of umbrellas in 1787; thereafter his references became numerous as it became an accustomed accessory.[27] The umbrella, destined to be a metonym of English ways, had gone from being a suspiciously foreign and feminine expression of courtly manners to being a fashionable device with which anyone might cope with the discomforts of the English climate.

Figure 5.7. Fashionable comfort. When a shower hits St. James Park, everyone is ready with an umbrella. Samuel Collings, *The Battle of Umbrellas* (London, 1784). Courtesy of the Lewis Walpole Library, Print Collection, Yale University.

When Adam Smith rehearsed the increase and the improvement of "the necessaries and the conveniencies of life" for England's laboring population, he confronted "the common complaint that luxury extends itself even to the lowest ranks of the people, and that the labouring poor will not now be contented with the same food, cloathing and lodging which satisfied them in former time." He acknowledged the force of traditional views on luxury by taking up the question of whether this improvement in popular standards of living should "be regarded as an advantage or as an inconveniency to the society." And he forthrightly repudiated traditional wisdom: "what improves the circumstances of the greater part can never be regarded as inconveniency to the whole." Social justice depended in part on the availability of everyday foods, such as cheaper potatoes, turnips, carrots, cabbages, apples, and onions, on "cheaper and better cloathing," on the availability of "many

agreeable and convenient pieces of household furniture," and on more affordable "soap, salt, candles, leather, and fermented liquors."[28]

Smith contrasted necessity and luxury, but he explicitly conceded Mandeville's relativism: "By necessaries I understand, not only the commodities
which are indispensably necessary for the support of life, but whatever the
custom of the country renders it indecent for creditable people, even of the
lowest order, to be without." He used the word *comfortably* to explain how
linen shirts could be a decency in contemporary Europe but unnecessary
among other civilized peoples such as the Greeks and Romans. (Here Mandeville almost certainly influenced Smith directly, since Mandeville used the
same example, linen shirts, to illustrate the same point.) Such comparisons
showed that decency was primarily a matter of social habit, not physical satisfaction. Lack of a linen shirt in eighteenth-century Europe would mark
"that disgraceful degree of poverty, which, it is presumed, no body can well
fall into without extreme bad conduct."[29]

Throughout the *Wealth of Nations* Adam Smith related "the necessities and
conveniences" of life to the material benefits of people's labor. Nowhere,
however, did he distinguish necessities *from* conveniences. Instead, he concluded the book's celebrated first chapter, that on the division of labor, with
a paean to the "universal opulence which extends itself to the lowest ranks
of the people." Among the items composing this opulence were a woolen
coat, a linen shirt, shoes, a bed, a kitchen-grate and its coals, "all the other
utensils of his kitchen, all the furniture of his table, the knives and forks, the
earthen or pewter plates upon which he serves up and divides his victuals,
bread, beer," and "the glass window which lets in the heat and the light, and
keeps out the wind and the rain . . . without which these northern parts of
the world would scarce have afforded a very *comfortable* habitation." The
diversity of production possible with a high degree of division of labor had
allowed the "accommodation" of "an industrious and frugal peasant" to
exceed that of a ruler in savage societies. (By "savage" Smith meant societies
in which subsistence depended on hunting and fishing.)[30]

According to Smith the primary imperative of satisfying necessity was to
avoid shame. Thus, anyone in England would be "ashamed to appear in
publick" without leather shoes, while among "the lowest order" in Scotland
only men, not women, felt such necessity. In France's "lowest rank of people" neither the men nor the women felt any "discredit" in appearing publicly either in wooden shoes or in bare feet. Smith distinguished between

necessities and luxuries, but he defined them both in reference to the same standard, the opinion of others. While respectability was crucial in the definition of necessities, the consumption of luxuries could be irrelevant to respectability, so long as it was "temperate." Luxuries were consumables from which people could abstain without suffering any "reproach"—as in forgoing beer or wine. Smith simultaneously disavowed an automatic disapproval of luxury and made popular consumption patterns respectable by definition.[31] Popular opinion determined what was a necessity, and comfort consisted in satisfying the necessities of life, so popular opinion now legitimized popular consumption.

ADAM SMITH'S analysis of consumption patterns showed how sympathy—the ability to understand other people by imaginatively experiencing their emotions and sensations—shaped material culture. In the latter decades of the eighteenth century, humanitarian reformers urged people to use sympathy to appreciate others' right to physical comfort. Consideration of others' physical discomforts fit well into the eighteenth century's thriving culture of sensibility, which encouraged people of social and economic privilege to empathize with the physical and psychological distress of those less fortunate than themselves. A prime manifestation of this philosophy was the campaign for prison reform. The preeminent prison reformer, John Howard, established a genre of social reporting that relied on a humanitarian aesthetic of sensitivity to others' miseries. His difficulties and perils in observing prisoners' miserable conditions were themselves sympathetic arguments for the need to design prisons with a view toward the prisoners' "cleanly and wholesome abodes." Most of the recent historiography on eighteenth-century English prison reform has followed the Foucauldian line of "discipline and punish" interpretations and has concentrated on the design of specialized facilities for the control and rehabilitation of criminals, but when Howard wrote *The State of the Prisons in England and Wales* in 1777, *distress*, a term conventionally used to arouse sympathy, was Howard's crucial word. In response to earlier findings by Howard about prisoners' critical liability to gaol fever, Parliament had in 1774 passed an act for preserving the health of prisoners. Howard's continuing investigation determined that prisoners' living conditions remained miserable: "any one may judge of the probability there is against the health, and life of prisoners crowded in close rooms, cells, and subterraneous dungeons, for fourteen or fifteen hours out of the four and twenty. In some of those caverns the floor is very damp: in others there is sometimes an inch or two of water: and the straw, or bedding is laid on such floors; seldom on barrack-bed steads." Howard's "proposed improvements" in the accommodation of prisoners included individual rooms for sleeping, bedsteads (preferably of iron), windows with shutters and barred doors for ventilation, and facilities for bathing with warm water. Howard even had to insist that jails have some heating: "this is not only what humanity demands in our climate, but . . . it is essential to the preservation of the health of prisoners, by promoting the circulation of air, and preventing those mortifications of the feet to which they are so liable." Similar concerns arose about the comfort of prisoners of war and were included in the negotiation of treaties in the 1780s as the United States sought to enlist allies in declarations of the rights of prisoners of war. The rights would include that prisoners should not be sent to "distant and inclement Countries" nor kept in "close and noxious places"; imprisoned officers should have "*comfortable* Quarters and the Commen Men be disposed in cantonments open and extensive enough for air and exercise, and lodged in barracks as roomly and good" as those provided the captor's troops.[32]

Similar terms began to inform commentary on the amenity of slave housing in the new United States. A Polish nobleman interested in prison reform (and himself a political prisoner for two years) invoked the humanitarian aesthetics of misery to report on slavery at George Washington's Mount Vernon plantation: "We entered one of the huts of the Blacks, for one can not call them by the name of houses. They are more miserable than the most miserable of the cottages of our peasants. The husband and wife sleep on a mean pallet, the children on the ground; a very bad fireplace, some utensils for cooking, but in the middle of this poverty some cups and a teapot." Earlier references to slaves' housing used a spectrum of generic terms that took poor quality for granted without further comment: *quarters, hovels, huts, cabins, cottages,* and *Negro houses.* After the Revolution, travelers used *comfort* when assessing slave housing, both positively and negatively, as "*comfortably* furnished" or having "no convenience, no furniture, no *comfort.*" Hygiene, warmth, and privacy came to define slaves' minimal entitlement to comfort. As *comfort* emerged in denunciatory descriptions of slaves' living conditions, slave owners increasingly prided themselves on building accommodation that met minimal standards for decent living, as measured by how poor European-Americans lived. This concern on the part of some slave owners was part of the broader humanitarian definition of comfort that developed in the second half of the eighteenth century. More pressingly, their application of that standard met a need to apologize for their treatment of human chattels in the face of antislavery developments throughout European Atlantic culture.[33]

The culture of sensibility identified the phenomenon of *discomfort* and made it susceptible to rational correction. Besides concern for the standards of housing for prisoners and slaves, humanitarians took particular responsibility for the design of comfortable cottages for the rural poor, as will be shown in a subsequent chapter. Housing for these groups had been miserable for a long time, but its inadequacy had not been regularly reported or studied until a new standard applied—comfort.

BY THE TURN of the nineteenth century Anglo-American social thought, in its denunciation of discomfort and its promotion of the acceptability of material consumption, had naturalized the desire for physical comfort. The mature work of Thomas Malthus represented and synthesized the invention of comfort in material culture and social thought: the undeterminability of distinctions between necessity and luxury, the acceptance of popular consumption patterns, the benevolist impulse to establish minimal standards of comfort, and the demonstrability of respectability in family life by the presence of a comfortable domestic environment. Between the first edition of the *Essay on the Principle of Population* in 1798 and the second edition in 1803, largely as a result of his travels to compare English living conditions with ones elsewhere in Europe, Malthus came to the realization that a desire for comfort and convenience was crucial to the "moral restraint" that allowed sufficient control over population to maintain happiness in a society. Comforts cost money, so people worked hard and postponed the gratifications of marriage in order to afford more amenities: "throughout a very large class of people [in England], a decided taste for the conveniences and *comforts* of life, a strong desire of bettering their condition (that master-spring of public prosperity), and, in consequence, a most laudable spirit of industry and foresight, are observed to prevail."[34]

Malthus's image of the comforts of English life came straight out of genre representations of happy cottagers: "a good meal, a warm house, and a *comfortable* fireside in the evening" (Figure 5.8). The desire for such comforts, said Malthus, "put in motion the greatest part of that activity, from which spring

Figure 5.8. Happy cottagers. Though close to nature, the romantically portrayed household amply meets its physical needs for shelter, food, heat, and light, while also having such manufactured items as shoes, stockings, ribbons, coats and gowns, tobacco, turned furniture, mirrors, and ceramics. David Allan, *Glaud, Jenny and Peggy*, from Alan Ramsay, *The Gentle Shepherd, a Pastoral Comedy* (Glasgow: A. Foulis, 1788), facing 92. Courtesy of the Yale Center for British Art, Paul Mellon Collection, Yale University.

the multiplied improvements and advantages of civilised life; and . . . the pursuit of these objects, and the gratification of these desires, form the principal happiness of the larger half of mankind, civilised or uncivilised, and are indispensably necessary to the more refined enjoyments of the other half."

What was minimally comfortable for the propertied was needed by the poor as well, and it was reasonable and desirable that the poor should want those "luxuries" of the propertied that were really comfortable: "It is the spread of luxury therefore among the mass of the people, and not an excess of it in a few, that seems to be most advantageous, both with regard to national wealth and national happiness . . . if it be observed that a taste for the *comforts* and conveniences of life will prevent people from marrying, under the certainty of being deprived of these advantages."[35]

Comfort had become a set of expectations, physical designs, and personal imperatives, as Robert Southey's fictional Spanish visitor to England in 1807 explained:

> There are two words in their language on which these people pride themselves, and which they say cannot be translated. *Home* is the one, by which an Englishman means his house . . . . The other word is *comfort;* it means all the enjoyments and privileges of *home;* and here I must confess that these proud islanders have reason for their pride. In their social intercourse and their modes of life they have enjoyments which we never dream of.

Southey went on to link these ideals with the consumer revolution:

> Saints and philosophers teach us that they who have the fewest wants are the wisest and the happiest; but neither philosophers nor saints are in fashion in England. It is recorded of some old Eastern tyrant, that he offered a reward for the discovery of a new pleasure;—in like manner this nation offers a perpetual reward to those who will discover new wants for them, in the readiness wherewith they purchase any thing, if the seller will but assure them that it is exceedingly convenient.[36]

Southey's examples of such conveniences included patent corkscrews, pocket fenders and toasting forks, lightweight fire irons, mechanical candle snuffers, pen cutters, nail clippers, cucumber slicers, and buttoners for knee britches.

6

ENLIGHTENED COMFORT

Stoves and Lamps

AS THE value of physical comfort became more explicit and desirable, the technology of its improvement gained intellectual prestige. Here Benjamin Franklin was the paragon among eighteenth-century philosophes, with his interest in the history, anthropology, and science of basic household comforts. He committed himself to closing the gap between the ideals and the technology of comfort. He promoted spermaceti candles for their steady, clean illumination; he suggested that people experiment with the ventilation in their sleeping quarters to improve their sleep; and his name became synonymous with smoke-free and draft-free heating.[1] He appreciated that the obstacles to improving comfort were more cultural than technical, and to remove these obstacles he urged his readers to question expert authority on material culture and to transcend their ethnocentrism regarding the domestic environment.

In Pennsylvania Franklin could consider a range of ethnic alternatives in domestic comfort. He was particularly attentive to the Dutch and German use of stoves that entirely enclosed the fire and used it only for heating purposes. Such stoves reduced drafts because they either drew combustion air from outside the room being heated (in the case of German jamb stoves) or closely regulated the combustion air in proportion to the desired intensity of the fire (in the freestanding Dutch stoves). Franklin contrasted the clean warmth of these stoves with that provided by the two fireplace types popular among English colonists: a traditional design with high, deep hearth openings and a "newer-fashion'd" style with "low Breasts, and narrow Hearths." In the large traditional fireplaces, people could sit warmly within the chimney itself, which was also used for drying and smoking foods, just as peasants had traditionally used rafters above open central hearths. With such fireplaces, the chief piece of furniture for daytime comfort, the settle bench, was effectively a fourth wall to the hearth, designed to isolate its occupants within the hearth space in order to block drafts from the rest of the room. These traditional fireplaces were being superseded and replaced by genteel designs, as people moved out of their fireplaces: "Most of these old-fashioned Chimneys in Towns and Cities, have been, of late Years, reduc'd to the second sort mention'd, by building Jambs within them, narrowing the Hearth, and making a low Arch or Breast." From Franklin's perspective both of these chimney fireplaces required an invidious trade-off between comfortable heat and smoky discomfort. When they became unbearably smoky it was necessary to increase the draft by opening an outside door, so it was impossible to heat an entire room with such fireplaces: "I suppose our Ancestors never thought of warming Rooms to sit in; all they purpos'd was to have a Place to Make a Fire in, by which they might warm themselves when cold."[2]

The traditional fireplace found in rural colonial American houses involved a physical proximity to the source of heat and light similar to that of the European peasantry's open hearth. The new, smaller fireplaces were improvements because their smaller chimneyface was less smoky, and they did not require an open door for draft; but they still needed room air for combustion, which they drew through all of the small openings in the walls. The new fireplaces only gave the illusion of separating domestic life from the elements. They were cleaner but not significantly more warming than the traditional fireplaces. Since they improved living style, not comfort, scientific solutions to their technical shortcomings could be neutralized by the force of "Custom and Fancy"—in this case, the ornamental chimneypiece. The desire to have "large and elegant Rooms" required "the Appearance of a larger Chimney" to display "expensive marginal Decorations in Marble, &c."

In time, perhaps, that which is fittest in the nature of things may come
to be thought handsomest. But at present when Men and Women in
different Countries show themselves dissatisfied with the Forms God
has given to their Heads, Waists, and Feet, and pretend to shape them
more perfectly, it is hardly to be expected that they will be content
always with the best Form of a Chimney. And there are some, I know,
so bigotted to the Fancy of a large noble Opening, that rather than
change it, they would submit to have damaged Furniture, sore Eyes,
and Skins almost smok'd to Bacon.

Franklin saw architects as servants of fashion rather than scientific enlightenment, bringing an entirely inappropriate set of concerns to the problem:
"Architects in general have no other Ideas of Proportion in the Opening of a
Chimney, than what relate to Symmetry and Beauty, respecting the Dimensions of the Room; while its true Proportion, respecting its Function and
Utility, depends on quite other Principles." He lamented that the practical
necessities of heating were usually secondary considerations in the design of
fireplaces; fashionable style for chimneypieces had priority over efficient
comfort.[3]

    Franklin appreciated that most people liked the way they lived and resisted
alternatives. Both five-plate German jamb stoves (heated by a fire outside
the room, usually in the kitchen) and Dutch six-plate stoves (fueled from
within the room being heated) were known and used in his native Boston in
the early eighteenth century, but not widely. English people resisted using
stoves precisely because of their technical virtues: they eliminated drafts so
efficiently that they made rooms seem stifling. The English had a long list of
prejudices against living with such stoves: they maintained a fetid atmosphere
of "Breath and Perspiration from one anothers Bodies, which is very disagreeable to those who have not been accustomed to it"; the stoves themselves gave off an unpleasant smell of cooked candle grease and spittle; and
their excessive warmth made people "tender and apt to catch cold." Franklin
knew that getting Anglo-Americans to adopt his stove would require more
fastidious domestic behavior: people would have to avoid the "inconsiderate,
filthy unmannerly custom" of spitting on the stove to see if it were hot, and
they would need to use soap more often to clean the stove's surface. But
the strongest resistance to using stoves arose from English people's insistence

on being be able to see an open flame, which a stove by definition obscured. Faced with a choice, they tolerated some smoke better than too much warmth.[4]

Franklin identified himself with members of a scientifically enlightened subculture who criticized the priority of fashion over comfort in the domestic environment. Rather than leave such technical problems aside once he had established a trans-Atlantic scientific reputation, Franklin became the Enlightenment's authority on smoky chimneys. He took no offense when David Hume's cousin, Lord Kames, wrote him for advice on such a mundane matter as smoky chimneys in a new house: "I have long been of an opinion similar to that you express," Franklin replied, "and think happiness consists more in small conveniences or pleasures that occur every day, than in great pieces of good fortune that happen but seldom to a man in the course of his life." Dr. Samuel Johnson voiced much the same opinion when commenting on the inadequacies of window glazing in Kames's homeland, Scotland:

> It must be remembered, that life consists not of a series of illustrious actions, or elegant enjoyments; the greater part of our time passes in compliance with necessities, in the performance of daily duties, in the removal of small inconveniencies, in the procurement of petty pleasures; and we are well or ill at ease, as the main stream of life glides on smoothly, or is ruffled by small obstacles and frequent interruption. The true state of every nation is the state of common life.[5]

The philosophes were putting comfort at the heart of the civilizing process: its improvement called for the rethinking of customary ways before new technology could have much social impact.

Science and Smoky Chimneys

Since the time of Prometheus residents of western Europe had lived with smoky interiors while expressing only the most passing of resigned complaints. They ignored alternatives to the open hearth, such as the ancient hypocaust and the airtight stoves of Germanic and Slavic cultures. But in the eighteenth century technologically minded reformers began to express the sentiment that they could no longer bear living amidst smoke. This sensibility was especially strong in France, where the use of stoves in Parisian apartments and houses was becoming frequent, as it became acknowledged that smoke from chimneys ("*cette vapeur meurtrière*") irritated the eyes, soiled the walls and furnishings, and menaced health. Diderot's *Encyclopédie* used the entry "*Cheminée*" to explain a reorientation of the domestic environment during the Enlightenment, from the smoky hearth to the mirror and its reflections of fashionable comfort, the result of a fashionable preoccupation with style in the domestic environment that aggravated the problem of smoky interiors:

> It is not to be mentioned without astonishment, that so many able and ingenious artists, who have travelled over Europe to acquire knowledge in architecture, and who have designed and erected buildings in this country, far superior for strength, lightness, and elegance, to any that are to be found abroad, should, nevertheless, have neglected to ascertain the principles of a conveniency, the due execution of which is necessary to render every habitation *comfortable*, from the cottage to the palace![6]

From the beginning to the end of the century, pamphlet after pamphlet used Newtonian physics, innovative technical illustrations, and practical experiments to explain how to alleviate the most objectionable household discomfort.

The fireplace itself, as a source of heat, became the object of scientific innovation. Reformers sought to shift priorities in the design of the domestic environment from style to the technology of comfort. The shift is evident in a comparison of how the two great eighteenth-century encyclopedias treated chimneys. In the middle of the eighteenth century the *Encyclopédie* used the entry "*Cheminée*" to discuss the domestic use of mirrors, while in the 1770s the *Encyclopaedia Britannica* dealt with chimneys under the entry "Smoke." This entry was an eight-page essay by James Anderson, a prominent Scottish political economist and agricultural reformer. Smoke, Anderson reminded his readers,

> is a dense elastic vapour, arising from burning bodies. As this vapour is extremely disagreeable to the senses, and often prejudicial to the health, mankind have fallen upon several contrivances to enjoy the benefit of fire, without being annoyed by smoke. The most universal of these con-

trivances is a tube leading from the chamber in which the fire is kindled, to the top of the building, through which the smoke ascends, and is dispersed into the atmosphere. These tubes are called chimneys; which, when constructed in a proper manner, carry off the smoke entirely; but, when improperly constructed, they carry off the smoke imperfectly, to the great annoyance of the inhabitants.

Since most of his readers lived with the discomforts of smoky chimneys, Anderson knew he could "hardly perform a more acceptable service to the public than to point out the manner in which [chimneys] ought to be constructed so as to carry off the smoke entirely; as well as to explain the causes from which the defects so often complained of generally proceed, and the method of removing them" (Figure 6.1). Anderson closely linked the technology of heating with the progress of civilization: "As mankind advance in civilization,—as they become easy in their circumstances, and come to form a more adequate idea of enjoyment,—when they acquire an idea of cleanliness, and feel what a high luxury it is to enjoy it, smoke in their houses becomes so exceedingly inconvenient, as to be accounted one of the greatest interruptions to domestic enjoyment."[7]

Anderson's essay summarized a century-long, trans-Atlantic effort in the European scientific community to apply the findings of Boyle's pneumatics and Newtonian physics to the basic problem of household comfort in northern temperate climates—how to have a clean, warm domestic space. Though chimneys had been in use in western Europe for centuries, it was only in the middle of the seventeenth century—and then for purposes of alchemy, not heating—that the effect of flues on combustion was first scientifically described. In 1713 Nicolas Gauger had defined the problem in relation to domestic heating with *La méchanique du feu, ou l'art d'en augmenter les effets, & d'en diminuer la dépense. Contenant le traité de nouvelles cheminées qui échauffent plus que les cheminées ordinaires, & qui ne sont point sujettes à fumer* (The mechanics of fire, or how to increase its effects and decrease its expenses: showing the design of a new kind of fireplace that heats more than ordinary ones without being smoky). When he published *La méchanique du feu* Gauger was a lawyer in his early thirties, serving the Parlement de Paris and working as a royal censor. He typified the *parlementaires* (nobles in provincial courts), who composed the most coherent French group supporting the experimental philosophy, and

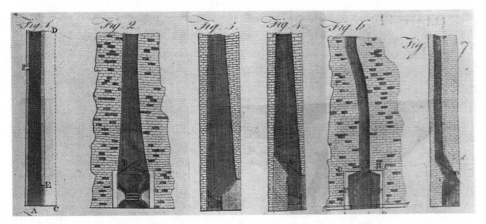

Figure 6.1. A comparison of chimney designs. James Anderson, *A Practical Treatise on Chimneys* (Edinburgh: T. Cadell, 1776), facing 130. Courtesy of the Winterthur Library, Printed Book and Periodical Collection, Winterthur, Delaware.

himself gave public demonstrations in physics and chemistry. His French education inevitably provided a Cartesian training, but his interests in the refraction of light led him to use Newtonian theories as well. He devoted his experimental efforts to the development of thermometers and barometers for atmospheric measurements and published his findings in 1710, shortly before *La méchanique du feu.*[8]

Gauger's scientific concerns with theory and experiment directly affected his technical work on smoky chimneys. As his title indicated, Gauger appropriated the mechanistic theory of light and applied it to heat: "the rays of heat" were "particles of the fuel which are darted from the fire." Once emitted, the rays of heat "follow the same laws as the rays of light." When they struck solid objects "their angle of incidence [was] equal to that of reflection." No sooner had Gauger proposed this mechanical account for the movement of heat, however, than he added a qualitative corollary from "experience," "that all little Bodies, heated, endeavour to go upwards": "A ray of heat then goes on by a compound motion made up of its impulse, according to the direction which it receives from the fire, and its constant tendency upwards." The heat of a fire came from the "motion of its parts," but in "common chimneys" "few direct rays, and fewer reflected ones" reached the occupants of a room to warm them. Gauger remedied this deficiency by applying some simple reflective geometry. Rather than rely on the random trajectories of a fire's rays for comfortable heat, Gauger designed a metal stove with parabolically shaped vertical surfaces at the back to direct heat rays toward the living space (Figure 6.2).[9]

Despite his allegiance to the mechanical theory of heat, Gauger applied most of his ingenuity to the delivery of comfortable heat by "transpiration" rather than by "direct or reflected rays." Gauger's fireplace brought air from outdoors (via *D*) directly into the airbox of the stove (via *y*), to be warmed without being first mixed with room air. This air from outside rose in temperature as it passed through baffles (*G, H, I*) in an airbox behind the hearth itself and then entered the room (via cylindrical register, *upper left*) to displace cold air. As it cooled in contact with colder air, this air, previously not directly exposed to the fire, returned to feed combustion and then passed up the chimney, to be replaced by newly warmed air from outside. Gauger described an experiment to measure the rate at which this process took place: "If a piece of paper P hangs from the ceiling by a thread, over against the hole R, thro' which the warm air comes into the room, that air will drive the paper before it as it comes into the Room: now if the paper be driven two foot in the fourth part of a second, the hole being six inches square, then will more than two square feet of air come into the room, in one second."[10] An extrapolation of this rate in relation to the volume of a room indicated how frequently the draft of the fireplace changed the air of a room.

Scientific theory and measurement provided the most explicit recommendations of Gauger's fireplace. He promised precise control over environmental insults to domestic life. His fireplace provided an alternative to the traditional trade-offs of drafts and smoke: "every crack or passage in a door or window, and every little cranny may be stopped up close without fear of the room smoking; whereas, when chimneys are built the common way, sometimes the external air must be let in at the door or window to keep the chimney from smoking." A valve at the warm air outlet allowed precise mixing of heated and fresh air in order to adjust the room's temperature in relation to the fire's need for draft air.[11]

Gauger discussed comfort primarily in relation to health. He sought to reverse a popular apprehension that "warm air is unwholsome," by showing that cold, not hot, air was injurious. Here Gauger's residual Cartesianism came through, as he considered heat and cold to be particles of different shapes and velocities. Only "very hot air" was unhealthy, and then because "its heat proceeds from a mixture of heterogeneous bodies, as parts of the

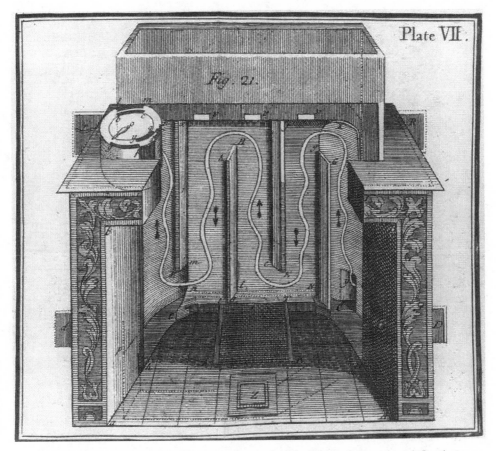

Figure 6.2. Cutaway section of Nicolas Gauger's stove. Outside air enters the stove through *D* and then travels either through *C* to the room's air by way of a warming airbox or through *Z* to combustion in the fireplace. [Nicolas Gauger], *Fires Improv'd* (London: J. Senex, 1715), pl. 7. Courtesy of the Winterthur Library, Printed Book and Periodical Collection, Winterthur, Delaware.

fuel from a very great fire, and as it is found in air heated by stoves." The "particles" of cold air were "so rigid, that the motion which the heat of our bodies can give them, makes 'em strike so forcibly, as in some measure to break the continuity of our parts, by tearing our fibres, and especially damaging our lungs (into which the air rushes continually) and so causing several distempers." Gauger also refuted the popular belief that "going out of a warm room into the cold air would make one apt to catch cold." The association of large fires with liability to colds arose, not from the warmth of the room one left, but from the disparities of heat and cold in the room itself, "when one part of the body is cold, whilst another is almost burned." Because Gauger's fireplace took the air to be heated entirely from external sources, it "regularly communicated" its heat to "the whole body [where] it is much longer retained." He testified that he had not had a cold in ten years of using his new fireplace.[12]

John Theophilus Desaguliers, who translated Gauger's work into English, was ideally situated to bridge French and English efforts in the practical application of Newton's physics. Desaguliers was a Huguenot, born in La Rochelle in 1683, whose parents fled immediately with him to England. He grew up in London and attended Christ Church, Oxford. In 1712 he began a career of lecturing in experimental philosophy by replacing James Keill at Hart Hall, Oxford. The next year, on Newton's recommendation, the Royal Society invited him to demonstrate some of Newton's experiments on heat. Soon a Fellow, he became the Society's technical expert on experiments, winning the Copley Medal for experimental innovation three times and publishing more than fifty papers in the *Philosophical Transactions*. He made the experimental demonstration the primary scientific activity by which to educate the learned public in Newtonian mechanics. Throughout his career he retained the interest in applied science that was marked initially by his 1715 translation of Gauger and later by his long-awaited two-volume *Course of Experimental Philosophy* (1733, 1744), which included discussions of such technical topics as waterwheels and railroads in addition to the conventional syllabus of mechanics.[13]

Desaguliers had a direct scientific influence on Benjamin Franklin, whose interest in smoky chimneys represented the epitome of Enlightenment concern with the subject. In the early 1740s Franklin commenced what would be a decade of research establishing his international authority on electricity, the crucial topic in eighteenth-century Newtonian physics. To begin his studies he read Desaguliers's *Course of Experimental Philosophy* and his translation of the Dutch Newtonian, Willem 'sGravesande's *Physices elementa mathematica* (1720). He also read Desaguliers's translation of Gauger's *La méchanique du feu*, with its telling English title, *Fires Improv'd: Being a New Method of Building Chimneys, So as to Prevent their Smoaking*. In his "Account of the New Invented Pennsylvanian Fire-Places" (1744) Franklin declared his indebtedness to Desaguliers for his "instructive writings," and at several points in the pamphlet he cited Desaguliers's findings on ventilation to confirm a technical point.[14]

With the guidance of Desaguliers's *Course of Experimental Philosophy* and

Martin Clare's *The Motion of Fluids* (1735), Franklin addressed the problem of smoky chimneys as an application of the physics of elastic fluids. (Both Desaguliers and Clare had written essays that explicitly considered the remedy for smoky chimneys.) As an elastic fluid, "rarefied by *heat*, and condens'd by *cold*," air "will rise in other Air of greater Density." A fire in a chimney heats air, which then rises, to be replaced as "other Air in the room (flowing towards the Chimney) supplies its place, is rarefied in its turn, and rises likewise." Because smoke is heavier than air and rises only when carried in rarefied air, the heated chimney's continuous need for air sets up an invidious balance: either there must be drafts of "fresh air coming in thro' Doors and Windows, or, if they be shut, thro' every Crevice with Violence," or else "Smoke being no longer driven up must come into the Room."[15]

Franklin acknowledged that many of his readers would still be familiar with "the large open Fire-places used in the Days of our Fathers, and still generally in the Country, and in Kitchens," where people could sit warmly within the fireplace itself. But such fireplaces had a long list of "inconveniencies":

> they are sometimes too hot to abide in, and at other times incommoded with the Smoke. . . . they almost always smoke if the Door be not left open. . . . they require a large Funnel, and a large Funnel carries off a great Quantity of Air, which occasions what is called a strong Draft to the Chimney; without which strong Draft the Smoke would come out of some Part or other of so large an Opening, so that the Door can seldom be shut; and the cold Air so nips the backs and Heels of those that sit before the Fire, that they have no *Comfort*, 'till either Screens or Settles are provided (at a considerable Expence) to keep it off, which both cumber the Room and darken the Fireside.

Most of these "old-fashion'd Chimneys" had been replaced in towns by "newer-fashion'd Fire-places, with low Breasts, and narrow Hearths." These new chimneys kept "Rooms generally free from Smoke, and, the Opening being contracted," allowed the door to be shut. But the open fire still needed draft air from the room, and the air rushed in "at every Crevice so strongly, as to make a continual Whistling or Howling," making it "very *uncomfortable* as well as dangerous to sit against any such Crevice." Women had particular liability to such cold drafts, "as they sit much in the House." They caught

"Colds in the Head, Rheums and Defluctions," illnesses as grievous for their effects on personal appearance as on health itself, because they caused loss of teeth, damage to the eyes, shriveling of the skin, and the general premature "Appearances of Old Age."[16]

Franklin credited Gauger's fireplaces with a technical solution to the trade-off between smoke and draft in the open fireplace, but he judged them too expensive and complicated to enjoy popularity. They also perpetuated the fireplace's traditional inefficiency by allowing the air directly heated by combustion to escape quickly up the chimney and to draw with it room air heated by radiation and convection. Franklin drew on his scientific work in physics to dissociate the fire's elements of smoke, heat, and light. The latter two elements radiated in straight lines, while smoke, as a part of the air, was carried around the house by drafts. To reduce drafts, Franklin designed a stove that cut off the air for ventilation from that for combustion by piping the latter directly to the fireplace from outside the house. Since room air circulated around the iron fireplace, the heat radiated by the fire could warm the room by convection around the metal plates (Figure 6.3). By separating radiant and convective heat this stove eliminated smoke while maximizing warmth. Franklin, hero of the Enlightenment for his control of electricity, proudly claimed control of smoke as well: "Smoke is a very tractable Thing, easily governed and directed when one knows the Principles, and is well informed of the Circumstances. You know I made it *descend* in my Pennsylvania Stove."[17]

Franklin's design separated the fire's heat from the undesirable element of smoke and the unnecessary element of light. He was not particularly interested in using the hearth fire for light, though he resignedly allowed for the atavistic English desire to view the fire's glow and flames. A sliding iron plate at the front of the fireplace provided a direct view of the fire, but its primary function was to regulate the amount of air admitted to the fire from its outside source. By reducing drafts and increasing conductive and convective heat, Franklin's fireplace made an entire room available for domestic activities, "so that People need not croud so close round the Fire, but may sit near the Window and have the Benefit of the Light for Reading, Writing, Needle-Work, etc. They may sit with *Comfort* in any Part of the Room."[18]

John Durno, the promoter of Franklin's design to consumers in England, was confident that "any attempt to make our Rooms more warm and *comfortable*, and that at a much less expence than usual; always free from smoke,

PROFILE of the Chimney and
FIRE-PLACE.

M The Mantle-piece or Breaſt
  of the Chimney.
C The Funnel.
B The falſe Back & Cloſing.
E True Back of the Chimney.
T Top of the Fire-place.
F The Front of it.
A The Place where the Fire is
  made.
D The Air-Box.
K The Hole in the Side-plate,
  thro' which the warm'd Air
  is diſcharg'd out of the Air-
  Box into the Room.
H The Hollow fill'd with freſh
  Air, entring at the Paſſage *I*,
  and aſcending into the Air-
  Box thro' the Air-hole in the
  Bottom-plate near
G The Partition in the Hollow
  to keep the Air and Smoke
  apart.
P The Paſſage under the falſe
  Back and Part of the Hearth
  for the Smoke.
↟↟↟↟↟↟ The Courſe of
  the Smoke.

The

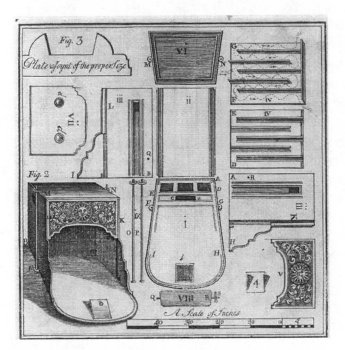

Figure 6.3.
Profile and section of
Benjamin Franklin's
Pennsylvania fire-
place. The smoke
descends behind the
ventilator, *D*, before
rising in the flue. *An
Account of the New
Invented Pennsylvanian
Fire-Places* (Philadel-
phia, 1744). Courtesy
of the Beinecke Rare
Book and Manuscript
Library, Yale
University.

and equally chearful as with the common fires; will meet with the favour of the publick." Just as Gauger, Desaguliers, and Franklin before him had done, Durno provided his readers an elementary physics lesson on the "properties of air and fire" to show that the elasticity of air made hot air rise. This phenomenon imposed the main technical problem in the design of stoves: how to conserve the "upright heat, which is at least three-fourths of what proceeds from the fire," but which "is almost wholly lost . . . in all the open fireplaces." Durno flattered his readers' empiricism by inviting them to test his claims "by trial and experience" with a demonstration model at his house. There they would find "that the warmth is diffused, more regularly and uniformly, over the whole room, than it was before." Durno developed his readers' technological literacy by comparing stove types: Gauger's (efficient but expensive), Desaguliers's (ditto), Dutch and German stoves (efficient but made the room stifling), French ceramic stoves (ditto), and stoves used in shops and coffee houses (efficient but noxious from leaky stovepipes). Durno had seen what he thought to be the only example in England of Franklin's Pennsylvania fireplace, and he concluded that it was superior to any of the other types of stoves: "you have a full sight of the fire, nor does it lose any of the upright heat, as in common fire-places. This stove has likewise the advantage of a constant supply of fresh air, coming in warm through a canal." Since the "chimney is so intirely closed up . . . if you sit near the fireplace, there is not the least cold air from the door, window, or any crevice, that can offend you, as in common fire-places; where, at the same time that you are burnt before, you are ready to freeze behind." Durno modified Franklin's design to burn coal, rather than wood, as its primary fuel, and he added an adjustable "register" to the chimney for regulating the intensity of the fire. The stove's effectiveness could be measured by thermometers "placed in the remotest parts of the room"; they provided "occular demonstration" that the stove was warming the room "equally all over." While reducing drafts, Durno's stove aided in the ventilation of rooms, since it still drew the air to be heated directly from outside. This reduction of drafts ensured that "candles, in all sorts of weather, will burn clear; the light will be pleasant, equal, and steady."[19]

As Durno's adoption of Franklin's redesign of Gauger's model shows, transatlantic interest in the technology of stoves ran both ways. In 1770 the royal governor of Virginia, Lord Botetourt, ordered a "Tripel Tier Patent Warming Machine" for the Virginia House of Burgesses. It would complement stoves he had already installed in the ballroom and supper room at the Governor's Palace, in a none-too-subtle but entirely effective effort to encourage associations between royal benevolence and fashionable taste (Figure 6.4). This stove was the top-of-the-line model among the designs of Abraham Buzaglo, a Moroccan Jew who immigrated to England in 1762 and devoted the rest of his life to improvements in heating and to cures of the gout. As outsiders, Franklin and Buzaglo (and soon Count Rumford) had some intellectual leverage in trying to reform English prejudices regarding comfortable warmth. Buzaglo advertised his stoves as "surpass[ing] in Utility, Beauty and Goodness anything hitherto Invented in all Europe." He claimed they "cast an equal & agreeable Heat to any Part of the Room, and are not attended by any Stench"; warmed "equally the whole Body, without scorching the Face or Legs"; and allowed "a bright Fire to be seen at Pleasure." Just as Franklin had, Buzaglo combined his recommendation of new standards of comfort with promises of improvements in health: his stoves were part of his cure for gout and they "preserve[d] Ladies Complexions and Eye sight."[20]

After corresponding for decades with other scientists on the subject of smoky chimneys, Franklin summarized his ideas in the *Transactions* of the American Philosophical Society, and they eventually replaced Anderson's essay on smoke in the *Encyclopaedia Britannica*. He lamented that the "Doctrine of Chimneys" remained poorly understood, "mistakes respecting them being attended with constant inconvenience," from irritated eyes and damaged furniture. Many still thought "that Smoke is in its Nature and of itself specifically lighter than Air. . . . Others think there is a Power in Chimneys to *draw* up the Smoke, and that there are different forms of Chimneys, which afford more or less of this Power." To correct these errors Franklin described several simple experiments to show that smoke was heavier than air and that it was "carried upwards only when attach'd to, or acted upon, by Air that is heated, and thereby rarefied and rendered specifically lighter than the Air in its Neighbourhood": "Having lit a pipe of tobacco, plunge the stem to the bottom of a decanter half fill'd with cold water; then putting a rag over the bowl, blow thro' it and make the smoke ascend in the stem of the pipe, from the end of which it will rise in bubbles thro' the water; and, being thus cool'd, will not afterwards rise to go out thro' the neck of the decanter, but remain spreading itself and resting on the surface of the water." The lack of understanding of "these first principles of chimneys" allowed people to refer

Figure 6.4. Buzaglo stove in the Governor's Palace, Williamsburg, Virginia. Botetourt's patronage demonstrated how English people used stoves much more readily for public than domestic spaces. Courtesy of Colonial Williamsburg Foundation.

to chimneys' *drawing*, "when in fact it is the superior Weight of the surrounding Atmosphere that *presses* to enter the Funnel below, and so *drives up* before it the Smoke and warm Air it meets with in its Passage." If atmospheric pressure determined whether air, and the smoke it carried, rose or fell in a chimney, then a room's own air could not supply the fire without constant drafts from outside. In a chilling analogy readily familiar to his scientific readership, Franklin compared this experience to living in an air pump: if a fire required the replacement of air in a room, "it will appear absolutely impossible that this Operation should go on if the tight Room is kept shut; for, were there any Force capable of drawing constantly so much Air out of it, it must soon be exhausted like the Receiver of an Air pump, and no Animal could live in it." When there was an open fireplace in a well-appointed house with tight-fitting wainscoting, doors, and sashes, the only way to avoid a smoky chimney was to open the door to equalize the pressure—thereby compromising the reason to have the fire in the first place.[21] Franklin referred his readers to Gauger for principles of designs that avoided such invidious choices between heat and smoke. Every room should have separate and precisely regulated external supplies of air for ventilation and for combustion respectively.

At the end of the century Benjamin Thompson, Count Rumford, brought the problem of smoky chimneys back very nearly to square one, with the design of what became the standard nineteenth-century English source of domestic heating—a small open fireplace. No participant in the Enlightenment's efforts to improve domestic heating had wider experience with the possibilities. He grew up on a farm in New Hampshire; a Loyalist, he moved to London during the American War of Independence and began an administrative and military career; during the war he became attached to the army of the Bavarian Elector, which he eventually headed as an imperial count. Thus, he lived with the large chimneys of traditional rural society, with the elegant chimneypieces of London's cosmopolitan elite, and with the stoves of Central Europe. Though most famous as a scientist for his refutation of the caloric (fluid) theory of heat, he worked continuously on practical applications of the physics of heat: standards for the quality of gunpowder, standards for luminosity (candlepower), cold-weather clothing for soldiers, and nutrition for large dependent populations (soldiers and the urban poor). His work on feeding large populations applied physics to the invention or sponsorship of promising appliances for cooking, such as the kitchen range with fitted pots, the double boiler, the pressure cooker, and an enclosed convection roaster.[22]

But with respect to domestic heating, Rumford proposed only minor modifications to the prevailing designs of English fireplaces. In order to eliminate smoke while minimizing the loss of heated room air up the chimney, he advocated a shallow hearth with widely beveled sides and a narrow throat to the flue (see Figure 6.5). The shallow hearth and narrow flue throat would limit the quantity of warm air passing up the flue to that actually exposed to combustion in the fire. The obliquely beveled sides would reflect heat into the room. A smoke chamber above the hearth would contain smoke until it could rise up the flue, and a damper would regulate the draft necessary to carry off the smoke. The damper was the only innovation. Rumford gave up entirely on using convective heat for domestic heating, finding that it "combined with the smoke, vapour, and heated air." He also knew he could not persuade English people to use stoves, which they felt made for stifling rooms. He remodeled chimney fireplaces only to make use of radiant heat, even though he calculated it to be less than one-third the heat available from convection.[23] Rumford's fireplace may have symbolized warmth and efficiency, but its deference to traditional expectations of an open fireplace compromised both supposed advantages.

What had at the start of the century been identified as a problem in domestic comfort—that the open fireplace encouraged the escape of the very air it warmed—had by the end of the century become a crucial reason to retain the design. English people thought that domestic space needed fresh air, lots of it, and preferably on the cold side. Otherwise they would be subjected to "a confined atmosphere of suffocating air, loaded with the perspiration of their own bodies, very injurious to the constitution." Although a warm, smoke-free, and draft-free living space became a technical feasibility with the introduction of stoves, English experts began to back off from recommending them: "Stoves do not promote a discharge of air from rooms, which yet is every moment more and more replete with vapours dispersed from burning candles, the breath and perspiration of the company, and occasionally from other sources; whence the air inspired becomes noxious. Fresh air cannot be duly circulated where stoves are used; nor can health be maintained where impure air is confined." Nor was it generally acceptable to the English to introduce combustion air from a source external to the room being heated, as proposed by Gauger and Franklin: "it stops the current, and keeps

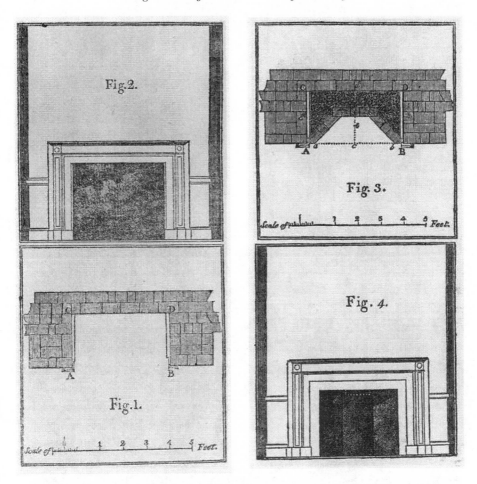

Figure 6.5. *Left* (Figs. 1 and 2), a fireplace of "the common construction," and *right* (Figs. 3 and 4), one with Rumford's "improvement." "Of Chimney Fireplaces" (London, 1796). Courtesy of the Winterthur Library, Printed Book and Periodical Collection, Winterthur, Delaware.

the air in the room in a state of stagnation, and thus prevents a free circulation of air in the room." Instead much ingenuity went into *designing* drafts into rooms, by strategically locating holes through the walls, since windows and doors had become relatively tight-fitting. "Cold air would force in at the external aperture, ascend into the room, and gradually mix with the heated air, in an imperceptible manner, dispersing itself through the room to the fire, carrying off the foul stagnated air. . . . the company will enjoy sweet, pure, and fresh air. . . . On this account, nothing is more desirable than open fire-places; they perform the part of a perpetual ventilator."[24] The contradictory role of open fires' introducing fresh air into a room as well as heating it needed to be maintained. Chilly drafty rooms were good for you.

Lighting the Enlightenment

Franklin's iron fireplace would make domestic life freer of elemental constraints by reducing the hearth's traditional association of heat and light. It made artificial illumination more available by enhancing the use of glass windows to illuminate whole rooms, though nightfall would still cut short activities requiring sharp vision. Since stoves provided draft-free warmth throughout a room, members of a household would be freer to spend time together out of choice rather than physical necessity for the fire's heat and light, while at the same time being able to pursue their individual activities.

Franklin was particularly attentive to the relationship, developing in Pennsylvania and throughout the Anglo-American world, between genteel domestic culture and improved artificial illumination. He grew up in an environment of dissatisfaction with traditional artificial illumination. His father ran a tallow chandlery, and Benjamin worked there as a boy. Neither of them liked the trade: his father had taken it up only because he could not find sufficient employment in his trade as a cloth dyer. When Franklin's brother John left for Rhode Island to take up their father's adopted trade, Benjamin had such a strong aversion at the prospect of replacing his brother in the shop that he wanted to run away to sea. On the other hand, his mother was a Folger, from Nantucket, the center of production for the new illuminants, whale oil and spermaceti wax. Franklin used spermaceti candles in his experiments on light and heat and applied the results to the invention of his iron fireplace.[25]

Franklin's sentiments about the intellectual respectability of improving everyday comforts applied particularly to lighting. By the third quarter of the eighteenth century there was a great deal of learned attention to the improvement of the fuels, appliances, and distribution of artificial illumination. In the seventeenth century there had been experiments for the Royal Society simply to show that coal gas would burn, but from the 1760s on, such efforts were specifically directed at producing artificial illumination. The physics of the flame had been studied in the seventeenth century, but flame as a source of illumination was a scientific topic of the second half of eighteenth century. Joseph Priestley renewed study of the flame itself, and under his influence Lavoisier made the study of combustion inseparable from the study of illumination. Rumford carefully measured the deterioration in the output of light from an unattended tallow candle: in just ten minutes it lost three-fifths of its brightness, and after twenty minutes it had lost another fifth; in the meanwhile it burned at twice the rate of a wax candle or a properly trimmed tallow candle. These concerns with the technology of lighting developed in response to an increased popular demand for artificial illumination. Gilbert White, in his charming *Natural History of Selburne,* calculated how for three shillings spent on rushes and grease a family could make sixteen hundred rushlights, enough for a year's domestic lighting.[26]

People wanted more light. Interest in the improvement of domestic lighting was especially keen in America. Americans had a near monopoly on the new spermaceti industry, extracting from sperm whales an oil that flowed well in temperate climates and also provided a new candle material, spermaceti wax, which burned cleanly and gave a reliably bright light. (A spermaceti candle would eventually provide the standard for "candlepower.") These fuels' potential to improve illumination was promptly recognized. A 1748 *Boston News Letter* extolled the virtues of the new wax:

> Sperma Ceti candles, exceeding all others for beauty, sweetness of scent when extinguished; duration being more than double tallow candles of equal size; Dimensions of flame, nearly four times more, emitting a soft, easy expanding light, bringing the object close to the sight, rather than causing the eye to trace after them, as all tallow candles do, from a constant dimness which they produce. One of these candles serves the use and purpose of three tallow ones, and upon the whole are much pleasanter and cheaper.

Benjamin Franklin promoted the spermaceti candle for these qualities, and experimented with multiple-wick oil lamps in order to determine the most efficient arrangement for a bright light. Thomas Jefferson, while ambassador to France in the 1780s, also experimented with different oils to determine which gave the most economical light. In an effort to increase Franco-American trade, he sought to convince French authorities of the superiority of whale oil over vegetable oil as an illuminant fuel. Francis Hopkinson, newly appointed editor of the *American Museum,* wrote Jefferson about having "invented this Winter a cheap, convenient and useful Appendage to a common candlestick, which keeps the flame from being flared by the Wind in summer or the fire in Winter, and makes it give a pleasant and steady Light to read or write by."[27]

These efforts to improve the technology of lighting culminated when the Swiss physicist Aimé Argand invented a cylindrical wick for oil lamps, producing a much brighter flame than did candles or lamps with string wicks. François-Pierre Aimé Argand (1750–1803) grew up in a Genevan watchmaker's family. At the University of Geneva he studied science with Henri-Benedict de Sassure and then left for the scientific demimonde in Paris. In the late 1770s he applied to Jacques Necker's ministry of finance for a monopoly on a new process to distill alcohol. At the ministry's urging he established contact with the Académie de Montpelier in order to test his process in the field. In Montpelier the Treasurer of the Etats du Languedoc, a member of the Académie there, became Argand's patron in the distilling industry. The scale of lighting needed for his industrial operations apparently challenged Argand to experiment with designs for more powerful forms of illumination. Argand came to France schooled in the phlogiston theory, but in Paris he became aware of Lavoisier's critique and in the mid-1770s began to develop his own theory of combustion. By 1780 he had applied his theory to developing the defining characteristic of the Argand lamp, a hollow, cylindrical wick that passed air for combustion along both outside and inside of the circular flame. In 1782 he successfully demonstrated a prototype of the lamp to the Assemblé Générale of the Etat du Languedoc, from where word quickly spread of its superior qualities of bright light, cleanliness, and ease of use.[28]

Meanwhile Argand's interests were shifting away from the distilling business as he began to work with the Montgolfier brothers in their design of a hot-air balloon, and in 1783 he accompanied them to Paris for their enormously successful demonstrations. When the Montgolfiers' balloon flights eclipsed fashionable French scientific interest in Argand's lamp, he went to London. There his contacts in the Royal Society secured for him a royal audience at which to demonstrate both the hot-air balloon and his lamp. The demonstrations won him royal support for a patent, and British manufacturing of his lamp began in 1784. While Argand was in England an improved version of his lamp went into production in France, under the direction of a pharmacist, Quinquet, and a distiller to the king, Lange. Lange modified Argand's own improvement, a chimney above the flame, by design-

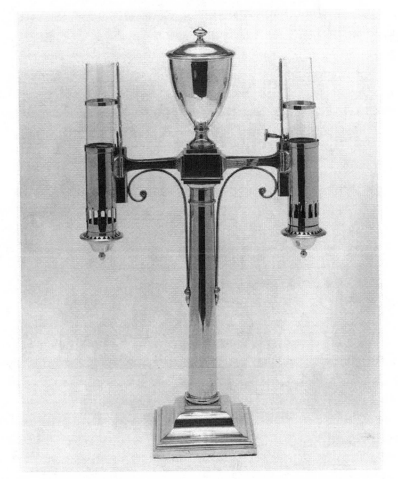

Figure 6.6. Argand lamp (England 1780–1800). Having two light sources on the lamp reduced shadows cast by the oil reservoir. Courtesy of the Winterthur Museum, Winterthur, Delaware.

ing a glass chimney with a neck that further intensified combustion by having air speed up as it passed the top of the flame. (See Figure 6.6.)

As a revolution in lighting, the Argand lamp was more important symbolically than practically, as was the case with the contemporaneous Rumford fireplace. Ownership of the lamps signified technological sophistication; presidents, nobles, and ambassadors were eager to have them and to recommend them to friends. Jefferson sent one to Madison and described its virtues: "There is a new lamp invented here lately which with a very small consumption of oil (of olives) is thought to give a light equal to six or eight candles. The wick is hollow in the middle in the form of a hollow cylinder, and permits the air to pass thro' it. It requires no snuffing. They make shade candlesticks of them at two guineas price, which are excellent for reading and are much used by studious men." Contrary to Jefferson's recommendation, Argand lamps usually illuminated fashionable public spaces such as shops, or reception areas in domestic settings. After hearing about "Patent lamps" that "consume their own smoke—do no injury to the furniture—give more light—and are cheaper than candles," George Washington ordered a dozen for the "Hall, Entries, and Stairs" of his presidential mansion in New York.[29]

Argand lamps were luxury items, expensive to buy and to use. (Washington ordered two fancy ones at three guineas, the rest at one or two guineas.) To provide their bright flame Argand lamps needed a steady and abundant supply of oil from gravity fed or mechanically pressured reservoirs. They put out a brighter light than candles, but candles could provide a given period of illumination much more cheaply. Candles continued to be the usual means of domestic artificial illumination well into the nineteenth century. As a technical breakthrough for popular lighting, the Argand lamp mattered less than subsequent improvements in the materials and manufacturing of candles. Stearine wax, developed by French chemists in the 1820s from fatty acids, provided a material with a melting temperature high enough to fuel a braided wick that burned without leaving a string of ash. The harder, smoother stearine allowed the mechanization of candle molding, and stearine candles were competitive with wax candles in their virtues for illumination. Only in the middle decades of the nineteenth century did oil lamps, using a flat woven wick inside a chimney and burning refined whale, or later paraffin, oil, finally displace the candle in domestic lighting.[30]

The Obsession with Comfort

Ridicule of the philosophes' commitment to improving the technology of daily life was sure proof of heightened interest in the enhancement of comfort. British satiric art, long a rich source of social commentary, developed a new theme in the latter decades of the eighteenth century—discomfort (Figure 6.7). Beginning with prints inspired by the Macaroni phenomenon, as in *Darly's Comic Prints* (1776), satires on dress emphasized the irrationality inher-

Figure 6.7. Fashionable people expressing a variety of discomforts: tight-fitting clothes, slipping wigs, stifling air, and crowded rooms. Thomas Rowlandson, *The Comforts of a Modern Gala. Where Now the Routs Full Myriad Clos the Staircase and the Dore* (London: Thomas Tegg, 1807). Courtesy of the Lewis Walpole Library, Print Collection, Yale University.

ent in the priority of fashion over ease. The outlandish wigs of male Macaronis contrasted with the downright styles of other men, while female Macaronis wore torturing "Bath Stays or the Ladys Steel Shapes" to have an ideal figure. When less constraining clothing became fashionable in the 1790s, it too was satirized. James Gillray, for example, mocked both male and female fashions for informality: in "The Fashionable Mamma—or—the Conveniency of Modern Dress" (1796) an elegant mother nurses her child while wearing a gown without stays, and in "Wigs All the Rage, or a Debate on the Baldness of the Times" (1798) both men and women with shaved heads hold their wigs aloft during a debate on the desirability of baldness.

Satirical prints also played on the practical inconveniences of devices supposed to provide comfort, such as umbrellas, Rumford stoves, prosthetics for gout, hand muffs, and Argand lamps. The foremost British satirical artists, James Gillray and Thomas Rowlandson, and later George Cruickshank, established this genre by publishing many dozens of prints in a variety of series under the generic labels "Miseries" and "Comforts": "Miseries of Human Life," "Miseries Personified," "Miseries of London," "Miseries of Travelling," "Miseries Personal," "Comforts of High Living," "Comforts of a Modern Gala," "Comforts of Bath," "Comfort in the Gout," "Comforts of Matrimony." The prints frequently have elaborate captions carefully explaining how the physical circumstances of the pictured scene represent either misery or a false comfort.

Satire of the new culture of comfort had its sharpest focus in James Beresford's *The Miseries of Human Life; or the Last Groans of Timothy Testy and Samuel Sensitive, with a Few Supplementary Sighs from Mrs. Testy.* Within a year of its initial publication in 1806, there were eleven editions, including four of an expanded two-volume edition. Both John Augustus Atkinson and Thomas Rowlandson illustrated several dozen of the more than three hundred miseries itemized by Testy and Sensitive in a series of categories: miseries of the body, of the table, of the home, of travelling, of social life, of the country, of the town, of watering places, of fashionable life, and of reading and writing.

The book's two men—and the miseries identified were invariably ones supposedly experienced by men—were martyrs to irritations of their exquisite nervous systems (Figure 6.8). Sensitive asks rhetorically, "What, my poor sir, are the senses, but five yawning inlets to hourly and momentary molestations?" Such sensitivity made a mockery of the supposed comforts of home: "What is your house, while you are in it, but a prison filled with nests of little reptiles—of insect-annoyances—which torment you more because they cannot kill you? What are the familiar operations of dressing and undressing, but stinging remembrances of the privileged nakedness of the Savage?" Testy and Sensitive alleviated their miseries by describing them with ironic aphorisms, in response to the malfunctions of the material culture of modern comforts.

Sitting for hours before a smoky chimney, like a Hottentot in a kraal; then, just as your sufferings seem at last to be at an end, puff, puff, whiff, whiff, again far more furious than ever. Add to this a scolding wife.

The machinery of the window-sash rudely and furiously slapping down, without a moment's warning, with the force (if not the effect), of a guillotine.

Figure 6.8. A well-kept house takes precedence over the "warmth and comfort" of the household's head, who, coming downstairs on a winter morning, finds an empty grate, the window open, and the floor being scrubbed. Thomas Rowlandson, *Miseries of Human Life, Getting up Early on a Cold Gloomy Morning* (London: Thomas Tegg, 1807). Courtesy of the Lewis Walpole Library, Print Collection, Yale University.

Just in that period of your walk when you are overtaken by a torrent of rain, and secretly applauding your own caution in having provided yourself with an umbrella, said umbrella is suddenly and furiously reversed by a puff of wind and shredded to ribbons in an instant.

After long reclining, with every limb disposed in some peculiarly luxurious manner, to be suddenly routed from your sofa! Then, endeavouring in vain to reestablish yourself in your former posture, of which you have forgotten the particulars, though you recollect the enjoyments, every new attempt leaving a certain void in your *comfort*, which nothing can supply.[31]

As the book's title indicates, the miseries catalogued were overwhelmingly of apparently masculine, often misogynistic, discomforts, as "During the

endless time that you are kept waiting in a carriage while the ladies are shop-
ping having our impatience soothed by the setting of a saw close at your
ear." The gout embodied this dyspeptically tragic view of masculine life.
Men with gout—women were never so represented—could never know real
comfort, while they were constantly at risk to excruciating misery: "When in
the gout receiving the ruinous salutation of a muscular friend (a sea captain),
who, seizing your hand in the first transports of a sudden meeting, affec-
tionately crumbles your chalky knuckles with the gripe of a grasping-iron,
and then further confirms his regard for you by greeting your tendrest toe
with the stamp of a charger." Only at the book's conclusion did Mrs. Testy
have an opportunity to voice her complaints, which were chiefly about
housekeeping and entertaining. She too was often misogynistic, as when list-
ing as a "misery personal" how "after dinner when the ladies retire with you
from a party of very pleasant men, having to entertain as you can half a
score of empty or formal females."[32]

All of these miseries, and worse, had been available for visual satire for
decades and even centuries without calling for such explicit commiseration.
Discomfort became the object of satire's commentary on social tensions precisely because physical comfort had become such a powerful imperative in
Anglo-American material culture. Unlike most twentieth-century historians
of the Anglo-American consumer revolution, eighteenth-century satirists
recognized the development of the culture of comfort as a historical phenomenon: they did not assume its imperatives to be natural. Satires of the
culture of comfort sharply identified it as a social phenomenon that shaped
a middle class by articulating and distinguishing masculine and feminine
realms on the basis of the genders' respective needs for comfort in the material culture of domesticity. Initially, however, male voices prevailed in articulating the discomforts needing redress.

Thomas Jefferson's design and furnishing of Monticello epitomized the
new obsession with comfort, as he sought to improve the heating, ventilation,
illumination, privacy, and hygiene of conventional architecture. According
to biographer Jack McLaughlin, "his design style was to choose what was
often an impractical but aesthetically satisfying architectural motif, and then
modify it to make the space as comfortable and livable as possible." For
warmth Jefferson installed Count Rumford's newly designed fireplaces and
stoves, and for insulation the north-facing tea room had triple-glazed windows and double sliding glass doors. His alcove bed had a papered screen

that raised and lowered depending on his relative needs for ventilation or privacy. He relished natural illumination: his bedroom had a skylight, the tearoom and parlor had half-octagonal plans in order to maximize their glazing, and triple-sashed windows in the dining room doubled as doors onto the terrace. Elaborate attention went to providing shade and ventilation while maintaining privacy from visitors outside the house: he designed (but may not have installed) hinged blinds between the porticoes so that they could fold up into the ceiling, louvred verandahs at the corners of his most-private library-bedroom suite, and louvred shades both inside and out. Jefferson loved Venetian blinds because they admitted light while providing insulation and privacy; most of the first-floor windows had them.[33]

Jefferson, a man of infinite physical and mental energy, was obsessed with improving the physical efficiency of furniture. He shopped for tables and chairs that used rotating mechanisms to reduce the need to move about a room, and he encouraged the furniture makers at Monticello to improve on these designs. He designed a Windsor armchair with a revolving seat that enabled him to work at more than one desk without getting up. Complementing the chair were writing tables that spun so that he could take maximum advantage of the desktop's area and work on different materials without stacking them on top of each other, and he designed a rotating bookstand that made up to five books instantly readable. Jefferson also had a passion for furniture that could perform more than one function: candlestands whose tops flipped ninety degrees to serve as firescreens when they were not contributing to illumination, a bench with concave ends to fit the rotating Windsor chair so it made a leg rest, a rotating reading chair with candlesticks fitted to both arms. He loved adjustable furniture that he could position exactly for his changing physical needs—such as a candelabrum in which both the height of the two candles and the angle of their reflector could be adjusted.[34]

Jefferson was incapable of self-parody, but some of his recommendations of convenient devices could have struck his correspondents as an unconscious contribution to the satire of comfort. For example, along with his urging to Madison of the virtues of the Argand lamp, he also described a wonderful new means to light lamps and candles, phosphorus matches. The match was a wax taper impregnated with phosphorus at one end and then sealed in a glass tube. Using the match was simple: the tube was warmed in one's mouth, and then broken, which immediately ignited the match: "By having them at your bedside with a candle, the latter may be lighted at any moment of the night without getting out of bed." Such convenience came with a bit of risk: "Great care must be taken in extracting the taper that none of the phosphorous drops on your hand, because it is inextinguishable and will therefore burn to the bone if there be matter enough. It is said that urine will extinguish it." Rowlandson would have relished the opportunity to portray consumers' quandary whether to keep a glass of urine handy on the night table or to rely on fresh supplies in the excitement of the moment.[35]

Jefferson never elaborated on what he meant by "the pursuit of happiness," the second most famous phrase in American culture (after "all men are created equal"); but given his lifelong obsession with the improvement of convenience and comfort, it seems reasonable to infer that he believed their successful pursuit would result in happiness. Indeed, in his own time equality and comfort had become closely linked, if only implicitly, as misery became associated with the abuse of social privilege. Yet, in his concern with comfort, as well as in his assumption of equality, Jefferson was articulating ideals whose attainment would continually recede from realization, as they were redefined with each achievement.

PART THREE

The Landscape of Comfort

PICTURESQUE COMFORT

The Cottage

IN *Sense and Sensibility* the egregious Robert Ferrars expresses his envy for the new cottage life of the Misses Dashwood:

> I am excessively fond of a cottage; there is always so much *comfort*, so much elegance about them. And I protest, if I had any money to spare, I should buy a little land and build one myself within a short distance of London, where I might drive myself down at any time and collect a few friends about me and be happy.

Austen's satire marked a recent fashion for cottages. For Austen *cottage* implicitly referred to a house, the acceptability of which arose from its modesty and physical comfort. Not only was this usage a new meaning for cottages; it employed a new concept in talking about any house, namely comfort.[1]

Before 1750 it was unlikely that a cottage would have been *designed*, much less have *comfort* among its architectural priorities. Historically, *cottage* and *cottager* had been synonymous with poverty and misery. Etymologically, *cottage* referred to a social and legal status (cottars, cottiers), not a building. It signified an insecure tenure. Cottagers were by definition tenants, usually with inadequate holdings in land to support a family; they had to sell their labor or household manufactures in order to have money to buy food and to pay rent. Their dwellings had close associations with the legal definitions of poverty. The Poor Law Amendment Act of 1662, for example, associated cottages with vagabonds, "who endeavour to settle themselves in those parishes where there is the best stock, the largest commons or wastes to build cottages, and the most woods for them to burn and destroy." Gregory King's analysis of England's social structure in 1688 put four hundred thousand families (one quarter of the English population) in the category of "cottagers and paupers." In the middle of the eighteenth century Samuel Johnson still defined a cottage as "a hut; a mean habitation; a cot; a little house. . . . A cottager, in law, is one that lives on the common, without paying rent, and without any land of his own" (Figure 7.1).[2] Over the next few decades, however, architecturally designed cottages became synonymous with comfort, the first house type to have this equivalence.

The association of the cottage with physical comfort originated obliquely from fashions in landscape architecture after 1750. These fashions encouraged exotic and primitivist styles in the incidental architecture of garden buildings, among which were buildings in rustic styles resembling cottages. During the same period, roughly the third quarter of the century, the culture of sensibility made physical comfort an objective problem that tested people's moral and technical enlightenment. This problem focused initially on the philanthropic intention of designing model cottages to meet standards of minimal comfort, standards that such designs would actually come to define. In the 1790s the picturesque aesthetic was used to explain how freedom from formal architectural imperatives gave the cottage an inherent potential for comfortable design. By the end of the century the cottage was the archetypally comfortable house in England.

Architectural Primitivism in Landscape Gardens

Two sets of architectural pattern books illustrate the new association of the cottage with comfort. A succession of pattern books for garden buildings was published largely from the 1750s through the 1780s, and from the 1790s through the 1820s British architectural writers produced dozens of pattern

Figure 7.1. Dilapidated cottage. Traditional cottages became features of genre art in the late eighteenth century, just when architects began to design nominal cottages for propertied families. John Thomas Smith, *Remarks on Rural Scenery* (London: Nathaniel Smith, 1797), pl. 14. Courtesy of the Winterthur Library, Printed Book and Periodical Collection, Winterthur, Delaware.

books with designs for cottages. Publications in the latter series have been studied for their relationship to neoclassical architectural theory, to picturesque aesthetics, to enclosure and agricultural improvement, to paternalistic responses to popular radicalism and insurgency, and of course to the rise of the middle class. But when these studies consider comfort at all, they take for granted its architectural embodiment in the cottage. In fact, architectural pattern books provide crucial evidence for the *invention* of the image of the cottage as a comfortable house: they demonstrate the historical contingency of comfort as a value. Most pattern book authors were below the top rank

of contemporaneous architects; they openly solicited business from a readership they described hopefully as "genteel," people of at least "moderate"
gentry or mercantile fortune who sought rural accommodation for "retreat"
and "retirement." They were gauging a market as much as dictating taste.
These authors did not invent physical comfort; they gave architectural focus
to a concept and a set of values that had developed in the middle decades of
the eighteenth century. Cottages (by which is meant what people in the latter half of the eighteenth century called cottages) were regarded as comfortable only because their designers and owners described them so. Pattern
books, with their orientation toward shaping the taste of genteel consumers
of at least moderate fortune, provide just this sort of normative evidence.[3]

Around the turn of the nineteenth century, for the first time, architectural
publications carried the term *comfort* in their titles, and then only in association with cottages. Humphry Repton, then Britain's leading landscape
architect, explained the new priority among the classical principles of "convenience, duration and beauty." Convenience corresponded closely with
comfort: "in architecture and gardening, the present era furnishes more examples of attention to *comfort* and convenience than are to be found in the
plans of Palladio, Vitruvius, or Le Nôtre, who, in the display of useless symmetry, often forget the requisites of habitation." Earlier in the century *convenient* had meant "commodious" for Palladio's English readers.[4]

This earlier definition of convenience still applied to the initial discussion
of cottages as architecture, which took place only tangentially and rhetorically when analyzing farm architecture. Farmhouses achieved respectability in the middle of the eighteenth century as architects began to capitalize
on landowners' realization that architecture was a crucial part of agricultural "improvement." Landlords intent on improving their farms used well-
designed and carefully constructed buildings to attract the best tenants, and
they further rationalized such fixed capital expenditures as savings in long-
term expenditure. Previous architectural theory had conscientiously neglected
rural architecture. Fifteenth-century Italian architect Leone Battista Alberti
dismissed farm buildings, indeed "anything that is immediately necessary for
any particular purpose," as "not so much the business of the architect, as of
a common workman." Isaac Ware, writing in the 1760s, implicitly acknowledged the previous lack of architectural respect for the design of farmhouses
when he argued that an architect should not consider "common houses" as
beneath his talents: "he must be ready to make the best design for the ser-

vice of the proprietor, whether it be of the meanest cottage, or the most magnificent palace." Early rural architects designed farm buildings rather than cottages; their "convenience" was mainly spatial and nonresidential. Yard plans for barns, stables, hog styes, cow houses, and dairies received at least as much attention as farm*houses*.[5] Some farmyard plans included a one-room "cottage," but such a cottage was usually symmetrical with the stable in the plan and could itself be converted into a stable. With farmhouses, design of accommodations for the human inhabitants was secondary to that for animals.

If not in rural architecture, where did cottages come to be identified with comfort? The answer lies in English landscape architecture, in which architecturally sophisticated buildings could be both nostalgic and radical. There was no well-established learned tradition in garden architecture to be overset. In the first half of the eighteenth century, British landscape architects claimed to have repudiated artificiality, as associated with the formal garden and identified with the straight lines, topiary, and parterres attributed to French and Dutch influences. But the types and number of garden buildings proliferated across the eighteenth-century British landscape. Alexander Pope's paradigmatic garden at Twickenham had, besides its celebrated grotto, a shell temple, three mounts, an obelisk, a "stove" (heated room for plants), and an orangery—all presented as alternatives to artifice. William Kent's landscaping at Stowe, where Horace Walpole found the source of the modern English landscape garden, epitomized the appropriateness of garden buildings in landscape design. William Chambers, designer of Kew's many garden buildings, reported invitingly how Chinese gardens, synonymous with naturalistic irregularity, had innumerable "seats or buildings, adapted to the different purposes of mental or sensual enjoyments." Capability Brown included numerous highly stylized garden buildings in his "natural" landscapes; they seemed natural to Walpole, the first historian of the English landscape garden, because they were not French and because they had garden buildings in the properly English style, Gothic.[6]

During the period of Capability Brown's career, from 1749 when he began to work independently until his death in 1783, pattern books for garden buildings flourished as never before. Such buildings manifested the stylistic avant-garde in the eighteenth century, especially in its neoclassical varieties. Their relatively small size and relative impermanence allowed experimentation on a manageable scale at comparatively low costs, both in money and design failures. Doric, Palladian, Gothic, rustic, and grotesque styles all were revived for garden buildings. Grotesque architecture for "rural amusement" now included an extraordinary variety of types of buildings, to which art history's generic categorization as "temples," "pavilions," and "follies" hardly does justice. A far from exhaustive list of garden structures, taken from title pages alone, would include "garden-seats, banqueting houses, summerhouses, lodges, terminies, piers," "huts, retreats, summer and winter hermitages, terminaries, chinese, gothic, and natural grottos, cascades, rustic seats, baths, mosques, moresque pavilions, grotesque seats, green houses," "a bath, a dog-kennel, pavilions, . . . fishing-houses, sporting-boxes, shooting-lodges, single and double cottages."[7]

The cottage became the object of architectural design as just one type among a plethora of garden buildings. Its deliberate rusticity mirrored that of vernacular cottages, but as a professional design the cottage was not a frequent type of building in landscape architecture until the 1760s. Its predecessor among garden buildings was the yet meaner "hut."

As garden buildings, huts were studies in rusticity, either as hermitages or as neoclassically primitive dwellings. Hermitages made use of elementary materials to experiment with the minimal necessities for comfort—floors "paved with sheep marrow-bones placed upright" but provided with a "couch" and "seats of retirement," walls "lined with wool or other warm substance intermixed with moss" for winter use, seats "composed of large irregular stones, roots of trees," interior lighting by a "gazebo, supported by trunks of trees twined about ivy." Hermitages were huts by definition; in pattern books sometimes an illustrative plate corresponding with the description of a "hermitage" is labeled "primitive hut." The garden buildings identified as huts allowed direct analogy with existing vernacular cottages because they were small and constructed of local materials. One ten-foot-square hut for a garden was "faced with Flints, or other rough Stones, and lined with Billet of Wood and Moss; the Floor to be of Mortar made for that Purpose, and the Roof to be covered with Thatch." The stylized rusticity of huts transferred readily to nominal cottages, so that "shepherds' huts, or cottages" could have facades "formed of rough trunks of trees, and the walls built with the arms of trees. . . . The lining of the door jambs, &c. may be of oak or beech slabs; and the building covered with reed flag, straw, or heath thatch."[8]

Architectural primitivism focused on the design of huts and cottages.

Robert Morris, the foremost architectural theorist in mid-eighteenth-century Britain, epitomized this linkage in *Rural Architecture*. Confronted with "the Gaiety, Magnificence, the rude Gothic, or the Chinese unmeaning Stile" studied by "our modern Architects," Morris urged a return to "Grecian and Roman Purity and Simplicity": "I have chose to copy the harmonious Dictates which Nature and Science teach; preferring Plainness and Utility to Gaiety and Ornament." In his book on rural architecture Morris rehearsed Vitruvius's speculation that the origin of architecture lay in the building of huts to replace caves as dwellings: "The *Science* I am treating on, is made universal through Necessity: It sprung from Distress, and Utility was the view of the Designer. . . . in every Structure, in every Climate, Nature had dictated the Architect to the Disposal of it, for Use and Convenience." According to such primitivist theory, houses were initially made with materials at hand— tree branches, moss, and turf (Figure 7.2). Reminders of such primitive houses could be seen in the "thousands of Mudwall, and Thatched buildings" in England and Wales, where "we see Huts and Cottages built in the same Manner, just as if the Inhabitants had newly started into Being, and were led, by Nature and Necessity, to form a Fabric, for their own preservation, from the Inclemencies of the Season." Such architectural primitivism led to consideration of the minimal necessities for comfort, which became associated with cottages, and a determination that "From the Hut arose the Cottage" as more extensive land was cultivated and people settled in groups. The leaders among such groups supposedly put a new premium on "convenience" in the "disposition of the apartments" so that there would be shelter from the wind, shade, and accessibility to food, fuel, and water.[9]

The primitivist impulse shifted the meaning of convenience toward comfort. The Abbé Laugier's *Essay on Architecture*, published in English translation in 1755, reinforced Morris's association of the primitive hut with questions of minimal comfort and, more importantly, included an illustrated frontispiece providing an iconography for the primitive hut: "The little rustic cabin that I have just described, is the model upon which all the magnificences of architecture have been imagined, it is coming near in the execution of the simplicity of this first model, that we avoid all essential defects, that we lay hold of true perfection." Laugier borrowed his analysis of the origins of architecture from Vitruvius, but he too, like Morris, explained basic architectural needs in terms of comfort as well as structural integrity: the sun was too hot out in the open; caves protected from rain but their air was too

Figure 7.2. Architectural development from primitive huts. William Chambers, *A Treatise on Civil Architecture . . .* (London: J. Haberkorn, 1759), facing 1. Courtesy of the Winterthur Library, Printed Book and Periodical Collection, Winterthur, Delaware.

stifling; so our ancestors built a house of branches, which in turn proved inadequate when there were no walls to shield from heat and cold. Neoclassical primitivism virtually required that experimental and innovative styles be brought to bear on architecture in the countryside. The use of elementary materials for wall surfaces emphasized the lack of classical ornament and moldings generally, while columns of tree trunks supporting overhangs of thatched roofs reminded viewers to consider how Baroque style had distorted classical architecture from the pure forms of the Greeks (Figure 7.3).[10]

Exploring the elementary necessities of comfort in the construction of huts in the garden made sense, for buildings there were by definition for "pleasure and recreation." Such garden and park buildings as lodges, gatehouses, keeper's houses, and summerhouses allowed experimentation with plans and designs that provided full-fledged residential accommodation for dining, entertaining, and sleeping. Many garden buildings incorporated more sophisticated hygiene in relation to water than was likely to be found in permanent dwellings, where specialized space for bathing or water closets was practically unknown. John Plaw designed a "Wood Pile House" to serve as a water closet "intended for a convenience in a park or plantation where the walks or rides are extensive." As so often was the case with garden buildings, rustic ornament gave a counterpoint to the basic comfort of this water closet: "built with the arms and boughs of oak trees, not too large, cut into regular lengths, and bedded in tempered clay, mixed up with straw; the roof is thatched, and the inside, above the lining, is stuck with moss" (Figure 7.4). People interested in the newly fashionable practice of full-immersion bathing were more likely to take a bath in the garden than in the house. Bathing, like water closets, initially had associations with leisure out-of-doors, particularly in gardens. Hermitages in gardens might incorporate both libraries and baths (Figure 7.5). Bathhouses advertised a closeness to elemental nature, but actually they had far more careful designs for the control of air and water temperature than most luxurious houses. Plaw explained how "a circular duck pond, within a clump of beautiful fir trees, gave rise to this idea [for a bath]. . . . it is situated a small distance from the brew-house and reservoir, by which it is supplied with hot and cold water, sufficient to make a tepid bath: there are provisions also for a shower bath occasionally. The dressing room is furnished with a couch and stove." Designs for an orangery might include an *apartement de bains* with a privy as well as provision for both hot and cold baths.[11]

Figure 7.3. The garlands, log colonnade, and thatch roofing identify this plan for Strawberry Hill as that of a cottage. Robert Adam, *Front of a Cottage for the Honorable Horace Walpole* (1768). Courtesy of the Lewis Walpole Library, Print Collection, Yale University.

Figure 7.4. Wood pile house for water closet. John Plaw, *Ferme Ornée; or, Rural Improvements* . . . (London: I. & J. Taylor, 1795), pl. 3. Courtesy of the Winterthur Library, Printed Book and Periodical Collection, Winterthur, Delaware.

Since landscape garden architecture was deliberately unconventional, it suited the development and application of the new value of comfort. Dairies, in particular, exquisitely combined fashionable naturalness with careful control over environmental insults to human experience. On farms, dairies were the province of women and were separated from the rest of the farmyard to avoid contamination, so they adapted well to placement in a garden or park as a highly decorated leisure space, where their premium on cleanliness and temperature control presented new standards for comfort. Genteel women designed and supervised dairies that integrated function with ornament. Extensive tinted glazing provided a diffuse bright light by which to gauge the stages of processing. Dairies were tiled for coolness and cleanliness, and the emphasis on clean utensils allowed for lavish display of porcelain and other ceramics. The most desirable porcelain was Chinese, and dairies often had appropriately exotic designs. In the 1760s Josiah Wedgwood developed cream-colored Queen's Ware, which was ideal for dairies, since they often included tea rooms for entertaining. Wedgwood expected that "the consumption [of "Cream-colour Tyles"] will be great for Dairys, Baths, Summer Houses, Temples." Genteel dairies virtually cried out on functional grounds for picturesque handling. Verandahs shielded the interior from glare while complementing the thatched roof in moderating temperature changes outside.[12] With such vernacular elements, plus accommodation for a milkmaid, the designs of dairies elided with those for cottages. (See Figure 7.6.)

The emphasis on aesthetics in late-eighteenth-century landscape design

Figure 7.5. Hermitage with library and bath. William Wrighte, *Grotesque Architecture; or, Rural Amusement* (1767; reprint London: I. & J. Taylor, 1790), pl. 7. Courtesy of the Winterthur Library, Printed Book and Periodical Collection, Winterthur, Delaware.

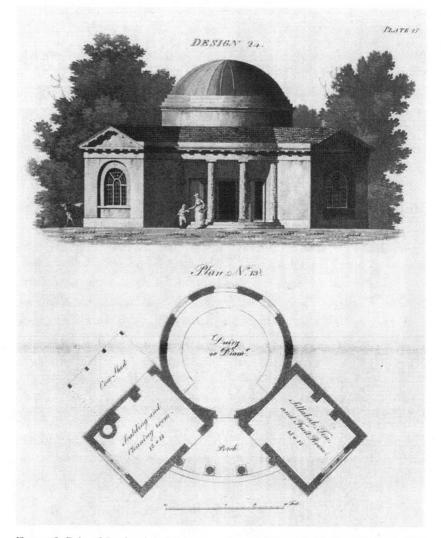

Figure 7.6. Dairy of "cool and rustic appearance." James Malton, *A Collection of Designs for Rural Retreats, as Villas, Principally in the Gothic and Castle Styles of Architecture* (London: J. & T. Carpenter, 1802), pl. 27. Courtesy of the Winterthur Library, Printed Book and Periodical Collection, Winterthur, Delaware.

focused architectural attention on spatial location of the cottage, which had the inherent capacity to make a landscape picturesque. Landscape architect Thomas Whately observed that "the same ground which in the fields is no more than rough, often seems to be romantic, when it is the site of a village; the buildings and other circumstances mark and aggravate the irregularity:

to strengthen this appearance, one cottage may be placed on the edge of a steep, and some winding steps of unhewn stone lead up to the door; another in a hollow, with all its little appurtenances hanging above it." "Though small and familiar," cottages did not need to be "insignificant objects" in "a very spacious field, or sheep-walk." In views across parkland cottages presented "ideas of retirement in the midst of so much open exposure." They added variety to views that might otherwise be monotonous or too familiar: "a small single building diverts the attention at once from the sameness of the extent, which it breaks, but does not divide, and diversifies, without altering its nature."[13]

Sentimental associations with the cottage also developed in the cultural context of landscape design. Oliver Goldsmith's poem, *The Deserted Village* (1770), so often cited as a condemnation of the social injustices of agricultural enclosure, actually dealt with an occasion when villagers were relocated to improve Lord Harcourt's view of the landscape at Nuneham Courtney. The poem related to landscape gardening, not intensive agriculture, and condemned the enclosure (landlords' legal expropriation of the rural poor's customary rights to common lands) of *park*land, not fields.

> Thus fares the land, by luxury betrayed,
> In nature's simplest charms at first arrayed,
> But verging to decline, its splendours rise,
> Its vistas strike, its palaces surprize;
> While scourged by famine from the smiling land,
> The mournful peasant leads his humble band;
> And while he sinks without one arm to save,
> The country blooms—a garden, and a grave.

In "The Removal of the Village at Nuneham," William Whitehead, poet laureate, depicted the cottagers as appreciating Lord Harcourt's benevolence:

> The careful matrons of the plain
> Had left their cots without a sigh,
> Well pleased to shroud their little train
> In happier mansions, warm, & dry.

In the 1770s cottages and their sentimentalized occupants began to prolifer-
ate on the cultural landscape. They figured importantly in genre scenes, as
cottagers displaced livestock, pets, and conversation pieces as privileged figures in English landscape painting.[14] Before 1780 the word *cottage* appeared
in the titles of British publications less than once a year, but between 1780
and 1800 more than one hundred titles included the word, most of them publications in the pastoral tradition.

Sympathetic Humanitarianism in Philanthropic Cottages

This sentimentalization of the cottager developed simultaneously with architectural interest in cottages, first in landscape architecture, then in philanthropic designs, and finally in residential architecture for the propertied.
No British architectural publication had the word *cottage* in its title before
1780; in the next two decades at least seventeen did. The first type of house
in which comfort had explicit priority in design was the model cottage. In
the last quarter of the eighteenth century, humanitarian reform for the first
time gave priority to architectural standards of comfort. While it might be
taken for granted that humanitarian reformers would want to enable the
poor to have comfortable housing, this assumption falsely begs the question
that comfort was an architectural priority.

In the latter decades of the eighteenth century, humanitarian reform had
a new architectural standard—minimal necessities for physical comfort.
Consideration of the architectural adequacy of cottages simultaneously
tested social and aesthetic sensitivity. Humanitarian concern with the physical miseries of poverty took particular responsibility for the design of comfortable cottages. Nathaniel Kent and John Wood established the genre of
the philanthropic model cottage; their designs had a generic quality that
allowed frequent imitations and borrowings (Figure 7.7). Kent's *Hints to
Gentlemen of Landed Property* contained a chapter entitled "Reflections on the
great importance of cottages." Kent was the king's bailiff at Windsor and the
estate surveyor for Thomas William Coke, the preeminent agricultural im-
prover. As a professional estate surveyor he spoke authoritatively on cottagers' physical conditions. Since Wood had designed Bath's Royal Crescent
and New Assembly Rooms, his architectural credentials were unassailable
when he called for the application of architectural expertise to ordinary

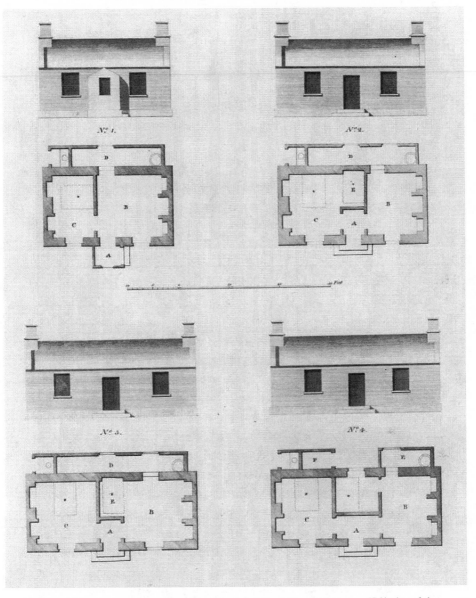

Figure 7.7. Two-room model cottages. John Wood, *A Series of Plans for Cottages or Habitations of the Labourer* . . . (1781; reprint, London: J. Taylor, 1806), pl. 5. Courtesy of the Winterthur Library, Printed Book and Periodical Collection, Winterthur, Delaware.

buildings. He capitalized on the neoclassical context to assert the need for attention to cottages: "no architect had, as yet, thought it worth his while to offer to the publick any well constructed plans for cottages; considering the regular gradation between the plan of the most simple hut and that of the most superb palace; that a palace is nothing more than a cottage improved; and that the plan of the latter is the basis as it were of plans for the former." His book, *A Series of Plans for Cottages or Habitations of the Labourer,* helped put the cottage in the architectural mainstream as a generic design. As a member of the Society Instituted at Bath for the Encouragement of Agriculture, Arts, Manufactures and Commerce, Wood, like Kent, had the breadth of knowledge to link cottage designs with social and economic improvement.[15]

In the last decades of the eighteenth century, public attention focused on cottagers' social and economic plights. Parliamentary acts enclosing commons enabled landlords to consolidate their holdings and to displace smallholders from housing and familiar livelihoods. Agricultural "improvement" supposedly compensated for this displacement by providing increased opportunities for paid labor, but real wages declined. Social criticism accused large tenant farmers, the spearheads of the agricultural revolution, of ignoring accustomed paternalistic roles and deliberately reducing the number of cottagers in order to lower their poor rates. But with the population of England nearly doubling during the eighteenth century, there would have been a housing shortage in any case. Those involved in formulating public policy affecting the rural poor debated whether the circumstances of the poor were a social matter, to be addressed through reform of the Poor Law, or whether the market in labor should be allowed to determine their fate. The Speenhamland system used wage supplements as an awkward resolution.

Philanthropists advised enlightened landlords to build model cottages for their own best interest as well as charity. Such designs, which usually included gardens, ovens, and grazing for a cow as resources for subsistence, would keep down a farmer's poor rates and provide labor from healthy, numerous families. With crushing condescension, reformers argued that well-designed cottages harmonized aesthetic, social, and economic priorities:

> As a number of labourers constitutes one of the requisites of grandeur, *comfortable* habitations for its poor dependents ought to be provided. It is not more necessary that these inhabitants should be seen immediately near the palace than that their inhabitants should dine at the same

table, but if their humble dwelling can be made a subordinate part of the general scenery, they will, so far from disgracing it, add to the dignity that wealth can derive from the exercise of benevolence.[16]

The assertion of basic architectural needs for physical comfort was one of the ways humanitarians identified a common humanity across social gulfs. In presenting model cottages as tests in the efficient design of minimal comfort, housing reformers urged magnanimous landlords to consider comfort to be a right: "it is as necessary to provide plain and *comfortable* habitations for the poor as it is to provide *comfortable* and convenient buildings for cattle. . . . we bestow considerable attention upon our stables and kennels, but we are apt to look upon cottages as incumbrances, and clogs to our property."[17]

Cottages had been built before for charitable purposes, but from the mid-1770s onwards their comfortable design took on new social and moral importance. Kent, Wood, and other agricultural reformers interested in housing tested their readers' sensitivity by challenging them in their imaginations to enter

the shattered hovels which half the poor of this kingdom are obliged to put up with . . . those who condescend to visit these miserable tenements, can testify, that neither health or decency can be preserved in them. The weather frequently penetrates all parts of them: which must occasion illness of various kinds, particularly agues; which more frequently visit the children of cottagers than any others, and early shake their constitutions. And it is shocking that a man, his wife, and half a dozen children should be obliged to lie all in one room together; and more so, that the wife should have no more private place to be brought to bed in.

Encounters with miserable housing allowed the "man of feeling" to find a common humanity in the experiences of others: "This would be dealing with the poor as we would wish to be dealt with ourselves, in a similar situation." Such sympathy provided a guide to design: "in order to make myself master the subject, it was necessary for me to feel as the cottager himself. . . . no architect can form a convenient plan, unless he ideally places himself in the situation of the person for whom he designs . . . and for that end to visit him; to enquire after the conveniencies he wanted, and into the inconveniencies he laboured under."[18]

Architectural, philanthropic, and agricultural reform converged on the cottage. The design of comfortable cottages proceeded from an analysis of the architecture of *dis*comfort. Cottages built in "low *dreary* spots," sometimes with floors below grade, were inevitably "*wet and damp.*" If doors opened directly into them from outside, rooms would be "*cold and cheerless.*" The "steepness, straitness and bad situation of the stairs," usually beside the chimney, made houses "*inconvenient* from their want of room."[19]

The supposedly simple needs of cottagers were a measure of virtue as well as a gauge of minimal comforts: "they are bred up in greater simplicity; live more primitive lives, more free from vice and debauchery, than any other set of men of the lower class."

> The wants of man in the lowest stage of society ["laboring poor and inferior tradesmen"] are comparatively few: they are only those of simple nature; and nature, always consistent with herself, affords obvious and simple means of resource. The part acted by the cottager in the great drama of life, though important when viewed collectively, is nevertheless, as to the operations of the individual, scarcely discernible. The first and last time that we see him is in the field or in the highway at hard labour; when he is no longer capable of toil, he retires under the shelter of his cottage, and leaves the world as obscurely as he came into it.

Housing reformers reminded genteel readers that they shared a common humanity with cottagers: "so like the feelings of men in a higher sphere, are those of a poor cottager, that if his habitation be warm, cheerful, and *comfortable,* he will return to it with gladness, and abide in it with pleasure."[20]

Condescension was a humanitarian strategy. The real physical needs of cottagers were so minimal that a little generosity could provide a radical improvement. Investment in comfortable housing would provide those without property with a stake in society:

> these sort of cottages will tend to enhance [the landlord's] property for [the occupants] will be permanently fixed to the soil and having some Interest in their Dwellings and possessing *comforts* superior to those who have not the same advantages will be the last men to risk them by joining occasional Tumults but will on the contrary be the best props a

farmer can lean upon in the case of any such calamity and will be the least likely to become a burden upon the parish.[21]

The design of philanthropic model cottages defined comfortable housing, at least minimally. In 1793 Parliament established the Board of Agriculture and charged it with proposing ways of reducing rural disturbances. In 1797 the board published the results of its national inquiry concerning the best form for a cottage. Many were two-storied, because "upper apartments are more wholesome to sleep in than ground floor," but they seldom had a full two stories in elevation. The basic plan was two rooms, with floor plans generally twelve by sixteen feet. The main, multipurpose downstairs room had a fireplace and measured about twelve by twelve feet. It might be called by any of a variety of names, such as "living room," "dwelling room," or "working room." The room was seldom called "kitchen," although it often had an oven. Also on the ground floor there were usually one or more service rooms, such as a dairy, pantry, or cellar. First-floor plans often identified space for a bed and made provision for shelving and storage as well. The second story might have a fireplace too, but if there were two chambers upstairs, the second would be unheated, since cottages seldom had more than one chimney. Designers, however, favored having two bedrooms and even then worried about the propriety of children of both sexes sleeping in the same room. Southern orientation of the house was recommended for the advantages of natural light. Windows were glazed but with casement rather than sash windows. There was only one window per room, with about ten square feet of glazing, and upstairs chambers sometimes shared a window. Local materials were recommended, as were alternative construction materials—mud walls, pisé, frame, brick. Roofs were thatched, and floors were sometimes earthen. Despite these seemingly picturesque design features, philanthropic designs for cottages did not include landscaping. Indeed John Barrell has argued that most people with a professional interest in agricultural improvement felt ambivalent at best about the picturesque aesthetic. Most illustrations of model cottages presented them in stark views and elevations, or with only minimal suggestions of setting. Yet, at a time when house plans for the wealthy usually failed to include sanitary facilities, plans for cottages often identified privies, albeit outside.[22]

The minimal necessities of comfort stopped short of genteel, bright space, as would have been provided by parlors and cross lighting: "I am far from wishing to see the cottage improved, or augmented so as to make it fine, or expensive. . . . All that is requisite, is a warm *comfortable*, plain room, for the poor inhabitants to eat their morsel in, an oven to bake their bread, a little receptacle for their small beer and provision, and two wholesome lodging apartments, one for the man and his wife, and another for his children." This definition seems entirely reasonable. "Of course" people would want housing of at least the standard of the model cottage. But architectural reformers thought that many propertied families in the countryside also lived indifferently in houses liable to the following description: "*unhealthy* from the lowness and closeness of the rooms; from their facing mostly the north and west; and from the chambers being crowded into the roof, where having nothing to defend them from the weather but the rafters and bare roof without ceiling, they were stifling hot in the summer, and freezing cold in the winter; the triangular shape of the roof rendered them also incommodious; the dormer windows being continually out of repair, and the dormers leaky, added greatly to the dampness, unhealthiness, and decay."[23]

As a public issue, the miserably *un*comfortable cottage of the mass of the rural population was a new historical phenomenon. In the 1780s and 1790s reports on vernacular architecture became a convention in travel literature from all locales in Britain as well as abroad. Arthur Young, the preeminent agricultural reformer in late-eighteenth-century Britain, included the adequacy of peasant housing in his inventory of questions when assessing a region. When touring Catalonia, for example, he noted repeatedly how the houses lacked chimneys and glazed windows. In the valley of Aran he found "abodes of poverty and wretchedness; not one window of glass to be seen in the whole town; scarcely any chimnies, both ground floor and the chambers vomiting the smoke out of the windows." Young was perplexed to explain "a poverty which hurt our feelings," among a people whom he found highly industrious in their use of agricultural resources. He tentatively attributed the disparity to an absentee landholding class that neglected its social responsibilities: "the whole country is thus abandoned to the very lowest classes, and the wealth and intelligence, which might contribute to its improvement diverted into distant and very different channels." In England, however, the apparent comfort of cottages contributed, he thought, to the beauty of the landscape that kept the English landholding classes on the land:

To the taste of a man that is fond of a country in a northern climate, there are few objects more pleasing to the eye, or more refreshing to the imagination, than the natural landscape scenes of a well-cultivated and well-peopled country. These have, in England, features that charm and instruct. Inequalities of country, not too abrupt, woods that present rich masses of shade, rivers that offer the contrast of their silver bosoms, gliding gently through vales of constant verdure, which are neither hurt by their rapidity, nor rendered marshy by their sluggishness; inclosures, which mark the value and the culture of the soil; and scattered habitations of the poor, clean and *comfortable*, mixed with the houses of farmers, in a state of ease and prosperity; and with the seats of gentlemen, who find society and liberal pleasures, without deserting the fields, which give them their support, for the profusion and taste of a capital.[24]

Peasant housing had been miserable for a long time before, but its inadequacy had not previously been regularly reported or studied. Now, in the process of applying to it the standard of comfort, it was being assessed and considered.

The Picturesque Aesthetic in Suburban Housing

British humanitarian concern with model cottages encouraged the potential in landscape architecture for the design of comfortable cottages. The same architects—Repton, Plaw, John Soane, Charles Middleton, James Malton, and John Claudius Loudon—designed model cottages for laboring families as well as picturesque cottages for propertied people. Some of the best known among them were primarily landscape architects. After all, model cottages might not have much ornament themselves, but they enhanced the appearance of the estate: "cottages . . . would be of great use and ornament to a country, and a real credit to every gentleman's residence; as, on the contrary, nothing can reflect greater disgrace upon him, than a shattered, miserable hovel at his gate, unfit for human creatures to inhabit." Richard Payne Knight, archtheorist of the picturesque, criticized the transposition of rustic style from the garden to domestic architecture in the last quarter of the eighteenth century, deftly noting the style's influence: "Rustic lodges to parks, dressed cottages, pastoral seats, gates and gateways, made of unhewn branches and stems of trees, have all necessarily a still stronger character of affectation . . . for to adapt the genuine style of a herdsman's hut or a plough-man's cottage to the dwellings of opulence and luxury, is as utterly impossi-ble, as it is to adapt their language, dress, and manners to the refined usages of polished society." Knight's comment emphasizes how garden buildings ran the architectural liability of being victims of their own stylistic success, and indeed there was a fashionable reaction against the proliferation of tem-ples, rotundas, ruins, and pagodas. But he erred about the adaptability of the cottage to polite taste. Cottages enjoyed stylistic privilege because they were both exotic—for the propertied classes—and authentically English.[25]

Architectural pattern books of the 1790s and early 1800s identified the cottage's irregularity with the newly fashionable picturesque aesthetic. In his *Essay on British Cottage Architecture*, Malton confidently presented a verbal image to guide aesthetic responses to the cottage's physical appearance:

> When mention is made of the kind of dwelling called a Cottage, I figure in my imagination a small house in the country; of odd, irregu-lar form, with various, harmonious colouring, the effect of weather, time, and accident; the whole environed with smiling verdure, having a contented, cheerful, inviting aspect, and the door on the latch, ready to receive the gossipy neighbour, or weary, exhausted traveler. There are many indescribable somethings that must necessarily combine to give a dwelling this distinguishing character. A porch at entrance; irregular breaks in the direction of the walls; one part higher than another; var-ious roofing of different materials, thatch particularly, boldly project-ing; fronts partly built of walls of brick, partly weather boarded, and partly brick-noggin dashed; casement window lights are all conducive, and constitute its features.

(See Figure 7.8.) How could genteel people imagine living in houses of a type previously identified with rural poverty? Ann Bermingham has shown how the picturesque aesthetic eulogized a landscape that was disappearing, pushed out by agricultural development: the aesthetic simulataneously ad-mired a landscape and put it at a safe distance socially and historically. Once aestheticized, architectural irregularity and crude materials could be used as signs that rural necessity had been transcended while its traditional virtues had been maintained. Designedly picturesque cottages for the propertied

Figure 7.8. Cottage designed "agreeably to the principles of the picturesque." James Malton, *An Essay on British Cottage Architecture* (London: Hookham & Carpenter, 1798), pl. 9. Courtesy of the Winterthur Library, Printed Book and Periodical Collection, Winterthur, Delaware.

complemented the generic architecture of cottages intended for laboring households.[26]

The picturesque cottage could take shape fast because of the preceding half-century of rustic architecture in landscape design. By the time Malton published his *Essay on British Cottage Architecture*, he could take for granted that the harmony of (nominal) cottages with the landscape made them a housing option for virtually all social groups: "These [designs] are humbly presented as hints to those Noblemen and Gentlemen of taste, who build retreats for themselves, with desire to have them appear as cottages, or erect habitations for their peasantry or other tenants: And to the Farmer, as a guide in the construction of his dwelling, that it may agree and correspond with the surrounding scenery." Malton criticized the prevailing use of "cottages" as garden buildings, and sought to make domesticity the priority in their design, noting that they could "as well be the habitation of a substantial farmer or affluent gentleman, as the dwelling of the hedger or ditcher. . . . With reference to its decay, or with regard to its moveables, any dwelling may be rendered mean; but where *comfort*, plenty, and hospitality reign; or where cleanliness, content, and smiles appear, meanness must necessarily be excluded."[27]

In comparison with philanthropic model cottages, cottages for families of property had more privacy. They had many more bedrooms and additional types of rooms such as halls, parlors, kitchens, and water closets. A spectrum of leisure spaces—studies, dining rooms, withdrawing rooms, conservatories—provided both psychological and physical comforts to "a family with a small independent fortune, or a retreat occasionally to relax from the bustle of business." Not bound by regularity, the cottage particularly lent itself to convenient designs: "there will always be opportunity of making matters accord to desire by additions to the main dwelling, without injury to the design."[28]

Images of the cottage closely associated comfort and the picturesque. Robert Payne Knight could take for granted that comfortable cottages defined the picturesque landscape:

> We are delighted with neat and *comfortable* cottages, inhabited by a plain and simple, but not rude or vulgar peasantry; placed amidst cultivated, but not ornamented gardens, meads, and pastures, abounding in flocks and herds, refreshed by bubbling springs, and cooled by overhanging shade. Such scenery we call *pastoral;* and, though the impressions, which it makes upon the sense, be pleasing; yet this pleasure is greatly enhanced, to a mind conversant with pastoral poetry, by the association of the ideas excited with those previously formed.[29]

Neoclassical sensibilities encouraged consideration of the "graduation of buildings, from the primitive Hut, to the superb Mansion." This explicit primitivism took an evolutionary perspective on household amenities. The simplest of buildings, the one-room "primitive hut" formed by a circle of limbs propped against one another, lacked windows, a chimney, or a hinged door. The simplest rectangular building was also built of unshaped logs and limbs propped against one another, but it had a door and windows, though only one room and no chimney. The introduction of a chimney and the use of stone or framing for the walls corresponded with the separation of a bedroom from the kitchen. With the further addition of a parlor (with its own chimney) on the ground floor came the use of stairs to reach upstairs chambers. As wealthy households became more complex political and economic institutions, they added more specialized rooms—sculleries, store rooms, sitting rooms, dressing rooms, and halls.[30]

Repton carried this evolutionary perspective on comfort forward from its

neoclassical context: "The present style of living in the country is so different from that of former times, that there are few houses of ancient date
which would be habitable, without great alterations and additions." He lists
the "eating room," library, drawing room, music room, biliard room, con-
servatory, boudoir, wardrobe, and the amenity of "hot and cold baths" and
labels them all "modern appendages unknown in Queen Elizabeth's days.
Under these circumstances, it is difficult to preserve the ancient style of a
mansion without considerable additions." If comfort had a history, then it
could still be changing in contemporary England. If it was changing in England, and comfort was a priority, then, Repton argued, the picturesque style
was peculiarly suited to the design of English dwellings, not just on grounds
of appearance but because of its functional adaptability:

> When we look back a few centuries, and compare the habits of former
> times with those of the present, we shall be apt to wonder at the pre-
> sumption of any person who shall propose to build a house that may
> suit the next generation. Who, in the reign of Queen Elizabeth, would
> have planned a library, a music-room, a billiard-room, or a conserva-
> tory? Yet these are now deemed essential to *comfort* and magnificence:
> perhaps, in future days, new rooms for new purposes will be deemed
> equally necessary. But to a house of perfect symmetry these can never
> be added.[31]

When discussing the cottage, comfort became critical in arguments about
style.

Once the design of cottages had solidly established comfort as a priority
in domestic architecture, excesses in the application of the picturesque aesthetic could be criticized in the name of comfortable design. Repton warned
against translating picturesque poetic images into architectural reality: a
house "whose chimney is choked up with ivy . . . may perhaps yield a residence for squalid misery and want." Just as other arts struck balances
between extremes, "gardening must include the two opposite characters of
native wildness, and artificial *comfort*, each adapted to the genius and character of the place; yet ever mindful that near the residence of man, convenience, and not picturesque effect, must have the preference."[32]

No sooner had convenience and comfort gained priority over pictur-
esqueness in the design of cottages than cottages gained potential for a new

virtue, elegance. Usage of the term *elegance* increased dramatically in the 1790s. Of the 839 books published in eighteenth-century England with that word in their titles, nearly half—402—appeared in the 1790s. (It will be recalled that Robert Ferrars admired cottages for their elegance as well as their comfort.) Johnson defined *elegance* as "beauty rather soothing than striking; beauty without grandeur; the beauty of propriety not of greatness . . . anything that pleases by its nicety . . . pleasing by minuter beauties." It implied neatness rather than extravagance. Particularly as a standard for interior finish and plan, elegance could complement the cottage's exterior rusticity: "Elegance is a term applied to such objects as show a degree of refinement, or smoothness of surface, a delicacy of proportion, when compared with the general appearances of such objects." By the first decade of the nineteenth century assertions of elegant design cautioned against building *only* with a concern for comfort. The "ornamented cottage"—also referred to as the "cabâne ornée" and "cottage orné"—met this test, but still gave priority to comfort:

> a building that owes its origin to the taste of the present day, and though humble in its appearance affords the necessary conveniences for persons of refined manners and habits, and is, perhaps, more calculated than any other description of building for the enjoyment of the true pleasures of domestic life, unincumbered with the forms of state and troublesome appendages. The leading feature of this style of building is to appear in every respect a dwelling calculated for *comfort* and convenience, without minute attention to the rules of art; every part having its uses apparent, and this appearance not in any case sacrificed to regularity.

Ornamented cottages could be elegant if they looked manifestly comfortable, as marked by verandahs and trellises.[33]

By 1800, villas and ornamented cottages were suburban cousins. Many pattern books presented both types of buildings on a continuum of design along the axis of comfort and elegance—from laborer's cottage through ornamented cottages to villas. Villas needed to have an identifiable style but the choices were eclectic. They could be Roman, Greek, Gothic, Italianate, neoclassical, even "cottage," but it was required that "an elegant simplicity reign throughout the whole, and the general forms and construction be such, as plainly demonstrate at the first view, that nothing grand and magnificent is attempted." Cottages were meant to be seen, villas to provide vantage points. Villas had balconies and conservatories; cottages had rustic detail. Cottages were intimate, whether for entertainment or domestic life. Villas provided space for elaborate entertainment, while maintaining opportunities for domestic retreat in a range of rooms implying fine gradations between privacy and interaction with outsiders. A specific plan for a villa would have some, though not necessarily all, of these rooms: vestibule, anteroom, drawing room, parlor, music room, billiard room, dining room, breakfast parlor, library, cabinet, study, and dressing room. Villas necessarily employed entourages of servants but maintained exclusive space for their owners by means of separate passageways for servants about the house. The manifest elegance of villas set them between the rusticity of cottages and "the magnificence and extensive range of the country seats" of nobility and "opulent gentry." Their supposed lack of pretension implied their comfort, which their frequent association with cottages underlined.[34]

The design of cottages had created a single type of house acceptable to a wide range of society, from the worthy poor to people who were wealthy but not landlords. The basis for this acceptability was comfort. Three aspects of eighteenth-century British culture—architectural primitivism, sympathetic humanitarianism, and the picturesque aesthetic—had dealt with comfort in ways that could be explored in the design of cottages. Each movement addressed markedly different architectural contexts—landscape gardens, farms, and suburbs. In landscape gardens comfort gained association with leisure pursued in small groups; on improved farms comfort redressed poverty; and in the suburbs comfort expressed elegant taste. In each of these contexts cottages represented how the realization of comfort tested sensibility as well as technology. The architecturally designed cottage symbolized comfort, as the bungalow and the suburban house would later.[35]

8

HEALTHY COMFORT

The Piazza

DURING THE eighteenth century the porch became a common element in British domestic architecture around the world. Since that time the porch or verandah has been one of the strongest and most evocative images of comfort in North America. The association of the porch with comfort is a particularly apt test of the naturalness of comfort, because the porch's technology and design are simple, and its respective adoptions always seemed in retrospect to have been eminently sensible adaptations to climate. But there was nothing inevitable about the need or lack of need for a porch in a particular climate, since many cultures in hot and humid climates do not have them and some cultures in cold climates do.

Architectural etymology shows the peculiarity of designing an English domestic space with exposure to the elements. English vernacular architecture had several semienclosed structures—the lean-to *linney* in Devon for storing carts, the spinning gallery in the Lake District, the single-sloping *pentice* roof for passage along a wall, and the ubiquitous *shed*—but none of these terms was applied to comparable structures in fashionable architecture. *Porches* were spaces enclosed on all sides to protect an entrance. *Porch* is a Middle English borrowing from the Old French *porche*, which had derived from the Latin *porticus* (portico). The Latin root of *porch* and *portico* is *porta*, meaning "gate," which emphasizes entering the house, not remaining outside. *Porticos* were open, but their provision of covered social space was subsidiary and almost accidental to their monumental function, derived from their association with classical architecture. When late-sixteenth- and early-seventeenth-century English palace architects designed arcaded spaces in Renaissance style, they identified the new feature with such terms as *cloister, gallery, open gallery, terrace, open terrace, lodge,* and the Italian *loggia*. These terms already referred to spaces for leisure walking, and indeed loggias were initially used on garden facades for strolls and banquets (exquisite small meals in intimate settings). In the early seventeenth century, loggias became fashionable as entrance facades also.[1]

The term *piazza* apparently entered generic English usage in connection with the house front arcades that Inigo Jones designed for two sides of Covent Garden in the early 1630s. By the eighteenth century this Italian misnomer was the usual term for a structure that provided partially enclosed domestic space and would later be known as a *porch* or *verandah*. The term originally referred to a public space in Italian towns, where arcaded buildings defined the piazza. The arcades' covered but open spaces, where one could socialize outside while protected from the elements, deeply impressed English travelers of the sixteenth and seventeenth centuries. By association they referred to these arcaded spaces as "piazzas." (Mispronunciation marked the unfamiliarity, so that *piazza* in print when read aloud initially came out as "P-H," which then became one of the variant spellings of *piazza* in vernacular publications such as real estate advertisements.) Meanwhile in seventeenth-century and early-eighteenth-century India, British people were encountering piazzalike features in indigenous domestic architecture. Eighteenth-century British commentators in India used a variety of associations—piazza, shed, portico—to describe the entity, but eventually the term *verandah* entered English. Back in Britain, the term first appeared in an architectural publication when John Plaw published a design for a cottage "with a viranda, in the manner of an Indian bungalow," in his *Sketches for Country Houses, Villas and Rural Dwellings* (1800).[2]

Climate and Comfort in the Carolinas and West Indies

THE CHARLESTON SINGLE HOUSE AS THE EPITOME OF COMFORT

If piazzas were naturally desirable because they alleviated uncomfortable climatic excesses of heat and humidity, then northern Europeans living in the American South should readily have adopted them. In early American architectural history the Charleston "single house," with its "open, airy verandas and verdant gardens," has pride of place for climatic adaptation (Figure 8.1). But this naturalistic explanation depends on a woefully vague chronology. Charleston summers were hot and humid long before piazzas became typical, and Charleston architecture incorporated several new designs before piazzas became frequent. The double-storied pedimented portico of Drayton Hall (c. 1738) was supposedly "well suited to the hot Southern climate," but during the next half-century in South Carolina virtually no other residence (with the possible exception of the Miles Brewton house) shared its most distinctive feature, despite numerous reminders in widely used Palladian design books. South Carolina's public buildings had arcaded gathering spaces, and Charleston streets had covered walkways as well, but neither facility markedly influenced domestic architecture in the city's early decades. Before 1740, houses along the Charleston waterfront had balconies, but other architectural adaptation to a supposedly benign climate seemed largely unnecessary. During the 1740s and 1750s, however, in the face of feverish epidemics, environmental perceptions changed and Charleston now seemed a refuge from the liability to fevers in swampy areas.[3] The city's exposure to cool, dry sea breezes supposedly had hygienic effects, and people of means adopted new designs accordingly.

Concerns for health, not comfort, began to provide the strongest imperatives for architectural adaptations to South Carolina's climate. The writings of George Cheyne and William Buchan in the middle decades of the eighteenth century popularized classical and medieval theories about the need to maintain health by avoiding the *miasma* of air that had lost its elasticity from exposure to excesses of heat, dampness, subterranean minerals, and putrification:

The *Air* is attracted and received into our *Habit*, and mixed with our *Fluids* every Instant of our *Lives;* so that any ill *Quality* in the *Air* so con-

Figure 8.1. Piazzas (added after 1800) on single houses (built c. 1760–90), 90–94 Church Street, Charleston, South Carolina. Courtesy of the South Carolina Historical Society, Charleston.

tinually introduced, must in Time produce *fatal* effects on the animal *OEconomy:* And therefore it will be of the utmost Consequence to every one, to take Care what kind of *Air* it is they sleep and watch, breathe and live in, and are perpetually receiving into the most intimate *Union* with the *Principles* of Life.

By the 1760s the "double house," two rooms deep, typically had a full-story basement above ground level, with impressive stairways providing entrance to the first floor. On the same principle that higher was better when it came to ventilation, the drawing room was on the second floor.[4]

Despite being promoted by some for their healthfulness, through the 1760s piazzas seldom figured as selling features in real estate advertisements in South Carolina newspapers. Houses were regularly recommended for their kitchens, cellars, gardens, orchards, chair houses and stables, for having a fireplace in each room, and for their materials of construction, but only exceptionally for having a piazza. When advertisements did mention piazzas, they did not usually correspond with the two-story piazzas on side-wall courtyards that later characterized single houses. Instead they were on the front and/or back of houses, taverns, plantation dwellings, and vestry houses in the country. By the mid-1770s piazzas had associations with both healthful ventilation and climatic comfort:

> Now most houses are built of brick, three storys high, some of them elegant, and all neat habitations; within they are genteelly furnished, and without exposed as much as possible to the refreshing breezes from the sea. Many of them are indeed encumbered with balconies and piazzas, but these are found convenient and even necessary during the hot season, into which the inhabitants retreat for enjoying the benefit of fresh air, which is commonly occasioned, and always increased, by the flux and reflux of the sea.[5]

Piazzas were not unknown in Charleston before the 1770s, but their very infrequency implies that their appropriateness for the climate was subsidiary to other architectural, social, and cultural priorities.

The piazza did not originally define the single house. Single houses, one room deep, with their gable end on the street, coexisted with double houses, which were the more prestigious design and apparently did not have piazzas before the 1790s. Single houses originally "accommodated commercial and domestic functions," with entrance directly from the street into a shop, and residential spaces upstairs and further back in the lot. Their yards, which a piazza would overlook, gave little apparent priority to amenity, since archaeologists have found them strewn with house and kitchen refuse. Among the one hundred or so references to domestic architecture in Henry Laurens's correspondence in the 1760s, none discusses piazzas. Nowhere in his many detailed reports in 1773 of Charleston's elegant sociability did Josiah Quincy, Jr., record use of piazzas for entertainment or leisure.[6]

A vagueness in the chronology of architectural history has allowed the piazza to become synonymous with the single house, but virtually none of the datable surviving piazzas were built before the late 1780s. Piazzas became frequent in Charleston's domestic architecture in the 1790s, following shortly on the fashion for garden parterres that typically took up over half the area of exiguous town lots. Piazzas now represented a new sensitivity to comfort:

> Everything peculiar to the buildings of this place is formed to moderate the excessive heats; the windows are open, the doors pass through both sides of the houses. Every endeavor is used to refresh the apartments within with fresh air. Large galleries are formed to shelter the upper part of the house from the force of the sun's rays; and only the cooling northeast wind is admitted to blow through the rooms. In Charlestown persons vie with one another, not who shall have the finest, but who the coolest house.

Charleston newspapers now advertised "New Invented Patent Sun-shades," and explained why people might want them: "The utility of this invention has been fully proved, by the universal approbation of every person of science and taste in England. They are peculiarly adapted to repel the rays of the sun, promote ventilation, and at the same time ornament the building." By the 1790s fashion-conscious families throughout the eastern seaboard had adopted piazzas from features of garden architecture.[7]

ADAPTING TO THE "MIASMIC" CARIBBEAN

Because Europeans colonized South Carolina from Barbados and the mainland colony continued to have regular trade with the West Indies, architectural historians have readily attributed the distinctive features of Charleston's domestic architecture to West Indian influences. The West Indies being south of South Carolina, so the inferences seem to run, they must have been even more subject to heat and humidity, and therefore likely to have developed piazzas as functional adaptations to the climate. But how prevalent were piazzas in the seventeenth-century and early-eighteenth-century British West Indian colonies? Well into the eighteenth century people there with the means to build as they pleased were notorious either for architectural eccentricity, building weird imitations of English manors, or else for skimping on their houses in order to give architectural priority to the plantations' productive facilities. Codrington House (1660) on Barbados is reported to have had a gallery and a loggia (as did a contemporaneous oddity, Governor

Berkeley's Greenspring, in Virginia), but those features made it exceptional among other manors built in the seventeenth-century British West Indies. Many housing traditions in coastal tropical Africa had architectural elements similar to verandahs in design and function, but their influence on British colonial architecture was slight. Spanish arcaded and galleried houses survived on Jamaica, but there is no conclusive evidence that they served as examples for further building. Hans Sloane's 1689 observations on architecture in Jamaica are repeatedly and exclusively cited to prove the influence of Spanish architecture on British housing there, but Sloane was actually pointing out an exception, an Englishman, Colonel Barry, who lived in a Spanish house "all galleried round," while observing that in general "the houses built by the English, are, for the most part brick, and after the English manner, which are neither cool nor able to endure the shocks of earthquakes."[8]

British planters in the seventeenth-century Caribbean resisted the innovation of piazzas. Richard Ligon, a gentleman who spent the period 1647–50 in self-imposed royalist exile on Barbados, made the most self-consciously analytical assessment of the housing needs peculiar to British people living in the West Indies. When illness terminated his efforts at sugar planting, he sought to capitalize on his classical education and travels in France and Italy to reform everything on the island, from diet and cuisine to music and architecture. He found planters, servants, and slaves living in similarly stifling accommodation, "rather like stoves than houses." In such a hot climate, he had expected to find houses with "thick walls, high roofs, and deep cellars," but found exactly the opposite, "for the most of them are made of timber, low rooft keeping out the wind, letting in the Sun." To improve the houses' ventilation and dryness, he made such simple recommendations as adding shutters to keep out the rain while allowing ventilation at other times, and siting houses under trees for shade. He urged that houses be built with two perpendicular wings, a higher one to the west in order to provide afternoon shade to the lower east-west oriented wing, which should have the best rooms and be built off the ground to provide ventilation underneath. By 1700, possibly from the influence of the very few planters who took Ligon's advice, vernacular Anglo-Caribbean housing featured elevated floors and rooms (called "shades") with amply shuttered windows at each end. But wealthy colonists still tended to build multistoried buildings whose numerous glazed windows were their most prized features. Thomas Thistlewood's diary as an overseer, the fullest surviving first-hand account of life in eighteenth-century

Jamaica, describes houses that drew on Spanish and African building traditions but did not include piazzalike structures.[9]

As in subtropical South Carolina, considerations of health mattered at
least as much as ones of comfort when eighteenth-century planters built
houses specifically for the tropical British colonies. The heat and dampness
of tropical climates took away the air's "elasticity," which was necessary for
healthy vitality. Medically informed opinion in the West Indies attributed
much of the islands' morbidity to the "malignancy" of the air. This malignancy arose from the sun's heat exciting the "exhalations" "from foul, oozy
shores, the nauseous stagnant water of lagoons, and the fetid mud or soil of
low, swampy grounds." Such air, literally "morbid," induced a "disposition
to putrecency, and rendered those disorders of the frame malignant, which
otherwise, perhaps, the efforts of nature alone, or but slightly assisted, might
have thrown off."[10]

Wariness, not leisure, should be the predisposition when considering the
relation between one's house and the atmosphere. Because people needed
protection from these exhalations, especially at night, they should build their
houses elevated off the damp ground, but opening them to the atmosphere
was contraindicated. Heat per se was less dangerous than fluctuations in
temperature, which encouraged both vaporization and condensation: "A
close, sheltered, and covered place," was "the best preservative against the
mischievous impressions of a putrid fog, [or] a swampy or marshy exhala-
tion." Fresh air was a good thing, but only so long as it was well removed
from malignant exhalations.

> Those Damps, Vapours, and Exhalations, that are drawn up in to the
> higher Regions, and are so rarified by the Heat and Action of the Sun,
> as to become innocent or very weak in the Day-time; are condensed,
> sink low, near the Surface of the Earth, and are perpetually dropping
> down in the Night Season; and consequently must be injurious to those
> tender Persons, that unnaturally watch in that Season; and must neces-
> sarily obstruct the Perspiration, which the Activity of Watching, and
> the motion of Labour promotes. . . . our bodies suck and draw into
> them, the good or bad qualities of the circumambient Air, through the
> mouths of all the perspiratory Ducts of the skin. . . . On the contrary,
> the Heat of the Sun in the Day-time, by its Action on human Bodies,
> the very Light, and free Air, and the Motions of things about us, dis-

turbing the Quiet of the Air, must necessarily disorder the equable course of the perspiration, the Tenour of the secondary Concoctions, and the Tranquillity of the Spirits so necessary to Rest and Quiet.

Medical advice in the West Indies recommended seeking healthful air by moving up to cleared hillsides, where the air was drier and temperatures fluctuated less. Simply opening up the side of the house, regardless of its location, was irresponsible.[11]

During the third quarter of the eighteenth century, however, radically different designs, low-storied houses with piazzas, began to be reported in the British West Indies. In his *History of Jamaica,* based on his experience there as an officeholder in the 1760s, Edward Long reported on piazzas as an English innovation for a crucial leisure space:

> [The Spanish] houses had no piazzas originally: the English made these additions, in order to render them more cool and pleasant. . . . In the piazzas many families may be said to live the greater part of their time; the shade and refreshing breeze inviting them to employ most hours there, that are not devoted to eating, drinking, and sleeping: nor can there be a more agreeable indulgence enjoyed by the master of the house, than to sit in an elbow-chair, with his feet resting against one of the piazza-columns; in this attitude he converses, smoaks his pipe, and quaffs his tea, in all the luxury of indolence.

When Janet Schaw, en route from England with her brother to inspect recently inherited properties in North Carolina, visited Antigua and St. Kitts in the winter of 1774–75, she noted, "every house has a handsome piazza"; she often had an "airy" bedroom that opened onto a "parterre." Gardens marked the stylized comfort of such houses: "You reach the house by a Serpentine walk, on each side grows a hedge of Cape Jasmine. The verdure which appeared here is surprising, and shews that it only required a little care to exclude that heat which ruins everything. The sun was now high, yet it was so cool, that we were able to walk a great way under these trees." Maria Skinner Nugent, wife of the newly arrived governor of Jamaica in 1801, remarked similarly that the "usual" design for a plantation house was one story above a ground floor with a piazza, which she too associated with the surrounding garden and "picturesque" prospects of the countryside. As eminent visitors, Schaw and Nugent were being shown a skewed sample of plantation houses—those in picturesque settings in the islands' hills.[12]

PIAZZAS FOR MILITARY HYGIENE

Adoption of piazzas for West Indian plantation houses has drawn little consideration by architectural historians because it was thought to be a necessary indigenous development. A factor not taken into account by such naturalistic explanations is that British army and navy officers played crucial roles in the introduction of this house design. As permanent military and naval forces became part of the national strategies of France and Great Britain in the eighteenth century, preparedness for war depended critically on the health of troops and sailors. In the eighteenth century, warships were more dangerous to the men aboard them than to the enemy whom they battled, just as troops were more likely to die from life in barracks than on the battlefield. Commanders dealt obsessively with questions bearing on the health of men in their command—particularly questions of cleanliness, diet, and ventilation—and seized on expert opinion in such matters. For example, Stephen Hales, the distinguished physicist, and in-law of Admiral Edward Boscawen, devoted himself to the technical problem of mechanical ventilation aboard ship, and the Royal Navy rapidly adopted his recommendations.

The armed services also contributed more directly to expertise on hygiene. Hales collaborated with the army physician John Pringle, whose *Observations on the Nature and Cure of Hospital and Jayl-Fevers* (1750) and *Observations on the Diseases of the Army, in Camp and Garrison* (1752) analyzed how corrupted air caused illness. Pringle—royal physician and president of the Royal Society—authoritatively identified proper ventilation as the precondition for health: "a corruption of the air, pent up and deprived of its elastic parts by the respiration of a multitude, and more particularly vitiated with the perspirable matter, which, as it is the most volatile part of the humours, is also the most putrescent." Because military hospitals and naval ships, even more so than jails, exposed their occupants to such dangerous air (because of the prevalence of open wounds), the armed services intensely studied the design of hygienic living spaces. In the course of studying morbidity in hospitals, Pringle and other military physicians had come to the surprising conclusion that temporary facilities such as tents and huts, inherently well ventilated because of their improvised construction, had lower rates of fatality than more specialized hospitals or rented dwellings. The design of the Royal Naval Hospital at Plymouth (1765) eventually applied Pringle's findings on a triumphant scale. Its widely spaced, low density pavilions set the European standard for effectively ventilated hospital wards. Piazzas for convalescent airing connected the pavilions.[13]

William Buchan's *Domestic Medicine,* the most widely read British guide to hygiene and medical self-treatment in the eighteenth century, made Pringle's views conventional learning. (He dedicated the work to Pringle, to whom he was related by marriage.) Buchan warned that the lessons learned about the need for greater ventilation in jails, ships, and slums applied to genteel living as well: "The various methods which luxury has invented to make houses close and warm, contribute not a little to render them unwholesome. No house can be wholesome unless the air has a free passage through it. For which reason houses ought daily to be ventilated by opening opposite windows, and admitting a current of fresh air into every room." Such lessons were particularly applicable in the tropics: "Air not only loses its spring, and becomes unwholesome from heat and stagnation, but likewise from moisture. Thus, in low marshy countries, the air is generally bad, as also in countries over run with wood, or any thing that sends forth moist exhalations."[14] Buchan's concern with the prevention of "infection" from stagnant air ("miasma") and putrescence was consistent with classical and medieval medical theory, but he gave it new therapeutic and prophylactic priorities.

Decades earlier piazzas had become a regular feature of military hospitals and quarters in the West Indies. When the Royal Navy built permanent facilities for naval stores and careening yards on Lynche's (later Navy) Island at Port Antonio, Jamaica, in the early 1730s, a structure with a verandah, presumably quarters for officers, crowned the island's hilltop. Shortly thereafter double-storied civilian houses with verandahs appeared, judging from contemporary illustrations.[15]

During the 1740s the Royal Navy adopted a policy of building its own hospitals, in place of the previous practice of contracting out care for ill and injured sailors. The most important of such hospitals was New Greenwich, built across the harbor from Port Royal, Jamaica, at the instigation of Admiral Edward Vernon, hero of the capture of Porto Bello in 1740 and paragon of paternalistic concern for his men's health. (He had instituted the practice of issuing a ration of grog to his men, meeting their thirst with diluted rum in hopes of curtailing off-post consumption.) Of all places that British men

in arms might find their health at immediate risk, the West Indies aroused
the most frequent dread; and Vernon had the largest fleet in the Royal Navy,
fifty-two ships and sixteen thousand men. Vernon appealed to the Navy
Board for funds to build a permanent hospital in order to reduce the morbidity of hospitalized sailors and to prevent the drunkenness and desertion
allowed by lodging them in private facilities. The Navy Board approved the
proposal and sent Vernon a plan for a single-story building, forming a quadrangle more than one hundred yards square, "with a piazza on every side."
In the middle of the quadrangle would be two buildings to house mates and
surgeons, and they would be provided even better ventilation, "with piazzas
on each side of them." Besides the emphasis on piazzas, the Navy Board's
design further anticipated the eventually "typical" plantation with a recommendation that the buildings be two-storied—but only if the ground floor
could be built of stone or brick, since timber decayed too fast in the West
Indies to warrant its use in multistoried buildings.[16]

Officers so unfortunate as to have a land station in the West Indies looked
for ways to maintain the exposure to fresh air they had known above decks
at sea. The Navy Board's design, particularly the recommendation of a
second-story piazza, became the desired standard for barracks and officers'
quarters in the West Indies. By the 1770s military surgeons in the West Indies
knew from Pringle's research what caused the high rates of morbidity and
mortality among troops stationed there—"the low situation of, and confined
air in, the barracks." And they knew how to lessen these conditions: move
the barracks and hospitals from the coastal plains to the hills and build them
with piazzas: "we are the more confirmed in this our opinion, as a company
quartered in an upstair barrack, with a balcony, have neither lost half the
number of the other companies, or at any time had so many sick." Pringle
had found that "great heats were never so much the immediate, as the re-
moter cause of a general sickness, by relaxing the fibres, and disposing the
humours to putrefaction" by air rising from the damp ground. Hence the
need to elevate living areas. By the 1780s the standard design of barracks for
troops in the British West Indies shared a number of characteristics with
what has been identified as the typical plantation houses there: "The main
floor was raised from ground level by a terrace, often supported by rounded
arches, access to which was provided by a double flight of stone steps leading to the verandas which surrounded the whole building and on which so
much leisure-time was spent."[17]

PIAZZAS IN THE OTHER CAROLINA

Mid-eighteenth-century houses in coastal *North* Carolina bore a closer resemblance than Charleston's to the plantation architecture becoming fashionable in the contemporaneous British West Indies. Wilmington's and Brunswick's early piazzas are better documented and studied than those supposed to have existed in Charleston. In the late 1750s Wilmington reportedly had numerous brick houses with "double Piazzas w[hi]ch made a good appera[nce]." Historical record indicates that, as in the West Indies, military officers took the initiative in introducing piazzas to fasionable architecture. A naval commander, newly stationed on the Cape Fear River in 1751 in response to Spanish attacks on Brunswick, soon built the first house there known to have had a piazza. At Russellborough, on the Cape Fear River just above Brunswick, Captain John Russell built brick foundations for the piazza and frame of his house, but he died before finishing the interior. Governor Arthur Dobbs soon accepted Brunswick's offer of the house and moved there from New Bern to recover his health. His successor, William Tryon, lived there after 1765 during construction of his monumental palace in New Bern and reported happily on its most prominent feature: "There is a Piaza Runs Round the House both Stories of ten feet Wide with a Ballustrade of four feet high, which is a great Security for my little girl."[18]

By the 1770s houses in towns on Pamlico Sound and Albemarle Sound as well as in the Cape Fear region had a distinctive design that used piazzas on both the front and the rear of the house, one set facing the water and the other landward. The ability of such houses to moderate climatic effects caught the interest of the naturalist John Bartram when he observed them throughout the low country on his travels in 1765–66: "the inhabitants of both Carolina & Georgia generally buildes piazas on one or more sides of thair houses which is very commodious in these hot climates[.] thay screen of the violent scorching sunshine & draws the breese finely[,] & it must be extream hot indeed if one cant sit or walk very *comfortably* in these when out of employ[.] & much conversation both sitting & walking is held in these." This design apparently combined the fashionable attraction of piazzas as leisure spaces with a vernacular tradition of shedlike structures in domestic architecture. "Shades" and "sheds" at the back and/or front had been integral parts of framed houses in coastal North Carolina since the late seventeenth century. They initially provided enclosed space for sleeping and working, rather than open space for leisure, but the middle of the porch was sometimes left open to provide direct access to the shed rooms. In the mid-eighteenth century such sheds, when left open to the front and sides, became piazzas, and when houses had two stories the piazzas could be double-storied too. Caribbean trade with coastal North Carolina may have served as a vector for architectural influences from the islands to the mainland, but the shedlike features of North Carolina's housing first received recorded notice, in 1734, as "built after the Dutch fashion."[19]

Sociability on the Dutch Stoop

Where did the piazza develop most markedly in early British America? In Dutch settled areas. The stoop as a semipermanent, partially enclosed architectural feature intended for outdoor leisure apparently developed as a part of Dutch-American vernacular architecture. Its design drew on customs and features of Netherlandish residential life, and then innovated from them. From the Middle Ages, town ordinances in the Netherlands had required the owner of a house to pave the area between the house front and the street gutter; in compensation for this responsibility the householder was given the right to use that public space for private leisure, including the placing of seats there. Exercise of this conjoint responsibility and right often resulted in the laying of a raised area of paving, hence *stoep* (step). The *stoep* itself was the paved area, without superstructure, though benches might be built along the house wall and/or at right angles to it. If steps led from the stoop to the door, the stair railing could provide a backrest to a bench at right angles to the doorway. In the seventeenth-century Netherlands, such elevated stoops had associations with wealthy merchants' houses, so there may have been an emulative aspect to their initial fashionability in eighteenth-century North America.[20] The stoop as a small piazza or verandah, providing a roof over fixed seating, developed in Dutch colonial architecture, and as an English word *stoop* has currency only in Canada, South Africa, and the United States. (In present-day Dutch and Flemish small towns, an identifiable space in front of the house is customarily used for leisure, even though it lacks specialized facilities or structures; it is now known as the *trottoir* in the Netherlands but still as the *stoep* in Flanders.)

By the middle of the eighteenth century, houses in the Dutch-settled areas of New York and New Jersey had a variety of structures apparently providing semiprotected space for social purposes. The stoop facilitated the vernacular formalities of an intense out-of-doors sociability in these regions. In his account of travels in North America (1747–51), Swedish scientist Peter Kalm described some houses in New Brunswick, New Jersey, that presented a brick gable-end front to the street: "before each door there was an elevation, to which you ascend by some steps from the street; it resembled a small balcony, and had some benches on both sides, on which the people sat in the evening, to enjoy the fresh air, and to have the pleasure of viewing those who passed by." In Albany, Kalm noted house roofs that extended beyond the walls to provide a stooplike space for leisure: "The street-doors are generally in the middle of the houses; and on both sides are seats, on which, during fair weather, the people spend almost the whole day, especially on those which are in the shadow of the houses. In the evening these seats are covered with people of both sexes; but this is rather troublesome, as those who pass by are obliged to greet every body, unless they will shock the politeness of the inhabitants of this town." Such flared eaves apparently derived from designs to protect the unmortared fabric of rural buildings in the damp, temperate climate of coastal Holland, Flanders and adjacent France. Paradoxically, in the architecture of the middle colonies the extent of the overhang increased as walls themselves became more durable with the use of mortared stone or shingled cladding.[21]

What Kalm took to be architectural adaptation to climate with incidental social advantages actually was inspired first by social considerations. By the middle of the eighteenth century in New Jersey and New York, the stoop had acquired furnishings, and the definition of a leisure space under the eaves could extend beyond the doorway's stoop to include the entire frontage of a house. Just as the benches on the stoop often had a railing behind them, now a railing and/or pillars often marked this extension of domestic space outside the house walls. This space under the flared eaves often had wooden flooring or stone flagging.[22]

These covered spaces caught the intrigued attention of visitors to New York, particularly those with highly developed interests in design, such as artists and engineers. John Singleton Copley, while in New York in 1771 to paint a series of commissioned portraits, wrote his half brother, Henry Pelham, who was supervising extensive renovations to Copley's house near Boston: "Should I not add Wings I shall add a peazer when I return, which

is much practiced here, and is very beautiful and convenient." Pelham asked
Copley to explain, because he had not a clue about "peazers." Copley replied:

> You say you don't know what I mean by a Peaza. I will tell you than. It
> is exactly such a thing as the cover over the pump in your Yard, suppose
> no enclosure for Poultry their, and 3 or 4 Posts added to support the
> front of the Roof, a good floor at bottum, and from post to post a Chi-
> nese enclosure [railing]. These posts are Scantlings of 6 by 4 inches
> Diameter, the Broad side to the front, with only a little moulding round
> the top in a neat plain manner. Some have Collumns but very few, and
> the top is generally Plasterd, but I think if the top was sealed with neat
> plained Boards I should like it as well. These Peazas are so cool in
> Sumer and in Winter break off the storms so much that I think I should
> not be able to like an house without.

After receiving this elaboration, Pelham realized how piazzas would be "very
convenient, as well as pleasant."[23]

Among Copley's portrait subjects in New York was the British military
engineer, John Montresor. Montresor was the son of the chief engineer of
British forces in North America and himself served in North America from
1754 to 1778. Few Europeans in North America had a more professional or
wide-ranging view of architecture. He supervised surveys and military construction projects throughout the British North American colonies from
Pennsylvania northward, but he made his home in New York and married
into a colonial family there. Shortly after his marriage in 1764 he sketched a
design for a "Country House for this Climate," presumably to share with his
new bride. It had a verandah with railings and pillars on the front and sides.
Montresor, in his travels, delivered some of Copley's correspondence to
Henry Pelham, and in it Copley advised his brother to ask Montresor for
authoritative advice on how to design the perplexing piazzas.[24]

In rural New York, stoops and piazzas featured in the most socially prominent as well as more modest households and carried strong associations with
regular sociability. Anne MacVicar Grant extolled these associations in her
*Memoirs of an American Lady: With Sketches of Manners and Scenery in America, as
they Existed Previous to the Revolution.* Born in Scotland in 1755, she lived, between
the ages of three and thirteen, in Albany, the station of her father, a British

army captain. Four decades later and long repatriated to Britain, she published a deeply nostalgic and yearningly picturesque memoir of those years, which she recalled as "a state of society so peculiar, so utterly dissimilar to any other that I have heard or read of, that it exhibits human nature in a new aspect, and is so far an object of rational curiosity as well as a kind of phaenomenon in the history of colonization." Albany, she wrote, was unique for its "tranquillity and *comfort*." During her childhood there she frequently visited the household of Margaretta Schuyler, who was the wife and first cousin of Philip Pieterse Schuyler and from whom she apparently learned a benignly paternalistic view of social relations around Albany. Grant's strongest architectural memory of the Schuylers' mansion was its "large portico at the door, with a few steps leading up to it and floored like a room; it was open at the sides and had seats all round. Above was either a slight wooden roof, painted like an awning, or a covering of lattice-work, over which a transplanted wild vine spread its luxuriant leaves and numerous clusters."[25]

The Schuyler's "portico" was only picturesquely more elaborate than the stoop that Anne MacVicar Grant represented as the crux of life around Albany. The town of Albany was really "a kind of semi-rural establishment," where, unlike the urban norm, there was a tree planted in front of every house in order to provide "the most agreeable shade to the open portico at [the] door, which was surrounded by seats, and ascended by a few steps." On summer evenings families gathered on these stoops "to enjoy the balmy twilight, or serenely clear moonlight." Seated on their stoops "in easy indolence, or social intercourse, clothed in the plainest habits, and with minds as undisguised and artless," they watched their comparably contented cows find their ways home through the main street of town. The stoop provided the social space for this bucolic life:

> These primitive beings were dispersed in porches grouped according to similarity of years and inclinations. At one door young matrons, at another the elders of the people, at a third the youths and maidens, gaily chatting or singing together, while the children played round the trees, or waited by the cows, for the chief ingredient of their frugal supper, which they generally ate sitting on the steps in the open air.[26]

The development of the stoop is fascinating in its own right, but it also has a symptomatic significance for the realization of comfort. About the middle of the eighteenth century outsiders to Dutch-American culture began to notice the stoop and to report favorably on it, using the language of the picturesque aesthetic. By the 1760s and 1770s vernacular designs of the piazza in the middle colonies were inspiring people with a professional eye for design—Copley as an artist, Montresor as an architect, MacVicar Grant as a belletrist—to adapt its features for use elsewhere. In 1778 Montresor returned to England, where between then and 1795 he built "American cottages," with piazzas on three sides. In 1795 John Plaw published this new building design in *Ferme Ornée; or Rural Improvements,* where it represented "the first publication of an [Anglo-]American building in an English or European architectural book" (Figure 8.2). Plaw published the design to show its "extreme singularity" since "the East, West, and South aspects have a piazza around them."[27] Montresor designed the building to house two laborers' households. He did not live there himself: in the perspective of an English gentleman the piazzas appeared too shedlike to be the most prominent feature of a respectable primary residence.

The Anglo-Indian Verandah and the Imperial Picturesque

In 1800 Plaw published a new book of house plans for ornamental cottages, including one "with a Viranda in the manner of an Indian Bungalow." Unlike the piazzas for Montresor's New York Cottage, the verandah of this bungalow surrounded the house. This feature of verandahs also appeared in plans of cottages "calculated for persons of moderate income and for *comfortable* retirement," which came in versions for both single- and double-household occupancy. Plaw capitalized on the picturesque aesthetic to encourage associations between "the real *comforts* of life" and architecture whose exotic rusticity proclaimed its lack of pretension.[28]

The verandah had only recently been added to the British architectural vocabulary, as a result of British imperial expansion to new continents. During the period 1770–1830, as the East India Company extended its domain to the subcontinental interior, adaptation of Bengali hut designs by the company's commanders resulted in the verandahed bungalow's becoming the typical exurban dwelling for the company's officers and civilian administrators. The initial physical bases of the company's operations were the military cantonments, where troops lived in tents and barracks and officers lived in

Figure 8.2. John Plaw's "American cottages." John Plaw, *Ferme Ornée; or Rural Improvements* (London: I. & J. Taylor, 1795), pl. 19. Courtesy of the Winterthur Library, Printed Book and Periodical Collection, Winterthur, Delaware.

temporary buildings constructed by indigenous laborers using traditional materials and according to vernacular housing designs. From this European appropriation of indigenous vernacular architecture resulted the bungalow, with the verandah as its most impressive structural feature. In Bengali vernacular architecture the thatched overhang served primarily to protect the supporting walls of sun-dried brick and mud from exposure to rain, but British officers had the eave extended to provide a multipurpose space for sleeping, washing, eating, and leisure. Though only of semipermanent construction, the bungalow symbolized colonial rule, by its location and layout as well as by its occupants. Its location in a compound empty of other buildings differentiated it from indigenous life, and the open verandah testified to confidence in rule while providing surveillance of the surrounding society. The bungalow was not a building for nabobs: whether in Indian cities or the English countryside, nabobs built mansions.[29]

ANTIPODEAN VERANDAHS

British military rulers, virtually all of whom had served in India and/or the West Indies, also built the first verandahs in Australia. The colony's second lieutenant governor, Major Francis Grose, built one of the earliest, in 1793, as an addition to his predecessor's single-storied residence, which was located in the military district of Sydney, between the parade grounds and the soldiers' barracks. This military residence, which appeared as "a big bungalow, with a wide roof, and verandah posts so closely spaced that they were more like vertical louvres," contrasted sharply with the governor's residence, which had been constructed in 1788 and 1789. The first governor, Admiral Arthur Phillip, had built Government House as "a symmetrical, two-storied, hip-roofed and stuccoed-brick rectangle." Phillip's successor, Admiral John Hunter, subordinated these Palladian features by adding a verandah that crossed the entire front of the building. In 1802, Anna Josepha King, wife of Hunter's successor, Philip Gidley King, the first governor to bring his wife to Australia, had the verandah extended on one side to complement a new drawing room. And by the first decade of the nineteenth century the verandah marked commandants' residences at British settlements elsewhere in Australia, at Norfolk Island and Newcastle. Early New South Wales—virtually "a vast anchored warship with a pressed crew and a few officers' wives secreted aboard"—seems a peculiar locale for innovations in domestic comfort. Military officials, despite their presumable insistence on formal rank, were introducing architectural designs that set aside Georgian considerations of symmetry, vertical hierarchy, and formal precision in order to give apparent priority to climatic considerations. In the 1810s Governor Lachlan Macquarie, who served in India for seventeen years before going to Australia, encouraged architectural adaptation to Australian conditions by commissioning the construction of barracks and hospitals with verandahs. By the 1820s civilian houses in Australia often had verandahs too.[30]

SUBBOREAL VERANDAHS

At the same time that British military officers in Australia—and their wives—were using the verandah to adapt to a new colonial landscape, their comrades in Canada—and their respective spouses—were doing exactly the same thing. In 1780 the governor of Quebec, Sir Frederick Haldimand, an army officer, built the earliest British Canadian house with a verandah, after having been military governor of Trois-Rivières, where he would have encountered the verandahlike *galeries* characteristic of Québecois architecture. He used this verandah to picturesque effect, orienting it toward a view of Mortmorency Falls. When Elizabeth Simcoe, wife of the first lieutenant governor of Upper Canada, visited the wife of Captain Gilbert Tice of the Indian Department at her Niagara Falls home in August 1795, she made a similar connection between verandahlike structures, comfort, and the picturesque potential of the site. She noted how its "peculiarly dry & healthy" situation took advantage of "a shed or gallery before the House & some oak trees close to it, therefore there is always shade & cool air here, when we are suffering from intense heat at Navy Hall" (Figure 8.3). Navy Hall was a collection of buildings on Lake Ontario at the mouth of the Niagara River, where the naval commander and sailors had previously wintered over. The new lieutenant governor expected to make his residence there, but his wife found the buildings uninhabitable and insisted on renovations. On the other side of the river's mouth was the garrison her husband commanded, but she hated staying there, too, because the garrison's "huts" either stifled in the heat or caused colds when it rained, so "the Gov. ordered 3 Marquees to be pitched for us on the Hill above the House which is very dry ground & rises beautifully." Elizabeth Simcoe preferred these tentlike structures for much the same reasons that she found the verandahs at the Tice's residence so pleasant: they "command a beautiful view of the River & the Garrison on the opposite side, which from its being situated on the Point has a fine effect & the poorness of the Building is not remarked at this distance from whence

Figure 8.3. Picturesque Upper Canada. Elizabeth Simcoe, *Mrs. Tyce's near the Falls* (1795). Courtesy of Archives of Ontario, F 47-11-1-0-171 (106d), Toronto.

a fine picture might be made." She responded to this picturesque imperative by sketching many watercolors of the colonial scenery.[31]

In the autumn of 1793, at the end of their first full year in Upper Canada, Elizabeth Simcoe and her husband began to build a rural retreat near York (later renamed Toronto) on land owned by their young son, Francis. They had designed a picturesque cottage with a fondly facetious name: "It is called Castle Frank built on the plan of a Grecian Temple, totally of wood the Logs squared & so grooved together that in case of decay any log may be taken out. The large Pine trees make Pillars for the Porticos which are at each end 16 feet high." Despite the classical association and the monumentality implied by the term "portico," the building's style, construction, and use were those of a deliberately unpretentious bungalow with verandah: "The Porticos here are delightful pleasant & the Room cool from its height and the thickness of the logs of which the House is built." The house was so unfinished that at night she could hear "an Insect [probably a Pine Beetle] which is not to be got rid of, it bores into the Timber, & is heard at night it is like a large maggot." The Simcoes never finished the building. They once had to pitch a tent *inside* to stay dry, but they loved Castle Frank and made a sentimental point of visiting it before their return to England in 1796.[32]

The verandahs so characteristic of the houses of early Upper Canada's military rulers went largely unemulated by Loyalists who moved there from the United States—with the significant exception of those who had migrated from New York, where such structures had a strong place in vernacular architecture. The transplanted elite built mostly in the Georgian styles to which they were accustomed; for the first generation only their military rulers built homes in picturesque styles, with the nearly inevitable verandah.[33]

Professional circumstances inclined military commanders to define comfort as a problem in hygiene. Physical adaptation was therefore a professional necessity for military engineers designing barracks and quarters and for commanders responsible for hospitals. Among their resources for survival in alien climates were tactics they had learned from other cultures: no institutionalized profession except the Church had such a cosmopolitan exposure to different material cultures. Officers' mobility exposed them to diverse cultures, and this allowed them to consider design alternatives to the everyday practices of the environment in which they found themselves.

In two phases—the first from the 1740s to the 1760s in the Mississippi and St. Lawrence valleys and the interior domains of the East India Company (and on a new permanent scale in the West Indies), and the 1780s and 1790s for Australia and Upper Canada—British military and naval officers established themselves as governing presences in a newly expanded empire. Successful rule depended on coming to terms with an alien culture. Governing presence, not military action, was the strategic priority. The officers' own presence, however, was semipermanent at best, lasting only until the inevitable next station. Manors did not suit their ambitions and careers overseas. Military officers, disproportionately among the population, made the earliest and most innovative architectural adaptations to unfamiliar environments precisely because they were *not* going to colonize and stay to replicate the mother country. Adaptability was a professional imperative: they had to survive in order to serve at another station. A worldwide token of that adaptability was the piazza.[34]

From the Pavilion to the Piazza

By the 1760s cosmopolitan British American colonists too were adding piazzas to their residences, and the practice had become architecturally fashionable. Had British military officers in Australia, India, North America, and the West Indies become culture heroes of domestic comfort? Their mobility, professional adaptability, and cultural exposure gave them a role in the *diffusion* of innovative designs, but the actual adoption of design features depended on the architectural authorities who mediated between the diffusion of styles in Britain's commercial empire and a metropolitan taste for exotic architectural ornament and style. These authorities were the interpreters and popularizers of picturesque landscape architecture.

The so-called portico on George Washington's Mount Vernon epitomizes how imperial military culture and picturesque landscape architecture encouraged adoption of the piazza. On his only trip outside mainland North America, Washington visited Barbados, in 1751, to accompany his half-brother Lawrence on a trip for the cure of his respiratory illness. While looking for accommodation George thrilled at being "perfectly ravished by the beautiful prospects which on every side presented to our view the fields of cane, corne, fruit trees, in a delightful green." He rented a hillside villa outside Bridgetown from a fellow British officer, Captain Croftan, commander of James Fort. Although the revolution cut short Washington's direct participation in Britain's imperial military culture, the style of his domestic life corresponded to that of his former comrades in arms. At Mount Vernon, which he had inherited from his brother, a recently retired General Washington used an innovative design for a piazza to put before his compatriots a new self-image. (Serendipitously for this interpretation, Lawrence had named Mount Vernon after Admiral Vernon, his commander in the West Indies.) Immediately after the American War of Independence he recommenced the English-style landscaping he had been working on before the war and renovated a verandahlike portico to provide a setting for his role as retired hero. With typical overstatement of his professed desires for a modest retirement, he had built "a lofty portico, ninety-six feet in length, supported by eight pillars, [which] has a pleasing effect when viewed from the water." This piazza—Washington never referred to it as a portico—ran across the entire east front of the house, with a view that spread down to the Potomac across a garden of struggling ornamental plants and a lawn newly planted in English grass. In contrast to the west side of Mount Vernon, where the new serpentine drive brought visitors to a courtyard enclosed by the facade of the "mansion house" and symmetrically placed outbuildings connected by colonnade, no buildings interrupted the prospect from the piazza.

Out of unfamiliarity with such a structure's purposes in a fine house, his visitors usually called it a portico, but Washington referred to it as a piazza and a "long open Gallery" because he intended it to be a social space, not a token of Palladian style. He used English flagstones to pave the piazza in order to integrate it with the landscape gardening while providing a space for informal leisure and entertainment.[35]

During a visit to Mount Vernon in the summer of 1796, as Washington's third retirement neared, the architect Benjamin Henry Latrobe recorded the success of Washington's design and use of his piazza. Most American paintings and engravings of Mount Vernon in the 1790s naively exaggerated the monumentality of the portico. Latrobe too sketched architectural views of the portico, but he devoted more attention to the prospects *from* the piazza and the intimate groups socializing *on* it (Figure 8.4). The "prospect from the lawn" gave him a topic for conversation with Martha Washington, and the piazza provided a meeting place for her family and its house guests. They gathered there for easy conversation before dinner, and they took tea there. Washington and Latrobe lingered there all evening over coffee discussing the vicissitudes of wheat farming. Latrobe, recently arrived in the United States with formal training as an engineer and architect, and having an aesthetic interest in landscape theory, appreciated that these activities fulfilled the piazza's picturesque and neoclassical intents.[36]

The piazza at Mount Vernon dates from the late 1770s. In the two previous decades devotees of landscape gardening in the Chesapeake region had been exploring the possibilities of adapting piazzalike features of garden pavilions for actual residences. In the late 1750s Washington's neighbor, George Mason, made the connection between piazzas and garden pavilions stylistically explicit by incorporating gothic ogee arches into the piazza on the garden side of Gunston Hall; in the garden itself were probably "matching Chinese Chippendale pavilions." Contemporaneous English handbooks, such as Charles Over's *Ornamental Architecture in the Gothic, Chinese and Modern Taste* recommended an eclectic application of exotic styles to a wide variety of garden structures: seats, umbrellos, grottoes, hermitages, temples—everything but residences. Mason's architect, William Buckland, recently emigrated from England, apparently translated a design for a freestanding pavilion into an attached piazza. At about the same time, fellow Virginian John Tayloe was building Mount Airy with loggias similar to designs for houses and garden pavilions in James Gibbs's *A Book of Architecture, Containing Designs*

Figure 8.4. Sketch of a group for a drawing of Mount Vernon. Benjamin Latrobe Sketchbook, 1796, II:21. Courtesy of the Maryland Historical Society, Baltimore.

of Buildings and Ornaments (1728), and nearby a few years later Landon Carter added a piazza at Sabine Hall.[37]

In the 1760s Thomas Jefferson borrowed Gibbs's designs of garden pavilions for the first two plans of Monticello. One plan depended on Gibbs's design for "a Temple, made for a Person of Quality, and proposed to have been placed in the Center of four Walks; so that a Portico might front each Walk"; the other used a design for a "Menagery . . . having a Room at each end, and two Rooms behind for the person that looks after the Pheasants" (Figure 8.5). In later plans Jefferson incorporated a piazza into his design for the residence's portico, and he intended to build flanking outbuildings with open loggias much like the pavilion spaces of the first two plans. Shortly after construction of the residence began in 1769 Jefferson again turned his architectural energies toward ornamental garden architecture. During the next decade, under the particular influence of Thomas Whately's recently published *Observations on Modern Gardening* (1770), Jefferson designed more than twenty pavilions for Monticello's gardens. Only one was built, but the designs themselves used the whole range of styles for exotic garden archi-

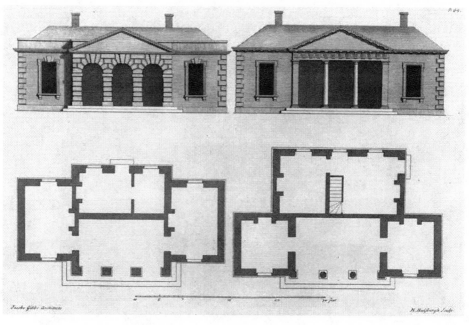

Figure 8.5. A garden pavilion. Jefferson's initial plans for Monticello drew on these designs for a menagery at Harkwood, even though some of the rooms lacked interior communication. James Gibbs, *A Book of Architecture, Containing Designs of Buildings and Ornaments* (London, 1728), pl. 84. Courtesy of the DalTech Library, Dalhousie University.

tecture—gothic, Chinese, neoclassical, rustic hermitages, even picturesque grottoes for a nymphaeum. Such garden pavilions and summerhouses were virtually piazzas without houses attached to them.[38]

The connection between piazzas and the picturesque aesthetic arose from the fashions for two types of buildings in eighteenth-century landscape architecture whose names indicate their manifest *im*practicality—garden pavilions and ornamental cottages. Pavilions were semipermanent structures for taking leisure out-of-doors in order to appreciate picturesque surroundings. Their name derives from ornate medieval tents that had a metaphorical association with butterflies (*papillon*). Most ornamental cottages signified their lack of architectural pretension by featuring a piazzalike structure that associated them with certain types of rustic buildings in landscape architecture, such as hermitages (Figure 8.6).

In early America, garden pavilions and ornamental cottages were initially most frequent on the grounds of the country houses near Philadelphia that became so numerous from the 1740s onwards. Around Baltimore more than

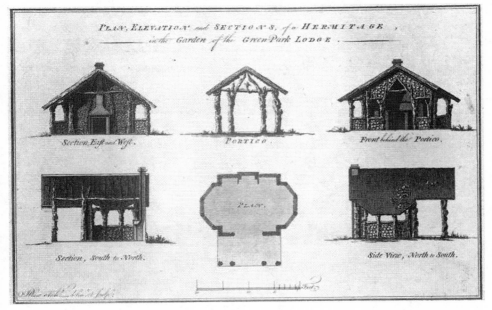

Figure 8.6. The open architecture of a hermitage. Many types of garden pavilions imitated the shedlike details of rustic farm buildings. John Plaw, *Rural Architecture; or Designs, from the Simple Cottage to the Decorated Villa* (London: I. & J. Taylor, 1796), pl. 1. Courtesy of the Winterthur Library, Printed Book and Periodical Collection, Winterthur, Delaware.

seventy pleasure gardens were built in the last quarter of the eighteenth century, featuring a variety of garden structures.[39] Such garden architecture, with its manifestations of "philosophical rural retreat," could profoundly impress visitors from other colonies, as it did Massachusetts's Josiah Quincy, Jr., when he visited Fairhill, John Dickinson's "country seat" near Philadelphia, in 1773:

> This worthy and arch-politician . . . here enjoys *otium cum dignitate* as much as any man. Take into consideration the antique look of his house, his gardens, green-house, bathing-house, grotto, study, fish-pond, fields, meadows, vista, through which is a distant prospect of the Delaware River, his paintings, antiquities, improvements, etc., in short his whole life, and we are apt to think him the happiest of mortals.

Otium cum dignatate, "the relaxing improvement of mind and body," had been an ideal of the Roman senatorial class. Descriptions and evocations of the villa by Pliny the Younger and Horace were full of self-conscious satisfaction with physical circumstance. But by definition these pleasures were alternatives to daily or popular life, and Roman comfort privileged aristocratic and male self-realization, not family happiness. The very fact that the ideal of these comforts had so much latent potency to shape material culture— witness the villa's influence in Renaissance Italy—and yet was relatively *in*significant in British contexts until the middle third of the eighteenth century, indicates that cultural choice rather than naturalistic determinism was at work. In eighteenth-century Britain, as well as in Augustan Rome and Renaissance Italy, comfort was, initially, episodic and recreational. Therefore, much of the experimentation in the culture of comfort occurred in settings of gardens and landscape architecture, places designed to stimulate a special sense of well-being from physical accommodation. The dramatic increase of pleasure gardens in America and the simultaneous building of piazzas on American villas exemplify such experimentation.[40]

The piazza as an element of Anglo-American architecture also arose in response to the picturesque aesthetic. It will be recalled how many of the observers quoted in this chapter, particularly women, associated the piazza with landscape gardening and the prospects it afforded. Why were piazza-like structures making such an impression on people with an eye toward aesthetic discrimination in landscape architecture? By the end of the eighteenth century few Americans had adopted more than various details of "modern" English landscape design, such as serpentine walks, while geometric parterres remained typical. As traditional pleasure gardens became frequent, the design elements of what would have been temples, hermitages, and pavilions in a picturesque English garden became increasingly likely to appear as piazzas on *fermes ornées* (Figure 8.7). Applying ornamental detail to a house was easier than designing an estate's entire domain in accordance with an unfamiliar aesthetic, however enticing its descriptive language. American piazzas initially served the same function as garden pavilions in modish English gardening: they directed the view toward a designed prospect, whether an ornamental garden or a more distant landscape.[41]

The fashionability of the piazza developed from architectural adaptations to the cultural construction of the landscape. Rather than meet "natural" needs for comfort, technological "improvements" like the piazza redefine comfort. (In recent years, air conditioning has had a similar effect.) Part of that redefinition in the eighteenth century involved notions of entitlements

Figure 8.7. Villa in the style of a *ferme ornée*. Anna Maria Thornton, *West Lawn of Monticello* (1802). Courtesy of the Museum of Early Southern Decorative Arts, Winston-Salem, North Carolina.

to comfort. Here the military provided a precocious example. As a governing warrior order, military officers were the classically leisured class in British society. They had entitlements to comfortable leisure well before the middle class could confidently assert that prerogative. By the middle of the eighteenth century their experiences in North America, India, and the West Indies had exposed them to a wide variety of foreign vernacular architectures, which, in the colonies at least, they could adopt without losing respectability. The imperial and revolutionary wars from the Seven Years War through the Napoleonic Wars, with their abrupt changes of dominion and migrations of peoples into new cultural environments, introduced Anglo-Americans to further designs for the piazza—African, French colonial, French-Creole, and Spanish.[42] For fashion-conscious civilians the picturesque aesthetic had by the 1760s provided a rationale and a taste that allowed the attachment of exotic, semipermanent architectural features to the residential fabric. With their piazzas, people of northern European cultures communicated the desire to establish an easy relation between the domestic and the natural environments. A community of comfort could be imagined from their piazzas.

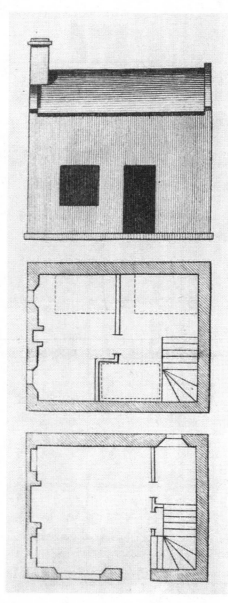

Figure 9.1. Laborer's cottage. The first architectural drawing of a cottage published in America. J. B. Bordley, *Essays and Notes on Husbandry and Rural Affairs* (2nd ed., Philadelphia: Thomas Dobson, 1801), pl. 5. Courtesy of the Winterthur Library, Printed Book and Periodical Collection, Winterthur, Delaware.

9

GENDERED COMFORT

House Design Books

THE IDEA of the comfortable cottage entered American housing culture decades later than it did Britain's. The first American design for a "cottage" was published in 1798, and it was presented as an elevation of popular housing standards. It was an example of the model cottages recommended by agricultural reformers, and there was nothing picturesque about it. With a fourteen-by-ten-foot floor plan, it had a masonry or brick chimney with fireplaces on both floors, one window each for the living room and pantry on the first floor, and three beds in the two rooms in the loft (one of the rooms was windowless) (Figure 9.1).[1]

Beginning in the late eighteenth century and continuing for several decades, there was a housing boom in the United States, in response to a broadening of demand for greater permanency in construction, higher standards of finish, and more spatial differentiation. More tradesmen's houses had parlors, with work and service areas separated behind or below domestic space. In New England more households built houses with multiple chimneys to serve double-storied and/or double-pile houses. In German-settled areas symmetrical houses of frame and brick displaced asymmetrical ones of stone or log. In North Carolina and Virginia changes in plan and size were less widespread than changes in quality of finish: more brick chimneys and brick foundations, more sawn weatherboards and plastering, more glazed sash windows.[2]

This "transformation of living standards" took place during a period not noted for increases in per capita wealth, which by some estimates may even have fallen. The priority of housing in household consumption had increased but still remained generally low: "most Americans were still living in small, mean, vernacular houses." Two-room houses were the modal plan. The size of houses need not have increased to meet the new standards of decoration and finish, because those standards were focused largely on the front parts of the house, particularly the areas for entertaining, while the areas for everyday domestic activity—the kitchen and chambers—changed little in their degree of finish. In the early nineteenth century, household comfort had not yet become so popular as the display of refinement and gentility. Areas for polite behavior had priority in the housing revolution.[3]

The Marketability of Comfort

In the initial decades of the American republic, the pursuit of happiness began to give a higher priority to housing. More spending, especially among merchants and artisans in towns and cities, went into permanency of construction, stylish exteriors, and refined interior spaces for entertaining.[4] But American architects' explicit articulation of comfortable housing, specifically as represented by the cottage, waited for more than a generation to borrow from developments in Britain. The apparent precondition for this borrowing was a broadening of interest in horticulture and landscape architecture, particularly in the 1830s.

The writings of the British landscape architect, John Claudius Loudon, especially his *Encyclopaedia of Cottage, Farm and Villa Architecture and Furniture*, first published in 1833, served as the acknowledged intermediary between American architects and British authorities on the comfortable cottage. In 1838, in an effort to improve the "bald and uninteresting aspect of our houses . . . to those who are familiar with the picturesque Cottages and Villas of England," Alexander J. Davis published the first cottage in an American architectural pattern book. The bucolic landscape setting, columns of unhewn logs, and open porch signified harmonious relations between the inhabitants of the cottage and their immediate physical environment. (See Figure 9.2.) With Davis's assistance in an extraordinarily successful series of publications over the next decade, Andrew Jackson Downing made the cottage an American byword for comfort, and he made comfort the crucial consideration in the design of houses. No American's work manifested the links among improvements in horticulture, landscape architecture, and cottage architecture more clearly than Downing's, and he forthrightly acknowledged his inspiration from British landscape architecture and theory.[5]

The two most widely read authorities on residential architecture in the mid-nineteenth-century United States were Catherine Beecher (1800–1878) and Andrew Jackson Downing (1815–1852). In 1841 Beecher published *A Treatise on Domestic Economy for the Use of Young Ladies at Home and at School.* It made her the foremost authority on homemaking and showed her to be the most technologically minded commentator on the domestic environment in Victorian America.[6] Her technological concerns focused on house designs that gave priority to the imperatives of housework, as housework became a distinct type of labor. In the same year that Beecher's *Treatise* appeared, Downing began his decade-long series of books linking landscape architecture with the design of houses. He was the first significant American publicist of the "modern" English garden and the most popular theorist of the picturesque aesthetic in the United States. His discussions and illustrations of the picturesque style made the house pattern book the most popular type of American architectural publication in the nineteenth century.

As professional writers Beecher and Downing were cultural rather than business entrepreneurs, but they quite literally authored markets in mid-nineteenth-century America. Each of them reoriented a genre of publication—Beecher the manual of housekeeping, Downing the house pattern book—in ways intended to shape consumption patterns in the domestic environment. Beecher itemized "a proper supply of utensils and conveniences for housekeeping," including a "settee ironing-table," kitchen scales, numerous cooking pans such as fish kettles and preserving kettles, and a variety of utensils such as egg beaters, apple corers, and rolling pins. Downing moved beyond generic recommendations to provide specific consumer advice on the best brands of furniture, furnaces, and flush toilets and where to buy them—such as "complete sets of *chamber* or *bed-room furniture* got up at the manufactory of Edward Hennessey, 49 and 51 Brattle Street, Boston," or "the best

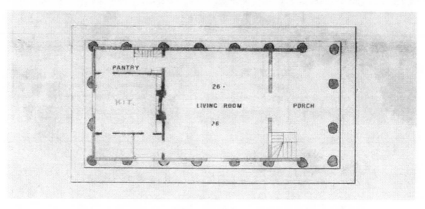

Figure 9.2. Log cottage. The first architectural drawing of a picturesque cottage published in America. Alexander Jackson Davis, *Rural Residences . . . with a View to the Improvement of American Country Architecture . . .* (New York, 1837–38). Courtesy of the Winterthur Library, Printed Book and Periodical Collection, Winterthur, Delaware.

hot-air furnace yet invented in this country" from Chilson's in Boston.[7] Both Downing and Beecher made comfort and convenience critical issues in the design of houses. A comparison of their respective ideologies, publishing strategies, and designs helps identify the meanings of comfort and the corresponding priorities for household spending in mid-nineteenth-century America.

Beecher's and Downing's books appeared just as industrialization of the publishing industry's organization, technology, and marketing made it possible for publications to have readerships in the many thousands. Journeymen became wage laborers, while printers became managers of printing plants. With the deskilling of the printing craft and the division of labor, capitalist reorganization enabled firms to increase their profits and to generate capital for reinvestment in machinery. Mechanization of papermaking and printing processes, such as the appearance of reliable steam-powered presses in the 1830s, raised the output and lowered the production costs of books and periodicals. To supply the increased output of the presses, by 1840 most American mills produced paper by machine in continuous rolls instead of hand-laid paper. The marketing of books became a separate function within publishing firms. Books became commodities.[8]

Both Beecher's and Downing's books were published by companies that had based themselves in New York, in order to produce and sell books in the enormous integrated markets being created as railroads linked the northeastern and the northwestern states; Beecher was published by Harper and Brothers, Downing by Appleton and by Wiley and Putnam. The scale of these authors' markets required and warranted investment in equipment to publish large-scale editions of several thousand copies. When the state of Massachusetts approved Beecher's *Treatise* as a text for its schools, the book was printed by stereotype, a costly process per se but economical for books likely to be reprinted, since it captured an image of an entire page of type that could be reprinted without resetting. Downing's books were produced by industrial processes too. As luxury items, architectural publications had previously used manual printing technology, were bound in sheep skin, and included illustrations from copperplate engravings. Downing's *Landscape Gardening* was the first American architectural publication issued in machine-sewn cloth bindings and the first to extensively use wood engravings. These so-called engravings actually produced a relief image making it possible to set illustrations on the same page as text.[9]

Beecher's and Downing's respective publications integrated their devoted efforts to improve the design of Americans' domestic environments. Beecher devoted her life to women's education and the professionalization of female educators; Downing undertook private and public commissions to provide examples of appropriate taste in landscape and domestic architecture for each part of the country.[10] Both wrote for homeowners who were likely to employ servants; both dealt condescendingly with farmers' and mechanics' households; and both reacted against the potential for vulgarity among the newly enriched.

They sought to reform the very society whose urbanization, industrialization, and democratic culture made such expansive publishing possible. American social mobility troubled both Beecher and Downing in ways that directly affected their designs for the domestic environment. Both of them acknowledged that reading Tocqueville's *Democracy in America* had shaped their understanding of the development of American society. (*Democracy's* crucial second volume—with its identification of individualism as Americans' national trait—had appeared just the year before they published their first books.) Tocqueville's analysis of American individualism reinforced Beecher's anxiety that high rates of horizontal and vertical mobility in an expanding democracy portended chaotic social and political conflict. She explained how westward settlement was breaking down social and political hierarchies, so that people floundered when looking for rational models of household economy:

> The sons of the wealthy are leaving the rich mansions of their fathers, to dwell in the log cabins of the forest, where very soon they bear away the daughters of ease and refinement, to share the privations of a new settlement. . . . there is a constant comparison of conditions, among equals, and a constant temptation presented to imitate the customs, and to strive for the enjoyments, of those who possess larger means.

She intended her book to convert "the daughters of ease and refinement" to resist such social competition by assuming the burden of housework themselves in order to understand the social realities of their families.[11]

Downing was less antidemocratic but more forthrightly snobbish about the implications of vertical mobility for taste. He perceived that houseowners were finding it increasingly difficult to use tasteful residential design to signify their personal character. In the American context, where "extraordinary display" had become "the common property of the sovereign people," gentlemen with "the taste for private display" were liable to confound themselves by seeming "vulgar." Instead, "the gentleman who wished his house to be distinguished by good taste" had to restrain such impulses and "choose the opposite course, viz. to make its interior remarkable for chaste beauty,

and elegant simplicity, rather than for elaborate and profuse decorations."
Downing's concentration on "country" houses was critical to his ideal of un-
derstated good taste: "it is in the country, if anywhere, that we should find
essential ease and convenience always preferred to that love of effect and
desire to dazzle, which is begotten, for the most part, by rivalry of mere
wealth in town life."[12] Downing urged all homeowners to consider the *apparent* comfort of their houses as an indication to the public of their commitment to domestic virtues. His designs symbolized their owners' concern with
domesticity, and he signified the importance of women in the household with
apparently feminine external ornamentation and architectural features. Picturesque semipermanent structures like arbors, trellises, stoops, and verandahs, where women could find space for tender leisure with their children,
ideally expressed the owner's commitment to domestic virtues.

More than the sheer fact of Beecher's being a woman and Downing
a man make gender relevant in a comparison of their work. Beecher published in a "women's" genre—housekeeping manuals; Downing published
in a "men's" genre—architectural treatises. But both of them also crossed
previous gender boundaries in their participation in the creation of a culture
of domesticity. Downing used architectural design to symbolize domestic
priorities, and Beecher asserted women's architectural prerogative to define
domestic convenience and comfort.

Andrew Jackson Downing on Taste and Comfort

Downing was the youngest child of a Newburgh, New York, wheelwright.
His father had changed his livelihood to commercial gardening when his
health began to fail, and he had run a nursery for about five years before
Andrew was born. (Having been born in 1815, he must have been named for
the general, not the president.) A few years later, an older brother, Charles,
succeeded to the business on their father's death, and Andrew joined his
brother as a partner in 1831 at the age of sixteen. By the time Andrew left
school to go into this business, he had several years' formal education at local
academies, which he immediately turned to advantage to advertise his expertise. From the age of seventeen he was publishing articles on landscape
gardening in local and national journals. The ambition evident in his early
publishing was apparent in his personal life as well: in 1838, at the age of

twenty-three, Downing married Caroline De Wint, a great-granddaughter of John Adams and from a prominent Hudson Valley family. Downing used this connection to dedicate his first book to John Quincy Adams, his wife's granduncle. A fatal ship accident in 1852, while Downing was on the way to his most important commission, the Public Grounds in Washington, cut short a brilliant career.[13]

By the mid-1830s the Downing brothers had a national clientele for their nursery, with a reputation for international correspondence on horticultural science and specimens. Downing reinforced and capitalized on these connections by publishing *A Treatise on the Theory and Practice of Landscape Gardening with a View to the Improvement of Country Residences*, the first American book consistently linking practical gardening advice with the aesthetic issues that British landscape architecture had dealt with for over a century. Published when he was twenty-six, it immediately gained recognition as *the* American "treatise on landscape gardening." His second book, published a year later, in 1842, claimed to be the first American book "devoted to Rural Architecture" and was similarly successful. Its architectural focus developed a minor but winning feature of the first book, perspective views of houses in landscaped settings (like the illustration of his own house shown in Figure 9.3). In *Landscape Gardening* Downing had identified "the proper characteristics of a rural residence": "a dwelling, as from its various accommodations, not only gives ample space for all the *comforts* and conveniences of a country life, but by its varied and picturesque form and outline . . . also appears to have some reasonable connection, or to be in perfect keeping, with surrounding nature." Downing's books helped inaugurate and long dominated the field of house pattern books. *Landscape Gardening* went through sixteen printings in eight editions before 1879; *Cottage Residences* thirteen printings before 1887; and *The Architecture of Country Houses* (1850) nineteen printings before 1887.[14]

Downing reoriented the market for architectural publishing from the house carpenter, who needed books with precise up-to-date stylistic details, to the potential owner, who could demonstrate his taste as a consumer of overall designs. Publication of his three books in less than a decade marked how house pattern books had replaced builders' guides as the most popular form of architectural publication. Builders' guides, especially those of Asher Benjamin, with such titles as *The American Builder's Companion* (1806) and *The Practical House Carpenter* (1830), had provided house carpenters with precise detail of stylistic ornament, while largely disregarding questions of archi-

Figure 9.3. Residence of Andrew Jackson Downing, Newburgh, New York. Downing's illustrations of houses in landscape settings provided the most influential model for house pattern books. Andrew Jackson Downing, *A Treatise on the Theory and Practice of Landscape Gardening, Adapted to North America* (New York: Wiley & Putnam, 1844), facing 371. Courtesy of the Winterthur Library, Printed Book and Periodical Collection, Winterthur, Delaware.

tectural design or the use of space. They seldom provided plans or elevations and entirely disregarded questions of siting and landscape design.

By espousing the picturesque aesthetic, with its admiration for the rural cottage, Downing's designs could have an appeal across virtually the whole social spectrum of home builders. Downing emphasized that taste should be the prerogative of all people of property, not just the rich. *Elegance* was the key aesthetic term in his first book, *Landscape Gardening*, which addressed a clientele of wealthy Hudson Valley estate owners; but the book also reminded its readers that just as money alone could not guarantee taste, so real beauty could be found in modest settings: "Rural bedlams, full of all kinds of absurdities, without a leading character or expression of any sort, cost their owners a vast deal of trouble and money, without giving a tasteful mind a shadow of the beauty which it feels at the first glimpse of a neat cottage residence, with its simple, sylvan character of well kept lawn and trees."[15]

His later books drew on the preceding half-century of British publications on rural architecture to demonstrate how tasteful examples of cottages and villas were affordable over a wide social range, from tradesmen and workingmen to wealthy businessmen. The books' perspective views of houses in landscape settings encouraged potential builders to imagine living in a picturesque setting. In Downing's reshaping of the genre, house pattern books disregarded details of construction and presented people with instruction on the display of taste.

Much of the success of Downing's books depended on their effective use of recently developed techniques for illustration. More skilled with verbal than graphic images, he forthrightly recruited the best architectural draftsman and engraver in the country, Alexander J. Davis and Joseph A. Adams respectively, and then coordinated their translations of his designs into publishable illustrations. Davis, who had worked as a printer and architectural illustrator before his distinguished career as an architect, had already published the first house pattern book, but he lacked Downing's commercial shrewdness and literary fluency with the picturesque aesthetic. Davis's *Rural Residences*, published in 1837–38, provided the graphic model for the house pattern book by exploiting the imperatives of the picturesque aesthetic for variety in style, structure, and ornament. Rather than emphasize the floor plan as a guide to construction, Davis illustrated houses with "perspective views in landscape settings" to aid prospective owners in choosing among designs. *Rural Residences* had been an effort by Davis to advertise his architectural practice among wealthy New Yorkers, but each of its six volumes was to include only four plates, and the expense of the hand-colored lithographs so limited the market for the books that the project ended after only two volumes. Davis's books had little of the evaluative commentary on tasteful choices that contributed to the success of Downing's, but the fine illustrations impressed Downing, who recruited Davis to prepare finished drawings from Downing's sketches. (Ironically, Downing the landscape architect could sketch houses rather well, but was hopeless with their landscape settings, while Davis the architect often provided such elaborate landscapes for his architectural drawings that the buildings themselves were nearly lost from view.) Joseph Adams, who had engraved the plates for *Rural Residences*, used the drawings by Davis based on Downing's sketches to engrave the wooden blocks used to print Downing's illustrations.[16]

The critical antecedents for Downing's house pattern books were archi-

Figures 9.4. A small bracketed cottage, without (*top*) and with (*bottom*) the picturesque features of trellises, arbored seat, and bay window, showing how tasteful ornament could be added to modest houses. Andrew Jackson Downing, *The Architecture of Country Houses* (New York: Appleton, 1852), facing 80, 78. Courtesy of the Winterthur Library, Printed Book and Periodical Collection, Winterthur, Delaware.

tectural illustrations in agricultural and gardening magazines. Architectural illustrations in the gardening press were infrequent because of the high expense of lithographs, but publishers wanted to show buildings in picturesque landscape settings. By the late 1830s gardening magazines had started using a technique of illustration that had been employed in the agricultural press since the 1810s for farm buildings, namely "engraved" woodcuts, which were cheaper than lithographs and could be integrated with the text. At the same time, agricultural magazines began to publish house designs, often the results of competitions, which were still typically classical in style. Downing, who was already writing for the horticultural press, integrated landscape gardeners' interest in picturesque country buildings with wealthy townspeople's interest in stylish designs for villas. He brought together the aesthetic interests of the gardening press with the commercial practicality of the agricultural press.[17]

One of Downing's biographers, George Tatum, has explained how Downing popularized the "modern" English garden and its picturesque aesthetic in the United States: "Downing set out to show how the Natural, or English, style of gardening might be adapted to a simple cottage or a modest farm, and by convincing the average man that taste was not the exclusive property of the rich, he succeeded in interesting thousands of middle-class Americans in the appearance of their homes." (See Figure 9.4.) Although writing half a century after the period of most intense discussion in British eighteenth-century aesthetic theory, Downing followed it in trying to distinguish between the beautiful and the picturesque in modern landscape gardening. The beautiful landscape was curvaceous yet smooth, with rounded outlines for the main features of its terrain and trees and gradual complex curves for streams and bodies of water. In contrast, picturesque landscapes surprised, with their juxtaposition of such raw features as dead trees, exposed rocks, and thorny underbrush, and they silhouetted architectural and botanical angularity. The picturesque had "outlines of a certain spirited irregularity, surfaces comparatively abrupt and broken, and growth of a somewhat wild and bold character."[18] *Picturesque* referred generally to the visually informal and naturalistic; if the terms were applied strictly, Downing really designed "picturesque" houses for "beautiful" landscapes. When he used contrasting illustrations to demonstrate the distinction, that for the picturesque showed a man and his dog in a woodland setting while that for the beautiful presented a woman and her child on a house lawn (Figure 9.5).

Figure 9.5. The beautiful, or "graceful," style (*top*) and the picturesque style (*bottom*) in landscape gardening. Andrew Jackson Downing, *A Treatise on the Theory and Practice of Landscape Gardening* (New York: Wiley & Putnam, 1844), facing 55. Courtesy of the Winterthur Library, Printed Book and Periodical Collection, Winterthur, Delaware.

By coyly excusing his comments on what he considered to be feminine preserves of taste, Downing hinted at his awareness of women's privileges in the previously male domain of domestic architecture. He half-heartedly apologized for comments on interior decoration, lest they seem to intrude on women's realm of expertise. He acknowledged that women had "natural good taste" regarding decorative fabrics and furniture but justified his advice on those subjects as providing rational criteria for what otherwise would be just "a matter of fancy." "Our fair readers will doubtless pardon us for the seeming intrusion on their province, when we say that our object is mainly to furnish them with the reasons for the natural good taste which they usually show in this department, and point out the shoals on which those few who fail from want of native perception are wrecked, so that they may, if possible, be avoided."[19] Downing's sensitivity to the cult of domesticity and his awareness of the relevance of gender to domestic architecture enabled him to produce residential designs for a culture that had enhanced women's say on architecture. The person who most forcefully asserted that prerogative was Catherine Beecher.

Catherine Beecher on Domesticity and Comfort

Catherine Beecher came from a highly literate, high-minded family.[20] She was the sister of Harriet Beecher Stowe, author of *Uncle Tom's Cabin,* and her father, Lyman Beecher, was a nationally prominent evangelical minister. At the age of sixteen, as the eldest of eight children in the household, Catherine readily assumed maternal responsibilities when her mother died, until her father remarried a year later. In her early twenties she began to work as an independent schoolteacher, first in New London and later in Hartford, Connecticut. At her father's urging, despite her own reluctance, she became engaged to a Yale professor, but when the young man died in a shipwreck she soon decided to remain unmarried. Thereafter she lived in a series of complicated households—usually involving her father or siblings—while pursuing her career as an administrator and advocate of women's education. Although her father was a Christian evangelist and she one of the objects of his zeal, when she herself led a religious revival, something respectable ladies did not do, he disapproved. Nevertheless, she inspired a group of women from elite families in Hartford and then used this group to gain support for the endowment of what became the Hartford Female Seminary.

Beecher reiterated her real priorities by turning away from her evangelical success to commit herself to secular means of social reform. She began to gain national prominence as an educator when she established the Female Seminary, which had a new building and a staff of eight. Beecher taught moral philosophy there, and in 1831 she published her first book, *The Elements of Mental and Moral Philosophy, Founded upon Experience, Reason, and the Bible.* The book articulated an ideological conviction that women were morally superior to men because they had a greater willingness for self-sacrifice, which Beecher had determined to be the test of morality.

Beecher committed herself to a career as a reformer in order to help women realize their capacity for self-sacrifice. She sought to make teaching a women's profession by establishing a nationwide system of schools to train them as teachers.[21] When her father moved to Cincinnati in 1831 to become president of the Lane Theological Seminary, she moved there too, in order to take advantage of its strategic location on the Ohio River to advance her program in the rapidly growing population of the old Northwest and upper South. A decade of social and political disasters followed the Beechers' move west. Her imperious New England snobbishness alienated an initially supportive local elite, and her father was blamed for Lane Seminary's harboring of abolitionists. Yet, in a bitter controversy with the abolitionist Angelina Grimké, Catherine Beecher distanced herself from a nascent feminist movement by extravagantly repudiating women's participation in any political capacity, because it would compromise their monopoly of moral authority within the home. Failure in Cincinnati made it all the more imperative that her ideas have a national exposure.

With her interest and experience in the education of young women, Beecher wanted to write for the secondary school market. She thought one of her works, *The Moral Instructor* (1838), had potential as a text in the new common school systems recently established in several states at public expense. Her brother-in-law, Calvin Stowe, had become a national authority on public education after the Ohio legislature commissioned him to report on European elementary school systems. Beecher used her connection with him to introduce herself and her book to the new directors of public education in Pennsylvania and Massachusetts. When it became apparent that sectarian defensiveness and jealousies would be obstacles to the adoption of any text on moral instruction, Beecher sought sponsorship from ladies' magazines. She wrote to one editor, "Cannot you help forward the introduction of such a work into schools, by a little notice of it in the *Mothers Magazine*—for if mothers will interest themselves to have moral instruction in schools the thing will be done." She also frankly acknowledged that she needed to have a higher literary profile if she was to sell her work: "to make myself known, and as popular as I can, with all classes of readers—I need not tell you that this may be aimed at without any craving for fame or notoriety, but as one means of increasing the sphere of usefulness."[22]

As the commercial disappointment of *The Moral Instructor* became apparent, Beecher started working on *The Treatise on Domestic Economy for the Use of Young Ladies at Home and at School*. Since the seventeenth century, manuals of practical advice on housework had provided recipes and home remedies in a piecemeal fashion. Beecher reoriented the genre by personalizing its advice to encourage women's self-consciousness about their roles as homeworkers, by providing medical and technical explanations for the particular advice regarding health and housekeeping, and by framing the practical advice with an analysis of the social importance of domesticity. Beecher intended *The Treatise on Domestic Economy* to be a schoolbook as well as a tract of domestic feminism. Her success in having the book approved in 1842 for use in Massachusetts schools guaranteed her sales and livelihood, and reversed a decade of failure in cracking the new textbook market. The contract she eventually would have with Harper and Brothers allowed the publisher 5 percent of sales as security against bad debts, an additional 20 percent of sales "for commissions paid to retailers," plus "current market prices" for "the expenses of printing, paper, and binding." The net profits after these charges were to be split equally between the publisher and a "board of gentlemen" who would hold the copyright. This board would pay Beecher "a moderate compensation . . . for the time and labour spent in preparing these works" and apply "the remainder paid over by the publishers, to aid in educating and locating such female teachers as wish to be employed in those portions of our country, which are most destitute of schools." The book was republished yearly for over a decade, and its commercial success would give Catherine Beecher the economic independence necessary to pursue her reformist goals.[23]

In the first edition of the *Treatise*, published by a medium-sized Boston firm, Beecher modestly presented herself as writing the book out of reluctant necessity. Only personal knowledge of the calamitous state of American women's health had led her undertake the work.

> How came the Author to write such a book? She answers, Because she has herself suffered from the want of such knowledge, in early life; because others, under her care, have suffered from her ignorance; and because many mothers and teachers, especially in reference to matters pertaining to health, have so much occasion to sympathize in the regret with which this acknowledgement is made.
>
> The care of a female seminary, for some twelve years, and subsequent extensive travels, have given such a view of female health, in this Nation, and of the causes which tend to weaken and destroy the constitution of young women, together with the sufferings consequent on a want of early domestic knowledge and habits.

She had hoped to have the material on "physiology and hygiene" presented by "medical gentlemen." She was more confident of her expertise on "domestic duties," saying of herself, "Being the eldest of a large family, she has, from early life, been accustomed to the care of children, and to the performance of most domestic duties." But even on domestic matters, she assured her readers, she had learned from others, since it had been "her good fortune to reside, most of her life, in the families of exemplary and accomplished housekeepers, and under the supervision of such friends, most of the domestic operations, detailed in this work, have been performed by the writer." The second edition, published by another Boston firm, reiterated this modest authorial persona but noted as well that the book now enjoyed "the sanction of the Massachusetts Board of Education[;] it has been furnished with additional engravings, a copious Glossary, and a full Index."[24]

Where Downing's audience was only implicitly male—men who would build homes for their families—Beecher's was forthrightly female—young women who would eventually marry and run households. Beecher worked within a literary tradition of advice to women on housekeeping, but a more general influence on her thought was political economy. She took a critical view toward received wisdom on virtually all topics, and she analyzed the female role of domesticity as a contractual, not natural, division of labor. The division arose from a social contract that gave men authority in public affairs while women would be authoritative in domestic matters. Beecher wanted to make women's work more efficient and rational, but she expressed no resentment that women did all the housework nor that the amount of work was oppressive. Beecher, the advocate of women's education, actually called for *less* formal education for women in the liberal arts, so that they might devote more time to systematic study of domestic science. She wanted middle-class women to do more work: too many of them had been debilitated in their health by relying on servants and thereby denying themselves the beneficial exercise of housework.[25]

Once she had a commercial success on her hands, Beecher reedited the *Treatise* and switched publisher again, forcing her second Boston publisher to sell back the contract so that Harper and Brothers in New York could begin its many editions of the book. With the book being published by the largest book company in the country, she forthrightly cited testimonials to its worthy success as a schoolbook. She claimed that its lessons on architecture had been particularly successful and recounted the testimony of one teacher, who

> remarked that she had never known a school-book that awakened more interest, and that some young girls would learn a lesson in this when they would study nothing else. She remarked, also, that when reciting the chapter on the construction of houses, they became greatly interested in inventing plans of their own, which gave an opportunity to the teacher to point out difficulties and defects. Had this part of domestic economy been taught in our schools, our land would not be so defaced with awkward, misshapen, inconvenient, and, at the same time, needlessly expensive houses, as it now is.

As with her previous texts, she promoted the book to "leading minds in the country already interested on the subject of *popular education.*" She particularly appealed to Mary Lyon, head of Mount Holyoke, the foremost "female seminary" for training women as teachers, to give her approval and support for the introduction of domestic economy to the curriculum of women's formal education:

> The truth is that even in this democratic nation labor is considered vulgar and degrading, and none of the associations of taste and science

have been thrown round the peculiar profession of a woman. And one grand step towards remedying the evils from this cause, will be to have young ladies find at the highest seminaries for their sex, their peculiar profession required as a science as honorable and important as any in their course of study.

And again she made the self-denying claim that the proceeds of the book's sales would go toward the cause of educational reform.[26]

The Treatise, Beecher claimed, would make it possible to teach "domestic economy" as "systematically" as "political economy" or "moral science." The system of political economy particularly suited architectural analysis. She addressed women's architectural issues under the rubrics of the "economy of labor, economy of money, economy of health, economy of *comfort,* and good taste." Conversely, architectural metaphors established the importance of domestic economy. Women, in contributing "to the intellectual and moral elevation" of their country—as mothers, wage-earners, and servants—were "building a glorious *Temple.*" Women should appropriate architectural issues as peculiarly their own. Beecher asked rhetorically, "Are not the principles that should guide in constructing a house, and in warming and ventilating it properly, as important to young girls as the principles of the Athenian Constitution, or the rules of Roman tactics?" She intended to make women architecturally sophisticated so they could influence their husbands when together they formed "plans for a future residence." Thus, she introduced her readers to such architectural terminology as *plan* and *elevation,* and she carefully explained how to read a plan for the layout and scale of walls, windows and doors.[27] The plans her readers would look at were likely to be Andrew Jackson Downing's.

For Downing "the porch, the verandah, or the piazza," were the arch signifiers of domestic comfort: "no dwelling house can be considered complete without one or more of them." They protected the entrance to the house and provided a place to walk in poor weather; their shade made them "necessary and delightful" in summer; and for much of the year they were "the favorite lounging apartment of the family," especially if they had an agreeable prospect (Figure 9.6). But *representing* these possibilities mattered more than the practical advantages themselves: "a broad shady verandah suggests ideas of *comfort* and is highly expressive of purpose," in the same way that "bay or oriel windows, balconies, and terraces, added to villas," denote "ele-

Figure 9.6. The cynosures of trellis and verandah in cottage architecture. Andrew Jackson Downing, *The Architecture of Country Houses* (New York: Appleton, 1852), facing 112. Courtesy of the Winterthur Library, Printed Book and Periodical Collection, Winterthur, Delaware.

gant enjoyments which belong to the habitation of man in a cultivated and refined state of society." To be without a "vine covered porch" expressed contentment "to live in a clumsy, badly contrived, and uncouth habitation," "to have in [one's] heart but a scanty flow of genial domestic sympathies."[28]

Beecher shared Downing's picturesque aesthetic, and on matters of landscape gardening she acknowledged his authority. When she represented her dream house, "a Gothic cottage, which secures the most economy of labor and expense, with the greatest amount of convenience and *comfort* which the writer has ever seen," it had not one but two "piazzas," opening respectively from the parlor and the dining room. She illustrated another Gothic cottage—built by her graphic artist, Daniel Wadsworth—in picturesque detail, with a summerhouse and barn decorated with battlements, and the portico of the cottage supported with pillars "made simply of the trunks of small trees, giving a beautiful rural finish" (Figure 9.7). Her landscaping of this idealized cottage was similarly picturesque: "instead of planting shade-trees in straight lines, or scattering them about, as single trees, they should be arranged in clusters, with large openings for turf, flowers, and shrubbery." This landscaping aimed to "give the graceful ease and variety seen in nature."[29]

But Beecher would not give picturesque ideals priority over practical considerations in the design of houses. Domestic priorities justified skepticism of the need for porches or any other architectural symbol of domesticity. "Good taste" was desirable but less important than the "economy of *comfort*": "Cramping the conveniences and *comfort* of a family, in order to secure elegant rooms, to show to company, is a weakness and folly." She generally condemned "piazzas and porticoes" as "very expensive," particularly when their "cost would secure far more *comfort*, if devoted to additional nursery or kitchen conveniences." Money spent on porches could instead be "devoted to providing a *comfortable* kitchen and chambers for domestics" or "back-door accommodations" such as privies and a "bathing tub" with running water, which saved women "much hard labor and perplexity."[30]

Beecher associated domesticity with work; Downing associated domesticity with leisured privacy. When he dealt with the use of space inside the

Figure 9.7. Gothic cottage. Catherine E. Beecher, *A Treatise on Domestic Economy* (New York: Harper & Brothers, 1848), 274. Courtesy of the Winterthur Library, Printed Book and Periodical Collection, Winterthur, Delaware.

house, he was more concerned to get servants out from underfoot than to lessen women's housework. Dumbwaiters and speaking-tubes mattered just as much as water pumps in saving domestic labor: "The maximum of *comfort* . . . is found to consist in employing the smallest number of servants actually necessary." Downing expressed no interest in the workings or location of kitchens, except to insulate them from the awareness of people elsewhere in the house. The only male space in Downing's houses was a retreat, the library. Female spaces ranged from the kitchen and boudoir to "the garden, the lawn, [and] the pleasure-grounds," while the family collectively used the parlor, veranda, and dining room.[31]

In this context of blissful masculine indifference to household workings, Beecher asserted that "there is no point of domestic economy, which more seriously involves the health and daily *comfort* of American women, than the proper construction of houses." Beecher treated "good taste" in the design of houses as "a desirable, though less important" consideration than the economies of labor, expense, health, and comfort. She had little more to say about taste except to assert that "it is always as cheap, and generally cheaper, to build a house in agreement with the rules of good taste, than to build an awkward and ill-proportioned one." Economy of labor meant that men should not build large houses that were difficult to run if they lacked the means to hire sufficient service and/or if their wives were "feeble": "Every room in a house adds to the expense involved in finishing and furnishing it, and to the amount of labor spent in sweeping, dusting, cleaning floors, paint, and windows, and taking care of, and repairing, its furniture." For economy in labor and money, houses square in plan, which enclosed the largest space for the least expense of construction and were most efficiently heated and ventilated, were preferable to ones with picturesquely irregular projections and wings. Piazzas, porticoes, and verandahs—Downing's arch symbols of domesticity—were particularly irrational in their expense: "their cost would secure far more *comfort*, if devoted to additional nursery and kitchen conveniences"[32] (Figure 9.8).

Beecher related problems of residential design to the experience of *living* in houses, rather than *looking* at them. For her the plan was more important than the view. The layout of rooms, "and the proper supply of conveniences" called for "economy of labor and *comfort*." Rooms that women used frequently—kitchen, sitting room, and nursery—should be on the same floor, and handy to each other: "Nothing is more injurious, to a feeble woman, than going up and down stairs; and yet, in order to gain two large parlors, to show to a few friends, or to strangers, immense sacrifices of health, *comfort*, and money, are made." She was particularly attentive to considerations of storage and carefully noted the layout of closet and shelf space, especially in rooms that were likely to be used as nurseries.[33]

Beecher advised that facilities for handling water have priority in the design of conveniences, so that women did not have to function as human plumbing systems. "With half the expense usually devoted to a sideboard or sofa, the water used from a well or cistern can be so conducted, as that, by simply turning a cock, it will flow to the place where it is to be used." Unlike Downing, who only noted a general desirability for indoor plumbing and seldom included it in his plans, Beecher provided a rationale—it was unhealthy for people "in the perspiration of labor, or the debility of disease [to be] obliged to go out of doors in all weather"—and she actually designed plumbing facilities into her plans. Beecher designed a complete plumbing system to provide cold water for kitchen use and hot water for bathing and laundry. She devoted a separate plan to these and other "backdoor accommodations," including privies, ash bins, and woodpile (Figures 9.9 and 9.10). "Every woman," Beecher advised, should use her influence to secure all these conveniences; even if it involves the sacrifice of the piazza, or "the best parlor."[34]

The Respectability of Comfort

Downing paid more attention to the appearance of houses from the outside than to the use of their space. When designing the "convenient arrangement of the rooms" he gave primary consideration to the "aspect" and "view" from them. How household spaces were used mattered less than assuring their separation from each other: "the ideal of domestic accommodation [is to have] each department of the house being complete in itself, and intruding itself but very little on the attention of family or guests when not required to be visible."[35] His archetypal family member was implicitly the father, who should not be bothered.

Downing allowed women architectural initiative with one archly picturesque symbol of domesticity—the twisted vine. Not every cottage could "display science or knowledge, because science demands architectural education in its builder or designer," but everyone had a "feeling" for beauty,

Fig. 22.

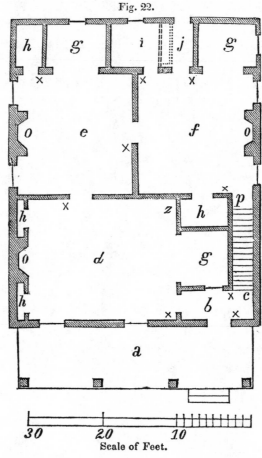

Scale of Feet.

a, Porch.
b, Entry.
c, Stairs.
d, Parlor, 16 by 20 feet.
e, Dining-room, 16 by 16 feet.
f, Kitchen.

g, g, g, Bedpresses.
h, h, h, h, Closets.
i, Store-closet.
j, Back entry and Sink.
p, Cellar stairs.
o, o, o, Fireplaces.

Figure 9.8. Plans for houses with (*left*) and without (*right*) piazza, costing the same amount to build. Plan on right has two stories. Catherine E. Beecher, *A Treatise on Domestic Economy* (New York: Harper & Brothers, 1848), 266, 267. Courtesy of the Winterthur Library, Printed Book and Periodical Collection, Winterthur, Delaware.

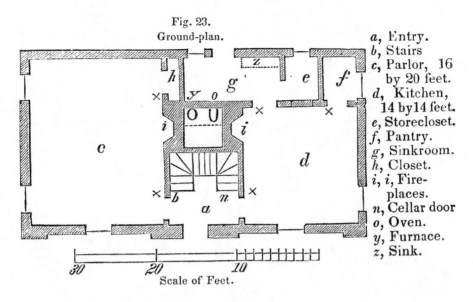

Fig. 23.
Ground-plan.

a, Entry.
b, Stairs
c, Parlor, 16 by 20 feet.
d, Kitchen, 14 by 14 feet.
e, Storecloset.
f, Pantry.
g, Sinkroom.
h, Closet.
i, i, Fireplaces.
n, Cellar door
o, Oven.
y, Furnace.
z, Sink.

Scale of Feet.

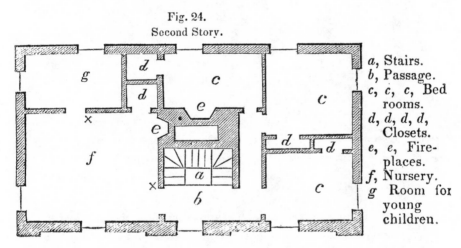

Fig. 24.
Second Story.

a, Stairs.
b, Passage.
c, c, c, Bed rooms.
d, d, d, d, Closets.
e, e, Fireplaces.
f, Nursery.
g Room for young children.

and "permanent vines" expressed it most effectively, "because mere utility would never lead any person to plant flowering vines." The "architects, masons, carpenters" who actually constructed a cottage never planted vines. They were only planted by those who "live in it, and make it truly a home, and generally by the mother or daughter, whose very planting of the vines is a labor of love offered up on the domestic altar." "By the most direct and natural associations" with femininity, "vines on a rural cottage always express domesticity and the presence of heart." The twisted vine was the

Fig. 34.

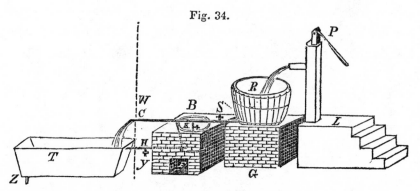

P, Pump.   *L*, Steps to use when pumping.   *R*, Reservoir.   *G*, Brickwork to raise the Reservoir.   *B*, A large Boiler.   *F*, Furnace, beneath the Boiler.   *C*, Conductor of cold water.   *H*, Conductor of hot water.   *K*, Cock for letting cold water into the Boiler.   *S*, Pipe to conduct cold water to a cock over the kitchen sink.   *T*, Bathing-tub, which receives cold water from the Conductor, *C*, and hot water from the Conductor, *H*.   *W*, Partition separating the Bathing-room from the Wash-room.   *Y*, Cock to draw off hot water.   *Z*, Plug to let off the water from the Bathing-tub into a drain.

Figure 9.9. "Accommodations" for securing water with the least labor. Catherine E. Beecher, *A Treatise on Domestic Economy* (New York: Harper & Brothers, 1848), 275. Courtesy of the Winterthur Library, Printed Book and Periodical Collection, Winterthur, Delaware.

model of Downing's other twisted symbol, the "wreathed column" such as could be found in Rhenish architecture. Downing saves his modern readers from a tendentious reading of this "natural symbol or emblem of affectionate embrace":

> Wherever there is a twining vine or climber that, obeying the law of its vital force, ascends in spiral lines around a naked stem or branch of a tree, there you have the twisted column. It is the delicate, clinging for support to the strong—the frail, upheld by the powerful—in short, the poet's own type of affectionate, loving, trusting womanhood.

Worthy domesticity required that women simultaneously depend on men physically but support them emotionally.[36]

Beecher's and Downing's respective dispositions toward the multipurpose use of space corresponded to gender experience. Divisions of labor in housework did not cross gender lines, and in most households, including middle-

class ones, the most intense forms of domestic labor—involving food preparation, textiles, and child care—usually involved overlapping uses of spaces.
Having argued for the design of smaller and simpler houses as a desirable
convenience in itself, and not just a concession to economic necessity, Beecher
was exceptionally willing to use the same space in different ways according
to the season or time of day. She recommended floor-length windows in lieu
of verandahs and/or outside doors from sitting rooms. In summer such windows could open to the fresh air, but in winter they could be securely closed
and caulked against cold and drafts. She also designed "bedpresses," sleeping alcoves off sitting rooms that could be opened at night so the sitting room
became a bedroom. (See Figure 9.8A.)

Figure 9.10. Plan of a building with "back-door accommodations," and fragment of caption. Catherine E. Beecher, *A Treatise on Domestic Economy* (New York: Harper & Brothers, 1848), 276. Courtesy
of the Winterthur Library, Printed Book and Periodical Collection, Winterthur, Delaware.

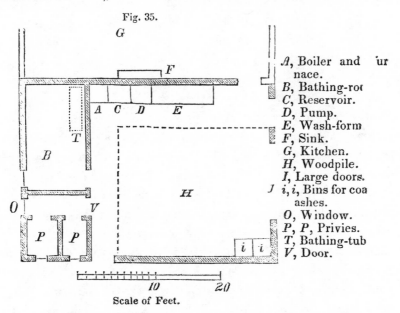

Fig. 35, is the plan of a building for back-door
accommodations. At *A, C, D, E,* are accommoda
tions shown in Fig. 34. The bathing-room is adjacent
to the boiler and reservoir, to receive the water. The
privy, *P, P,* should have two apartments, as indispensa-

The residential designs of Beecher and Downing perpetuated longstanding gender relations in the domestic environment. Beecher thought of the
house from the experience of working in it, and she concerned herself with
the multipurpose use of domestic space for house work. Downing gave priority to male leisure and the symbolic importance of the house's external
appearance.[37] But they each appropriated the other gender's traditional pre-
rogatives on the domestic environment—Downing with his sentimentalization of domestic relations, Beecher with her technological expertise in residential design.

How was this appropriation possible? As a precondition, at least, part of
the answer may be biographical. Their experience allowed a certain abstrac-
tion of the issues. Neither of them actually lived typically gendered domestic
roles: Downing was childless, and Beecher remained single by choice. Could
the picturesque aesthetic have enabled their cross-gendering of authority?
Certainly its emphasis on sentimental subjectivity in taste allowed Downing
to evoke the emotions of domestic life in reference to his designs. In addition, its rusticity of design and exoticism of style self-consciously provided
an alternative to the symmetry, hierarchy, and canonical style of Georgian
and neoclassical residential architecture.

Both the picturesque aesthetic and the cult of domesticity involved a
dialogue between and about genders. By the end of the 1840s Catherine
Beecher seemed to have been prescient in her call for women to educate
themselves architecturally in order to articulate women's interests in the
design of houses. By mid-century women predominated in the American
reading public, and women wrote the most popular books and edited the
most popular magazine. In the decade following publication of Beecher's
Treatise, the agricultural press began to feature women's designs and commentary on vernacular houses, out of recognition of their expertise on the
efficient functioning of the farm household. Downing's last book, *The Architecture of Country Houses*, paid sustained attention to questions bearing on comfort and interior decoration, as is forthrightly indicated by its subtitle, *with
Lengthy Discussions of Furniture as well as Ventilation and Heating*. Published in 1850,
this book was liable to influence by new women's publications—devoted to
the domestic environment—such as Beecher's book and Godey's *Lady's Book*,
edited by Sara Josepha Hale. In September 1846 Godey's *Lady's Book* began
to publish house designs regularly, in a section called "Model Cottages." As
the most widely circulated monthly publication in the United States, with

over sixty thousand copies per issue in 1850, it remained the most important popular publication on domestic architecture for several decades. British designs, mainly from Loudon's *Encyclopaedia of Cottage, Farm and Villa Architecture*, predominated in the early years, but by the mid-1850s American work, including Downing's, prevailed.[38]

What architectural influence did Beecher and Downing have? Features of Downing's designs were recognizable in suburban and small town architecture for decades. Beecher's designs, though often republished in the *Treatise*, had little apparent direct influence on the design of houses. Though she was deeply concerned with improvements in the design of the domestic environment for the benefit of women, her own strategy for such improvements made architectural design a subsidiary matter. To exploit the picturesque aesthetic architecturally would have compromised her principle of giving housework priority in the design of houses. Her designs appeared in a chapter of a book directed exclusively at young women; an amateur architect prepared the crude though precise reproductions of her designs for the book. In the generation after her *Treatise on Domestic Economy* first appeared, even as women's magazines provided the widest exposure for designs of houses, the trend in American domestic architecture contradicted her advice. It developed the American cottage and villa styles popularized by Downing, with the elaboration of parlors, the increase in bedrooms, the proliferation of verandahs, and irregular houseplans.[39] The culture of comfort was more readily symbolized than realized.

CONCLUSION

I STARTED this study with two assumptions: people can usually get used to anything, and most people think that the way they live is the right way to live. From this perspective there is little surprise that the amenities of physical comfort did not change much over time in medieval and early modern Britain and during the first two centuries in British America. Nor is it surprising how similar the basic standards of physical accommodation were across the social spectrum throughout that period—the hall, the chamber, the chimney fireplace, and the bed. There was not much demand for their improvement. There was increasing demand for items to display and with which to assert social status. Fashions in clothing, furniture, and architecture inspired dramatic changes in the design of material culture, even in this pre-industrial society. Household amenity in medieval and early modern British culture changed primarily not in relation to domestic life but to hospitality, cleanliness, and the healthfulness of the air. The changes in material culture that sprang from these concerns would later be understood as enhancements in personal and domestic comfort.

What would eventually be considered minimal comfort for all people developed initially for people of exceptional status. Many of the early and most influential innovations in the design of the domestic environment were associated, paradoxically, with the ascetic, nonparochial clergy. Precisely because they cut themselves off from ordinary daily life, they viewed their society's material culture more critically than did those who were at home in it.

Consequently, they designed living arrangements with fewer traditional and habitual constraints on innovation. Chimney fireplaces, glazed windows, and parlors were regular features of clerical accommodation well before most of the laity adopted them as part of their standard of living.

The other large social category that was set apart in feudal society, besides the clergy, was women. The desire to create separate spaces for women's protection and the designation of certain tasks to women were critical to sixteenth- and seventeenth-century changes in the design of the domestic environment—the chambers, beds, kitchens, and areas of the fire. The sexual politics of consumption favored men, since a family's wealth was legally theirs, and they used parlors to display goods they had purchased. The parlor differentiated domestic space more sharply along gender lines than the hall-and-chamber had. If the household areas of primary interest to women—the hearth, chamber, and yard—were second in line for innovations in household spending, then the priority of physical comfort was likely to remain low as well.

My biggest surprise in this research was to find how much of the culture of comfort developed in conjunction with landscape architecture—witness the piazza, the cottage, and the house pattern book. Because in eighteenth-century Britain comfort was, initially, episodic and recreational, garden and landscape architecture offered a wealth of opportunities to explore the culture of comfort.

These developments show how culture shapes consumption. This relationship becomes particularly interesting when applied to the society of self-conscious consumers oriented toward the satisfaction of new needs that developed in the early modern British world. Participation in a domestically oriented consuming public requires households to increase their technological specialization and to lessen their primary production for subsistence. Artificial illumination and new facilities for heating defined the space as well as the time during which newly fashionable forms of sociability would take place. Technological changes in heating and lighting symbolized an environment in which domestic activities, and their attendant patterns of consumption, would take place with fewer of their traditional elemental constraints.

Historical changes in the technology of elementary comforts depended on the existence of a fashion-conscious public that was made aware of the *dis*comfort of what had previously been considered functionally adequate. The processes by which cultural imperatives shaped new patterns of consumption are particularly evident in the preindustrial context, where changes in the design and use of domestic space and its facilities were far more dramatic than can be accounted for by technological innovations alone. These processes included vernacular emulation of the court and aristocracy as metropolitan cultures developed, exposure to new possibilities for design and consumption from contact with the material cultures of non-European societies as a world economy developed, and the intensification of secular and vernacular graphic communication after the invention of printing.

The eighteenth-century consumer revolution in Anglo-American society developed a culture of comfort that synthesized *comfort*'s new physical meanings with traditional ones of moral support. This sensibility recognized that comfort was culturally progressive rather than physically natural. Concern with comfort provided a rationale for moderate but innovative patterns of consumption that transcended both the aristocratic imperatives of luxury and the necessities of poverty.

By 1800 physical comfort had developed into a culture to be learned and demonstrated as a sign of social progress. Satisfaction with a comfortable home became one of the most convincing ways to give meaning to consumption patterns. In the early decades of the nineteenth century the ideal of comfort provided values, consumption patterns, and behaviors crucial to the formation of a middle class. The culture of comfort that developed in eighteenth-century British and Anglo-American society asserted its essential domesticity, its technological promise, and its universality: all people were entitled to physical comfort, and all people could be comfortable the same way.

NOTES

PREFACE

1. On the study of comfort in architecture schools, see Witold Rybczynski, *Home: A Short History of an Idea* (New York: Penguin Books, 1987), vii. For architectural efforts to measure comfort, see T. C. Angus, *The Control of Indoor Climate* (Oxford: Pergamon Press, 1968); Reyner Banham, *The Architecture of the Well-tempered Environment* (London: Architectural Press, 1969); P. O. Fanger, *Thermal Comfort: Analysis and Applications of Environmental Engineering* (New York: McGraw-Hill, 1970). On the cultural relativity of comfort, see Bernard Rudofsky, *Now I Lay Me Down to Eat: Notes and Footnotes on the Lost Art of Living* (New York: Anchor Books, 1980); Amos Rapoport, *House Form and Culture* (Englewood Cliffs, N.J.: Prentice-Hall, 1969); Brent C. Brolin, *The Failure of Modern Architecture* (New York: Van Nostrand Reinhold, 1976); Paul Oliver, *Dwellings: The House across the World* (Austin: University of Texas Press, 1987); Ronald G. Knapp, *The Chinese House: Craft, Symbol, and the Folk Tradition* (Oxford: Oxford University Press, 1991). On the cultural constitution of needs, see Don Slater, *Consumer Culture and Modernity* (Cambridge, England: Polity Press, 1997); Marshall Sahlins, *Culture and Practical Reason* (Chicago: University of Chicago Press, 1976). On the "development" of comfortable seating, see Siegfried Giedion, *Mechanization Takes Command: A Contribution to Anonymous History* (1948; repr. New York: W. W. Norton, 1969), 309–18; Galen Cranz, *The Chair: Rethinking Culture, Body, and Design* (New York: W. W. Norton, 1998); cf. Bernard E. Finneson and Arthur S. Freese, *Dr. Finneson on Low Back Pain* (New York: G. P. Putnam, 1975), 239. For cross-cultural comparisons of seating postures, see John Gloag, *The Englishman's Chair: Origins, Design, and Social History of Seat Furniture in Eng-

land (London: George Allen & Unwin, 1964), 2–5; Joseph Rykwert, "The Sitting Position: A Question of Method," *The Necessity of Artifice* (New York: Rizzoli, 1982), 23–31.

2. Adam Smith, *An Inquiry into the Nature and Causes of the Wealth of Nations* [1776], ed. R. H. Campbell and A. S. Skinner, 2 vols. (Oxford, 1976; repr. Indianapolis: Liberty Classics, 1981), 10, 47, 51, 95, 176, 927.

CHAPTER I   COMMODIOUS COMFORT

1. Colin Platt, *Medieval England: A Social History and Archaeology from the Conquest to A.D. 1600* (London: Routledge & Kegan Paul, 1978), 182; W. A. Panting, "Medieval Priests' Houses in South-West England," *Medieval Archaeology* 1 (1957): 119. On the relative priority of comfort in medieval design, see Witold Rybczynski, *Home: A Short History of an Idea* (New York: Penguin Books, 1987), 31–36; and Siegfried Giedion, *Mechanization Takes Command: A Contribution to Anonymous History* (1948; repr. New York: W. W. Norton, 1969), 258–304.

Comfort and its cognates have been italicized in quotations throughout.

2. Ulrich Wyrwa, "Consumption and Consumer Society: A Contribution to the History of Ideas," in *Getting and Spending: European and American Consumer Societies in the Twentieth Century* (Cambridge: Cambridge University Press, 1998), 432–33; A. J. Greimas, *Dictionnaire de l'ancien français jusqu'au milieu du XIVe siècle* 2nd ed. (Paris: Librairie Larousse, 1977), s.v. "conforter"; *The Oxford English Dictionary*, 2nd ed. (Oxford: Clarendon Press, 1989), s.v. "comfort"; Samuel Johnson, *A Dictionary of the English Language*, 2 vols. (London: J. F. & C. Rivington et al., 1785), s.v. "comfort," "comfortless," "discomfort."

3. Gwyn Jones and Thomas Jones, eds., *The Mabinogion* (London: J. M. Dent, 1949), 137–39; reference from M. W. Thompson, *The Rise of the Castle* (Cambridge: Cambridge Unviersity Press, 1991), 115. On medieval standards of housekeeping, see Barbara A. Hanawalt, *The Ties That Bound: Peasant Families in Medieval England* (New York: Oxford University Press, 1986), 37. *Le ménagier de Paris* (*The Goodman of Paris: A Treatise on Moral and Domestic Economy by A Citizen of Paris*) (*c. 1393*), ed. and trans. Eileen Power (London: George Routledge, 1928), 171–76, see also 190. Power notes that Chaucer twice used the same proverb about what drove a man from his house; ibid., 320; see also, *The Oxford Dictionary of English Proverbs*, comp. William George Smith (Oxford: Clarendon Press, 1935), 491.

4. Penelope Eames, "Documentary Evidence Concerning the Character and Use of Domestic Furnishings in England in the Fourteenth and Fifteenth Centuries," *Furniture History* 7 (1971): 50, quoting R. W. Chambers, ed., *A Fifteenth-Century Courtesy Book* (London: Early English Tract Society, 1914), 11; Thomas Wright, *A History of Domestic Manners and Sentiments in England during the Middle Ages* (London: Chapman & Hall, 1862), 59, 156–57, 259; Georges Duby, "Solitude: Eleventh to Thirteenth Century," in

A History of Private Life ed. Georges Duby, trans. Arthur Goldhammer, 5 vols. (Cambridge: Harvard University Press, 1988), 2:524–26; Philippe Braunstein, "Toward Intimacy: The Fourteenth and Fifteenth Centuries," in *History of Private Life*, 2:600–610; Hanawalt, *Ties That Bound*, 61; Barbara Harvey, *Living and Dying in England, 1100–1540: The Monastic Experience* (Oxford: Clarendon Press, 1993), 131; G. H. Cook, *English Monasteries in the Middle Ages* (London: Phoenix House, 1961), 69–70.

5. Thomas Wright, *A Volume of Vocabularies*, 2 vols. (London: Thomas Wright, 1857), as quoted in LeRoy Dresbeck, "Winter Climate and Society in the Northern Middle Ages: The Technological Impact," in *On Pre-Modern Technology and Science: A Volume of Studies in Honor of Lynn White, Jr.*, ed. Bert S. Hall and Delno C. West (Malibu, Calif.: Undena Publications, 1976), 194; Giedion, *Mechanization*, 270–76; Margaret Wade Labarge, *A Baronial Household of the Thirteenth Century* (New York: Barnes & Noble, 1965), 34; John Gloag, *A Social History of Furniture Design from B.C. 1300 to A.D. 1960* (New York: Bonanza, 1966), chap. 1; Eric Mercer, *Furniture, 700–1700* (New York: Meredith Press, 1969), 17.

6. Giedion, *Mechanization*, 260–67; Hanawalt, *Ties That Bound*, 46, 49.

7. Eames, "Documentary Evidence," 41–60; Wright, *History of Domestic Manners*, 45–46, 110, quoted 256; M. W. Barley, *The House and Home* (London: Vista Books, 1963), 21; Gloag, *Social History of Furniture Design*, 74, 78, 86; Lawrence Wright, *Warm and Snug: The History of the Bed* (London: Routledge & Kegan Paul, 1962), 18, 58–59, 71–73, 79–86, 93–100; Philippe Contamine, "Peasant Hearth to Papal Palace: The Fourteenth and Fifteenth Centuries," in *A History of Private Life*, ed. Georges Duby, trans. Arthur Goldhammer, 5 vols. (Cambridge: Harvard University Press, 1988), 2:489–99.

8. Robert Delort, *Life in the Middle Ages*, trans. Robert Allen (New York: Universe Books, 1973), 35–37, 158; James Laver, *Costume and History: A Concise History* (London: Thames & Hudson, 1982), 17, 56–60.

9. Jean Chapelot and Robert Fossier, *The Village and the House in the Middle Ages*, trans. Henry Cleere (French ed. 1980; London: B. T. Batsford, 1985); Contamine, "Peasant Hearth," 2:444–48. Castles cost in the thousands of pounds, a castle tower in the several hundreds, the hall and chamber of a modest manor house a few dozen, and a carpenter-built house for a peasant about £2; Christopher Dyer, *Standards of Living in the Later Middle Ages: Social Change in England c. 1200–1520* (Cambridge: Cambridge University Press, 1989), 80, 166. M. W. Thompson, *The Medieval Hall: The Basis of Secular Domestic Life, 600–1600 A.D.* (Aldershot, Hampshire: Scolar Press, 1995), 3, defines the hall in sociological, not architectural, terms as the possession of a noble, but it is unique as a book-length treatment of this architectural element. Thompson's social definition of the hall strains some comparisons with the houses of knights and peasants, since the aristocratic hall was used for feasting but not cooking or sleeping.

10. Peter Smith, *Houses of the Welsh Countryside: A Study in Historical Geography* (Lon-

don: Her Majesty's Stationery Office, 1975), 39–40. *The Oxford English Dictionary*, 2nd ed., 20 vols. (Oxford: Clarendon Press, 1989), s.v. "hearth"; *An Anglo-Saxon Dictionary*, ed. T. Northcote Toller (Oxford: Oxford University Press, 1898), s.v. "heorþ"; Gwyn I. Meirion-Jones, "The Long-house in Brittany: A Provisional Assessment," *Post-Medieval Archaeology* 7 (1973): 7–8; Nicholas Orme, "The Culture of Children in Medieval England," *Past and Present* 148 (May 1995): 65, 86.

11. Swaddling corresponded closely with the open hearth and was used across the social spectrum and over the whole medieval period, since it allowed children to be safely placed on the ground near the hearth for warmth; Wright, *History of Domestic Manners*, 48–51. To reduce the threat of fire while people slept, the fire was covered with a pierced lid that allowed the embers to smolder overnight but not to flame; Hanawalt, *Ties That Bound*, 40, 175. For exaggerated anachronism about the desirability of chimney fireplaces, see Leroy Joseph Dresbeck, *The Chimney and Fireplace: A Study in Technological Development Primarily in England during the Middle Ages* (Ph.D. diss., University of California–Los Angeles, 1971), 94–97. The open central hearth has less atavistic connotations in Scottish architectural history; Alexander Fenton, *The Hearth in Scotland* (Dundee: National Museum of Antiquities, 1981). On the anthropology of the relations of heating, lighting, and ventilation, see John Fitchen, "The Problem of Ventilation through the Ages," *Technology and Culture* 22 (1981): 485–511; James Marston Fitch and Daniel P. Brance, "Primitive Architecture and Climate," *Scientific American* 203, no. 6 (December 1960): 134–44; Peter Nabokov and Robert Easton, *Native American Architecture* (New York: Oxford University Press, 1989).

12. *Oxford Dictionary of English Proverbs*, 348. L. A. Shuffrey, *The English Fireplace: A History of the Development of the Chimney, Chimney-piece and Firegrate with Their Accessories, from the Earliest Times to the Beginning of the Nineteenth Century* (London: B. T. Batsford, 1912), 4; George Caspar Homans, *English Villagers of the Thirteenth Century* (1941; repr. New York: Russell & Russell, 1960), 111, 142, 180, 190–91; F. Pollock and F. W. Maitland, *The History of English Law before the Time of Edward I*, ed. S. F. C. Milsom, 2nd ed., 2 vols. (Cambridge: University Press, 1968), 2:285; R. Ross Noble, "Turf-Walled Houses of the Central Highlands: An Experiment in Reconstruction," *Folk Life* 22 (1983–84): 69. The anthropology of fire shows that its use for heating has often been subsidiary to other purposes, such as defense, light, ritual, and cooking; Kenneth Oakley, "The Earliest Fire-Makers," *Antiquity* 30, no. 118 (June 1956): 102ff. Bede quoted in Wright, *History of Domestic Manners*, 19.

13. Georges Duby, "Private Power, Public Power," in *A History of Private Life*, ed. Georges Duby, trans. Arthur Goldhammer, 5 vols. (Cambridge: Harvard University Press, 1988). 2:19; idem, "The Aristocratic Households of Feudal France," *History of Private Life*, 2:72–73.

14. Thompson, *Rise of the Castle*, 1; W. A. Pantin, "Medieval English Town-House

Plans," *Medieval Archaeology* 6–7 (1962–63): 202–9; Robert Taylor, "Town Houses in Taunton, 1500–1700," *Post-Medieval Archaeology* 8 (1974), 63–79.

15. Margaret Wood, *The English Medieval House* (London: Phoenix House, 1965), 35, 208; Wright, *History of Domestic Manners*, 11, 16, 26–27; John G. Hurst, "A Review of Archaeological Research (to 1968)," in *Deserted Medieval Villages*, ed. Maurice Beresford and John G. Hurst (London: Lutterworth, 1971), 90, 100. On chamber blocks, see John Blair, "Hall and Chamber: English Domestic Planning, 1000–1250," in *Manorial Domestic Buildings in England and Northern France*, ed. Gwyn Meirion-Jones and Michael Jones (London: Society of Antiquaries of London, 1993), 1–21. On the introduction of aisles after the Conquest, see Thompson, *Medieval Hall*, 26–27.

16. Patrick Faulkner, "Domestic Planning from the Twelfth to the Fourteenth Centuries," *Archaeological Journal* 115 (1958): 150–83; Duby, "Solitude," quoting de Mondeville, 2:522.

17. Peter Smith, "The Architectural Personality of the British Isles," *Archaeologia Cambrensis* 129 (1980): 7; J. T. Smith, "Medieval Roofs: A Classification," *Archaeological Journal* 115 (1960): 111–49; M. W. Barley, *The English Farmhouse and Cottage* (London: Routledge & Kegan Paul, 1961), 21.

18. J. T. Smith, "Medieval Aisled Halls and Their Derivatives," *Archaeological Journal* 112 (1955): 76–93; Eric Gee, "Heating in the Late Middle Ages," *Transactions of the Ancient Monuments Society* (London), 31 (1987): 88–105; Shuffrey, *English Fireplace*, 5–9; Thompson, *Medieval Hall*, 120, 141.

19. Geoffrey Chaucer, "The Nun's Priest Tale," 253, lines 2822, 2832; "The Wife of Bath's Prologue," 109, line 300; "The Wife of Bath's Tale," 117, line 869; "The House of Fame," 362, line 1186, in *The Riverside Chaucer*, ed. Larry D. Benson, 3rd ed. (Boston: Houghton Mifflin, 1988); John S. P. Tatlock and Arthur G. Kennedy, *A Concordance to the Complete Works of Geoffrey Chaucer and to the Romaunt of the Rose* (Washington, D.C.: Carnegie Institution, 1927); A. Hamilton Thompson, "The English House," in *Social Life in Early England*, ed. Geoffrey Barraclough (London: Routledge & Kegan Paul, 1960), 139; *Oxford English Dictionary*, s.v. "bower," "chamber"; *Anglo-Saxon Dictionary*, s.v. "búr," "solor," "sollar"; *Grand Larousse de la langue française*, 6 vols. (Paris: Librairie Larousse, 1971), s.v. "chambre"; Gwyn I. Meirion-Jones, "The Vernacular Architecture of France: An Assessment," *Vernacular Architecture* 16 (1985): 14–15; Maurice Barley, "Glossary of Names for Rooms in Houses of the Sixteenth and Seventeenth Centuries," in *Culture and Environment: Essays in Honour of Sir Cyril Fox*, ed. Idris Llewelyn Foster and Leslie Alcock (London: Routledge & Paul, 1963), 496–97.

20. Thomas Wright, "Illustrations of Domestic Architecture," *Archaeological Journal* (London: British Archaeological Association, 1846), 1:213–15; Kate Mertes, *The English Noble Household, 1250–1600: Governance and Politic Rule* (Oxford: Basil Blackwell, 1988), 43, 57–58; Mark Girouard, *Life in the English Country House: A Social and Architectural History* (New Haven: Yale University Press, 1978), 27.

21. Wood, *English Medieval House*, 214.

22. Roberta Gilchrist, "Medieval Bodies in the Material World: Gender Stigma and the Body," in *Framing Medieval Bodies*, ed. Sarah Kay and Miri Rubin (Manchester: Manchester University Press, 1994), 53–55; Norman John Greville Pounds, *The Medieval Castle in England and Wales: A Social and Political History* (Cambridge: Cambridge University Press, 1990), 86–87.

23. Girouard, *Life in the English Country House*, 45–47; Wright, *History of Domestic Manners*, 40.

24. Eric Mercer, "'Domus Longa' and 'Long House,'" *Vernacular Architecture* 3 (1972): 9–10; C. A. Ralegh Radford, "The Saxon House: A Review and Some Parallels," *Medieval Archaeology* 1 (1957): 27–38; Eric Mercer, *English Vernacular Houses: A Study of Traditional Farmhouses and Cottages* (London: Her Majesty's Stationery Office, 1975), 37; J. T. Smith, "The Long-house in Monmouthshire: A Re-appraisal," in *Culture and Environment: Essays in Honor of Sir Cyril Fox*, ed. Idris Llewelyn Foster and Leslie Alcock (London: Routledge & Paul, 1963), 411–12; cf. Meirion-Jones, "Long-house in Brittany," 17–18. On medieval Germanic and Scandinavian hall-houses, see Morine Krissdotter, "Ingolf's Pillars: The Changing Icelandic House," *Landscape* 26, no. 2 (1982): 7–14; Karl Baumgarten, "Some Notes on the History of the German Hall House," *Vernacular Architecture* 7 (1976): 15–20; Robert C. Hekker, "Farmstead Villages in the Netherlands," *Vernacular Architecture* 4 (1973): 7–12. Meirion-Jones would argue that longhouses have been used widely throughout the British Isles, while a preference for a single-celled dwelling space was more nearly definitive of housing traditions in Celtic regions of Brittany and Ireland; "Some Early and Primitive Building Forms in Brittany," *Folk Life* 14 (1976): 46.

25. Maurice Beresford and John Hurst, *Wharram Percy: Deserted Medieval Village* (London: B. T. Batsford, 1990), 31–51, 69–100; Guy Beresford, "Three Deserted Medieval Settlements on Dartmoor: A Report on the E. Marie Minter's Excavation," *Medieval Archaeology* 23 (1979): 98–158; Smith, "Long-house in Monmouthshire," 393, 412–13.

26. Dyer, *Standards of Living*, 166; John Walker, "Wynter's Armourie: A Base-Cruck Hall in Essex and Its Significance," *Vernacular Architecture* 18 (1987): 25–33; Hurst, "Review of Archaeological Research," 99–100.

27. Platt, *Medieval England*, 40; Smith, *Houses of the Welsh Countryside*, 19.

28. Platt, *Medieval England*, 42, 105, 107; Helen Clarke, *The Archaeology of Medieval England* (Oxford: Basil Blackwell, 1986), 33–36; Mercer, *English Vernacular Houses*, 47–48.

29. Christopher Dyer, "English Peasant Buildings in the Later Middle Ages," *Medieval Archaeology*, 30 (1986): 19–43. On the effort required to maintain houses of semi-permanent construction, often equivalent to at least three or four weeks of household labor per year, see Noble, "Turf-Walled Houses," 68–83.

30. Mercer, *English Vernacular Houses*, 20–23; J. T. Smith, "The Evolution of the English Peasant House to the Late Seventeenth Century: The Evidence of Buildings,"

Journal of the British Archaeological Association, 3rd ser., 33 (1970): 122–47. For an example of a Downland (Sussex) timber-framed house remodeled in the early sixteenth century but retaining an open hearth and chalk floor, see F. G. Aldsworth, "A Medieval and Seventeenth-Century House at Walderton, West Sussex, Dismantled and Re-erected at the Weald and Downland Open Air Museum," *Sussex Archaeological Collections* 120 (1982): 45–92.

31. *Oxford Dictionary of English Proverbs,* 283, 316, 323, 461; Hurst, "Review of Archaeological Research," 106–11, 114; Mercer, *English Vernacular Houses,* 8, 13–14.

32. D. Hawes Richards, "The Chimney," *Journal of the British Archaeological Association,* 3rd ser., 24 (1961): 67–79; Eurwyn Wiliam, "Yr Aelwyd: The Architectural Development of the Hearth in Wales," *Folk Life* 16 (1978): 85–100; Sir Cyril Fox and Lord Raglan, *Monmouthshire Houses: A Study of Building Techniques and Smaller Houseplans in the Fifteenth to Seventeenth Centuries* (Cardiff: National Museum of Wales, 1954), 45.

33. There are no surviving French examples of aristocratic halls with central open hearths; Meirion-Jones, "Vernacular Architecture of France," 11, 16. M. E. Wood, "Norman Domestic Architecture," *Archaeological Journal* 92 (1935): 167–242; J-C. Bans, P. Gaillard-Bans, and Peter Smith, "Le Manoir de Saint Lô, Aclou," *Vernacular Architecture* 26 (1995): 26–32; *Oxford Latin Dictionary,* 2 vols. (Oxford: Clarendon Press, 1968), s.v. "caminus"; *Dictionnaire historique de la langue française,* 2 vols. (Paris: Dictonnaires Le Robert, 1992), s.v. "cheminée"; *Grand Larousse de la langue française,* 6 vols. (Paris: Librairie Larousse, 1971), s.v. "cheminée"; *The Oxford English Dictionary,* 2nd ed., 20 vols. (Oxford: Clarendon Press, 1989), s.v. "chimney"; *An Anglo-Saxon Dictionary,* ed. T. Northcote Toller (Oxford: Oxford University Press, 1898), s.v. "fýr."

34. Walter Horn and Ernest Born, *The Plan of St. Gall: A Study of the Architecture and Economy of, and Life in a Paradigmatic Carolingian Monastery,* 3 vols. (Berkeley: University of California Press, 1979), 2:124, 128; Dresbeck, *Chimney and Fireplace,* 48–49, 59, 83; David Lord, "Power Applied to Purpose: Towards a Synthesis of Climate, Energy and Comfort," *Journal of Architectural Education* 37, nos. 3, 4 (Spring–Summer 1984): 38–42.

35. Horn and Born, *Plan of St. Gall,* 2:348; Dresbeck, *Chimney and Fireplace,* 93; on stoves in Eastern Europe, see Chapelot and Fossier, *Village and House,* 210; "Plaster and Wicker Chimneys" in Wood, *English Medieval House;* E. W. Parkin, "A Unique Aisled Cottage at Petham," in *Collectanea Historica: Essays in Memory of Stuart Rigold,* ed. Alec Detsicas (Maidstone: Kent Archaeological Society, 1981), 227–30.

36. Hugh Braun, *English Abbeys* (London: Faber & Faber, 1971), 114–15; "From Hildemar's Commentary on St. Benedict's Rule (c. 850)," "A Description of the Monastery of Farfa (Cluny II, c. 1042–1049)," in Wolfgang Braunfels, *Monasteries of Western Europe: The Architecture of the Orders* (Princeton: Princeton University Press, 1972), 237–39.

37. Girouard, *Life in the English Country House,* 59, 103; Cook, *English Monasteries,* 74; Braun, *English Abbeys,* 127, 155, 179; Wright, *History of Domestic Manners,* 1862), 134.

Bishops' palaces introduced the parlor in North Wales in the fourteenth century; Smith, *Houses of the Welsh Countryside*, 48.

38. The undercroft, or subdorter, of the dormitory (dorter), was usually the warming room or *calefactorium*, the only heated place in the claustral precincts besides the kitchen. True to the Roman origins of monastic architecture, braziers initially provided the heat. Cistercians, however, used warming *houses*, smaller in floor plan than subdorters; they had dual chimney fireplaces (as at Rievaulx and Fountains) or else (as at Tintern) carefully louvered open hearths on the model of monastic kitchens; R. Liddesdale Palmer, *English Monasteries in the Middle Ages: An Outline of Monastic Architecture and Custom from the Conquest to the Suppression* (London: Constable, 1930), 149; Georges Duby, "Aristocratic Households of Feudal France," in *A History of Private Life*, ed. Georges Duby, trans. Arthur Goldhammer, 5 vols. (Cambridge: Harvard University Press, 1988), 2:48–49; J. C. Dickinson, *Monastic Life in Medieval England* (London: Adam & Charles Black, 1961), 34; Harvey, *Living and Dying in England*, 130.

39. Wright, "Illustrations of Domestic Architecture," 1:213.

40. Contamine, "Peasant Hearth," 2:482–84, 487; Leroy Joseph Dresbeck, "The Chimney," *Albion* 3 (1971): 25, cites an early-thirteenth-century reference to Carthusians' having chimney fireplaces in their cells.

41. Platt, *Medieval England*, 165–72; Harvey, *Living and Dying*, 77, 89–90, 130.

42. C. R. Peers, "Finchale Priory," *Archaeologia Aeliana*, 4th ser., no. 4 (1927): 193–220; William Greenwell, *Durham Cathedral*, 6th ed. (Durham, England: Andrews, 1904), 107.

43. Eileen Power, *Medieval English Nunneries, c. 1275–1535* (1922; repr. New York: Biblo & Tannen, 1964), 316–22.

44. Howard Morris Stuckert, *Corrodies in the English Monasteries: A Study in English Social History of the Middle Ages* (Philadelphia: University of Pennsylvania Press, 1923), 44; Platt, *Medieval England*, 149–54; Contamine, "Peasant Hearth," 2:488–89.

45. Wood, *English Medieval House*, 183, 200, 202; Panting, "Medieval Priests' Houses," 118–46.

46. Duby, "Solitude," 2:530; Girouard, *Life in the English Country House*, 56.

47. The following discussion is based on Dominique Barthélemy, "Civilizing the Fortress: Eleventh to Thirteenth Century," in *A History of Private Life*, ed. Georges Duby, trans. Arthur Goldhammer, 5 vols. (Cambridge: Harvard University Press, 1988), 2:396–423; John Burke, *Life in the Castle in Medieval England* (1978; repr. New York: British Heritage Press, 1987); Norman John Greville Pounds, *The Medieval Castle in England and Wales: A Social and Political History* (Cambridge: Cambridge University Press, 1990), 232–39; Thompson, *Rise of the Castle*, 136–37; Lawrence Wright, *Home Fires Burning: The History of Domestic Heating and Cooking* (London: Routledge & Kegan Paul, 1964), 19–24; Thompson, *Medieval Hall*, 62–98; Shuffrey, *English Fireplace*, 14–23; Janet Burton, *Monastic and Religious Orders in Britain, 1000–1300* (Cambridge: Cam-

bridge University Press, 1994), 132; Cook, *English Monasteries*, 41–42. While chimneys were being introduced to Anglo-Norman castles, stoves became frequent in Germanic castles; Bernard Metz, "A propos de quelques eléments du confort dans les chateaux fort alsaciens," in *Le chateau mediéval, forteresse habitée (XIe–XVIe): Archaeologie et histoire: Perspectives de la recherche en Rhone-Alpes, Documents d'Archaeologie Française*, no. 32 (Paris: Editions de la Maison des Sciences de l'Homme, 1992), 143–46, 149.

48. Burke, *Life in the Castle*, 11; Platt, *Medieval England*, 11, 13; Barthélemy, "Civilizing the Fortress," 2:404.

49. Platt, *Medieval England*, 16; Thompson, *Rise of the Castle*, 39, 59, 74–75.

50. D. F. Renn, *Norman Castles in Britain*, 2nd ed. (London: John Baker, 1973), 120, 130, 151, 255, 262, 265; cf. 143, 155–57, 191, 262; on castles as symbolic representations of royal authority, see T. A. Heslop, "Orford Castle, Nostalgia and Sophisticated Living," *Architectural History* 34 (1991): 36–58, esp. 42, 44.

51. For an exceptional emphasis on the continuing importance of the open hearth in medieval culture, see Thompson, *Medieval Hall*, 101, 110.

52. P. A. Faulkner, "Castle Planning in the Fourteenth Century," *Archaeological Journal* 120 (1963): 215–35.

53. Wright, "Illustrations of Domestic Architecture," 302–3, 305; Dresbeck, *Chimney and Fireplace*, 188–92; L. F. Salzman, *Building in England down to 1540: A Documentary History* (Oxford: Clarendon Press, 1967), 384–86.

54. Susan Margaret Conrad, *The Household Structure of the Medieval Castle and the Organization of Space: From the Eleventh through Fourteenth Centuries* (master's thesis, California State University at Fullerton, 1992), 103–5.

55. M. W. Thompson, *The Decline of the Castle* (Cambridge: Cambridge University Press, 1987), 68–69; Mertes, *English Noble Household*, 186–87.

56. Girouard, *Life in the English Country House*, 5–56; Andrew Ayton, *Knights and Warhorses: Military Service and the English Aristocracy under Edward III* (Woodbridge, Suffolk: Boydell Press, 1994), 10–11, 88–96, 232–46. Felicity Heal, "The Idea of Hospitality in Early Modern England," *Past and Present* 102 (February 1984): 66–67, 81–82; Thompson, *Medieval Hall*, 152–55.

57. On the late medieval "aversion to wintertime" (179), see Dresbeck, "Winter Climate and Society," 223–30; Contamine, "Peasant Hearth," 428, 429.

58. "The Boke of Kervynge" [1413], in *Early English Meals and Manners*, ed. Frederick J. Furnivall (London: Early English Text Society, 1868), 169; John Russell, "The Boke of Nurture folowyng Englondis gise" (c. 1450) (Harleian MS 4011), "The Office off a Chamburlayne," lines 875–78, 887–90, in *Early English Meals*, 60, 61.

59. William Langland, *The Book Concerning Piers the Plowman*, ed. Rachel Attwater (London: J. M. Dent, 1957), passus X, 78; Burke, *Life in the Castle*, 108–9, 116; Girouard, *Life in the English Country House*, 46–47; Wright, *History of Domestic Manners*, 150–54, 168; *Book of Kervynge*.

60. For an exaggerated account of the need for, social extent of, and social impact of the chimney in medieval Europe, see Dresbeck, *Chimney and Fireplace,* e.g., 8, 36. "By the twelfth century, the fireplace, in conjunction with the flue and chimney stack, had become the major source of heating for buildings in Western Europe"; ibid., 101, cf. 200n.

61. Wright, *History of Domestic Manners,* 83, 123; Andrew Boorde, *A Compendyous Regyment or a Dyetary of Helth,* ed. F. J. Furnivall ([1547]; London: Early English Text Society, 1870), quoted 247.

62. Smith, *Houses of the Welsh Countryside,* quoted 266. Eleanor S. Godfrey, *The Development of English Glassmaking, 1560–1640* (Chapel Hill: University of North Carolina Press, 1975), 207.

63. Godfrey, *Development of English Glassmaking,* 157–59; most of the following discussion of glassmaking is taken from this account.

64. Radford, "The Saxon House," 32–34; C. F. Innocent, *The Development of English Building Construction* (1916; repr., Newton Abbot: Charles & David Reprints, 1971), 249.

65. R. J. Charleston, *English Glass and the Glass Used in England, Circa 400–1940* (London: George Allen & Unwin, 1984), 13–14, Bede quoted 12; D. B. Harden, "Domestic Window Glass: Roman, Saxon and Medieval," *Studies in Building History: Essays in Recognition of the Work of B. H. St. J. O'Neil,* ed. E. M. Jope (London: Odhams Press, 1961), 48, 52–54.

66. Salzman, *Building in England,* 175, 356, Malmesbury quoted 365.

67. Peter Fergusson, *Architecture of Solitude: Cistercian Abbeys in Twelfth-Century England* (Princeton: Princeton University Press, 1984), 10, quoted 64.

68. Salzman, *Building in England,* 379.

69. Ibid., 379–80 (quoting Piers Plowman), 387, 398; Panting, "Medieval Priests' Houses," 1:122–23, 134.

70. Guy Beresford, "The Medieval Manor of Penhallam, Jacobstow, Cornwall," *Medieval Archaeology* 18 (1974): 90–145; Pantin, "Medieval Town-House Plans," 209.

71. Salzman, *Building in England,* 384 (insertions Salzman's).

72. Geoffrey Chaucer, "The Book of the Duchess," *The Riverside Chaucer,* ed. Larry D. Benson, 3rd ed. (Boston: Houghton Mifflin, 1988), lines 322–27, 335–38; Salzman, *Building in England,* 174–75, 384–85; Walker, "Wynter's Armourie," 30. Desiderius Erasmus, *The Correspondence of Erasmus,* trans. R. A. B. Mynors and Alexander Dalzell (11 vols.), vol. 10, *1523–1524* (Toronto: University of Toronto Press, 1992), Erasmus to John Francis, c. 27 December 1524, 10:471. *The American Heritage Dictionary of the English Language,* ed. William Morris (Boston: Houghton Mifflin, 1969), s.v. "story."

CHAPTER 2   CIVIL COMFORT

1. Colin Platt, *The Great Rebuildings of Tudor and Stuart England: Revolutions in Architectural Taste* (London: UCL Press, 1994); Mark Girouard, *Life in the English Country House: A Social and Architectural History* (New Haven: Yale University Press, 1978), 85, quoted 88; Kate Mertes, *The English Noble Household, 1250–1600: Governance and Politic Rule* (Oxford: Basil Blackwell, 1988), 103; Christopher Dyer, *Standards of Living in the Later Middle Ages: Social Change in England c. 1200–1520* (Cambridge: Cambridge University Press, 1989), 83; Felicity Heal, *Hospitality in Early Modern England* (Oxford: Clarendon Press, 1990), 36–48.

2. Mertes, *English Noble Household*, 51, 190–91; M. W. Barley, "Rural Housing in England," in *The Agrarian History of England and Wales (1560–1640)*, ed. Joan Thirsk, 7 vols. to date (Cambridge: Cambridge University Press, 1967–), 4:699.

3. Maurice Howard, "Self-Fashioning and the Classical Moment in Mid-Sixteenth-Century English Architecture," in *Renaissance Bodies: The Human Figure in English Culture c. 1540–1660*, ed. Lucy Gent and Nigel Llewllyn (London: Reacktion Books, 1990), 198–217; Mark Girouard, *Hardwick Hall* (London: National Trust, 1989), 15–16; Eric Mercer, *Furniture, 700–1700* (New York: Meredith Press, 1969), 100; Lord Raglan, "The Origin of Vernacular Architecture," *Culture and Environment: Essays in Honour of Sir Cyril Fox*, ed. Idris Llewelyn Foster and Leslie Alcock (London: Routledge & Paul, 1963), 373–87.

4. Barley, "Rural Housing," 4:696–766, esp. 720, 752; C. F. Innocent, *The Development of English Building Construction* (1916; repr., Newton Abbot: Charles & David Reprints, 1971), 248–69; Christopher Dyer, "English Peasant Buildings in the Later Middle Ages (1200–1500)," *Medieval Archaeology* 30 (1986): 19–45; J. T. Smith, "The Evolution of the English Peasant House to the Late Seventeenth Century: The Evidence of Buildings," *Journal of the British Archaeological Association*, 3rd ser., no. 33 (1970): 122–47; C. A. Hewett, "The Development of the Post-Medieval House," *Post-Medieval Archaeology* 7 (1973), 60–78; Matthew Johnson, *Housing Culture: Traditional Architecture in and English Landscape* (Washington D.C.: Smithsonian Institution Press, 1993), 44–63, 142–44; A. Emery, "Ralph, Lord Cromwell's Manor at Wingfield (1439–c. 1450): Its Construction, Design and Influence," *Archaeological Journal* 142 (1985): 276–339, esp. 291.

5. Howard Colvin and John Newman, eds., *Of Building: Roger North's Writings on Architecture* ([1698]; Oxford: Clarendon Press, 1981), xiv–xv. On the continuation of the hall as a space for open hospitality in gentry households, see Felicity Heal and Clive Holmes, *The Gentry in England and Wales, 1500–1700* (Stanford, Calif.: Stanford University Press, 1994), 282–89.

6. Desiderius Erasmus, *The Correspondence of Erasmus*, trans. R. A. B. Mynors and Alexander Dalzell (11 vols.), vol. 10, *1523–1524* (Toronto: University of Toronto Press,

1992), Erasmus to John Francis, c. 27 December 1524, 10:471. Erasmus's prejudice against dirt floors may have biased his perceptions, since maintaining a clean floor to reduce fire hazards was a high priority in medieval housekeeping. John G. Hurst, "A Review of Archaeological Research (to 1968)," in *Deserted Medieval Villages*, ed. Maurice Beresford and John G. Hurst (London: Lutterworth, 1971), 98–99; Gwyn I. Meirion-Jones, "Some Early and Primitive Building Forms in Brittany," *Folk Life* 14 (1976): 55–56. *The Complete Works of Saint Thomas More*, vol. 4, *Utopia*, ed. Edward Surtz, S.J., and J. H. Hexter, 15 vols. (New Haven: Yale University Press, 1961), 4:121; Sebastiano Serlio, *Regole generali di architettura* (Venice, 1537), book 4.

7. W. G. Hoskins, "The Great Rebuilding of Rural England, 1570 to 1640," *Past and Present* 4 (1953): 44–59; M. W. Barley, *The English Farmhouse and Cottage* (London: Routledge & Kegan Paul, 1961), 46, 62; Anthony Quiney, "The Lobby-Entry House: Its Origins and Distribution," *Architectural History* 27 (1984): 456–66. The best study of the transition is Johnson, *Housing Culture*, 64–121.

8. William Harrison, *The Description of England*, ed. Georges Edelen ([1587]; Ithaca: Cornell University Press, 1968), 200–201, 205, 276. The other two alterations Harrison noted were the replacement of straw pallets with beds and of wooden dining ware with glass and metal vessels and spoons. Harrison drafted *The Description of England* in the 1560s and then revised it over the next two decades as it was published with Holinshed's *Chronicles* in 1577 and issued separately in 1587; D. M. Palliser, *The Age of Elizabeth: England under the Later Tudors, 1547–1603* (London: Longman, 1983), 390–91.

9. Eric Mercer, *English Vernacular Houses: A Study of Traditional Farmhouses and Cottages* (London: Her Majesty's Stationery Office, 1975), 60–63.

10. Linda Hall, "Yeoman or Gentleman? Problems in Defining Social Status in Seventeenth- and Eighteenth-Century Gloucestershire," *Vernacular Architecture* 22 (1991): 5. Sylvia Colman, "Two Small Mediaeval Houses: Walnut Tree Cottage, Wattisfield, and Friars Hall, Rattlesden: The Effects of Modernisation," *Proceedings of the Suffolk Institute of Archaeology* 31 (1967): 68–70; John Walker, "Wynter's Armourie: A Base-Cruck Hall in Essex and Its Significance," *Vernacular Architecture* 18 (1987): 30; Frank E. Brown, "Continuity and Change in the Urban House: Developments in Domestic Space Organisation in Seventeenth-Century London," *Comparative Studies in Society and History* 28, no. 3 (July 1986): 583–84.

11. Peter Smith, *Houses of the Welsh Countryside: A Study in Historical Geography* (London: Her Majesty's Stationery Office, 1975), 232; M. W. Barley, "Rural Building in England," in *The Agrarian History of England and Wales (1640–1750)*, ed. Joan Thirsk (Cambridge: Cambridge University Press, 1985): 5:659.

12. Barley, *English Farmhouse and Cottage*, 43, 63, 88–89, 134, 139–40.

13. Ibid., 44–45, 74.

14. Margaret Wood, *The English Medieval House* (London: Phoenix House, 1965), 247; Maurice Barley, "Glossary of Names for Rooms in Houses of the Sixteenth and Sev-

enteenth Centuries," *Culture and Environment: Essays in Honour of Sir Cyril Fox*, ed.
Idris Llewelyn Foster and Leslie Alcock (London: Routledge & Paul, 1963), 492–93;
H. M. Spufford, "The Significance of the Cambridgeshire Hearth Tax," *Cambridge
Antiquarian Society Proceedings* 55 (1962): 53–59.

15. Barley, *English Farmhouse and Cottage*, 141, 149, 172, 239; Ursula Priestley and
P. J. Cornfield, "Rooms and Room Use in Norwich Housing, 1580–1730," *Post-
Medieval Archaeology* 16 (1982): 105–6, 108–9.

16. Priestley and Cornfield, "Rooms and Room Use," 101, 104–5, 108.

17. John Bell Henneman, *Royal Taxation in Fourteenth-Century France: The Develop-
ment of War Financing, 1322–1356* (Princeton: Princeton University Press, 1971), 4–5;
C. Clegg, "Hearth and Window Taxes," *Halifax Antiquarian Society* (1913): 275–76; *The
Economic Writings of Sir William Petty*, ed. Charles Hunt Hull (Cambridge: Cambridge
University Press, 1899), "Verbum Sapienti" (MS [1665], publ. [1691]), 1:115, "A Trea-
tise of Taxes and Contributions" [1662], 1:94.

18. C. D. Chandaman, *The English Public Revenue, 1660–1688* (Oxford: Clarendon
Press, 1975), 77–109; Lydia M. Marshall, "The Levying of the Hearth Tax, 1662–
1688," *English Historical Review* 51 (1936), 628–46; William Kennedy, *English Taxation,
1640–1799: An Essay on Policy and Opinion* (London: G. Bell & Sons, 1913), 58; John Pat-
ten, "The Hearth Taxes, 1662–1689," *Local Population Studies* 7 (1971): 15–16. The
statute with which Parliament legislated the hearth tax was 14 Charles II, c. 10; the
tax was repealed with 1 William & Mary, c. 10.

19. Tim Unwin, "Late Seventeenth-Century Taxation and Population: The Not-
tinghamshire Hearth Taxes and Compton Census," *Historical Geography Research Series*,
no. 16 (1985; Norwich: Institute of British Geographers, 1985); cf. Gwyn I. Meirion-
Jones, "The Use of Hearth Tax Returns and Vernacular Architecture in Settlement
Studies, with Examples from North-East Hampshire," *Transactions of the Institute of
British Geographers* 52 (March 1971), 133–60.

20. Andrew Boorde, *A Compendyous Regyment or a Dyetary of Helth*, ed. F. J. Furnivall
([1542]; London: Early English Text Society, 1870), 233, 235, 237, 239, 246–47; Harrison, *Description of England*, 200–201, 205, 276.

21. *Oxford Dictionary of English Proverbs*, 232. Spufford, "Significance of Hearth Tax";
Carole Shammas, *The Preindustrial Consumer in England and America* (Oxford: Oxford
University Press, 1990), 164–65.

22. *Rutland Hearth Tax 1665*, ed. Jill Bourne and Amanda Cole (Rutland Record
Society, 1991); W. G. Hoskins, *The Midland Peasant: The Economic and Social History of a
Leicestershire Village* (London: Macmillan, 1965), 299–307. In the early eighteenth century it cost £6–10 to renovate a house to the new standard of brick chimney, staircase, glazed windows, ceilings above the first floor, and plastering. That amount was
equivalent to the profit of two good years from a thirty-acre farm or one year's profit
from a sheep farm of that size; R. Machin, "The Mechanism of the Pre-Industrial

Building Cycle," *Vernacular Architecture* 8 (1977): 817. On chimney construction, see Colin Platt, *Medieval England: A Social History and Archaeology from the Conquest to A.D. 1600* (London: Routledge & Kegan Paul, 1978), 178; Jane E. Wight, *Brick Building in England from the Middle Ages to 1550* (London: John Baker, 1972), 98; L. F. Salzman, *Building in England down to 1540: A Documentary History* (Oxford: Clarendon Press, 1967), 98–100; E. L. Jones and M. E. Falkus, "Urban Improvement and the English Economy in the Seventeenth and Eighteenth Centuries," *Research in Economic History* 4 (1979): 198–203.

23. Barley, *English Farmhouse*, 188–90; Arthur Percival, "The Dutch Influence on English Vernacular Architecture with Particular Reference to East Kent," *Blackmansbury* 3, nos. 1, 2 (1966): 38–39; Gwyn I. Meirion-Jones, "The Domestic Buildings of Odiham, Hampshire," *Folk Life* 9 (1971): 130–34; Hoskins, *Midland Peasant*, 302; Robin Lucas, "When Did Norfolk Cross 'The Brick Threshold'?" *Vernacular Architecture* 28 (1997): 68–80; Abraham de la Pryme, "History and Antiquities of Hatfield Chase, Yorkshire," British Library, Manuscript Collection, Lansdowne MS 897, fol. 40r (courtesy of Daniel Woolf).

24. Richard Carew, *Survey of Cornwall*, ed. F. E. Halliday (MS c. 1582, publ. 1602, repr. London, 1969), 138, 124; William Smith (MS on Cheshire, c. 1585, publ. in Daniel King, *The Vale-Royal of England* [1656]), quoted in Palliser, *Age of Elizabeth*, 111.

25. Carew, *Survey of Cornwall*, 138, 124; Harrison, *Description of England*, 195; William Smith, MS on Cheshire, in Palliser, *Age of Elizabeth*, 111; Richard Gough, *The History of Myddle*, ed. David Hey (MS [1701–1702]; London: Penguin Books, 1981), 234–35; John Aubrey, *Natural History of Wiltshire* [1847], quoted in Mildred Campbell, *The English Yeoman under Elizabeth and the Early Stuarts* (1942; repr. New York: Barnes & Noble, 1960), 232.

26. R. Plot, *The Natural History of Staffordshire* (Oxford, 1686), quoted in Palliser, *Age of Elizabeth*, 113–14; Harrison, *Description of England*, 195; Andrew Boorde, "The First Boke of the Introduction of Knowledge," ed. F. J. Furnivall, *Andrew Boorde's Introduction and Dyetary, with Barnes in the Defence of the Berde* ([1547]; London: Early English Text Society, 1870), 136.

27. William Horman, *Vulgaria* (1519; repr. Norwood, N.J.: Walter J. Johnson, 1975), 242; M. W. Barley, *The House and Home* (London: Vista Books, 1963), 45; Christopher Hibbert, *The English: A Social History 1066–1945* (New York: Norton, 1987), 12; W. G. Hoskins, "An Elizabethan Provincial Town: Leicester," in *Provincial England: Essays in Social and Economic History* (London: Macmillan, 1963), 107; Eleanor S. Godfrey, *The Development of English Glassmaking, 1560–1640* (Chapel Hill: University of North Carolina Press, 1975), 207; Salzman, *Building in England*, 185; Barley, *English Farmhouse*, 70. Yeomen, too, bequeathed "glass in and about my house"; Campbell, *English Yeoman*, 232; John Henry Parker, *Some Account of Domestic Architecture in England, from Richard II to Henry VIII*, 2 vols. (Oxford: John Henry & James Parker, 1859), 1:122.

28. R. J. Charleston, *English Glass and the Glass Used in England, Circa 400–1940* (London: George Allen & Unwin, 1984), 80–81.

29. Godfrey, *Development of English Glassmaking*, 9–13, 209; Charleston, *English Glass*, 72–73, 78.

30. Godfrey, *Development of English Glassmaking*, 211–15; Charleston, *English Glass*, 79.

31. Godfrey, *Development of English Glassmaking*, 16–28.

32. Ibid., 202.

33. Ibid., 50–74, 82, 126, 139.

34. Innocent, *Development of English Building*, 258; Smith, *Houses of the Welsh Countryside*, 266.

35. Godfrey, *Development of English Glassmaking*, 205–6.

36. Laneham, *A Letter Whearin Part of the Entertainment, untoo the Queenz Majesty, at Killingwoorth Castl*, quoted in Mark Girouard, *Robert Smythson and the Architecture of the Elizabethan Era* (New York: A. S. Barnes, 1967), 33; see also 44–45, 71, 86–88, 99. Godfrey, *Development of English Glassmaking*, 205. Francis Bacon criticized as illogical the use of glass in architecture sheerly for display; *The Complete Essays of Francis Bacon* (1597; New York: Washington Square Press, 1963), 117–18.

37. Hurst, "Review of Archaeological Research," 97; Meirion-Jones, "Early and Primitive Building Forms," 56, 58; Caoimhín O'Danachair, "The Combined Byre-And-Dwelling," *Folk Life* 2 (1964): 70–71; Gwyn I. Meirion-Jones, "The Long-house in Brittany: A Provisional Assessment," *Post-Medieval Archaeology* 7, no. 2 (1973): 5–6.

38. Godfrey, *Development of English Glassmaking*, 208; Hoskins, *Midland Peasant*, 149, 291, 297, 298.

39. Abbott Lowell Cummings, *The Framed Houses of Massachusetts Bay, 1625–1725* (Cambridge: Harvard University Press, 1979), 145–56; idem, ed., "Massachusetts Bay Building Documents, 1638–1726," *Architecture in Colonial Massachusetts*, ed. idem (Boston: Colonial Society of Massachusetts, 1979), 193–221.

40. Abbott Lowell Cummings, "The Beginnings of Provincial Renaissance? Architecture in Boston, 1690–1725," *Journal of the Society of Architectural Historians* 42 (1983): 49; "Massachusetts Bay Building Documents," 196, 203, 208.

41. Clegg, "Hearth and Windows Taxes," 300–302. The statute for the window tax was 7 & 8 William III, c. 18.

42. Cummings, *Framed Houses*, 154–56; Charleston, *English Glass*, 195.

43. "Massachusetts Bay Building Documents," 194–95; Hall, "Yeoman or Gentleman?" 13–14, 19n. On the admirability of windows "sasht with Cristal Glass," see Robert Beverley, *The History and Present State of Virginia*, ed. Louis B. Wright (1705; repr. Chapel Hill: University of North Carolina Press, 1947), 289; Ivor Noel Hume, "A Window on Williamsburg: 'sasht with Cristal Glass,' the casement window swung outward," *Colonial Williamsburg* 20, no. 1 (Autumn 1997): 32–39.

44. *The Diary of Ralph Josselin, 1616–1683*, ed. Alan Macfarlane (London: Oxford

University Press for the British Academy, 1976), 3 (March 1632), 138 (13–14 September 1648), 217–18 (9 October 1650).

45. *The Oxford English Dictionary*, ed. J. A. Simpson and E. S. C. Weiner, 2nd ed., 20 vols. (Oxford: Clarendon Press, 1989), s.v. "ease." *Records of the Colony of New Plymouth in New England. Laws 1623–1682*, ed. David Pulsifer, 12 vols. (Boston: Commonwealth of Massachusetts, 1855–61), 6:125–26, 11:111 (1658); references from John Demos, *A Little Commonwealth: Family Life in Plymouth Colony* (New York: Oxford University Press, 1970), 76, 104. See also, Philip J. Greven, Jr., "Family Structure in Seventeenth-Century Andover, Massachusetts," *William and Mary Quarterly*, 3rd ser., 23, no. 2 (April 1966): 253; idem, *Four Generations: Population, Land, and Family in Colonial Andover, Massachusetts* (Ithaca: Cornell University Press, 1970), 145–46. Demos, *A Little Commonwealth*, 76, quoting deeds by John Branch and William White. Estate of John Boynton (1671), estate of Richard Dodge, Sr. (1671), *The Probate Records of Essex County Massachusetts*, 3 vols. (Salem: Essex Institute, 1916–1920), 2:215, 230–32.

46. Paul Drury, "'A Fayre House, Buylt by Sir Thomas Smith,' The Development of Hill Hall, Essex, 1557–1581," *Journal of the British Archaeological Association* 136 (1983): 98–123; "The Life of Adam Martindale Written by Himself," ed. Richard Parkinson, in *Remains Historical and Literary Connected with the Palatine Counties of Lancaster and Chester* (1845; repr. New York: Johnson Reprint, 1968), 4:12; cf. Barley, *English Farmhouse*, 114. Robert Blair St. George, "'Set Thine House in Order': The Domestication of the Yeomanry in Seventeenth-Century New England," in *New England Begins: The Seventeenth Century*, 3 vols., ed. Jonathan L. Fairbanks and Robert F. Trent (Boston: Museum of Fine Arts, 1982), 2:161–62, 166.

47. Gervase Markham, *Country Contentments, or the English Huswife* (London: R. Jackson, 1623), 154; Boorde, *Compendyous Regyment*," 235, 237, 249; Furnivall, *Andrew Boorde's Introduction and Dyetary*, "Extracts from Andrew Boorde, *Brevyary of Health*" (1547).

48. Boorde, *Compendyous Regyment*, 233, 235, 237, 239, 246–47; Bacon, *Complete Essays*, 115; John Worlidge, *Systema Agriculturae: The Mystery of Husbandry Discovered*, 2nd ed. (London: T. Dring, 1675), 231; John Shute, *The Theory and Practice of Architecture; or Vitruvius and Vignola Abridg'd* (London: R. Wellington, 1703), 17–18; John Shute, *The First and Chief Groundes of Architecture Used in All the Auncient and Famous Monumentes* (London: Thomas Marshe, 1563), Biiiv.

49. Norbert Elias, *The Civilizing Process*, trans. Edmund Jephcott, 2 vols. (orig. publ. in German, 1939; New York: Pantheon Books, 1978 [vol. 1]); Dora Thornton, *The Scholar in His Study: Ownership and Experience in Renaissance Italy* (New Haven: Yale University Press, 1997); Peter Thornton, *The Italian Renaissance Interior, 1400–1600* (London, Weidenfeld & Nicolson, 1991), 13, 15.

50. Shammas, *Preindustrial Consumer*; Campbell, *English Yeoman*, 238–40; Harrison, *Description of England*, 200.

51. Harrison, *Description of England*, 200–202. On the specialization of household

labor, see Jan de Vries, "Between Purchasing Power and the World of Goods: Under-standing the Household Economy of Early Modern Europe," in *Consumption and the World of Goods*, ed. John Brewer and Roy Porter (London: Routledge, 1993), 85–132. For similar developments in the Netherlands, see Jan de Vries, "Peasant Demand Pat-terns and Economic Development: Friesland 1550–1750," in *European Peasants and Their Markets: Essays in Agrarian Economic History*, ed. William N. Parker and Eric L. Jones (Princeton: Princeton University Press, 1975), 205–63; Simon Schama, *The Embarrassment of Riches: An Interpretation of Dutch Culture in the Golden Age* (Berkeley: Uni-versity of California Press, 1988), 290–322, 375–97; Witold Rybczynski, *Home: A Short History of an Idea* (New York: Penguin Books, 1987), 51–75.

52. Campbell, *English Yeoman*, quoted 235; Peter Thornton and Maurice Tomlin, *The Furnishing and Decoration of Ham House* (London: Furniture History Society, 1980), 31–32, 56.

53. Thornton and Tomlin, *Furnishing of Ham House*, 24, 56, 110, 145.

54. Markham, *Country Contentments*, 154; William Vaughan, "Fifteen Directions to Preserve Health" (from *Natural and Artificial Directions for Health* [1602]), in *Early English Meals and Manners*, ed. Frederick J. Furnivall (London: Early English Text Society, 1868), 136–37; Boorde, *Compendyous Regyment*, 244, 247, 249; Cotton Mather, *Comfort-able Chambers Opened and Visited* (Boston: J. Edwards, 1728).

55. Boorde, "First Boke," 132–33; Edmund Spenser, *A View of the Present State of Ire-land*, ed. W. L. Renwick ([1596]; Oxford: Clarendon Press, 1970), 51–53, 156–59.

56. William Petty, "The Political Anatomy of Ireland" (MS [1672]; publ. [1691]), in *A Collection of Tracts and Treatises Illustrative of the Natural History, Antiquities, and the Polit-ical and Social State of Ireland*, 2 vols. (Dublin: Alexander Thom & Sons, 1861), 2:19, 56, 58, 77.

57. Mercer, *English Vernacular Houses*, 8, 13–14, 30–32.

CHAPTER 3   COLONIAL COMFORT

1. William Bradford, *Of Plymouth Plantation, 1620–1647*, ed. Samuel Eliot Morison (New York: Alfred A. Knopf, 1952), 76, 136; Carl R. Lounsbury, ed., *An Illustrated Glos-sary of Early Southern Architecture and Landscape* (New York: Oxford University Press, 1994), 97; J. B. Bordley, "Thoughts on Hired Labourers and Servants, Cottages and Cottagers," in *Essays and Notes on Husbandry and Rural Affairs*, 2nd ed. (Philadelphia: Thomas Dobson, 1801), 389; Lucy Simler, "The Landless Worker: An Index of Eco-nomic and Social Change in Chester County, Pennsylvania, 1750–1820," *Pennsylvania Magazine of History and Biography* 114, no. 2 (April 1990): 168–69, 175–76, 179, 187; idem, "Tenancy in Colonial Pennsylvania: The Case of Chester County, Pennsylva-nia," *William and Mary Quarterly*, 3rd ser., 43, no. 3 (October 1986): 562–68; idem, let-ter to author 26 March 1996.

2. James Deetz, "Plymouth Colony Architecture: Archaeological Evidence from the Seventeenth Century," *Architecture in Colonial Massachusetts* (Boston: Colonial Society of Massachusetts, 1979), 43–60; Cary Carson, Norman F. Barka, William M. Kelso, Garry Wheeler Stone, and Dell Upton, "Impermanent Architecture in the Southern American Colonies," *Winterthur Portfolio* 16 (1981): 135–78; Mechal Sobel, *The World They Made Together: Black and White Values in Eighteenth-Century Virginia* (Princeton: Princeton University, 1987), 72–73, 104–5, 113, 119–26.

3. Father Andrew White, S.J., "A Briefe Relation of the Voyage unto Maryland, by Father Andrew White" (1634), in *Narratives of Early Maryland 1633–1684*, ed. Clayton Colman Hall (New York: Charles Scribner's Sons, 1910), 34–35; "Houses for New Albion, 1650," *Journal of the Society of Architectural Historians* 15, no. 3 (1956): 2; C. Carroll Lindsay, "Plantagenet's Wigwam," *Journal of the Society of Architectural Historians* 17, no. 4 (1958): 31–35; Amir H. Ameri, "Housing Ideologies in the New England and Chesapeake Bay Colonies," *Journal of the Society of Architectural Historians* 56, no. 1 (March 1997): 6–15.

4. D. M. Palliser, *The Age of Elizabeth: England under the Later Tudors 1547–1603* (London: Longman, 1983), 100; M. W. Barley, *The English Farmhouse and Cottage* (London: Routledge & Kegan Paul, 1961), 79–81, 91, 104–8, 115–19, 145, 175, 197, 205, 211, 222, 227–29, 235; W. G. Hoskins, *The Midland Peasant: The Economic and Social History of a Leicestershire Village* (London: Macmillan, 1965), 149, 187; Peter Smith, "The Architectural Personality of the British Isles," *Archaeologia Cambrensis* 129 (1980): 1–36.

5. Barry Harrison, "Longhouses in the Vale of York, 1570–1669," *Vernacular Architecture* 22 (1991): 31–39; M. W. Barley, "Rural Housing in England," in *The Agrarian History of England and Wales (1560–1640)*, ed. Joan Thirsk (Cambridge: Cambridge University Press, 1967), 4:749.

6. Dell Upton has interpreted this phenomenon to mean that "persons with access to elaborated codes might not use them in small communities where their status is unchallenged and needs no assertion"; Dell Upton, "Toward a Performance Theory of Vernacular Architecture: Early Tidewater Virginia as a Case Study," *Folklore Forum* 12, nos. 2 & 3 (1979): 184–85; James Horn, *Adapting to a New World: English Society in the Seventeenth Century Chesapeake* (Chapel Hill: University of North Carolina, 1994), 296–307, 328–30.

7. Carson et al., "Impermanent Architecture."

8. Fraser Neiman, "Domestic Architecture at the Clifts Plantation: The Social Context of Early Virginia Building," *Northern Neck of Virginia Historical Magazine* 28, no. 1 (December 1978): 3103–3104.

9. Robert Beverley, *The History and Present State of Virginia*, ed. Louis B. Wright (1705; repr., Chapel Hill: University of North Carolina, 1947), 289–90.

10. Dell Upton, "Vernacular Domestic Architecture in Eighteenth-Century Vir-

ginia," *Winterthur Portfolio* 17 (1982): 95–119; Cary Carson, "The 'Virginia House' in Maryland," *Maryland Historical Magazine* 69 (1974): 193–95.

11. Camille Wells, "The Eighteenth-Century Landscape of Virginia's Northern Neck," *Northern Neck of Virginia Magazine* 37 (1987): 4239–4245.

12. Dell Upton, "The Virginia Parlor: A Report on the Henry Saunders House and Its Occupants," (Washington, D.C.: National Museum of American History, Smithsonian Institution, 1981), 60–61; Donald W. Linebaugh, "'All the Annoyances and Inconveniences of the Country': Environmental Factors in the Development of Outbuildings in the Colonial Chesapeake," *Winterthur Portfolio* 20, no. 1 (Spring 1994): 1–18; Wells, "Eighteenth-Century Landscape," 4230, 4234–4235.

13. Lois Green Carr and Lorena S. Walsh, "Inventories and the Analysis of Wealth and Consumption Patterns in St. Mary's County, Maryland, 1658–1777," *Historical Methods* 13 (1980): 87–96; Carole Shammas, "The Domestic Environment in Early Modern England and America," *Journal of Social History* 14, no. 1 (Fall 1980–81): 1–24; Gloria L. Main, *Tobacco Colony: Life in Early Maryland, 1650–1720* (Princeton: Princeton University Press, 1982), 176.

14. Mark R. Wenger, "The Dining Room in Early Virginia," *Perspectives in Vernacular Architecture III*, ed. Thomas Carter and Bernard L. Herman (Columbia: University of Missouri, 1989), 149–59; Mark R. Wenger, "The Central Passage in Virginia: Evolution of an Eighteenth-Century Living Space," in *Perspectives in Vernacular Architecture II*, ed. Camille Wells (Columbia: University of Missouri, 1986), 137–49; Bernard L. Herman, *Architecture and Rural Life in Central Delaware, 1700–1900* (Knoxville: University of Tennessee Press, 1987), 20–49; Henry Glassie, *Folk Housing in Middle Virginia* (Knoxville: University of Tennessee Press, 1975), 28–31, 72–77, 84, 100, 104; Upton, "Vernacular Domestic Architecture," quoted 104.

15. Upton, "Vernacular Domestic Architecture," 106, 109–19.

16. Dell Upton, "Slave Housing in 18th-Century Virginia" (report to the Department of Social and Cultural History, National Museum of American History, Smithsonian Institution, July 1982), 22; Leland Ferguson, *Uncommon Ground: Archaeology and Early African America* (Washington, D.C.: Smithsonian Institution Press, 1992), 55–57; Philip D. Morgan, *Slave Counterpoint: Black Culture in the Eighteenth-Century Chesapeake and Lowcountry* (Chapel Hill: University of North Carolina Press, 1998), 104–24.

17. George W. McDaniel, *Hearth and Home: Preserving a People's Culture* (Philadelphia: Temple University Press, 1982), 54, 94; Upton, "Slave Housing," 30–34.

18. William M. Kelso, *Kingsmill Plantations, 1619–1800: Archaeology of Country Life in Colonial Virginia* (New York: Academic Press, 1984), 102–28. For a (regrettably static) comparison of slave and English servant accommodation, see Mark L. Walston, "'Uncle Tom's Cabin' Revisited: Origins and Interpretations of Slave Housing in the American South," *Southern Studies* 24, no. 4 (Winter 1985): 358–63.

19. John Michael Vlach, "Afro-American Domestic Artifacts in Eighteenth-Century Virginia," *Material Culture* 19, no. 1 (1987): 10.

20. McDaniel, *Hearth and Home*, 70–71, 78; Ferguson, *Uncommon Ground*, 57–58.

21. Upton, "Slave Housing," 35–37, 46–48.

22. Olaudah Equiano, *The Interesting Narrative of the Life of Olaudah Equiano, or Gustavus Vassa, the African*, 2 vols. (London, 1789; repr., Coral Gables, Fla.: Mnemosyne Publishing, 1989), 1:15; Jean-Paul Bourdier and Trinh T. Minh-Ha, *African Spaces: Designs for Living in Upper Volta* (New York: Africana Publishing, 1985).

23. Equiano, *Interesting Narrative*, 1:15.

24. Fritz Hamer and Michael Trinkley, "African Architectural Transference to the South Carolina Low Country, 1700–1880," *Tennessee Anthropologist* 22:1 (Spring 1997): 1–34; Thomas R. Wheaton, Amy Friedlander, Patrick H. Garrow, "Youghan and Curriboo Plantations: Studies in Afro-American Archaeology" (report to National Park Service, Southeast Regional Office, Archaeological Services Branch, April 1983), 169, 193–94, 340–41; Lesley M. Drucker, "The Spiers Landing Site: Archaeological Investigations in Berkeley County, South Carolina (report to U.S. Department of the Interior, Heritage Conservation and Recreation Service, Interagency Archaeological Services, Atlanta, 1979), 91, 93, 96.

25. Drucker, "Spiers Landing Site," 96, 123–27, 150; Wheaton, Friedlander, and Garrow, "Youghan and Curriboo Plantations," 338–39, 341; Ferguson, *Uncommon Ground*, 81, 145. On Jamaica slaves had even more control over the design and layout of housing. Only one-fifth of the plantations had plans showing that planters regimented the layout of slaves' accommodation, and the houses themselves represented several creole designs combining African and European building traditions; B. W. Higman, *Jamaica Surveyed: Plantation Maps and Plans of the Eighteenth and Nineteenth Centuries* (Kingston: Institute of Jamaica Publications, 1988), 245–46, 250.

26. Upton, "Slave Housing," 12, 15; McDaniel, *Hearth and Home*, 98–100.

27. Upton, "Slave Housing," 49; McDaniel, *Hearth and Home*, 47, 73.

28. Edward A. Chappell, "Housing a Nation: The Transformation of Living Standards in Early America," in *Of Consuming Interests: The Style of Life in the Eighteenth Century*, ed. Cary Carson, Ronald Hoffman, and Peter J. Albert (Charlottesville: University Press of Virginia, 1994), 181n, citing Maryland Orphans Court records.

29. Robert J. Turnbull, *A Refutation of the Calumnies* (1822), quoted in Ferguson, *Uncommon Ground*, 79; Bernard L. Herman, "Slave Quarters in Virginia: The Persona Behind Historic Artifacts," in *The Scope of Historical Archaeology: Essays in Honor of John L. Cotter*, ed. David G. Orr and Daniel G. Crozier (Philadelphia: Laboratory of Anthropology, Temple University, 1984), 274, et passim; Joyce E. Chaplin, "Slavery and the Principle of Humanity: A Modern Idea in the Early Lower South," *Journal of Social History* 24, no. 2 (Winter 1990): 299–313.

30. On Dutch windows, see Roderic H. Blackburn and Ruth Piwonka, eds., *Remem-*

brance of Patria: Dutch Arts and Culture in Colonial America 1609–1776 (Albany: Albany Institute of History and Art, 1988), 119–21, 133; Sarah Kemble Knight, *The Private Journal Kept by Madame Knight* [1704], quoted in ibid., 100; "A Glance at New York in 1697: The Travel Diary of Dr. Benjamin Bullivant," ibid., 146. In the second half of the eighteenth century virtually all Dutch fireplaces were modified to accommodate jambed fireplaces; ibid., 150. On Dutch use of stoves, "which keep the Room next to them, very warm, which is intirely disagreable to all Strangers & gives them an Headach", see Warren Johnson, "Journal of a Trip from New York to the Mohawk Region 1760–1761," quoted in ibid., 158.

31. William Woys Weaver, "The Pennsylvania German House: European Antecedents and New World Forms," *Winterthur Portfolio* 24, no. 4 (Winter 1986): 254–58; George Ellis Burcaw, *The Saxon House: A Cultural Index in European Ethnography* (Moscow: University of Idaho Museum, 1973), 50–51, 101.

32. Edward A. Chappell, "Acculturation in the Shenandoah Valley: Rhenish Houses of the Massanutten Settlement," *Proceedings of the American Philosophical Society* 124, no. 1 (1980): 55–89.

33. Henry Glassie, "Eighteenth-Century Cultural Process in Delaware Valley Folk Building," *Winterthur Portfolio* 7 (1972): 42, 47; Charles Bergengren, "From Lovers to Murderers: The Etiquette of Entry and the Social Implications of House Form," *Winterthur Portfolio* 20, no. 1 (Spring 1994): 48–53. On the compatibility of the "continental" three-room plan with British vernacular traditions, see W. John McIntyre, "Diffusion and Vision: A Case Study of the Ebenezer Doan House in Sharon, Ontario," *Material History Bulletin* 22 (Fall 1985): 11–20; Cary Carson, "The Consumer Revolution in Colonial British America: Why Demand?" in *Of Consuming Interests: The Style of Life in the Eighteenth Century,* ed. Cary Carson, Ronald Hoffman, and Peter J. Albert (Charlottesville: University Press of Virginia, 1994), 665–67.

34. Anthony Quiney, "The Lobby-Entry House: Its Origins and Distribution," *Architectural History* 27 (1984): 464; Symonds to Winthrop, 8 February 1638, "Massachusetts Bay Building Documents, 1638–1726," ed. Abbott Lowell Cummings, in *Architecture in Colonial Massachusetts,* ed. idem (Boston: Colonial Society of Massachusetts, 1979), 215–16.

35. J. F. Jameson, ed., *Johnson's Wonder-Working Providence, 1628–1651,* as quoted in Cary Carson, "Homestead Architecture in the Chesapeake Colonies" (presented at the Lives of Early Americans Conference: Archaeological Perspectives on Colonial Society, 30 April–2 May 1981, Millersville State College, Millersville, Pennsylvania), 7–8; Barley, *English Farmhouse and Cottage,* 142, 144–45; Barley, "Rural Housing," 4:765–66. In recent years there has been more historical archaeology of vernacular architecture in the British North American colonies than in Britain itself; J. T. Smith, "Short-Lived and Mobile Houses in Late Seventeenth-Century England," *Vernacular Architecture* 16 (1985): 33; Richard M. Candee, "A Documentary History of Plymouth

Colony Architecture, 1620–1700," part 1, *Old-Time New England* 59, no. 3 (January–March 1969): 61–69, Bradford quoted 61; idem, "A Documentary History of Plymouth Colony Architecture, 1620–1700," part 2, *Old-Time New England* 59, no. 4 (April–June 1970): 105–11; idem, "A Documentary History of Plymouth Colony Architecture, 1620–1700," part 3, *Old-Time New England* 60, no. 2 (October–December 1969): 37–50; idem, "First-Period Architecture in Maine and New Hampshire: The Evidence from Probate Inventories," *Early American Probate Inventories*, ed. Peter Benes (Boston: Boston University, 1989), 97–120.

36. Robert Blair St. George, "'Set Thine House in Order': The Domestication of the Yeomanry in Seventeenth-Century New England," in *New England Begins: The Seventeenth Century*, ed. Jonathan L. Fairbanks and Robert F. Trent, 3 vols. (Boston: Museum of Fine Arts, 1982), 2:161–62, 166; Abbott Lowell Cummings, "Inside the Massachusetts House," in *Common Places: Readings in American Vernacular Architecture*, ed. Dell Upton and John Michael Vlach (Athens: University of Georgia Press, 1986), 219–39; Abbott Lowell Cummings, "Three Hearths: A Socioarchitectural Study of Seventeenth-Century Massachusetts Bay Probate Inventories," *Old-Time New England* 75, no. 263 (1997): 5–49.

37. Candee, "Documentary History," part 1: 105, part 2: 47, 49; Dell Upton, "Architectural Change in Colonial Rhode Island: The Mott House as a Case Study," *Old-Time New England* 69, nos. 3, 4 (January–June 1979): 18–33; Norman Morrison Isham and Albert F. Brown, "Early Rhode Island Houses" [1895], in *Common Places: Readings in American Vernacular Aruchitecture*, ed. Dell Upton and John Michael Vlach (Athens: University of Georgia Press, 1986), 149–58.

38. Upton, "Architectural Change"; Abbott Lowell Cummings, *The Framed Houses of Massachusetts Bay, 1625–1725*, (Cambridge: Harvard University Press, 1979); John Demos, *A Little Commonwealth: Family Life in Plymouth Colony* (New York: Oxford University Press, 1970), 28–30.

39. Upton, "Architectural Change."

40. Abbott Lowell Cummings, "The Beginnings of Provincial Renaissance Architecture in Boston, 1690–1725," *Journal of the Society of Architectural Historians* 42 (1983): 43–53; P. Smith, "Some Reflections on the Development of the Centrally-Planned House," in *Collectanea Historica: Essays in Memory of Stuart Rigold*, ed. Alec Detsicas (Maidstone: Kent Archaeological Society, 1981), 192–212.

41. Kevin M. Sweeney, "Mansion People: Kinship, Class, and Architecture in Western Massachusetts in the Mid-Eighteenth Century," *Winterthur Portfolio* 19 (1984): 231–56.

42. Sweeney, "Mansion People," 237; David H. Flaherty, *Privacy in Colonial New England* (Charlottesville: University Press of Virginia, 1972), 41–42; Ernest Allen Connally, "The Cape Cod House: An Introductory Study," *Journal of the Society of Architectural Historians* 19 (1960): 49.

43. Sweeney, "Mansion People," 242; Cummings, "Inside the Massachusetts House."

44. Carol Shammas, *The Preindustrial Consumer in England and America* (Oxford: Oxford University Press, 1990), quoted 172; Michael Steinitz, "Rethinking Geographical Approaches to the Common House: The Evidence from Eighteenth-Century Massachusetts," *Perspectives in Vernacular Architecture III*, ed. Thomas Carter and Bernard L. Herman (Columbia: University of Missouri Press), 16–26.

45. Chappell, "Housing a Nation," 183–87, 190–91n.

46. Lee Soltow, "Egalitarian America and Its Inegalitarian Housing in the Federal Period," *Social Science History* 9, no. 2 (Spring 1985): 199–213; idem, *Distribution of Wealth and Income in the United States in 1798* (Pittsburgh: University of Pittsburgh Press, 1989), 53, 57, 99.

47. Lee Soltow, "Housing Characteristics on the Pennsylvania Frontier: Mifflin County Dwelling Values in 1798," *Pennsylvania History* 46 (January 1980): 57–70. On the colonial history of glass production, see Arlene Palmer, "Glass Production in Eighteenth-Century America: The Wistarburgh Enterprise," *Wintherthur Portfolio* 11 (1976): 75–101.

48. For use of the term *elegant* in congressional debate, see *The Debates and Proceedings in the Congress of the United States*, 42 vols. (Washington, D.C.: Gales & Seaton, 1834–56), 5th Cong., 2nd sess., (J. Williams, 30 May 1798, p. 1840), (N. Smith, 30 May 1798, p. 1846), (Harrison Gray Otis quoted, 30 May 1798, pp. 1842–43); "An act to provide for the valuation of lands and dwelling-houses, and the enumeration of slaves, within the United States," ibid., 3rd sess., 3763 (9 July 1798). Oliver Wolcott, Jr., to the House of Representatives, 14 December 1796, as quoted in *The Papers of Alexander Hamilton*, ed. Harold C. Syrett et al. (New York: Columbia University Press, 1974), 20:500n. By far the fullest study of the 1798 direct tax is Soltow, *Distribution of Wealth and Income*, see esp. 53–59, 75–76, 99.

49. Enclosure to Oliver Wolcott, 6 June 1797, *Papers of Alexander Hamilton*, 20: 502–4; Hamilton had sent a similar proposal, now lost, to Theodore Sedgwick in January 1797.

CHAPTER 4   DECENT COMFORT

1. F. W. Robins, *The Story of the Lamp and the Candle* (1939; repr. Bath: Kingsmead Reprints, 1970); William T. O'Dea, *The Social History of Lighting* (London: Routledge & Kegan Paul, 1958), 1, 223, and see 226, 232 for tall tales on lighting and sources of animal oils; Alastair Laing, *Lighting: The Arts and Living* (London: Her Majesty's Stationery Office, 1982), 8.

2. Fernand Braudel, *Capitalism and Material Life, 1400–1800* (New York: Harper & Row, 1973), 225–26.

3. On the physics and chemistry of flame, see Joseph T. Butler, *Candleholders in Amer-*

ica, 1650–1900: A Comprehensive Collection of American and European Candle Fixtures Used in America (New York: Crown, 1967); O'Dea, *Social History of Lighting*, 1–2, 13–15, 220.

4. David J. Eveleigh, *Candle Lighting* (Aylesbury, Buckinghamshire: Shire Publications, 1985); O'Dea, *Social History of Lighting*, 19, 32–34. The respective melting points of illuminants are: beef tallow 109°F, mutton tallow 117°F, beeswax 149°F.

5. O'Dea, *Social History of Lighting*, 6.

6. Ibid., 7, 20, 39; Leroy L. Thwing, "A Note about Rushlights," in *Lighting in America: From Colonial Rushlights to Victorian Chandeliers*, ed. Lawrence S. Cooke (Pittstown, N.J.: Main Street Press, 1984), 13–15. Monta Lee Dakin, *Brilliant with Lighting: A Reexamination of Artificial Lighting in Eighteenth-Century America* (M.A. thesis, George Washington University, 1983), as its title indicates, offers an optimistic assessment of the quality and quantity of artificial illumination in preindustrial America.

7. *The Book of Husbandry by Master Fitzherbert*, ed. Walter W. Skeat (1534; London: English Dialect Society, 1882), 101; Thomas Tusser, *Five Hundred Points of Good Husbandrie*, ed. W. Paine and Sidney Herrtage (1580; repr. London: English Dialect Society, 1878), 167, 177, 179; Francis Higginson, "A Catalogue of Such Needful Things as Every Planter Doth or Ought to Provide to Go to New England," in *Remarkable Providences*, ed. John Demos (New York: Braziller, 1972), 42–43; Rolla Milton Tryon, *Household Manufactures in the United States, 1640–1860* (Chicago, 1917), 81–85 (survey of inventories in Providence, R.I., 1716–25); Abbott Lowell Cummings, *Rural Household Inventories: Establishing the Names, Uses and Furnishings of Rooms in the Colonial New England Home, 1675–1775* (Boston: Society for the Preservation of New England Antiquities, 1964); Dakin, *Brilliant with Lighting*, 68, 138–39; Eliza Leslie, *The House Book: or, A Manual of Domestic Economy for Town and Country*, 3rd ed. (Philadelphia: Carey & Hart, 1840), 168–70.

8. O'Dea, *Social History of Lighting*, 2 (quoting Pepys), 114–15; *The Diary of Ralph Josselin, 1616–1683*, ed. Alan Macfarlane (London: Oxford University Press for the British Academy, 1976), 145–46 (6 November 1648, 16 November 1748), 180 (3 October 1649); Mario Praz, *Conversation Pieces: A Survey of the Informal Group Portrait in Europe and America* (University Park: Pennsylvania State University, 1971); James Horn, *Adapting to a New World: English Society in the Seventeenth-Century Chesapeake* (Chapel Hill: University of North Carolina, 1994), 312, 320–21, 324–25.

9. O'Dea, *Social History of Lighting*, 16–17, 140–41; Laing, *Lighting*, 13.

10. John Russell, *The Boke of Nurture folowyng Englondis gise* (c. 1450) (Harleian MS 4011), "The Warderober," lines 967–68, in *Early English Meals and Manners*, ed. Frederick J. Furnivall (London: Early English Text Society, 1868), 66; O'Dea, *Social History*, 141–43; Kate Mertes, *The English Noble Household, 1250–1600: Governance and Politic Rule* (Oxford: Basil Blackwell, 1988), 149; Peter Thornton and Maurice Tomlin, *The Furnishing and Decoration of Ham House* (London: Furniture History Society, 1980), 99; *The Diary of a Country Parson: The Reverend James Woodforde, 1758–1781*, ed. John Beres-

ford, 5 vols. (London: Oxford University Press, 1926–31), 2:223 (25 December 1785), 3:238 (25 December 1790).

11. Thomas Wright, *A History of Domestic Manners and Sentiments in England during the Middle Ages* (London: Chapman & Hall, 1862), 43–44, 93–94, 155, 246–49; Margaret Wade Labarge, *A Baronial Household of the Thirteenth Century* (New York: Barnes & Noble, 1965), 120.

12. "The Boke of Curtasye" (c. 1430–40), in *Early English Meals*, 189; *The Diary of Samuel Sewall, 1674–1729*, ed. M. Halsey Thomas, 2 vols. (New York: Farrar, Straus & Giroux, 1973), 2:622 (13 July 1709).

13. "Boke of Curtasye," 205; Barbara Harvey, *Living and Dying in England, 1100–1540: The Monastic Experience* (Oxford: Clarendon Press, 1993), 202; Wright, *History of Domestic Manners*, 108, 251.

14. Jonathan Bourne and Vanessa Brett, *Lighting in the Domestic Interior: Renaissance to Art Nouveau* (London: Sotheby's, 1991); Peter Thornton, *The Italian Renaissance Interior, 1400–1600*, (London: Weidenfeld & Nicolson, 1991), 277, 310; W. G. MacKay Thomas, "Old English Candlesticks and Their Venetian Prototypes," *Burlington Magazine* 80 (1942): 145–51.

15. Peter Hecht, "Candlelight and Dirty Fingers, or Royal Virtue in Disguise: Some Thoughts on Weyerman and Godfried Schalken," *Semiolis* 11 (1980): 28–29; Thomas Dekker, *The Seven Deadly Sins of London* (1601; repr. Cambridge: Cambridge University Press, 1905), 44–54; George Wither, *A Collection of Emblems, Ancient and Moderne* (London: Henry Taunton, 1635), 40, 169, 253.

16. O'Dea, *Social History*, 37, 154–61; Wolfgang Schivelbusch, *Disenchanted Night: The Industrialization of Light in the Nineteenth Century* (New York: Berg, 1988), 137–42; John Fowler and John Cornforth, *English Decoration in the Eighteenth Century* (Princeton: Pyne Press, 1974), 224; Charles Oman, "English Brass Chandeliers in American Churches," in *Lighting in America*, ed. Lawrence S. Cooke (Pittstown, N.J.: Main Street Press, 1974), 111–13; Jane C. Giffen, "Chandeliers in Federal New England," in ibid., 114–20.

17. Thornton and Tomlin, *Furnishing of Ham House*, 50, 68–69, 139.

18. Lorna Weatherill, *Consumer Behaviour and Material Culture in Britain 1660–1760*, (London: Routledge, 1988), 30.

19. 1 Corinthians 13:12, *The New English Bible: The New Testament*, 2nd ed. (London: Oxford University Press, 1970).

20. Thornton, *Italian Renaissance Interior*, 234. Chaucer's references to glass mirrors usually implied dullness; John S. P. Tatlock and Arthur G. Kennedy, *A Concordance to the Complete Works of Geoffrey Chaucer and to the Romaunt of the Rose* (Washington, D.C.: Carnegie Institution, 1927), s.v. "glass."

21. Dora Thornton, *The Scholar in His Study: Ownership and Experience in Renaissance Italy* (New Haven: Yale University Press, 1997), 167–74. D. B. Harden, "Domestic Window Glass: Roman, Saxon and Medieval," *Studies in Building History: Essays in*

Recognition of the Work of B. H. St. J. O'Neil, ed. E. M. Jope (London: Odhams Press, 1961), 40–45; Eleanor S. Godfrey, *The Development of English Glassmaking, 1560–1640* (Chapel Hill: University of North Carolina Press, 1975), 3–7, 235–37; Benjamin Goldberg, *The Mirror and Man*, (Charlottesville: University Press of Virginia, 1985), 96–99, 104–6, 110, 114–15, 138–42.

22. Ada Polak, *Glass: Its Makers and Its Public* (London: Weidenfeld & Nicolson, 1975), 114–39. Peter Thornton, *Authentic Decor: The Domestic Interior, 1620–1920*, (New York: Viking, 1984), 11, 19.

23. Thornton, *Authentic Decor*, 14–15; English visitors quoted in Charles Saumarez Smith, *Eighteenth-Century Decoration: Design and the Domestic Interior in England* (New York: H. N. Abrams 1993), 20.

24. Peter Thornton, *Seventeenth Century Interior Design in England, France and Holland*, (New Haven: Yale University Press, 1978), 36.

25. The design of chimneypieces became less important in France after 1720, but the Palladian orientation of English architecture continued to emphasize the sculptural importance of chimneypieces, and they remained the focus of attention in pattern books; Thornton, *Authentic Decor*, 17, 51, 97.

26. Charles Woolsey Cole, *Colbert and a Century of French Mercantilism*, 2 vols. (New York: Columbia University Press, 1939), 2:304–15; idem, *French Mercantilism, 1683–1700* (New York: Columbia University Press, 1943), 133–41; Thornton, *Authentic Decor*, 53–54.

27. Goldberg, *Mirror and Man*, 169–70.

28. "My Great Journey to New Castle and to Cornwall" [1698], *The Illustrated Journeys of Celia Fiennes 1685–c. 1712*, ed. Christopher Morris (London: Macdonald, 1982), 140–41.

29. Peter Earle, *The Making of the English Middle Class: Business, Society and Family Life in London, 1660–1730* (Berkeley: University of California Press, 1989), 25; Weatherill, *Consumer Behaviour*, 108, 110.

30. Weatherill, *Consumer Behaviour*, 76, 168; Earle, *Making of the English Middle Class*, 292.

31. Kevin M. Sweeney, "Furniture and the Domestic Environment in Wethersfield, Connecticut, 1639–1800," in *Material Life in America, 1600–1860*, ed. Robert Blair St. George (Boston: Northeastern University Press, 1988), 264–66, 268, 276, 280, 287; Laurel Thatcher Ulrich, *Good Wives: Image and Reality in the Lives of Women in Northern New England, 1650–1750* (New York: Knopf, 1982), 17, 69; Jack Michel, "'In a Manner and Fashion Suitable to Their Degree': A Preliminary Investigation of the Material Culture of Early Rural Pennsylvania," *Working Papers from the Regional Economic History Research Center*, ed. Glenn Porter and William H. Mulligan, Jr., vol. 5, no. 1 (Greenville, Del.: Eleutherian Mills–Hagley Foundation, 1981): 24.

32. Elisabeth Donaghy Garrett, *At Home: The American Family, 1750–1870* (New York:

Harry N. Abrams, 1990), 153–56; R. W. Symonds, "Eighteenth-Century Lighting Devices: Wall Fittings and Candlesticks," in *Lighting in America: From Colonial Rushlights to Victorian Chandeliers*, ed. Lawrence S. Cooke (Pittstown, N.J.: Main Street Press, 1984), 108; Hentie Louw, "Window Glass Making in Britain c. 1660–c. 1860 and Its Architectural Impact," *Construction History* 7 (1991): 50.

33. On the coronations, see Fowler and Cornforth, *English Decoration*, 222. "Copy of a Letter from an Officer at Philadelphia to his Correspondent in London, 23 May 1778," *Gentleman's Magazine* (July 1778): 356, 330; see also Ira D. Gruber, *The Howe Brothers and the American Revolution* (New York: Atheneum, 1972), 298–99.

34. Laing, *Lighting*, 59.

35. Symonds, "Eighteenth-Century Lighting Devices, 109.

36. Alexander O. Curle, "Domestic Candlesticks from the Fourteenth to the End of the Eighteenth Century," *Proceedings of the Society of Antiquaries of Scotland* 60 (1925–26): 183–214; Rupert Gentle and Rachael Feild, *English Domestic Brass 1680–1810 and the History of Its Origins* (London: Paul Elek, 1975), 62; John Kirk Richardson, "Brass Candlesticks," *Lighting in America: From Colonial Rushlights to Victorian Chandeliers*, ed. Lawrence S. Cooke (Pittstown, N.J.: Main Street Press, 1984), 83–88; Benjamin Ginsburg, "Dating English Brass Candlesticks," in ibid., 93–97; G. Bernard Hughes, "A Chronology of English Candlesticks," in ibid., 98–101.

37. Neil McKendrick, "The Consumer Revolution of Eighteenth-Century England," *The Birth of a Consumer Society: The Commercialization of Eighteenth-Century England*, ed. Neil McKendrick, John Brewer, and J. H. Plumb, (Bloomington: Indiana University Press, 1982), 9–33; Richard L. Bushman, "American High-Style and Vernacular Cultures," *Colonial British America: Essays in the New History of the Early Modern Era*, ed. Jack P. Greene and J. R. Pole (Baltimore: Johns Hopkins University Press, 1984), 345–83; Dakin, *Brilliant with Lighting*, 37; Little, "References to Lighting."

38. Gerard Brett, *Dinner Is Served: A History of Dining in England, 1400–1900* (Hamden, Conn.: Archon Books, 1969), 85–108.

39. On the precision of such symbolism in the Victorian period, see George H. Ford, "Light in Darkness: Gas, Oil, and Tallow in Dickens' *Bleak House*," in *From Smollett to James: Studies in the Novel and Other Essays Presented to Edgar Johnson*, ed. Samuel I. Mintz, Alice Chandler, and Christopher Mulvey (Charlottesville: University Press of Virginia, 1981), 183–210.

40. Carl Bridenbaugh, "Memoranda and Documents: The High Cost of Living in Boston, 1728," *New England Quarterly* 4 (1932): 800–811; [John] Trusler, *The London Adviser and Guide* (London: n.p., 1786), 167–68; Phyllis Deane and W. A. Cole, *British Economic Growth, 1688–1959: Trends and Structure* (Cambridge: Cambridge University Press, 1962), 57–58; O'Dea, *Social History of Lighting*, 219.

41. Adam Smith, *An Inquiry into the Nature and Causes of the Wealth of Nations* (1776), ed. R. H. Campbell and A. S. Skinner, 2 vols. (Oxford, 1976; repr. Indianapolis: Lib-

erty Classics, 1981), 1:23, 2:869–70. Leroy L. Thwing, "Lighting in Early Colonial Massachusetts," *New England Quarterly* 11 (1938): 168. Rita Susswain Gottesman, comp., *The Arts and Crafts in New York, 1726–1776: Advertisements and News Items from New York City Newspapers* (New York: New-York Historical Society, 1938), 194–97, 221–27; *Rivington's New York Gazetteer* (28 September 1775), quoted 227.

42. Dakin, *Brilliant with Lighting*, 65–67, 123–25 (for the list of Botetourt's lighting devices); Graham Hood, *The Governor's Palace in Williamsburg: A Cultural Study* (Williamsburg, Va.: Colonial Williamsburg Foundation, 1991), 187–205.

43. *The Diary of Colonel Landon Carter of Sabine Hall, 1752–1778*, ed. Jack P. Greene, 2 vols. (Charlottesville: University Press of Virginia, 1965), 243 (1 December 1763), 336 (4 March 1767), 349–50 (28 January 1770), 375 (24 March 1770), 530 (21 December 1770), 850 (15 August 1774).

44. Carter, *Diary*, quoted 1100 (25 April 1777); see also, 156 (March 1757).

45. Carter, *Diary*, 849 (12 August 1774), 996 (8 March 1776), 1002 (15 March 1776).

46. *Journal and Letters of Philip Vickers Fithian, 1773–1774: A Plantation Tutor of the Old Dominion*, ed. Hunter Dickinson Farish (Charlottesville: University Press of Virginia, 1957), 30 (14 December 1773), 31 (15 December 1773), 34 (18 December 1773), 39 (24 December 1773), 40 (25 December 1773), 44 (31 December 1773), 53 (8 January 1774), 59 (12 December 1773), 115 (5 June 1774), 125 (24 June 1774), 135 (9 July 1774).

47. Fithian, *Journal and Letters*, 34 (18 December 1773), 56–57 (18 January 1774), 125 (24 June 1774).

48. Fithian, *Journal and Letters*, 41 (25 December 1773), 61 (29 January 1774), 120 (14 June 1774).

CHAPTER 5   CONVENIENT COMFORT

1. *The Diary of a Country Parson: The Reverend James Woodforde, 1758–1781*, ed. John Beresford, 5 vols. (London: Oxford University Press, 1926–31), 4:245 (4 November 1795).

2. Thomas Jefferson, *Notes on the State of Virginia*, ed. Thomas Perkins Abernethy (MS [1785], orig. pub. 1861; New York: Torchbook, 1964; repr. Gloucester, Mass.: Peter Smith, 1976), 145–47; Benjamin Thompson, "Of Chimney Fire-places" [1796], *Collected Works of Count Rumford*, ed. Sanborn C. Brown, 5 vols. (Cambridge: Harvard University Press, 1968–70), 2:239.

3. Samuel Johnson, *A Dictionary of the English Language*, 2 vols. (London: J. F. and C. Rivington et al., 1785), s.v. "comfort," "comfortless," "discomfort."

4. Joan Thirsk, *Economic Policy and Projects: The Development of Consumer Society in Early Modern Britain* (Oxford: Clarendon Press, 1978); Neil McKendrick, John Brewer, and J. H. Plumb, eds., *The Birth of a Consumer Society: The Commercialization of Eighteenth-Century England* (Bloomington: Indiana University Press, 1982); Lorna Weatherill, *Con-*

sumer Behaviour and Material Culture in Britain, 1660–1760 (London: Routledge, 1988); Carole Shammas, *The Preindustrial Consumer in England and America* (Oxford: Oxford University Press, 1990); John Brewer and Roy Porter, eds., *Consumption and the World of Goods* (London: Routledge, 1993); Carole Shammas, "Explaining Past Changes in Consumption and Consumer Behavior," *Historical Methods* 22, no. 2 (Spring 1989): 61–67; Peter N. Stearns, "Stages of Consumerism: Recent Work on the Issues of Periodization," *Journal of Modern History* 69, no. 1 (March 1997): 102–17. Cary Carson, "The Consumer Revolution in Colonial British America: Why Demand?" in *Of Consuming Interests: The Style of Life in the Eighteenth Century,* ed. Cary Carson, Ronald Hoffman, and Peter J. Albert (Charlottesville: University Press of Virginia, 1994), 497; Richard L. Bushman, "American High-Style and Vernacular Cultures," *Colonial British America: Essays in the New History of the Early Modern Era,* ed. Jack P. Greene and J. R. Pole, (Baltimore: Johns Hopkins University Press, 1984), 345–83; Gerard Brett, *Dinner Is Served: A History of Dining in England, 1400–1900* (Hamden, Conn.: Archon, 1968), 85–108; Carole Shammas, "The Domestic Environment in Early Modern England and America," *Journal of Social History* 14, no. 1 (Fall 1980–81): 1–24; Lois Green Carr and Lorena S. Walsh, "Inventories and the Analysis of Wealth and Consumption Patterns in St. Mary's County, Maryland, 1658–1777," *Historical Methods* 13 (Spring 1980): 87–96; Lois Green Carr and Lorena S. Walsh, "Changing Lifestyles and Consumer Behavior in the Colonial Chesapeake," in *Of Consuming Interests,* 59–166; Peter Earle, *The Making of the English Middle Class: Business, Society, and Family Life in London, 1660–1730* (Berkeley: University of California Press, 1989), 290–301.

5. Margaret Spufford, *The Great Reclothing of Rural England: Petty Chapmen and Their Wares in the Seventeenth Century* (London: Hambledon Press, 1984), 111, 115, 119, 121. On the stylization of informality, see Geoffrey Squire, *Dress and Society, 1560–1970* (New York: Viking Press, 1974), 103–16; Erasmus Jones, *The Man of Manners,* 3rd ed. (London: J. Roberts, 1737; repr. Sandy Hook, Conn.: Hendrickson Group, 1993), 12.

6. Beverly Lemire, *Fashion's Favourite: The Cotton Trade and the Consumer in Britain, 1660–1800* (Oxford: Oxford University Press, 1991), 6–7; Patricia Trautman, "Dress in Seventeenth-Century Cambridge, Massachusetts: An Inventory-Based Reconstruction," in *Early American Probate Inventories,* ed. Peter Benes (Boston: Boston University Press, 1989), 55, 60, 70–71; François Boucher, *20,000 Years of Fashion: The History of Costume and Personal Adornment* (New York: Harry N. Abrams, 1987), 261, 273–74, 294–95, 448. On the need to wear stays, see Mrs. Delany to Mary Dewes Port, 1 October 1775, *The Autobiography and Correspondence of Mary Granville, Mrs. Delany,* 2nd ser., ed. Lady Llanover, 3 vols. (London: Richard Bentley, 1862), 2:160; Walpole to Richard Bentley, 6 March 1755, *The Yale Edition of Horace Walpole's Correspondence,* ed. W. S. Lewis et al., 48 vols. (New Haven: Yale University Press, 1937–83), 35:213; William Hogarth, *The Analysis of Beauty, with the Rejected Passages from the Manuscript Drafts and Autobiographical Notes,* ed. Joseph Burke ([1753]; Oxford: Clarendon Press, 1955), 65. For criticisms of

stays, see John Locke, *Some Thoughts Concerning Education*, ed. John W. and Jean S. Yolton ([1693]; Oxford: Clarendon Press, 1989), 90–91; Aileen Ribeiro, *The Art of Dress: Fashion in England and France, 1750–1820* (New Haven: Yale University Press, 1995), 62–75, quoting William Barker, *A Treatise on the Principles of Hair-Dressing* (c. 1780), 45; Anne Buck, *Clothes and the Child: A Handbook of Children's Dress in England, 1500–1900* (New York: Holmes & Meier, 1996), 74–75, 114, 185–86, 192, 210–11; Jane Ashelford, *The Art of Dress: Clothes and Society, 1500–1914* (London: National Trust, 1996), 191; Elizabeth Ham, *Elizabeth Ham by Herself, 1783–1820*, ed. Eric Gillett (London: Faber & Faber, 1945), 27.

7. Robert F. Trent, "Mid-Atlantic Easy Chairs, 1770–1820: Old Questions and New Evidence," *American Furniture 1993*, ed. Luke Beckerdite (Hanover, N.H.: Chipstone Foundation, 1993), 201–11; Clive Edwards, "Reclining Chairs Surveyed: Health, Comfort, and Fashion in Evolving Markets," *Studies in the Decorative Arts* 6, no. 1 (Fall–Winter 1998–99): 32–67; Elisabeth Donaghy Garrett, *At Home: The American Family, 1750–1870* (New York: Harry N. Abrams, 1990), 124–25. For a too-easy assertion of the easy chair's establishing "our standards of comfort," see John Gloag, *A Social History of Furniture Design from B.C. 1300 to A.D. 1960* (New York: Bonanza, 1966), 120. On the relation of chairs to social status, see ibid., 1, 63, 74, 93, 120, 127.

8. *The Gentleman and Cabinet-maker's Director*, 3rd ed. (London: Thomas Chippendale, 1762), 6, 17, 20; *Gentleman and Cabinet-maker's Director*, 1st ed., 11; A. Hepplewhite, *The Cabinet-Maker and Upholsterer's Guide* (London: I. and J. Taylor, 1788), preface, 1–24.

9. Francis Nivelon, *The Rudiments of Genteel Behavior* (London, 1737), 25. On gentility, see Norbert Elias, *The Civilizing Process*, trans. Edmund Jephcott, 2 vols. (orig. publ. in German, 1939; New York: Pantheon Books, 1982 [vol. 2]); Jacques Revel, "The Uses of Civility," in *A History of Private Life*, ed. Georges Duby, trans. Arthur Goldhammer, 5 vols. (Cambridge: Harvard University Press, 1988), 167–205; Roger Chartier, "From Texts to Manners: A Concept and Its Books: *Civilité* between Aristocratic Distinction and Popular Appropriation," in *The Cultural Uses of Print in Early Modern France*, trans. Lydia G. Cochrane (Princeton: Princeton University Press, 1987), 71–109; Richard L. Bushman, *The Refinement of America: Persons, Houses, Cities* (New York: Alfred A. Knopf, 1992), esp. 57–58 on "ease"; Carson, "Consumer Revolution."

10. Carr and Walsh, "Changing Lifestyles," 130–33; James Horn, *Adapting to a New World: English Society in the Seventeenth-Century Chesapeake* (Chapel Hill: University of North Carolina, 1994), 307–28.

11. John Sekora, *Luxury: The Concept in Western Thought, Eden to Smollett* (Baltimore: Johns Hopkins University Press, 1977), 1–62; Christopher J. Berry, *The Idea of Luxury: A Conceptual and Historical Investigation* (Cambridge: Cambridge University Press, 1994), chaps. 2–4; Johnson, *Dictionary of the English Language*, s.v. "necessity."

12. Joyce Oldham Appleby, *Economic Thought and Ideology in Seventeenth-Century England* (Princeton: Princeton University Press, 1978), 158–98, quoted 164–65; Joyce Old-

ham Appleby, "Ideology and Theory: The Tension between Political and Economic Liberalism in Seventeenth-Century England," *American Historical Review* 81, no. 3 (June 1976): 499–516, esp. 504; Gordon Vichert, "The Theory of Conspicuous Consumption in the Eighteenth Century," in *The Varied Pattern: Studies in the Eighteenth Century,* ed. Peter Hughes and David Williams, (Toronto: A. M. Hakkert, 1971), 253–67; Neil McKendrick, "The Consumer Revolution of Eighteenth-Century England," in *The Birth of a Consumer Society,* 9–33.

13. *Nicholas Barbon on A Discourse of Trade* ([1690]; repr. Baltimore: Lord Baltimore Press, 1905), 14, 21, 33; Ann Bermingham, *Landscape and Ideology: The English Rustic Tradition, 1740–1860* (Berkeley: University of California Press, 1980), 18–19, quoting Addison. Jules Lubbock, *The Tyranny of Taste: The Politics of Architecture and Design in Britain, 1550–1960* (New Haven: Yale University Press, 1995), 96–99; John Locke, *A Letter Concerning Toleration,* trans. from Latin by William Popple (London: Awnsham Churchill, 1689), 6; Lubbock, *Tyranny of Taste,* 100; E. J. Hundert, "Bernard Mandeville and the Enlightenment's Maxims of Modernity," *Journal of the History of Ideas* 56, no. 4 (October 1995): 590.

14. *The Oxford English Dictionary,* ed. J. A. Simpson and E. S. C. Weiner, 2nd ed., 20 vols. (Oxford: Clarendon, 1989), s.v. "commodious," "convenience." Henry Marty, "Considerations on the East-India Trade" [1691], in *A Select Collection of Early English Tracts on Commerce,* ed. J. R. McCulloch, (1856; repr. Cambridge: Cambridge University Press, 1954), 558; Erasmus Jones, *The Man of Manners* (1737; repr. Sandy Hook, Conn.: Hendrickson Group, 1993), 10, 12; [John] Trusler, *The London Adviser and Guide* (London: n.p., 1786), 120–24.

15. Joseph Addison and Richard Steele, *The Spectator,* ed. G. Gregory Smith, 8 vols. (New York: E. P. Dutton, 1930), no. 260 (28 December 1711), 1:35; no. 127 (26 July 1711), 2:165; see also no. 265 (3 January 1712), 4:54–55; no. 478 (8 September 1712), 7:18; John Brewer, "'The Most Polite Age and the Most Vicious': Attitudes towards Culture as a Commodity, 1660–1800," in *The Consumption of Culture, 1600–1800,* ed. Ann Bermingham and John Brewer (New York: Routledge, 1995). 342–50; Beth Kowaleski-Wallace, "Tea, Gender, and Domesticity in Eighteenth-Century England," *Studies in Eighteenth-Century Culture* 23 (1994): 133. On women's initiative in new consumption patterns, see Garrett, *At Home,* 249–60.

16. Bernard Mandeville, *The Fable of the Bees: Or Private Vices, Publick Benefits,* 6th ed. (1732), ed. F. B. Kaye, 2 vols. (repr. of 1924 ed.; Indianapolis: Liberty Classics, 1988), 1:25–26, 107–8, 169, 183.

17. Mandeville, *Fable of the Bees,* 1:107, 155.

18. Ian Watt, *The Rise of the Novel: Studies in Defoe, Richardson and Fielding* (Berkeley: University of California Press, 1957), 74, 86; Daniel Defoe, *The Life and Adventures of Robinson Crusoe* ([1719]; London: Penguin Books, 1965), 66–67.

19. Defoe, *Robinson Crusoe,* 72–75, 82, 84–85, 89, 91, 93.

20. Ibid., 112–15, 125, 129–34, 139–41, 144–46, 196–97; Andrew Varney, "Mandeville as a Defoe Source," *Notes and Queries*, n.s., no. 1 (vol. 228 in cont. series) (February 1983): 26–29. Daniel Defoe, *The Complete English Tradesman*, 3rd ed., 2 vols. (London: C. Rivington, 1732), 1:318.

21. David Hume, *Essays Moral, Political, and Literary*, ed. Eugene F. Miller, (rev. ed.; Indianapolis: Liberty Classics, 1987): "Of Refinement in the Arts" (1760), 268, 276; "Of the Delicacy of Taste and Passion" (1741), 5–6; "Of the Middle Station of Life" (1742), 546. Adam Ferguson, *An Essay on the History of Civil Society* (Edinburgh: A. Millar, T. Caddel, A. Kincaid, and J. Bell, 1767), 376–77; Francis Hutcheson, *A System of Moral Philosophy* (London, 1755), 1:287, as quoted in Adam Smith, *An Inquiry into the Nature and Causes of the Wealth of Nations* [1776], ed. R. H. Campbell and A. S. Skinner, 2 vols. (Oxford, 1976; repr. Indianapolis: Liberty Classics, 1981), 1:23–24n.

22. *The Good of the Community Impartially Considered* (Boston, 1754), quoted in T. H. Breen "The Meanings of Things: Interpreting the Consumer Economy in the Eighteenth Century," in *Consumption and the World of Goods*, ed. John Brewer and Roy Porter (London: Routledge, 1993), 258 (emphasis in original); John Brown, *An Estimate of the Manners and Principles of the Times* (Dublin: G. Faulkner, J. Hoey, and J. Exshaw, 1757), 17, 24–27; John Dickinson, *Letters from a Farmer in Pennsylvania to the Inhabitants of the British Colonies: The Writings of John Dickinson*, ed. Paul Leicester Ford, 2 vols. (Philadelphia: Historical Society of Pennsylvania, 1895), 1:354–55. On standards of living as a public issue, see James Raven, "Defending Conduct and Property: The London Press and the Luxury Debate," in *Early Modern Conceptions of Property*, ed. John Brewer and Susan Staves (London: Routledge, 1995), 308.

23. J. G. A. Pocock, *The Machiavellian Moment: Florentine Political Thought and the Atlantic Republican Tradition* (Princeton: Princeton University Press, 1975), chaps. 13, 14; John Robertson, "The Scottish Enlightenment at the Limits of the Civic Tradition," in *Wealth and Virtue: The Shaping of Political Economy in the Scottish Enlightenment*, ed. Istvan Hont and Michael Ignatieff (Cambridge: Cambridge University Press, 1983), 137–78; Istvan Hont, "The 'Rich Country–Poor Country' Debate in Scottish Classical Political Economy," in ibid., 271–317. John Adams to Abigail Adams, 5 July 1774, 20 September 1774; Abigail Adams to John Adams, 16 October 1774, *Adams Family Correspondence*, ed. L. H. Butterfield et al. (Cambridge: Harvard University Press, 1963), 1:125, 161, 173; David E. Shi, *The Simple Life: Plain Living and High Thinking in American Culture* (New York: Oxford University Press, 1985), 61–65. On stereotypes of women's simultaneous liability to luxury and their duty to moderate it with taste, see G. J. Barker-Benfield, *The Culture of Sensibility: Sex and Society in Eighteenth-Century Britain* (Chicago: University of Chicago Press, 1992), 190–214.

24. Adam Smith, "Report of 1762–3," *Lectures on Jurisprudence*, ed. R. L. Meek, D. D. Raphael, and P. G. Stein (1978; repr. Indianapolis: Liberty Classics, 1982), 334–39.

25. Josiah Tucker, "Instructions for Travellers" (1758), in *Josiah Tucker: A Selection from His Economic and Political Writings,* ed. Robert Livingston Schuyler (New York: Columbia University Press, 1931), 245–46; Adam Smith, "Of the Effect of Utility upon the Sentiment of Approbation," in *The Theory of Moral Sentiments* (1759), ed. D. D. Raphael and A. L. Macfie (Oxford, 1976; repr. Indianapolis: Liberty Press, 1982), part IV, chap. i, para. 1; IV.i.8; IV.i.9; IV.i.10; Smith, *Wealth of Nations,* book I, chap. i, para. 11; III.i.2.

26. The first French edition of *Robinson Crusoe* (1720), unlike early English editions, showed him with an umbrella; David Blewett, *The Illustration of "Robinson Crusoe" 1719–1920* (Gerrards Cross, Buckinghamshire: Colin Smythe, 1995), 26–32. On umbrellas as an item of French "populuxe" consumption, see Cissie Fairchilds, "The Production and Marketing of Populuxe Goods in Eighteenth-Century Paris," in *Consumption and the World of Goods,* ed. John Brewer and Roy Porter (London: Routledge, 1993), 235–39.

27. Walpole to John Chute (3 October 1765), Lady Hertford to Walpole (25 September 1775), *Horace Walpole's Correspondence,* 31:215, 35:112, 39:267; "The Battle of Umbrellas," *Wit's Magazine* (London, August 1784), 286–88; George Paston, *Social Caricature in the Eighteenth Century* (London: Methuen, 1905), 23–24, 30, pls. 18–19, 39; Woodeford, *Diary of a Country Parson*; Trusler, *London Adviser,* 115. On British usage, see William Edward Hartpole Lecky, *A History of England in the Eighteenth Century,* 8 vols. (London: Longmans, Green, 1887), 6:146–47; Jeremy Farrell, *Umbrellas and Parasols* (London: B. T. Batsford, 1985), 7–8, 19–37.

28. Smith, *Wealth of Nations,* (bk.)I.viii.35–36.

29. Ibid., V.ii.(sec.)k, 2–3.

30. Ibid., I.i.11, 23; for Smith's usage of "necessaries and conveniencies of life," see pp. 10, 47, 51, 95, 176, 927.

31. Ibid., V.ii.k.3, 869–70; Robert Boyden Lamb, "Adam Smith's System: Sympathy not Self-Interest," *Journal of the History of Ideas* 35, no. 4 (October–December 1974): 679–80; Nathan Phillipson, "Adam Smith as Civic Moralist," in *Wealth and Virtue: The Shaping of Political Economy in the Scottish Enlightenment,* ed. Istvan Hont and Michael Ignatieff (Cambridge: Cambridge University Press, 1983), 179–234.

32. On the heightened awareness in the eighteenth century of physical misery as an object for sentimental sympathy, see Thomas W. Laqueur, "Bodies, Details, and the Humanitarian Narrative," in *The New Cultural History,* ed. Lynn Hunt (Berkeley: University of California Press, 1989), 176–204; Jay Fliegelman, *Prodigals and Pilgrims: The American Revolution against Patriarchal Authority* (New York: Cambridge University Press, 1982), 25–26, 117–22; Barker-Benfield, *Culture of Sensibility,* 8–9, 215–20, 224–31; Karen Halttunen, "Humanitarianism and the Pornography of Pain in Anglo-American Culture," *American Historical Review* 100, no. 2 (April 1995): 303–9; Carolyn D. Williams, "'The Luxury of Doing Good': Benevolence, Sensibility, and the Royal Humane Society," in *Pleasure in the Eighteenth Century,* ed. Roy Porter and Marie Mul-

vey Roberts (Washington Square, N.Y.: New York University Press, 1996), 77–107. John Howard, *The State of the Prisons in England and Wales*, 3rd ed. (Warrington: William Eyres, 1784), 1–3, 22–23, 32, 38–39, quoted 7, 38. On prison furnishings, see Christopher Gilbert, *English Vernacular Furniture 1750–1900* (New Haven: Yale University Press, 1991), chap. 13. On prison reform, see Rod Morgan, "Divine Philanthropy: John Howard Reconsidered," *History* 62, no. 206 (October 1977): 388–411; Michael Ignatieff, *A Just Measure of Pain: The Penitentiary in the Industrial Revolution, 1750–1850* (New York: Pantheon Books, 1978); Robin Evans, *The Architecture of Virtue: English Prison Architecture, 1750–1840* (New York: Cambridge University Press, 1982). Robert Alan Cooper, in "Ideas and Their Execution: English Prison Reform," *Eighteenth-Century Studies* 10, no. 1 (Fall 1976): 80, points out that Howard himself was a "humanitarian" who "showed no interest in reducing the large number of capital crimes." On distress as a convention in sentimental literature, see Janet Todd, *Sensibility: An Introduction* (London: Methuen, 1986), 2–3. On the rights of prisoners of war, see "Projet of a Treaty Submitted by the American Commissioners" (1786), *The Papers of Thomas Jefferson*, ed. Julian P. Boyd, 27 vols. to date (Princeton: Princeton University Press, 1954), 9: 419–20; Joyce Appleby, "Consumption in Early Modern Social Thought," in *Consumption and the World of Goods*, ed. John Brewer and Roy Porter (London: Routledge, 1993), 169. Howard had reported on the condition of prisoners of war during the American War of Independence; see *State of the Prisons*, 184–94.

33. Julian Ursyn Niemcewicz, *Under Their Vine and Fig Tree: Travels through America in 1797–1799, 1805 with Some Further Account of Life in New Jersey* (Collections of the New Jersey Historical Society, Newark, item #14), ed. and trans. Metchie J. E. Budka (Elizabeth, N.J.: Grassman Publishing, 1965), 33–35, 100; Isaac Weld, *Travels through the States of North America, and the Provinces of Upper and Lower Canada, during the Years 1795, 1796, and 1797* (London: John Stockdale, 1799), 85; J. F. D. Smyth, *A Tour in the United States of America*, 2 vols. (London: G. Robinson, 1784), 1:76. Bernard L. Herman, "Slave Quarters in Virginia: The Persona Behind Historic Artifacts," *The Scope of Historical Archaeology: Essays in Honor of John L. Cotter*, ed. David G. Orr and Daniel G. Crozier (Philadelphia: Laboratory of Anthropology, Temple University, 1984), 274. On apologies for slavery in response to humanitarianism, see Joyce E. Chaplin, "Slavery and the Principle of Humanity: A Modern Idea in the Early Lower South," *Journal of Social History* 24, no. 2 (Winter 1990): 299–313; John Drayton, *A View of South Carolina, as Respects Her Natural and Civil Concerns* (Charleston: W. P. Young, 1802), 144–49. On the terminology applicable to slave accommodation, see Dell Upton, "Slave Housing in Eighteenth-Century Virginia: A Report to the Department of Social and Cultural History, National Museum of American History, Smithsonian Institution" (July 1982), 5; Philip D. Morgan, *Slave Counterpoint: Black Culture in the Eighteenth-Century Chesapeake and Lowcountry* (Chapel Hill: University of North Carolina Press, 1998), 104–21.

34. Thomas Malthus, "An Essay on the Principle of Population: The Sixth Edition (1826) with Variant Readings from the Second Edition (1803)," *The Works of Thomas Robert Malthus*, ed. E. A. Wrigley and David Souden, 9 vols. (London: William Pickering, 1986), 3:520; E. A. Wrigley, "Malthus on the Prospects for the Labouring Poor," *Historical Journal* 31, no. 4 (1988): 813–29; D. E. C. Eversley, *Social Theories of Fertility and the Malthusian Debate* (Oxford: Clarendon, 1959), 211.

35. Malthus, "Essay on the Principle of Population," 3:466–68.

36. Robert Southey, *Letters from England: By Don Manuel Alvarez Espriella. Translated from the Spanish*, 2 vols. (London, 1807), 1: 180, 182. On Republican optimism at "the prospect of the widespread enjoyment of *comforts*," see Joyce Appleby, *Capitalism and a New Social Order: The Republican Vision of the 1790s* (New York: New York University Press, 1984), 90–91.

CHAPTER 6   ENLIGHTENED COMFORT

1. Benjamin Franklin, "The Art of Procuring Pleasant Dreams" (1786), in *The Writings of Benjamin Franklin*, ed. Albert Henry Smyth, 10 vols. (New York: Macmillan, 1905–7), 10:132.

2. Benjamin Franklin, "An Account of the New Invented Pennsylvanian Fire-Places" (Philadelphia, 1744), in *The Papers of Benjamin Franklin*, ed. Leonard W. Labaree et al., 33 vols. to date (New Haven: Yale University Press, 1959–), 2:424–25. On settles, see Robert Blair St. George, "'Set Thine House in Order': The Domestication of the Yeomanry in Seventeenth-Century New England," in *New England Begins: The Seventeenth Century*, ed. Jonathan L. Fairbanks and Robert F. Trent, 3 vols. (Boston: Museum of Fine Arts, 1982), 2:220–21. On stoves in German housing culture, see Cynthia G. Falk, "Symbols of Assimilation or Status? The Meanings of Eighteenth-Century Houses in Coventry Township, Chester County, Pennsylvania," *Winterthur Portfolio* 33, no. 2–3 (Summer–Autumn 1998): 107–34; Henry C. Mercer, *The Bible in Iron, or The Pictured Stoves and Stove Plates of the Pennsylvania Germans* (Doylestown, Pa.: Bucks County Historical Society, 1914).

3. Benjamin Franklin to Jan Ingenhousz, 28 August 1785, *Writings of Benjamin Franklin*, ed. Smyth, 9:423, 425; see also Robert Clavering, *An Essay on the Construction and Building of Chimneys . . .* , 3rd ed. (London, 1743), 8. Franklin's original stove design did not catch on particularly well, despite advertisements for "New Invented Pennsylvanian Stoves . . . remarkable for making a Room Warm and *comfortable* with very little wood"; *New York Mercury*, 9 November 1761, as quoted in *The Arts and Crafts in New York, 1726–1776: Advertisements and New Items from New York City Newspapers* (New York: New-York Historical Society, 1938), 123. When he sought copies of the stove to give friends while in Paris, he learned that many had been "laid aside" and that "some parts of the plates have been apply'd for Backs or hearths of Chimneys or other

Jobs"; Franklin to Hugh Roberts, 9 August 1765; Hugh Roberts to Franklin, 27 November 1765, *Papers of Benjamin Franklin,* ed. Labaree et al., 12:236, 386–87. In the late eighteenth century Anglo-American use of stoves was still largely restricted to public buildings and houses of the wealthy; Samuel Y. Edgerton, "Heat and Style: Eighteenth-Century House Warming by Stoves," *Journal of the Society of Architectural Historians* 20 (1961): 20–26.

4. "Account of the New Invented Fire-Places," 2:438–39. On the use of stoves in Boston, see Josephine H. Peirce, *Fire on the Hearth: The Evolution and Romance of the Heating Stove* (Springfield, Mass.: Pond-Edberg, 1951), 36–38.

5. Franklin to Lord Kames, 28 February 1768, *Writings of Benjamin Franklin,* ed. Smyth, 5:107–10, quoted 107. Franklin respectfully explained that the problem was not one of poor construction of the flue but rather Lord Kames's apparent ignorance of the physics of heat on elastic fluids, which prevented him from compensating properly for the differences between the temperature of air in the chimney flue and the temperatures at the top and bottom of the flue. Franklin first worked out these ideas in a letter to James Bowdoin, 2 December 1758, *Papers of Benjamin Franklin,* ed. Labaree et al., 8:194–98. *Johnson's Journey to the Western Islands of Scotland and Boswell's Journal of a Tour to the Hebrides with Samuel Johnson, LL. D.,* ed. R. W. Chapman (Oxford: Oxford University Press, 1924), 19–20.

6. Clavering, *Essay on Chimneys,* quoted i; *Caminologie, ou traité des cheminées* (Dijon, 1756), ix–x; "Cheminée," *Encyclopédie, ou dictionnaire raisonné des sciences, des arts et des metiers,* ed. Denis Diderot and Jean d'Alembert (Paris, 1753), 3:281–82; Daniel Roche, *The People of Paris: An Essay in Popular Culture in the Eighteenth Century,* trans. Marie Evans and Gwynne Lewis (Berkeley: University of California Press, 1987), 137, 153–54; John F. Fitchen III, "The Problem of Ventilation through the Ages," *Technology and Culture* 22 (1981): 492–500; J. N. Goldsmith and E. Wyndham Hulme, "History of the Grated Hearth, the Chimney, and the Air-Furnace," *Transactions of the Newcomen Society for the Study of the History of Engineering and Technology* 23 (1942–43): 1–12.

7. *Encyclopaedia Britannica; or, A Dictionary of Arts and Sciences* (Edinburgh, 1771), 3:606–13. *James* Anderson expanded the essay into *A Practical Treatise on Chimneys, Containing Full Directions for Preventing or Removing Smoke in Houses* (Edinburgh, 1776).

8. *Dictionnaire de biographie française,* ed. M. Prévost et al. (Paris, 1982), 6:723–24. Gauger's work appeared simultaneously in a German edition, published in Hamburg. There were also at least three English editions, in 1715, 1716, and 1736, and two more in France, in 1714 and 1749. On predecessors to Gauger's design, see J. Pickering Putnam, *The Open Fireplace in All Ages* (Boston: James R. Osgood, 1881), 32–69.

9. [Nicolas Gauger], *Fires Improv'd: Being a New Method of Building Chimneys, So as to Prevent their Smoaking . . . ,* trans. J. T. Desaguliers (London: J. Senex, 1715).

10. Ibid., 7–9, 29.

11. Ibid., 8.

12. Ibid., 31, 38.

13. *Dictionary of Scientific Biography*, ed. Charles Coulston Gillispie, 18 vols. (Princeton: Princeton University Press, 1971), 4:43–46.

14. Franklin, "Account of the New Invented Fire-Places," 2:419–46; on the word *ventilation*, see Putnam, *The Open Fireplace*, 37. On the connections between Desaguliers and Franklin, see I. Bernard Cohen, *Franklin and Newton: An Inquiry into Speculative Newtonian Experimental Science and Franklin's Work in Electricity as an Example Thereof* (Cambridge: Harvard University Press, 1966), 243–61; Franklin may have met Desaguliers in London in 1726. Unlike Gauger, Desaguliers frankly acknowledged that little was known about the physics of heat and fire; Cohen, *Franklin and Newton*, 259.

15. Martin Clare, "A Digression to the Affair of Chimnies," *The Motion of Fluids, Natural and Artificial; in Particular that of the Air and Water* (London: Edward Symon, 1735), 220–26; J. T. Desaguliers, *A Course of Experimental Philosophy*, 2 vols. (London: W. Innys and T. Longman, 1744), 2:208–9; Franklin, "Account of the New Invented Fire-Places," 422–23.

16. Franklin, "Account of the New Invented Fire-Places," 424–25.

17. Franklin to Jan Ingenhousz, 28 August 1785, *Writings of Benjamin Franklin*, ed. Smyth, 9:439.

18. Franklin, "Account of the New Invented Fire-Places." On the use of stoves in Philadelphia later in the century, see John C. Wills, *The Politics of Taste in the New Republic: The Decorative Elaboration of the Philadelphia Household, 1780–1820* (Ph.D. diss., University of Michigan, 1994), chap. 6, "The Franklin Stove and the Changing Nature of Household Comfort and Display."

19. J. Durno, *A Description of a New Invented Stove-Grate* (London: J. Towers, 1753), 3–5, 13, 20, 23, 27, 29.

20. Graham Hood, *The Governor's Palace in Williamsburg: A Cultural Study* (Williamsburg, Va.: Colonial Williamsburg Foundation, 1991), 186–89, 269–71. At about the same time, similar Buzaglo stoves were installed in the hall at Knole Park, Kent, and in the Divinity School at Cambridge; Christopher Gilbert and Anthony Wells-Cole, *The Fashionable Fire Place, 1660–1840* (Leeds: Leeds City Art Galleries, 1985), 63–65. On Parisian usage of stoves, see Annik Pardailhé-Galabrun, *The Birth of Intimacy: Privacy and Domestic Life in Early Modern Paris*, trans. Jocelyn Phelps (Philadelphia: University of Pennsylvania Press, 1991), 120–22. On the heating of public spaces, see Todd Willmert, "Heating Methods and Their Impact on Soane's Work: Lincoln's Inn Fields and Dulwich Picture Gallery," *Journal of the Society of Architectural Historians* 52 (March 1993): 26–58; Benjamin L. Walbert, III, "The Infancy of Central Heating in the United States: 1803 to 1845," *Bulletin, Association for Preservation Technology* 3, no. 4 (1971): 76–87.

21. Benjamin Franklin, "A Letter from Dr. B. Franklin to Dr. Ingenhausz, Physician to the Emperor, at Vienna," *Transactions* [of the American Philosophical Society], 2

(pt. 1) (Philadelphia, 1786): 1–27; Franklin to Jan Ingenhousz, 28 August 1785, *Writings of Benjamin Franklin*, ed. Smyth, 9:413–43, quoted 414, 417–18; "Smoke," *Encyclopaedia Britannica*, 3rd edn. (Edinburgh, 1797), 7:547–56.

22. *Dictionary of Scientific Biography*, 13:350–52. Benjamin Thompson, "On the Construction of Kitchen Fire-places and Kitchen Utensils," *Collected Works of Count Rumford*, ed. Sanborn C. Brown, 5 vols. (1802; repr. Cambridge: Harvard University Press, 1968–70), 3:55–384.

23. Benjamin Thompson, "Of Chimney Fire-places" (1796), *Collected Works of Count Rumford*, 2:221–307, esp. 225–30, 235–36. Rumford's design of stoves for cooking ran against deep English prejudices in favor of roasting by open fire; David J. Eveleigh, "'Put Down to a Clear Bright Fire': The English Tradition of Open-Fire Roasting," *Folk Life* 29 (1990–91): 5–18. Charles Willson Peale experimented with both stoves and fireplaces: "The Improved Brick Stoves at Peale's Museum" (26 January 1796), "Description of Some Improvements in the Common Fire-Place" (17 March 1797), letter to the editor, *Weekly Magazine* (March 1798), in *The Selected Papers of Charles Willson Peale*, ed. Lillian B. Miller, 2 vols. (New Haven: Yale University Press, 1982), 2:140–41, 192–97, 209–15.

24. Clavering, *Construction and Building of Chimneys*, quoted 72–73, 76–78; John Whitehurst, *Observations on the Ventilation of Rooms; on the Construction of Chimneys* (London, 1794), 12, 23; cf. James Sharp, *An Account of the Principle and Effects of the Air Stove-Grates . . . Commonly Known by the Name of American Stoves* (London, [178?]). On the dangers of too warm a house, see Thomas Beddoes, *Essay on the Causes, Early Signs, and Prevention of Pulmonary Consumption* (Bristol: Biggs & Cottle, 1799), as quoted in Roy Porter, "Consumption: Disease of the Consumer Society?" in *Consumption and the World of Goods*, ed. John Brewer and Roy Porter (London: Routledge, 1993), 67. In the late eighteenth century and early nineteenth century technical concern with heating shifted to the special needs of large buildings, where questions of healthful ventilation had priority over ones of comfortable warmth; Robert Bruegmann, "Central Heating and Forced Ventilation: Origins and Effects on Architectural Design," *Journal of the Society of Architectural Historians* 37 (1978): 143–60.

25. *Benjamin Franklin's Autobiography*, ed. J. A. Leo Lemay and P. M. Zall (New York: W. W. Norton, 1986), 6, 8–9. Franklin's interest in artificial illumination ranged to public as well as domestic uses: he promoted public streetlighting and devised a superior lamp housing, and he coordinated efforts to expand the production of glass in the colonies, in which his son John took part. On Franklin's interest in lighting, see Esmond Wright, *Franklin of Philadelphia* (Cambridge: Harvard University Press, 1986), 61–62.

26. Arthur Elton, "Gas for Light and Heat," in *A History of Technology*, ed. Charles Singer et al., 8 vols. (Oxford: Clarendon Press, 1954–84), 4:258–59; Michael Schrøder, *The Argand Burner: Its Origin and Development in France and England, 1780–1800* (Odense,

Denmark: Odense University Press, 1968), 35, 592. Wolfgang Schivelbusch, *Disenchanted Night: The Industrialization of Light in the Nineteenth Century* (New York: Berg, 1988), 93; William T. O'Dea, *The Social History of Lighting* (London: Routledge & Kegan Paul, 1958), 42–43.

27. *Boston News Letter*, 30 March 1748, as quoted in *The Arts and Crafts in New England, 1704–1775*, ed. George Francis Dow (Topsfield, Mass.: Wayside Press, 1927). Francis Hopkinson to Jefferson, 14 April 1787, *The Papers of Thomas Jefferson*, ed. Julian P. Boyd et al., 27 vols. to date (Princeton: Princeton University, 1955–), 11:290.

28. Unless another source is cited, the information on Argand and his lamp derives from Schröder, *Argand Burner*, passim. On its use in the United States, see Wills, *Politics of Taste*, chap. 7, "The Argand Lamp and the Changing Awareness of Time and Self."

29. Jefferson to James Madison, 11 November 1784, *Papers of Thomas Jefferson*, 7:505; Jefferson sent practically the same message to Charles Thompson the same day; ibid., 7:518. Washington to Gouvernour Morris, 1 March 1790, *The Papers of George Washington. Presidential Series*, ed. Dorothy Twohig et al. (Charlottesville: University of Virginia Press, 1996), 5:192–93.

30. O'Dea, *Social History of Lighting*, 52–55.

31. James Beresford, *The Miseries of Human Life . . .* , comp. Michelle Lovric (1806; New York: St. Martin's Press, 1995), 8, 13, 21, 24, 44.

32. Ibid., 8–13.

33. Jack McLaughlin, *Jefferson and Monticello: The Biography of a Builder* (New York: Henry Holt, 1988), 5, 20, 254, 280, 298, 322–25, 383, 444, quoted 36, 254.

34. Susan R. Stein, *The Worlds of Thomas Jefferson at Monticello* (New York: Harry N. Abrams, 1993), 258–59, 264–67, 286–87, 290, 418–19.

35. Jefferson to Madison, 11 November 1784, *Papers of Thomas Jefferson*, 7:505.

CHAPTER 7 PICTURESQUE COMFORT

1. Jane Austen, *Sense and Sensibility* (1811; reprint, New York: Signet, 1995), 213–14, chap. 14.

2. Christopher Dyer, "Towns and Cottages in Eleventh-Century England," in *Studies in Medieval History Presented to R. H. C. Davis*, ed. Henry Mayr-Harting and R. I. Moore (London: Hambledon, 1985), 91–106; "Poor Law Amendment Act, 1662," in Peter Laslett, *The World We Have Lost Further Explored* (New York: Charles Scribner's Sons, 1984), 32–33; Samuel Johnson, *A Dictionary of the English Language*, 2 vols. (London: J. F. and C. Rivington et al., 1785), s.v. "cottage."

3. Studies of early architecturally designed cottages include: Sandra Blutman, "Books of Designs for Country Houses, 1780–1815," *Architectural History* 11 (1968): 25–33; Sutherland Lyall, "Minor Domestic Architecture in Britain and the Pattern

Books" (Ph.D. diss., University of London, 1974); Michael McMordie, "Picturesque Pattern Books and Pre-Victorian Designers," *Architectural History* 18 (1975): 43–59; David Paul Schuyler, "English and American Cottages, 1795–1855: A Study in Architectural Theory and the Social Order" (master's thesis, University of Delaware, 1976); Michael McMordie, "The Cottage Idea," *RACAR: Revue d'art canadienne / Canadian Art Review* 6, no. 1 (1979): 17–27; Sutherland Lyall, *Dream Cottages: From Cottage Ornée to Stockbroker Tudor, Two Hundred Years of the Cult of the Vernacular* (London: Robert Hale, 1988); James S. Ackerman, *The Villa: Form and Ideology of Country Houses* (Princeton: Princeton University Press, 1990), 212–27.

On architectural pattern books in Britain and America, see John Archer, *The Literature of British Domestic Architecture, 1715–1842* (Cambridge: MIT Press, 1985), esp. 21, 28–30, 56–71, 78–83; Dell Upton, "Pattern Books and Professionalism: Aspects of the Transformation of Domestic Architecture in America, 1800–1860," *Winterthur Portfolio* 19, no. 2–3 (Summer–Autumn 1984): 107–50; Charles B. Wood III, "The New Pattern Books and the Role of the Agricultural Press," in *Prophet With Honor: The Career of Andrew Jackson Downing, 1815–1852*, ed. George B. Tatum and Elisabeth Blair MacDougall (Washington, D.C.: Dumbarton Oaks Research Library and Collection, 1989), 165–89.

4. Humphry Repton, *Observations on the Theory and Practice of Landscape Gardening* (London: J. Taylor, 1803), 11; *The Four Books of Andrea Palladio's Architecture* (1738; reprint, New York: Dover, 1965), 1.

5. Leone Battista Alberti, *Ten Books on Architecture,* trans. James Leoni (1755), ed. J. Rykwert (London: Alec Tiranti, 1955), 205; Claudia Lazzaro, "Rustic Country House to Refined Farmhouse: The Evolution and Migration of an Architectural Form," *Journal of the Society of Architectural Historians* 44, no. 4 (December 1985): 346–67; Isaac Ware, *A Complete Body of Architecture* (1768; reprint, Westmead, England: Gregg International, 1971), 345. On farmhouse architecture, see Thomas Rawlins, *Familiar Architecture; Consisting of Original Designs of Houses for Gentlemen and Tradesmen, Parsonages and Summer-Retreats* (London: n.p., 1768), ii–iii; Daniel Garret, *Designs, and Estimates, of Farm Houses, etc.* (London: J. Brindley, 1747), 1–2; William Halfpenny, *Six New Designs for Convenient Farm-Houses* (London: Robert Sayer, 1751), preface; idem, *Twelve Beautiful Designs for Farm-houses,* 3rd ed. (London: Robert Sayer, 1774); Eileen Harris, "The Farmhouse: Vernacular and After," *Architectural Review* 130, no. 778 (December 1961): 377–79; John Martin Robinson, *Georgian Model Farms: A Study of the Decorative and Model Farm Buildings of the Age of Improvement, 1700–1846* (Oxford: Clarendon Press, 1983), 15, 19.

6. Batty Langley, *New Principles of Gardening* (London: A. Bettesworth & J. Batley, 1728), x–xi, 193–95; Laurence Fleming and Alan Gore, *The English Garden* (London: Michael Joseph, 1979), 18, 24, 27–29, 32, 34, 38, 60, 62, 92; George Mott, Sally Sample Aall, and Gervase Jackson-Stops, *Follies and Pleasure Pavilions: England, Ireland, Scotland, Wales* (New York: Harry N. Abrams, 1989), 9; H. F. Clark, "Eighteenth-Century

Elysiums: The Role of 'Association' in the Landscape Movement," *Journal of the Warburg and Courtauld Institute*, 6 (1943): 165–89; S. Lang, "The Genesis of the English Landscape Garden," in *The Picturesque Garden and its Influence outside the British Isles*, ed. Nikolaus Pevsner (Washington, D.C.: Dumbarton Oaks, 1974), 22–29; Tom Williamson, *Polite Landscapes: Gardens and Society in Eighteenth-Century England* (Baltimore: Johns Hopkins University Press, 1995), passim; Michel Saudan, Sylvia Saudan-Skira, and François Crouzet, *From Folly to Follies: Discovering the World of Gardens* (New York: Abbeville Press, 1988), viii; Margaret Jourdain, *The Work of William Kent, Artist, Painter, Designer, and Landscape Gardener* (New York: C. Scribner's Sons, 1948), 79; William Chambers, *A Dissertation on Oriental Gardening*, 2nd ed. (London: W. Griffin, 1773), 16, 21; idem, *Plans, Elevations, Sections and Perspective Views of the Gardens and Buildings at Kew* (London: J. Hakerkorn, 1763); Thomas Hinde, *Capability Brown: The Story of a Master Gardener* (New York: W. W. Norton, 1987), 134, 139; Roger Turner, *Capability Brown and the Eighteenth-Century English Landscape* (New York: Rizzoli, 1985), 86, 145–46, 181, 187; Dorothy Stroud, *Capability Brown* (London: Country Life, 1950), 87, 161, 180, 208–9.

7. Morrison Heckscher, "Eighteenth-Century Rustic Furniture Designs," *Furniture History* 11 (1975): 64n; Alistair Rowan, *Garden Buildings* (Feltham: Country Life Books, 1968), 3; Roger White, "Georgian Landscape Architecture," in *Georgian Arcadia: Architecture for the Park and Garden* (London: Colnaghi, 1987), 9–16. William Halfpenny and John Halfpenny, *Rural Architecture in the Gothick Taste* (London: Robert Sayer, 1752); William Wrighte, *Grotesque Architecture, or, Rural Amusement* (London: I. & J. Taylor, 1790); John Plaw, *Ferme Ornée; or Rural Improvements* (London: I. & J. Taylor, (1795); William Wrighte, *Ideas for Rustic Furniture Proper for Garden Seats, Summer Houses, Hermitages, Cottages* (London: I. & J. Taylor, c. 1790); Thomas Collins Overton, *Original Designs of Temples, and Other Ornamental Buildings for Parks and Gardens in the Greek, Roman, and Gothic Taste* (London: Henry Webley, 1766), pl. 34 [misprinted as 43]. For early examples of cottages as part of landscape architecture, see Nigel Temple, *John Nash and the Village Picturesque* (London: Alan Sutton, 1979), 5–7; Michael McCarthy, "Eighteenth Century Amateur Architects and Their Gardens," in *The Picturesque Garden and its Influence Outside the British Isles*, ed. Nikolaus Pevsner (Washington, D.C.: Dumbarton Oaks, 1974), 51; Timothy Mowl, "The Evolution of the Park Gate Lodge as a Building Type," *Architectural History* 27 (1984): 468.

8. Eileen Harris, *British Architectural Books and Writers, 1556–1785* (New York: Cambridge University Press, 1990), 221; White, *Georgian Arcadia*, 34–35; Wrighte, *Grotesque Architecture*, 3–5, pl. 1; William Halfpenny and John Halfpenny, *The Country Gentleman's Pocket Companion, and Builder's Assistant, for Rural Decorative Architecture* (London: Robert Sayer, 1753), 9; Plaw, *Ferme Ornée*, 6, pl. 12.

9. Robert Morris, *Rural Architecture* (1750; repr., Westmead, England: Gregg International, 1971), preface and introduction; cf. James S. Ackerman, "The Tuscan/Rus-

tic Order: A Study in the Metaphorical Language of Architecture," *Journal of the Society of Architectural Historians* 42, no. 1 (March 1983): 15–34.

10. Marc-Antoine Laugier, *An Essay on Architecture; in which its True Principles are Explained, and Invariable Rules Proposed* (London: T. Osborne and Shipton, 1755), 11–12 (*Essai sur l'architecture*, 2nd ed. [Paris: Duchesne, 1755], 9).

11. Thomas Collins Overton, *The Temple Builder's Most Useful Companion* (London: I. Taylor, 1774); William Halfpenny and John Halfpenny, *Rural Architecture in the Chinese Taste*, 3rd ed. (1755; repr., New York: Benjamin Blom, 1968), pls. 9–13; Halfpenny and Halfpenny, *Rural Architecture in the Gothick Taste*, 10–11, pls. 14, 15, 18. Jacques-François Blondel, *De la distribution des maisons de plaisance*, 2 vols. (Paris: Charles-Antoine Jombert, 1737), 1:71–72; 2:129, pl. 10; Plaw, *Ferme Ornée*, 2–3, 7; Charles Over, *Ornamental Architecture in the Gothic, Chinese and Modern Taste* (London: Robert Sayer, 1758), 4, pl. 16; John Soan[e], *Designs in Architecture . . . for Temples, Baths, Cassines, Pavilions, Garden-Seats, Obelisks, and other Buildings; for Decorating Pleasure-Grounds, Parks, Forests* (1778; reprint Westmead, England: Gregg International, 1968), pls. 9–10, 34; Pierre de la Ruffinière du Prey, *John Soane: The Making of an Architect* (Chicago: University of Chicago Press, 1982), 124–28. On the high-mindedness associated with hermitages, see Judith Colton, "Kent's Hermitage for Queen Caroline at Richmond," *Architectura* 2 (1974): 181–91.

12. Margaret Willes, "Country House Dairies," *Apollo* 149, no. 446 (April 1999): 29–32; Robinson, *Georgian Model Farms*, 82–96, pls. 84–96; Alison Kelly, *The Story of Wedgwood* (London: Faber & Faber, 1975), 21–22; Wedgwood quoted in Alison Kelly, *Decorative Wedgwood in Architecture and Furniture* (London: Country Life, 1965), 119–23, pls. 58–61; Johann Langner, "Architecture pastorale sous Louis XVI," *Art de France* 3 (1963): 170–86; James Malton, *A Collection of Designs for Rural Retreats* (London: J. & T. Carpenter, 1802), 33–34, pls. 27–28. On the connection in architectural design between cottages and dairies, see du Prey, *John Soane*, 245–55, 377.

13. Thomas Whately, *Observations on Modern Gardening, Illustrated by Descriptions*, 3rd ed. (London: T. Payne, 1771), 116–35, 231–32.

14. Oliver Goldsmith, "The Deserted Village," in *Collected Works of Oliver Goldsmith*, ed. Arthur Friedman, 5 vols. (Oxford: Clarendon Press, 1966), 4:298, lines 295–302. William Whitehead as quoted by Mavis Batey, "Oliver Goldsmith: An Indictment of Landscape Gardening," in *Furor Hortensis: Essays on the History of the English Landscape Garden in Memory of H. F. Clark*, ed. Peter Willis (Edinburgh: Elysium Press, 1974), 57–71. See also H. J. Bell, "'The Deserted Village' and Goldsmith's Social Doctrines," *Proceedings of the Modern Language Association* 59, no. 3 (September 1944): 747–72. John Barrell, *The Dark Side of the Landscape: The Rural Poor in English Painting, 1730–1840* (Cambridge: Cambridge University Press, 1980), 35–88; Ann Bermingham, *Landscape and Ideology: The English Rustic Tradition, 1740–1860* (Berkeley: University of California Press, 1986), 14–54; Christiana Payne, *Toil and Plenty: Images of the Agricultural Landscape in England, 1780–1890* (New Haven: Yale University Press, 1993), 23–66.

15. Harris, *British Architectural Books*, 490; John Wood, *Series of Plans for Cottages or Habitations of the Labourer . . . Tending to the Comfort of the Poor and Advantage of the Builder* (1781; reprint, London: J. Taylor, 1806); John Plaw, *Sketches for Country Houses, Villas, and Rural Dwellings; Calculated for Persons of Moderate Income, and for Comfortable Retirement* (London: J. Taylor, 1800); E. Gyfford, *Designs for Elegant Cottages and Small Villas, Calculated for the Comfort and Convenience of Persons of Moderate and of Ample Fortune* (1806; reprint, Westmead, England: Gregg International, 1972).

16. J. D. Chambers and G. E. Mingay, *The Agricultural Revolution, 1750–1880* (New York: Schocken Books, 1966), 95–102, 119–20, 141–43; Paul Langford, *A Polite and Commercial People: England, 1727–1783* (New York: Oxford University Press, 1992), 435–40, 458–59; Repton, *Observations*, quoted 137–38.

17. Nathaniel Kent to Coke of Norfolk, 1789, as quoted in Robinson, *Georgian Model Farms*, 109; Nathaniel Kent, *Hints to Gentlemen of London Property* (London: J. Dodsley, 1775), 230.

18. Kent, *Hints to Gentlemen*, 229, 237; Wood, *Series of Plans*, 3.

19. Wood, *Series of Plans*, 4.

20. Kent, *Hints to Gentlemen*, 230–31; John Loudon, *A Treatise on Forming, Improving, and Managing Country Residences*, 2 vols. (London: Longman, Hurst, Rees, & Orme, 1806), 1:124–25; Wood, *Series of Plans*, 5.

21. Kent to Coke of Norfolk, as quoted in Robinson, *Georgian Model Farms*, 109.

22. *Communications to the Board of Agriculture on Subjects Relative to the Husbandry and Internal Improvement of the Country*, 7 vols. (London: W. Bulmer, 1797), vol. 1, part 2, *Cottages*, 89, 96–98, 103–17, pls. 34–35; J. Miller, *The Country Gentleman's Architect* (London: I. & J. Taylor, 1791); James Malton, *An Essay on British Cottage Architecture*, (London: Hookham & Carpenter, 1798), 17–18; Wood, *Series of Plans*, 5, 22, pls. 1–28. On cottages actually built according to these models, see Robinson, *Georgian Model Farms*, 111; Lyall, *Dream Cottages*, 113–24. On the ambivalence of the "rural professional class" toward the picturesque, see John Barrell, *The Idea of Landscape and the Sense of Place, 1730–1840: An Approach to the Poetry of John Clare* (Cambridge: Cambridge University Press), 64–97.

23. Kent, *Hints to Gentlemen*, 231–32; Wood, *Series of Plans*, 4.

24. Arthur Young, "Tour in Catalonia," *Annals of Agriculture and Other Useful Arts* (Bury St. Edmunds: J. Rackham, 1787), 8:202, 207, 210, 263, 273. On the reporting of rural living conditions, see G. E. Fussell, *The English Rural Labourer: His Home, Furniture, Clothing & Food from Tudor to Victorian Times* (London: Batchworth Press, 1949), 50–67.

25. Kent, *Hints to Gentlemen*, 238; Richard Payne Knight, *An Analytical Inquiry into the Principles of Taste*, 2nd ed. (London: T. Payne, 1805), 222; S. Lang, "Richard Payne Knight and the Idea of Modernity," *Concerning Architecture: Essays on Architectural Writers and Writing Presented to Nikolaus Pevsner*, ed. John Summerson (London: Allen Lane,

1968), 91; Dora Wiebenson, *The Picturesque Garden in France* (Princeton: Princeton University Press, 1978), 60–63.

26. Malton, *Essay on British Cottage Architecture*, 2, 4–5; Bermingham, *Landscape and Ideology*, 40–41, 69–75.

27. Charles Thomas Middleton, *Picturesque and Architectural Views for Cottages, Farm Houses, and Country Villas* (London: Edward Jeffrey, 1793), 2; idem, *The Architect and Builder's Miscellany* (1795; repr., London: 1979), pls. 1–15; Malton, *Essay on British Cottage Architecture*, 4–5, 22; pls. 10, 11, 12, 14; E. A. Wade, "James Malton, Picturesque Pioneer," *The Picturesque* 3 (Summer 1993): 19–24.

28. Middleton, *Picturesque and Architectural Views*, 1; Gyfford, *Designs for Elegant Cottages and Small Villas*, 1–3, pls. 1–6; Plaw, *Sketches for Country Houses*, 11–12, pls. 8, 13; Malton, *Essay on British Cottage Architecture*, 27; Nigel H. L. Temple, *John Nash and the Village Picturesque: with Special Reference to the Reptons and Nash at the Blaise Castle Estate, Bristol* (Gloucester: Alan Sutton, 1979), 84. Nikolaus Pevsner, "Richard Payne Knight," *Art Bulletin* 31, no. 4 (December 1949): 311.

29. Knight, *Analytical Inquiry*, 193.

30. Middleton, *Architect and Builder's Miscellany*, pls. 1–12.

31. Repton, *Observations*, 177–79; Loudon, *Treatise on Country Residences*, 69–71; Humphry Repton and John Adey Repton, *Fragments on the Theory and Practice of Landscape Gardening* (London: J. Taylor, 1816), 15.

32. Richard Payne Knight, *The Landscape, a Didactic Poem in Three Books, Addressed to Uvedale Price, Esq.* (London: W. Bulmer, 1794), 36, lines 262–67; idem, *Analytical Inquiry*, 223–25; Uvedale Price, "Essay on Architecture and Building," in *Essays on the Picturesque, as Compared with the Beautiful; and, on the Use of Studying Pictures, for the Purpose of Improving Real Landscape*, 3 vols. (London: J. Mawman, 1810), 2:265–67, 341; Humphry Repton, *Sketches and Hints on Landscape Gardening* (London: W. Bulmer, 1794), 6, 59–62, 64, 70, 77.

33. Johnson, *Dictionary*, s.v. "elegance"; Thomas Dyche and William Pardon, *New General English Dictionary* (London: Catherine & Richard Ware, 1765), s.v. "elegance"; N. Bailey, *An Universal Etymological English Dictionary* (London: J. & A. Duncan, 1794), s.v. "elegant"; W. F. Pocock, *Architectural Designs for Rustic Cottages, Picturesque Dwellings, Villas* (London: J. Taylor, 1807), 1, 8–9; Edmund Bartell, *Hints for Picturesque Improvements in Ornamental Cottages* (London: J. Taylor, 1804); Lyall, *Dream Cottages*, 73–86.

34. James Randall, *A Collection of Architectural Designs for Mansions, Casinos, Villas, Lodges, and Cottages* (London: J. Taylor, 1806), iv–v; E. Gyfford, *Designs for Small Picturesque Cottages* (London: J. Taylor, 1807), v–vii; Plaw, *Sketches for Country Houses*, pls. 15, 16, 17, 21; T. R. Slater, "Family, Society and the Ornamental Villa on the Fringes of English Country Towns," *Journal of Historical Geography* 4, no. 2 (April 1978): 129–44; John Summerson, "The Classical Country House in 18th-Century England," *Journal of the Royal Society of Arts* 107 (1959): 539–87.

35. For later house types with similar symbolic importance, see Anthony D. King, *The Bungalow: The Production of a Global Culture* (London: Routledge & Kegan Paul, 1984); Alan Gowans, *The Comfortable House: North American Suburban Architecture 1890–1930* (Cambridge: MIT Press, 1986).

CHAPTER 8   HEALTHY COMFORT

1. Paula Henderson, "The Loggia in Tudor and Early Stuart England: The Adaptation and Function of Classical Form," in *Albion's Classicism: The Visual Arts in Britain, 1550–1600*, ed. Lucy Gent (New Haven: Yale University, 1995), 109–45; Rosalys Coope, "The 'Long Gallery': Its Origins, Development, Use and Decoration," *Architecture History* 29 (1986): 43–72.

2. *The Oxford English Dictionary*, 2nd edn. (Oxford: Clarendon Press, 1989), s.v. "piazza," "veranda, verandah"; Albert Matthews, "Piazza," *Nation*, 68 (1 June 1899): 416; Henry Yule and A. C. Burnell, *Hobson-Jobson: A Glossary of Colloquial Anglo-Indian Words and Phrases, and of Kindred Terms, Etymological, Historical, Geographical and Discursive*, 2nd ed. (London: Routledge & Kegan Paul, 1985), s.v. "veranda"; Anthony D. King, "An Architectural Note on the Term 'Verandah,'" *The Bungalow: The Production of a Global Culture* (London: Routledge & Kegan Paul, 1984), 265–67.

3. Jessie Poesch, *The Art of the Old South: Painting, Sculpture, Architecture and the Products of Craftsmen, 1560–1860* (New York: Alfred A. Knopf, 1983), 129; H. Roy Merrens and George D. Terry, "Dying in Paradise: Malaria, Mortality, and the Perceptual Environment in Colonial South Carolina," *Journal of Southern History* 50, no. 4, (November 1984): 547–49; Joyce E. Chaplin, *An Anxious Pursuit: Agricultural Innovation and Modernity in the Lower South, 1730–1815* (Chapel Hill: University of North Carolina, 1993), 93–108.

4. George Cheyne, *An Essay of Health and Long Life* (London: George Strahan, 1724), quoted 6–7.

5. For mention of piazzas in real estate advertisements, see *South Carolina Gazette*, 19 May 1746, 10 May 1747, 11 April 1748. [Alexander Hewatt], *An Historical Account of the Rise and Progress of the Colonies of South Carolina and Georgia*, 2 vols. (London: Alexander Donaldson, 1779), quoted 2:290. For an early illustration of a piazza on a plantation house, and perhaps on slave houses as well, see Philip D. Morgan, *Slave Counterpoint: Black Culture in the Eighteenth-Century Chesapeake and Lowcountry* (Chapel Hill: University of North Carolina Press, 1998), 107.

6. The best discussions of the single house are Bernard L. Herman, "Rethinking the Charleston Single House," *Exploring Everyday Landscapes: Perspectives in Vernacular Architecture, VII*, ed. Annmarie Adams and Sally McMurry (Knoxville: University of Tennessee Press, 1997), 41–57; and Martha A. Zierden and Bernard L. Herman, "Charleston Townhouses: Archaeology, Architecture, and the Urban Landscape, 1750–1850," *Landscape Archaeology: Reading and Interpreting the American Historical Landscape,*

ed. Rebecca Yamin and Karen Bescherer Metheny (Knoxville: University of Tennessee Press, 1996), 193–227, quoted 204. See also, George Waddell, "The Charleston Single House: An Architectural Survey," *Preservation Progress* 22, no. 2 (March 1977): 4–8; Albert Simons, "Architectural Trends in Charleston," *Antiques* 97, no. 4 (April 1970): 547–55; Poesch, *Art of the Old South,* 52–60, cf. 129–39; Peter Coclanis, "The Sociology of Architecture in Colonial Charleston: Pattern and Process in an Eighteenth-Century Southern City," *Journal of Social History* 18, no. 4, (Summer 1985): 607–23. *The Papers of Henry Laurens,* ed. Philip M. Hamer et al., 14 vols. to date (Columbia: University of South Carolina, 1968–); "Journal of Josiah Quincy, Junior, 1773," Massachusetts Historical Society, *Proceedings* 49 (October 1915–June 1916): 440–57.

7. Duc de La Rochefoucauld-Liancourt, *Travels through the United States of North America in the Years 1795, 1796, and 1797,* as quoted in Alice R. Huger Smith and D. E. Huger Smith, *The Dwelling Houses of Charleston South Carolina* (Philadelphia: J. B. Lippincott, 1917), 26; see also, John Drayton, *A View of SC, as respects Her Natural and Civil Concerns* (Charleston, S.C.: W. P. Young, 1802), 111–12; advertisement by Charles Stuart, *Charleston City Gazette and Advertiser,* 27 May 1793, as quoted in *The Arts and Crafts in Philadelphia, Maryland, and South Carolina: Gleanings from Newspapers,* comp. Alfred Coxe Prime, vol. 2, *1786–1800* (n.p.: Walpole Society, 1932), 228–29. Around 1800 Charles Fraser sketched numerous houses with piazzas; *A Charleston Sketchbook, 1796–1806,* ed. Alice R. Huger Smith (Charleston, S.C.: Carolina Art Association, 1940).

8. Ruth Little-Stokes, "The North Carolina Porch: A Climatic and Cultural Buffer," *Carolina Dwelling,* vol. 26, *Toward Preservation of Place: In Celebration of the North Carolina Vernacular Landscape,* ed. Doug Swaim (Raleigh: North Carolina State University, 1978), 104–11; Jay D. Edwards, "The Evolution of Vernacular Architecture in the Western Caribbean," *Cultural Traditions and Caribbean Identity: The Question of Patrimony,* ed. S. Jeffrey Wilkerson and Roy Hunt (Gainesville: University of Florida Press, 1980), 297–319; Thomas T. Waterman, "Some Early Buildings of Barbados," *Journal of the Barbados Museum and Historical Society* 13 (1945): 140–48.

On the likelihood of African origins for the piazza, see Fritz Hamer and Michael Trinkley, "African Architectural Transference to the South Carolina Low Country, 1700–1880," *Tennessee Anthropologist* 22, no. 1 (Spring 1997): 1–34; David S. Cecelski, "The Hidden World of Mullet Camps: African-American Architecture on the North Carolina Coast," *North Carolina Historical Review* 70, no. 1 (January 1993): 6–8; Robert Farris Thompson, "The Song that Named the Land: The Visionary Presence of African-American Art," *Black Art—Ancestral Legacy: The African Impulse in African-American Art* (New York: Harry N. Abrams, 1989), 119–22; Jay Edwards and Mary Lee Eggart, "Architectural Creolization: The Role of Africans in America's Vernacular Architecture" (paper, Department of Geography and Anthropology, Lousiana State University, 1 January 1996). On Greenspring, see *Latrobe's View of America, 1795–1820: Selections from the Watercolors and Sketches,* ed. Edward C. Carter II, John C. Van Horne, and Charles E. Brownell (New Haven: Yale University Press, 1985), 100–101. On the verandahlike structures in early-eighteenth-century French creole architecture in Saint Domingue (now Haiti) and Louisiana, see Philippe Oszuscik, "Passage of the Gallery and Other Caribbean Elements from the French and Spanish to the British in the United States," *Pioneer America Society Transactions* 15 (1992): 1–4; and idem, "The French Creole Cottage and Its Caribbean Connection," *French and Germans in the Mississippi Valley: Landscape and Cultural Traditions*, ed. Michael Roard (Cape Girardeau, Mo.: Center for Regional History and Cultural Heritage, Southeast Missouri State University), 61–78; Jay D. Edwards, "The Origins of the Louisiana Creole Cottage," ibid., 8–60, quoting Sloane, 30–31.

9. Richard Ligon, *A True and Exact History of the Island of Barbadoes* (London, 1657), 40–43, 102–4; Carl Bridenbaugh and Roberta Bridenbaugh, *No Peace Beyond the Line: The English in the Caribbean, 1624–1690* (New York: Oxford University Press, 1972), 134, 151–54; Richard S. Dunn, *Sugar and Slaves: The Rise of the Planter Class in the English West Indies, 1624–1713* (New York: W. W. Norton, 1973), 287–99; "The Diary of a Westmoreland Planter, Part 1: Thomas Thistlewood in the Vineyard, 1750–51," *Jamaica Journal* 21, no. 3 (August–October 1988): 20–21.

10. Edward Long, *The History of Jamaica*, 3 vols. (1774; reprint, London: Frank Cass, 1970), 2:505–20, quoted 515 (Edward Long left Jamaica in 1769 for reasons of health, never to return); Cheyne, *Essay of Health*, 81–83; Karen Ordahl Kupperman, "Fear of Hot Climates in the Anglo-American Colonial Experience," *William and Mary Quarterly*, 3rd ser., 41 (April 1984): 224–25.

11. Long, *History of Jamaica*, 2:505–20; Cheyne, *Essay of Health*, 81–83.

12. Long, *History of Jamaica*, 2:21; Janet Schaw, *Journal of a Lady of Quality; Being a Narrative of a Journey from Scotland to the West Indies, North Carolina, and Portugal, in the years 1774 to 1776*, ed. Evangeline Walker Andrews and Charles McLean Andrews (New Haven: Yale University, 1923), 90, 101–3, 122, 124; Maria Skinner Nugent, *Lady Nugent's Journal of her Residence in Jamaica from 1801 to 1805*, ed. Philip Wright (1839; rev. ed., Kingston, Jamaica: Institute of Jamaica Publications, 1966), 25–26. "One story" in English usage would have been one story above the ground floor. On the piazza as a standard feature of Jamaican architecture in the early nineteenth century and its relation to plantation prospects, see B. W. Higman, *Jamaica Surveyed: Plantation Maps and Plans of the Eighteenth and Nineteenth Centuries* (Kingston: Institute of Jamaica Publications, 1988), 237–40, 267–68.

13. John Pringle, *Observations on the Nature and Cure of Hospital and Jayl-Fevers* (1750), quoted in John D. Thompson and Grace Goldin, *The Hospital: A Social and Architectural History* (New Haven: Yale University Press, 1975), 149, 151; John Pringle, *Observations on the Diseases of the Army, in Camp and Garrison*, 3rd ed. (London: A. Millar, 1761), 125–28; Arnold Zuckerman, "Scurvy and the Ventilation of Ships in the Royal Navy: Samuel Sutton's Contribution," *Eighteenth-Century Studies* 10, no. 2 (Winter 1976–77): 222–34;

Christopher Lloyd and Jack L. S. Coulter, *Medicine and the Navy, 1200–1900*, vol. 3, *1714–1815*, 4 vols. (London: E. & S. Livingstone, 1961), 70–80; D. G. C. Allan and R. E. Schofield, *Stephen Hales: Scientist and Philanthropist* (London: Scolar Press, 1980), 48–64, 85.

14. William Buchan, *Domestic Medicine; or the Family Physician* (Edinburgh: Balfour, Auld, and Smellie, 1769), 84–85, see also 41–43; Charles E. Rosenberg, "Medical Text and Social Context: Explaining William Buchan's *Domestic Medicine*," *Bulletin of the History of Medicine* 57, no. 1 (Spring 1983): 22–42.

15. Samuel Vaughan, "A Perspective View of Navy or Lynches Island at Port Antoney in Jamaica," and inset detail on the map of Kingston c. 1738–47, both reproduced in Frank Cundall, *The Governors of Jamaica in the First Half of the Eighteenth Century* (London: West India Committee, 1937), plates facing 206 and 138 respectively.

16. N. A. M. Rodger, *The Wooden World: An Anatomy of the Georgian Navy* (London: Collins, 1986), 98–112; Vernon to the Navy Board, 30 August 1740; Vernon to the Secretary of the Admiralty, 5 September 1742, *The Vernon Papers*, ed. B. McL. Ranft (Greenwich: Navy Records Society, 1958), 324, 334; Navy Board to the Admiralty, 25 April 1740, *Vernon Papers*, 326.

17. Vernon fatally compromised the design with his contradictory disciplinary and hygienic purposes. He built the piazza on the *inside* of the quadrangle and used bricks contributed by the colonists to build a solid outer wall to prevent inmates' casual exit. His hospital did nothing to lessen morbidity, but naval inspectors attributed its shortcomings to inadequacies of administration and location, not design. Vernon to the Secretary of the Admiralty, 7 October 1740, 8 October 1740, 15 November 1742, *Vernon Papers*, 314–15, 325, 338; Military surgeons of the Fiftieth Regiment to Captain Ogilvy, December 1774, quoted in David Buisseret, "The Stony Hill Barracks," *Jamaica Journal* 7, nos. 1, 2 (March–June 1973): 22–23; Pringle, *Observations on Diseases of the Army*, 96–97, 118; Lloyd and Coulter, *Medicine and the Navy*, 3:101–3. Marion D. Ross, "Caribbean Colonial Architecture in Jamaica," *Journal of the Society of Architectural Historians* 3 (October 1951): 27; Edwards, "Evolution of Vernacular Architecture," 314, 324–32; David Buisseret, *Historic Architecture of the Caribbean* (London: Heinemann, 1980), 1–16; Jay D. Edwards, "The First Comparative Studies of Caribbean Architecture," *New West India Guide* 57, nos. 3, 4 (1983): 197.

18. Catherine W. Bishir, *North Carolina Architecture* (Chapel Hill: University of North Carolina Press, 1990), 26–27, 114–24; Stanley A. South, "'Russellborough': Two Royal Governors' Mansions at Brunswick Town," *North Carolina Historical Review* 44, no. 4 (October 1967): 360–61, 366; William Tryon to Sewallis Shirley, 26 July 1765, *The Correspondence of William Tryon and Other Selected Papers*, ed. William S. Powell, 2 vols. (Raleigh, N.C.: Department of Cultural Resources, 1980), 1:138.

19. John Bartram, "Diary of a Journey through the Carolinas, Georgia, and Florida from July 1, 1765, to April 10, 1766," ed. Francis Harper, *Transactions of the*

American Philosophical Society, n.s. 33, part 1 (December 1942): 30; William M. Kelso, *Captain Jones's Wormslow: A Historical, Archaeological, and Architectural Study of an Eighteenth-Century Plantation Site near Savannah, Georgia* (Athens: University of Georgia Press, 1979), 74; Frances Benjamin Johnston and Thomas Tileston Waterman, *The Early Architecture of North Carolina* (Chapel Hill: University of North Carolina Press, 1947), 35, 41–43; Doug Swaim, "North Carolina Folk Housing," *Carolina Dwelling*, 26:34, 36, 39; Bishir, *North Carolina Architecture*, 20–25; Carl R. Lounsbury, ed., *An Illustrated Glossary of Early Southern Architecture and Landscape* (New York: Oxford University Press, 1994), 210, 327; Henry J. MacMillan, "Colonial Plantations of the Lower Cape Fear," *Lower Cape Fear Historical Society Bulletin* 12, no. 2 (February 1969): quoted 3–4; Roger G. Kennedy, *Architecture, Men, Women, and Money in America 1600–1860* (New York: Random House, 1985), 60–72.

20. Henk J. Zantkuyl, "The Netherlands Town House: How and Why It Works," *New World Dutch Studies: Dutch Arts and Culture in Colonial America, 1609–1776*, ed. Roderic H. Blackburn and Nancy A. Kelley (Albany, N.Y.: Albany Institute of History and Art, 1987), 144–45; *Masters of Seventeenth-Century Dutch Genre Painting*, ed. Jane Iandola Watkins (Philadelphia: Philadelphia Museum of Art, 1984); plates 1–5, 31, 32, 45, 67, 87, 88, 100.

21. Peter Kalm, *Travels into North America*, trans. John Reinhold Forster (1772; repr., Barre, Mass.: The Imprint Society, 1972), 120, 131, 330–31; David Steven Cohen, *The Dutch-American Farm* (New York: New York University Press, 1992), 33–59; Rosalie Fellows Bailey, *Pre-Revolutionary Dutch Houses and Families in Northern New Jersey and Southern New York* (1936; repr., New York: Dover Publications, 1968), 21; Roderic H. Blackburn and Ruth Piwonka, eds., *Remembrance of Patria: Dutch Arts and Culture in Colonial America 1609–1776* (Albany, N.Y.: Albany Institute of History and Art, 1988), 27, 96–97, 100–102, 104–6, 109, 120–21.

22. James Thacher, *Military Journal During the American Revolutionary War* (Boston: Richardson & Lord, 1823); entry for 2 December 1778, quoted in Bailey, *Pre-Revolutionary Dutch Houses*, 15.

23. John Singleton Copley to Henry Pelham, 3 August 1771, Pelham to Copley, 25 August 1771, *Letters and Papers of John Singleton Copley and Henry Pelham*, Massachusetts Historical Society, *Proceedings* 71 (1914): 136–37, 147; Jules David Prown, *John Singleton Copley in America 1738–1774* (Cambridge: Harvard University Press, 1966), 79–82.

24. Copley to Pelham, 12 October 1771, 6 November 173, *Letters and Papers of Copley and Pelham*, 165, 175; Jessie Poesch, "A British Officer and His 'New York' Cottage: An American Vernacular Brought to England," *American Art Journal* 20, no. 4, (1988): 75–97, provided a crucial introduction to materials for this discussion of the piazza in New York.

25. Anne MacVicar Grant, *Memoirs of an American Lady: With Sketches of Manners and*

Scenery in America, as they Existed Previous to the Revolution, 2 vols. (London, 1808), 1:7, 45–47.

26. Grant, *Memoirs of an American Lady,* 1:7, 45–47, 51, 94.

27. John Plaw, *Ferme Ornée; or Rural Improvements* (London: I. & J. Taylor, 1795), 7; Poesch, "A British Officer and His Cottage," 76.

28. John Plaw, *Sketches for Country Houses, Villas and Rural Dwellings* . . . (London: J. Taylor, 1800), 11, 13.

29. King, *The Bungalow,* 23–38.

30. Robert Irving, "Georgian Australia," in *The History and Design of the Australian House,* ed. Robert Irving (Melbourne: Oxford University Press, 1985), 37–48, 51–54; J. M. Freeland, *Architecture in Australia: A History* (Melbourne: F. W. Cheshire, 1968), 12–49; Robin Boyd, *Australia's Home: Its Origins, Builders and Occupiers* (1952; repr., Penguin Books, 1968), 16–19; Brian Hudson, "The View from the Verandah: Prospect, Refuge and Leisure," *Australian Geographical Studies* 31 (1993): 70–78; Balwant Saini, *The Australian House: Homes of the Tropical North* (Sydney: Lansdowne Press, 1982), 20–55; King, *The Bungalow,* 230–33. Architectural historians of Australia refer to the verandah as a "climatic necessity" and "always an honest expression of the land, its climate, and its people"; Peter Moffit, *The Australian Verandah* (Sydney: Ure Smith, 1976), quoted 5–6. For the simile, see David Mackay, "Far-flung Empire: A Neglected Imperial Outpost at Botany Bay, 1788–1801," *Journal of Imperial and Commonwealth History* 9, no. 2, (January 1981): 133.

31. Sandy Easterbrook, "The Evolution of the Verandah in Canadian Architecture of the Pre-Confederation Period" (Environment Canada, Parks Service, National Historic Parks and Sites Directorate, Canadian Inventory of Historic Building, Architectural History Branch, 1978). *Mrs. Simcoe's Diary,* ed. Mary Quayle Innis (Toronto: Macmillan, 1965), 75, 98, 110, 160.

32. Ibid., 170, 177.

33. Janet Wright, *Architecture of the Picturesque in Canada* (Ottawa: Parks Canada, 1984); Marian Macrea, *The Ancestral Roof: Domestic Architecture of Upper Canada* (Toronto: Clarke, Irwin, 1963).

34. Peter Marshall, "Imperial Policy and the Government of Detroit: Projects and Problems, 1760–1774," *Journal of Imperial and Commonwealth History* 11, no. 2 (January 1974): 153–89; Gerald Bryant, "Officers of the East India Company's Army in the Days of Clive and Hastings," *Journal of Imperial and Commonwealth History* 6, no. 3 (May 1978): 203–27; G. J. Bryant, "Pacification in the Early English Raj, 1755–85," *Journal of Imperial and Commonwealth History* 14, no. 1 (October 1985): 3–19.

Military engineers had a strong presence in French Saint Domingue and Louisiana from the beginnings of colonization in the late seventeenth century, and galleries and verandahs promptly became fixtures in colonial and creole architecture there. "The earliest documented building with a full-length front gallery in North America [c.

1704]" was a barracks at Fort Lewis in Old Mobile: Jay D. Edwards, "The Origins of Creole Architecture," *Winterthur Portfolio* 29, no. 2–3 (Summer–Autumn, 1994): 164, 173, quoted 180n. Edwards found that the ornamentation of galleries in French creole architecture closely resembled the decoration of French naval ships.

35. *The Diaries of George Washington, 1748–1799,* ed. Donald Jackson and Dorothy Twohig, 6 vols. (Charlottesville: University Press of Virginia, 1976), 1:73; James Thomas Flexner, *George Washington and the New Nation (1783–1793)* (Boston: Little, Brown, 1969), 11, quoting David Humphrey (1785); Robert F. Dalzell, Jr., and Lee Baldwin Dalzell, *George Washington's Mount Vernon: At Home in Revolutionary America* (New York: Oxford University Press, 1998), 92. On Washington's use of the terms *piazza* and *gallery,* see *Diaries of George Washington,* 4:190, 192, 334, 336 (5, 10 September 1785; 22, 27 May 1786); Washington to William Hamilton, 15 January 1784, 6 April 1784, *The Writings of George Washington,* ed. John C. Fitzpatrick (Washington, D.C.: Government Printing Office, 1938), 27:303, 388; Washington to John Rumney, 3 July 1784, *Writings of George Washington,* 27:433–35. On the originality and stylistic contradictions of Washington's continual remodeling, see Hugh Morrison, *Early American Architecture: From the First Colonial Settlements to the National Period* (New York: Oxford University Press, 1952), 355–61.

36. *The Virginia Journals of Benjamin Henry Latrobe, 1795–1798,* ed. Edward C. Carter II, 2 vols. (New Haven: Yale University Press, 1977), 1:162–72; Charles E. Brownell, "An Introduction to the Art of Latrobe's Drawings," *Latrobe's View of America, 1795–1820,* ed. Carter, Van Horne, and Brownell, 18–34.

37. Dorothy Hunt Williams, *Historic Virginia Gardens: Preservations by The Garden Club of Virginia* (Charlottesville: University Press of Virginia, 1975), 99–104; *Gunston Hall: Return to Splendor* (Mason Neck, Va.: Board of Regents, Gunston Hall, 1991); Mark R. Wenger, "The Central Passage in Virginia: Evolution of an Eighteenth-Century Living Space," *Perspectives in Vernacular Architecture II,* ed. Camille Wells (Columbia: University of Missouri Press, 1986), 142–43; Thomas Tileston Waterman, *The Mansions of Virginia, 1706–1776* (Chapel Hill: University of North Carolina Press, 1945), 253–60.

38. James Gibbs, *A Book of Architecture, Containing Designs of Buildings and Ornaments* (London, 1728), notes for plates 67 and 84, xviii, xx; Gene Waddell, "The First Monticello," *Journal of the Society of Architectural Historians* 46 (March 1987): 8–14, 19, shows the connection between Gibbs's pavilions and Jefferson's house plans. William L. Beiswanger, "The Temple in the Garden: Thomas Jefferson's Vision of the Monticello Landscape," *Eighteenth-Century Life* 8, no. 2, (January 1983): 170–88.

39. *South Carolina Gazette,* 23 June 1766, as quoted in *The Arts and Crafts in Philadelphia, Maryland and South Carolina: Gleanings from Newspapers,* comp. Alfred Coxe Prime, vol. 1, *1721–1785* (n.p.: Walpole Society, 1929), 189. Barbara Wells Sarudy, "A Late Eighteenth-Century 'Tour' of Baltimore Gardens," idem, "A Chesapeake Craftsman's Eighteenth-Century Gardens," *Journal of Garden History* 9, no. 3, (September 1989):

125–52; James D. Kornwolf, "The Picturesque in the American Garden and Landscape before 1800," *Eighteenth-Century Life* 8, no. 2, (January 1983): 93–106.

40. Elizabeth McLean, "Town and Country Gardens in Eighteenth-Century Philadelphia," *Eighteenth-Century Life* 8, no. 2, (January 1983): 136–47, esp. 141; "Journal of Josiah Quincy," 473; James S. Ackerman, *The Villa: Form and Ideology of Country Houses* (Princeton: Princeton University Press, 1990), 60.

41. Peter Martin, *The Pleasure Gardens of Virginia: From Jamestown to Jefferson* (Princeton: Princeton University Press, 1991), 141, 158; Barbara Wells Sarudy, *Gardens and Gardening in the Chesapeake, 1705–1805* (Baltimore: Johns Hopkins University Press, 1998), 11, 22, 32; C. Allan Brown, "Eighteenth-Century Virginia Plantation Gardens: Translating an Ancient Idyll," *Regional Garden Design in the United States,* ed. Therese O'Malley and Marc Treib (Washington, D.C.: Dumbarton Oaks Research Library and Collection, 1995), 145–46.

42. Raymond Arsenault, "The End of the Long Hot Summer: The Air Conditioner and Southern Culture," *Journal of Southern History* 50, no. 4, (November 1984): 597–628. On the possible African–West Indian origins of the verandah, see Carl Anthony, "The Big House and the Slave Quarters, Part 1: Prelude to New World Architecture," *Landscape* 20, no. 3, (1976): 12–15. John Michael Vlach does not present conclusive evidence that the design of the shotgun house included a porch when it was introduced into New Orleans, but in the nineteenth century, shotgun houses in both the American South and Haiti, in both urban and rural contexts, usually had them; John Michael Vlach, "The Shotgun House: An African Architectural Legacy," *Common Places: Readings in American Vernacular Architecture,* ed. Dell Upton and John Michael Vlach (Athens: University of Georgia Press, 1986), 58–78; John Michael Vlach, *The Afro-American Tradition in Decorative Arts* (Cleveland: Cleveland Museum of Art, 1978), 121–38. Jay Edwards, "The Complex Origins of the American Domestic Piazza-Veranda-Gallery," *Material Culture* 21, no. 2, (Summer 1989): 3–58. Edwards's wide-ranging study advances a cautious hypothesis for "the Spanish-Antillian Creole house" as the "progenitor" of the American porch. For precisely dated references to piazzas in the mid-eighteenth-century South, see Lounsbury, *Illustrated Glossary of Early Southern Architecture,* 269.

CHAPTER 9   GENDERED COMFORT

1. The design was first published in J. B. Bordley, *Country Habitations* (Philadelphia, 1798) and subsequently appeared in J. B. Bordley, *Essays and Notes on Husbandry and Rural Affairs,* 2nd ed. (Philadelphia: Thomas Dobson, 1801), pl. 5.

2. Edward A. Chappell, "Housing a Nation: The Transformation of Living Standards in Early America," in *Of Consuming Interests: The Style of Life in the Eighteenth Century,* ed. Cary Carson, Ronald Hoffman, and Peter J. Albert (Charlottesville: Univer-

sity Press of Virginia, 1994), 193–209; Jane C. Nylander, *Our Own Snug Fireside: Images of the New England Home, 1760–1860* (New Haven: Yale University Press, 1993).

3. Chappell, "Housing a Nation," 208 (quoted), 212–20, 229; Dell Upton, "The Traditional House and Its Enemies," *Traditional Dwellings and Settlement Review* 1 (Spring 1990): 71–84.

4. Thomas Jefferson, *Notes on the State of Virginia* (MS [1785]; orig. publ. 1861; New York: Torchbook, 1964; repr. Gloucester, Mass.: Peter Smith, 1976), 145–48; Jack Larkin, "From 'Country Mediocrity' to 'Rural Improvement': Transforming the Slovenly Countryside in Central Massachusetts, 1775–1840," in *Everyday Life in the Early Republic*, ed. Catherine E. Hutchins (Winterthur: Henry Francis du Pont Winterthur Museum, 1994), 175–201; Lee Soltow, *Distribution of Wealth and Income in the United States in 1798* (Pittsburgh: University of Pittsburgh Press, 1989), 57; Bernard Herman, *Architecture and Rural Life in Central Delaware, 1700–1900* (Knoxville: University of Tennessee Press, 1987), 14–41, 109–14; idem, *The Stolen House* (Charlottesville: University Press of Virginia, 1992), 183–95, 206–10, 217–22; Carole Shammas, *The Preindustrial Consumer in England and America* (Oxford: Clarendon Press, 1990), 165–69.

5. Alexander Jackson Davis, *Rural Residences* (New York, 1837–1838); Andrew Jackson Downing, *Treatise on the Theory and Practice of Landscape Gardening* (New York: Wiley & Putnam, 1841); idem, *Cottage Residences* (New York: Wiley & Putnam, 1842); idem, *The Architecture of Country Houses* (New York: D. Appleton, 1850); David Schuyler, *Apostle of Taste: Andrew Jackson Downing, 1815–1852* (Baltimore: Johns Hopkins University Press, 1996).

6. Kathryn Kish Sklar, *Catherine Beecher: A Study in American Domesticity* (New York: W. W. Norton, 1976).

7. *Miss Beecher's Domestic Receipt Book: Designed as a Supplement to Her Treatise on Domestic Economy* (New York: Harper & Brothers, 1846), 252–69; Downing, *Architecture of Country Houses*, 476; Kenneth L. Ames, "Downing and the Rationalization of Interior Design," in *Prophet With Honor: The Career of Andrew Jackson Downing, 1815–1852*, ed. George B. Tatum and Elisabeth Blair MacDougall (Washington, D.C.: Dumbarton Oaks Research Library and Collection, 1989), 191–217. On the interest in comfort in the nineteenth century, see Elizabeth Donaghy Garrett, *At Home: The American Family, 1750–1870* (New York: Harry N. Abrams, 1990), chap. 8, "The Quest for Comfort: Housekeeping Practices and Living Arrangements the Year Round."

8. Ronald J. Zboray, "The Transportation Revolution and Antebellum Book Distribution Reconsidered," *American Quarterly* 38 (1986): 53–71; idem, "Antebellum Reading and the Ironies of Technological Innovation, *American Quarterly* 40 (1988): 65–82; Gail Caskey Winkler, *Influence of Godey's "Lady's Book" on the American Woman and Her Home: Contributions to a National Culture, 1830–1877* (Ph.D. diss., University of Wisconsin—Madison, 1988), 99–107.

9. Mary Woods, "The First American Architectural Journals: The Profession's

Voice," *Journal of the Society of Architectural Historians* 48 (1989): 118; Charles B. Wood III, "The New 'Pattern Books' and the Role of the Agricultural Press," in *Prophet With Honor*, 182.

10. Clifford E. Clark, Jr., "Domestic Architecture as an Index to Social History: The Romantic Revival and the Cult of Domesticity in America, 1840–1870," *Journal of Interdisciplinary History* 7 (1976): 33–56; Norma Prendergast, *The Sense of Home: Nineteenth-Century Domestic Architectural Reform* (Ph.D. diss., Cornell University, 1981).

11. Catherine Beecher, *A Treatise on Domestic Economy for the Use of Young Ladies at Home and at School* (New York: Harper & Brothers, 1846), 40; Andrew Jackson Downing, *A Treatise on the Theory and Practice of Landscape Gardening* (London: Longman, Brown, Green, and Longmans, 1849), viii–ix.

12. Downing, *Architecture of Country Houses*, 409–12. On the aptness of Downing's remarks, see Richard L. Bushman, *The Refinement of America: Persons, Houses, Cities* (New York: Alfred A. Knopf, 1992), 354–65.

13. George B. Tatum, "Introduction: The Downing Decade (1841–1852)," in *Prophet With Honor*, 1–42.

14. George Bishop Tatum, *Andrew Jackson Downing: Arbiter of American Taste, 1815–1852* (Ph.D. diss., Princeton University, 1949), 41, 50, 149; Downing, *Treatise on Landscape Gardening* (1849), 370; Vincent J. Scully, Jr., *The Shingle Style and the Stick Style: Architectural Theory and Design from Downing to the Origins of Wright*, rev. ed. (New Haven: Yale University, 1971), xxv–xxix.

15. Downing, *Treatise on Landscape Gardening* (1849), 79.

16. Jane B. Davies, "Davis and Downing: Collaborators in the Picturesque," in *Prophet With Honor*, 84.

17. Wood, "New 'Pattern Books,'" 182.

18. Tatum, "The Downing Decade," 2; Downing, *Treatise on Landscape Gardening* (1849), 74.

19. Downing, *Architecture of Country Houses*, 373.

20. Where not otherwise cited, the following biographical information is from Sklar, *Catherine Beecher*.

21. Catherine Beecher to Mary Lyon, 17 November 1844, Beecher Family Papers, Archives, Mount Holyoke College, South Hadley, Massachusetts.

22. Sklar, *Catherine Beecher*, 301–4; Lawrence A. Cremin, *American Education: The National Experience, 1783–1876* (New York: Harper & Row, 1980), 69.

23. Beecher, *Treatise on Domestic Economy* (1846), 9.

24. Catherine Beecher, *Treatise on Domestic Economy* (Boston: March, Capen, Lyon, and Webb, 1841), preface; Beecher, *Treatise on Domestic Economy* (Boston: T. Webb, 1842), preface.

25. Beecher, *Treatise on Domestic Economy* (1846), 5–6, 25–26, 39–45.

26. On switching publishers, see Catherine Beecher to Mrs. Z. P. G. Bannister, 20

January 1845, Beecher Family Papers. Beecher, *Treatise on Domestic Economy* (1846), 8; Beecher to Lyon, 17 November 1844; Catherine Beecher to the Rev. Gorham D. Abbott, 9 November 1843, Katharine Day Collection, Stowe-Day Foundation, Hartford, Conn.; Kathryn Kish Sklar, "The Founding of Mount Holyoke College," in *Women in America: A History,* ed. Carol Ruth Berkin and Mary Beth Norton (Boston: Houghton Mifflin, 1979), 177–98.

27. Beecher, *Treatise on Domestic Economy* (1846), 6, 8, 261–63; Catherine Beecher, circular to family, 11 December 1840 (Cincinnati), Katharine Day Collection, Stowe-Day Foundation, Hartford, Conn.

28. Andrew Jackson Downing, *Cottage Residences,* 2nd ed. (New York: Appleton, 1844), 21–22, 38, 53, 65, 89.

29. Beecher, *Treatise on Domestic Economy* (1846), 271–77, 331.

30. Ibid., 259–63, 265, 271, 276–77.

31. Downing, *Cottage Residences,* 5; Andrew Jackson Downing, "On Feminine Taste in Rural Affairs," in *Rural Essays,* ed. George William Curtis (1853; repr. New York, 1974).

32. Beecher, *Treatise on Domestic Economy* (1846), 258–63.

33. Ibid., 259, 271.

34. Ibid., 259–60, 277. On the relationship between hygienic concerns and domestic architecture, see Annmarie Adams, *Architecture in the Family Way: Doctors, Houses, and Women, 1870–1900* (Montreal and Kingston: McGill–Queen's University Press, 1996).

35. Downing, *Cottage Residences,* 10–12.

36. Downing, *Architecture of Country Houses,* 79, 346–47.

37. Witold Rybczynski, *Home: A Short History of an Idea* (New York: Penguin, 1987), 158–62.

38. Susan Geary, "The Domestic Novel as a Commercial Commodity: Making a Best Seller in the 1850s," *Papers of the Bibliographic Society of America* 70 (1976): 366; Winkler, *Influence of Godey's "Lady's Book,"* 32–41, 137–93; Sally McMurry, *Families and Farmhouses in Nineteenth-Century America: Vernacular Design and Social Change* (New York: Oxford University Press, 1988), 56–86; George L. Hersey, "Godey's Choice," *Journal of the Society of Architectural Historians* 8 (1959): 104–11.

39. Jan Jennings, "Drawing on the Vernacular," *Winterthur Portfolio* 27 (1992): 255–79; Dell Upton, "Pattern Books and Professionalism: Aspects of the Transformation of Domestic Architecture in America, 1800–1860," *Winterthur Portfolio* 19 (1984): 107–50.

INDEX

Adams, Abigail, 160

Adams, John, 160

Adams, Joseph A. (engraver), 270

aesthetic, picturesque. *See* picturesque aesthetic

Africa, architecture in, 91–2, 236–7

agricultural improvement, architecture and, 206–7, 221

Agriculture, Board of, inquiry into cottage by, 221

Analysis of Beauty (Hogarth), 131 fig. 4.3, 135

Anderson, James: on smoky chimneys, 175–7, 177 fig. 6.1, 185

antiquaries: and archaic housing, 49, 59–62, 61 fig. 2.6, 78; and open central hearth, 60–1

architecture: African, 91–2, 236–7; and convenience, 206, 209, 227; ecclesiastical, 5–6, 12, 22–7, 40, 44, 46, 66; Henry III, influence of, 31–2, 41; impermanent, 19, 80, 88; medieval, 3–44; More, Thomas, on Utopians', 49; naval, in colonies, 240–2; neoclassical, 207–8, 210, 218, 226–7, 288; primitivism in, 204–16, 210 fig. 7.2, 226; Renaissance styles of, 46–9, 72–3; Repton, Humphry,

on modern priorities in, 206; of prisons, 166–8; Spanish colonial, 236, 238; Vitruvius on origins of, 209; women and, 26, 274, 278–9, 281–3, 285–6, 288–9

Architecture françoise des bastimens particuliers, L' (Savot), 125

architecture, landscape. *See* landscape architecture

Architecture of Country Houses, The (Downing), 268, 288

architecture, publications about, 205–16, 224, 270, 288–9; *comfort* in titles of, 205–6; Andrew Jackson Downing's, 263–5. *See also* house design books

Argand, François-Pierre Aimé, 192–3

Argand lamp, 192–4, 193 fig. 6.6, 199

atrium (Roman living area), 22, 113

Aubrey, John (antiquary), 60, 65, 115

Austen, Jane: *Sense and Sensibility*, cottage in, 203

Australia: verandah in, 249–50, 344 n. 30

Barbon, Nicholas: on proclivity to consume, 150

Barrell, John, 221

Bartram, John, 242

349

The Library of Congress has catalogued the hardcover edition of this book as follows:

Crowley, John E.

The Invention of comfort : sensibilities and design in early modern Britain and early America / John E. Crowley.

p.   cm.

ISBN 0-8018-6437-2 (alk. paper)

1. Households—United States—History.   2. Households—Great Britain—History.   3. House furnishings—
United States—History.   4. House furnishings—Great Britain—History.   5. United States—Social life and
customs.   6. Great Britain—Social life and customs.   I. Title.

GT481.U6C76 2000

306'.0973—dc21   00-008958